COLLECTIVE BARGAINING BY OBJECTIVES

A Positive Approach

REED C. RICHARDSON

*Professor of Management and Economics
and
Director, Institute of Industrial Relations
University of Utah*

Prentice-Hall, Inc., *Englewood Cliffs, New Jersey 07632*

Library of Congress Cataloging in Publication Data

Richardson, Reed C.
    Collective bargaining by objectives.

    Bibliography
    Includes index.
    1. Collective bargaining—United States. 2. Management
by objectives. I. Title.
HD6483.R48   331.89'1'0973   76-44459
ISBN 0-13-140517-9
ISBN 0-13-140509-8 pbk.

Printed in the United States of America

10 9 8 7 6 5 4 3

Prentice-Hall International, Inc., *London*
Prentice-Hall of Australia Pty., Limited, *Sydney*
Prentice-Hall of Canada, Ltd., *Toronto*
Prentice-Hall of India Private Limited, *New Delhi*
Prentice-Hall of Japan, Inc., *Tokyo*
Prentice-Hall of Southeast Asia Pte. Ltd., *Singapore*
Whitehall Books Limited, *Wellington, New Zealand*

TO JUDITH

FOR EDITING AND ENCOURAGEMENT

AND, SPANNING THREE DECADES, TO

CHARLES GULICK

MAURICE NEUFELD

DALE YODER

GEORGE ODIORNE

MENTORS, COLLEAGUES AND FRIENDS

Contents

6

Part Two
COLLECTIVE BARGAINING PROCESS — NEGOTIATION

7

8

9

10

11

12

13

14

Part Three
COLLECTIVE BARGAINING PROCESS — CONTRACT ADMINISTRATION

Part Four
COLLECTIVE BARGAINING PROCESS — RESOLUTION OF CONFLICT

Appendix

COLLECTIVE BARGAINING BY OBJECTIVES —
SIMULATION EXERCISES AND NEGOTIATION GAMES

Foreword

This book may just become the most innovative book in the field of labor relations to emerge from the past ten years or more. Reed Richardson is an old hand at labor relations. Since obtaining his doctorate at Cornell over twenty years ago, he has been a prolific writer about labor relations and labor history. His history of work rules in the railroad industry over a 100-year period is a classic. But he has not confined himself solely to the past; he has become one of the leading labor arbitrators in the West. Beyond this, he has always been a topflight and inspiring teacher of industrial relations. The roster of top personnel and industrial relations managers and union officers and staff members who learned their labor relations in his classes would fill a sizeable auditorium or two. This includes a considerable number of professionals, including labor lawyers, who never would have specialized in labor relations as a life's work without having studied under Reed.

It is not surprising to any of these friends, then, that the melding of MBO with collective bargaining would have occurred first to Reed Richardson. Recently many large companies and unions have engaged in what William Usery, recent Director of the Federal Mediation Service and now Secretary of Labor, calls "relationships by objectives." Richardson had been teaching this to public-sector bargainers, students and mediators for at least five years before anyone else had seen the logic of it.

Today, his former graduate students are teaching Labor Relations by Objectives to their own classes in many large universities, and this book will fill a felt need for a concrete text on how to apply MBO to collective bargaining. It does not throw out conventional labor relations and collective bargaining theory in the process. There is a need to understand the history of labor if one is to understand the present, a principle that

Richardson has always been a leader in espousing. Furthermore, collective bargaining is well known to be a three-party relationship, with the government and labor laws being the third element in what to the public might seem to be a two-party adversary system.

The distinctive feature of this book is the excellent advice it gives on how the parties can define explicit, measurable objectives prior to the bargaining. This statement of objectives into three major categories—realistic, pessimistic, and optimistic levels of outcome—puts some rigor and sense into what has been done all along on an intuitive basis. It answers questions of how to delegate to bargainers the power to commit, without either the union membership or the management losing control of their own powers to commit. It is an altogether excellent work, badly needed. As I said, it is probably the major innovation in collective bargaining of the decade, or perhaps of the past thirty years.

George S. Odiorne
Amherst, Massachusetts
1976

Preface

Collective bargaining, a term introduced by Beatrice Potter Webb in 1891, has traditionally been associated with the trade union movement. In terms of numbers of agreements negotiated and individuals directly concerned, this is still the most common form of collective bargaining. Involved are approximately 150,000 contracts between employers and unions, covering about 20 million workers in the United States. However, in recent years, a new dimension has been added, with the increasingly active role being played by professional and state associations of employees in the negotiation of collective bargaining agreements. Although avoiding the name *union* or formal affiliation with the union movement, these associations have taken on many of the trappings of unions. As a result, while union membership has been leveling off and even declining as a percentage of the labor force over the last decade, collective bargaining has significantly increased in importance and outstripped the union movement proper. Today, through the bargaining activities of both unions and associations, about 24 million employees are covered by approximately 160,000 labor agreements.

Many reasons might be advanced for this increased status of collective bargaining in labor–management relations. Some of the more important reasons are (1) the impact of broad attitudinal changes in our society during the last decade, (2) a growing acceptance of collective bargaining as a respectable and preferred vehicle for settling differences between employers and employees in all conceivable areas, (3) the lack of viable alternatives to collective bargaining in a free society, (4) the way the environment of a free society fosters and makes possible such collective action, and (5) government's extension of collective bargaining rights to its own employees.

Collective bargaining in labor–management relations usually has reference to two areas of activity: the negotiation of the terms of the agreement and the administration ("contract administration") of these terms during the life of the agreement. A third area of activity is identified for the purposes of this book. This is the related activity of private and public means developed for the purpose of strengthening collective bargaining as a means of resolving conflict. Where not purposely considered an alternative to collective bargaining, these private and public aids to the resolution of labor–management conflict constitute a vital support to the collective bargaining process. Thus, in addition to Part I, which introduces the reader to labor–management relations and collective bargaining, there are three major divisions of the book proper: Part II, Negotiation; Part III, Contract Administration; Part IV, Resolution of Conflict.

But the book is intended to be more than just a source of information concerning the collective bargaining process. The highest priority is given in the subject matter and arrangement of material to the practical matter of bridging the gap for the reader between information on the one hand and the practice of collective bargaining on the other. A book confined merely to information is like providing the tools for a building project without showing how to use them efficiently. This book presents a methodology for bargaining—a systematic and methodical step-by-step way of preparing for and carrying on bargaining to provide the link between information and use. The result is a more positive thrust to the entire procedure, increasing the effectiveness of the negotiator, experienced or inexperienced. The key to this methodology is that the common, ordinary tasks that have to be done to be effective in collective bargaining are placed within a systematic and easily followed framework. The methodology is called Collective Bargaining by Objectives (CBO) and is an adaptation of Management by Objectives (MBO) to the collective bargaining process. Key chapters in the development of this methodology are Chapters 9 through 14.

To facilitate the reader's understanding and to minimize the confusion that results from a lengthy and too minute coverage, I have kept the main content of the book informative but as brief as possible. For a more intensive investigation into any area of the book, each subject includes a list of annotated reading materials.

For the person who wishes to use the book for a learning experience or training device in the practice of collective bargaining, the appendix provides four negotiation games to be used in simulation training: manufacturing, construction, municipal government, and federal government. Guidance and information in their use, based on the author's experience over a number of years, are included. The use of simulation is strongly recommended as a highly effective teaching device in applying the objectives (CBO) methodology.

Many people have been influential and helpful in the development of this material over the last seven years. I am grateful for the advice and reactions to the CBO approach from my friends and colleagues, Arben Clark, Kenneth Davies, Wallace Gardner, Gary Hansen, Herbert Heneman, Robert Henson, Richard Kinnersley, George Odiorne, John Seybolt, and Dale Yoder.

Two FMCS commissioners of mediation, Jack Garvey and Glen Bergeson, have been most supportive. To cooperating groups such as the FMCS, AAA, Civil Service Commission, Federal Labor Relations Council, Federal Impasses Panel, Prentice-Hall, and Bureau of National Affairs, my deepest appreciation. I should be most ungrateful if I failed to mention the hundreds of graduate students who have been exposed to the CBO method during the past seven years and whose comments have been most useful. And I thank Professors Howard Finston, Craig Overton, and Robert Wegner, who reviewed the manuscript. Finally, a special thanks to Valerie Lindley, Cecily Smart, Minell Mohr, Sharon Valentine, Louis Preysz, and James Peters for valuable assistance in research, editing, and typing.

Background

But though Collective Bargaining prevails over a much larger area than Trade Unionism, it is the Trade Union alone which can provide the machinery for any but its most casual and limited application.

Sidney and Beatrice Webb   *1902*

PART ONE

Evolution of Collective Bargaining— 1790-1890

CHAPTER 1

GENERAL INTRODUCTION

The objective in including a section on the evolution of collective bargaining in America is to provide a historical framework within which the remainder of the book may be more clearly understood.

Rather than an exhaustive account of collective bargaining, the emphasis is upon an overview through the selective use of historical materials. The materials chosen are those that identify the significant changes in collective bargaining from one historical period to another and the major environmental forces that have blended and molded collective bargaining into what it is today.

While the material is divided into two general periods of approximately a century each, there is a further identification of five subperiods for clarity. They are:

1. Foundation period, 1790–1890
2. Unilateralism to collective bargaining, 1890–1930
3. Collective bargaining and public policy, 1930–1945
4. Employer Acceptance, 1945–1962
5. Collective bargaining, an institution, 1962 to present

To facilitate the understanding of the processes of historical change, a standard format is used in each period: first, an overview of the major developments in collective bargaining for the period; second, a survey of changes occurring in the labor movement; third, a more detailed examination of the significant developments in collective bargaining, and their nature, extent, and form; and fourth, identification of environmental forces responsible for changes in collective bargaining during the period.

For purposes of clarification, the term *union* or *labor movement* is defined as the formal trade union movement; the term *employee organization* (especially pertinent to the contemporary period) is used in a broader sense to identify all forms of employee organizations, union or otherwise, engaged in collective bargaining or negotiation of labor–management agreements.

The term *collective bargaining* will be used throughout to identify developments in joint labor–management negotiation and/or administration of the labor agreement. It is recognized that the term did not originate until the end of the nineteenth century. It was coined by Beatrice Potter Webb to describe the bilateral negotiation process between labor and management.

FOUNDATION PERIOD—1790–1890

Introduction

It is customary to think of collective bargaining as coextensive with unionism; however, such was not the case in the first century of the American labor movement. More commonly, the relationship between employers and unions of the period was unilateral. The employees, through their union organization, normally looked upon their demands as being final demands, not subject to the give-and-take of negotiation or bargaining. As a result, employees approached employers with a "take it or we strike" attitude. The employer's approach was equally unilateral. If in a strong position, the employer simply ignored the union demands, or refused them and let the union action run its course. If in a weak position, the employer might accede to the union demands until a better day, when the tables could be turned on the union through a unilateral abolishment of the gains made.[1]

> The demands which the body drew up were demands which they expected to have met in full. They were not bargaining proposals, set two or three times higher than their settlement price, but an "actual bill of wages" sometimes printed and ready to be posted in the shops immediately upon acceptance. Compromise was therefore not intended. The union members had previously sworn among themselves not to work for less than the wages stated in their demands, and they were serious in that oath.

[1] In describing the historical development of collective bargaining in America, no serious labor historian can ignore the pioneering work of Neil Chamberlain, *Collective Bargaining* (New York: McGraw-Hill, 1951), and Vernon H. Jensen, "Notes on the Beginnings of Collective Bargaining," *Industrial and Labor Relations Review*, Vol. 9, No. 2 (January 1956).

This was not therefore a process of bargaining. It was a procedure for a trial of economic strength to determine whose wage decisions would prevail—the union's or the employer's.[2]

Even so, the roots of collective bargaining were established in this period. Prior to the Civil War, there were sporadic attempts at collective bargaining, although they were aptly described as "straws in the wind." Following the Civil War, in a few significant instances, unions established a formal and continuing bargaining relationship with their employers. What is equally important is that for the first time, these collective bargaining relationships were evidenced by written rather than verbal agreements.

The Labor Movement

This was not only a period of beginnings for the American labor movement, but a period of searching for self-realization and self-fulfillment. Characterized by constant experimentation by organized labor in the search for a workable mode of operation, it illustrates dramatically the way in which institutions are shaped and molded by their environment. By 1886, the American labor movement had evolved to the characteristic structure and philosophy that have typified it to the present day.

Developing a Structure

The organizational structure that characterizes the American labor movement today evolved by 1886 as a pragmatic response of labor groups to the competitive environment in which they had to operate. It began with the establishment of the first local labor organizations within two groups of skilled craftsmen: the journeymen shoemakers of Philadelphia in 1792, and the journeymen printers of New York in 1794. There was not an immediate surge of organizational activity, yet this marked the beginning of the organization of local groups of craft workers in other communities and crafts as the need and desire arose. These were initially spontaneous developments, unrelated to each other, dictated by the immediate needs of workers. Communities were somewhat isolated from each other then, and the local market dominated; as long as the employer was confined to the local market, the local union was sufficient to meet the needs of its members.

A second structural step was taken that still reflected the dominant influence of the local market but was intended to combine the strength of the various local unions within the local community or market area.

[2] Chamberlain, *Collective Bargaining*, pp. 6–7.

This was the establishment in 1827 of the Mechanics' Union of Trade Associations, a sort of citywide federation of local labor groups in Philadelphia. This organization was an outgrowth of a strike for a 10-hour day by some 600 journeymen carpenters, which stirred first the interest and then the aid of not only other building-trade groups (bricklayers, painters, glaziers, and so on) but other non-building-trade societies within the city. As a result of the interest aroused, it was decided to form a central organization for mutual aid and protection in similar disputes.

Other than a short-lived attempt to establish a National Trades Union, 1834–1837, no other structural changes were made until the 1850s and 1860s. The National Trades Union was a good example of a structural shift that was ahead of its time. It was an attempt to bring organization to the national level while the markets in which labor organizations functioned were still essentially local.

As the isolation of communities and markets began to break down under the impact of improved transportation (railroad) and communication (telegraph) in the 1850s and 1860s, local labor organizations found themselves subjected to influences from which they had been happily secure by the isolation of the local-market situation in earlier years. Local enterprise, heretofore protected from outside competition, now found itself subject to competition from other geographical markets. This brought new pressures on wages of workers in the local community. Moreover, as transportation improved, workers became more mobile, and the organized worker found himself now faced with competition from workers from other areas. As these external pressures were felt by local unions and the local unions were unable to cope, the need for organizational unity on a broader scale became apparent. The result was an impetus for local trade unions to join forces on a national craft basis for the protection of their common interests in their trade. A number of national trade unions were formed in the 1850s; most did not survive the economic crisis of 1857, but at least they paved the way for a more permanent development after the Civil War. As Commons notes:

There resulted a type of national unionism indicating the evolution to the period of nationalization which followed the war and, in a sense at least, preparing the local unions for such nationalization. The national unions as appeared in the decade of the fifties (with one notable exception—the typographical union) were organized for discussion rather than for administration and were, at their best, little more than advisory committees to aid the local union represented.[3]

[3] John R. Commons et al., *History of Labour in the United States* (New York: Macmillan, 1926), I, p. 620.

By 1872, some 26 national unions had been formed, constituting a membership of around 300,000. Included were such groups as carpenters, cigar makers, bricklayers, printers, shoemakers, coopers, plasterers, iron molders, machinists, blacksmiths, masons, painters, metal workers, locomotive engineers, and locomotive firemen, to name a few.

Establishment of the national trade union in response to the broadening of market forces was motivated primarily by the need to meet the specific pressures upon a particular trade or craft. However, as the nationalization of markets continued apace, as the Industrial Revolution began to have an impact on the economy, as employers were able to organize on a broader basis and to amass large funds and great power, as national legislation and politics became more important, and as money problems became nationwide, organized labor found an increasing need for organization on a broader base than the national union of a specific trade or craft. What was required was an effective combining of the strength of organized labor nationwide on matters of common interest. This pressure initially found fruition in the one-big-union idea of the National Labor Union in 1866 and the Knights of Labor in 1869. Neither was able to survive, because of its own inherent weaknesses. However, in the eighties, a nationwide structure was formed based on a federation of national trade unions, more narrowly defined than the one-big-union idea, stronger because its constituency was the craft worker, and more acceptable because it did not reflect ideas hostile to the American capitalistic system. This was the establishment of the American Federation of Labor in 1886, an outgrowth of the Federation of Organized Trades and Labor Unions in the United States and Canada, established in 1881.

Thus, by 1886 the question of a basic organizational structure for the American labor movement had been resolved. It is this structure, with only functional alterations, that still characterizes the American labor movement.

CHART 1–1

Philosophy or Mode of Operation

Perlman and Taft describe the activities of the American labor movement during its first century as

> . . . a record of continuous experimentation with programs and strategies, in an incessant search for a mode of operation which would secure to labor a maximum improvement in conditions together with a most stable organization and a minimum opposition from the remainder of the community.[4]

The search for a philosophy or workable mode of operation began immediately with the first organizations of workers in the 1790s and was not resolved finally until the year of the Great Upheaval in 1886. The details of organized labor's efforts in this quest are voluminous, but a brief account of the major shifts and changes of the labor movement reflects the adaptive process continually faced by any incipient organization, such as organized labor, that lacks the power to change its environment.

Wages were the focus of attention of the first labor organizations, to be joined later by the issue of hours. The problem was direct and easily defined—higher wages and shorter hours—and called for a pragmatic solution. The tool used was direct pressure on employers in the form of strikes, picketing, and boycotts. With the gradual extension of voting rights to workers, and with the impetus generated by the Jacksonian emphasis upon the rights of the common man, labor organizations from 1827 to 1832 shifted their direction to the goals of political and economic equality. Political action was initiated through the formation of labor parties in a number of major cities. When these political movements had run their course and were no longer exciting or fruitful, labor organizations turned back once again to economic objectives, primarily improvement in wages, from 1832 to 1837. This was a practical decision to counter employer pressures on existing wage scales and the deterioration of the real wage during the inflation of 1834–1837. The means used to achieve these ends was direct economic action in the form of strikes, boycotts, and picketing.

All this was brought to an abrupt halt by the panic of 1837 and the ensuing period of high unemployment and deprivation for the worker. Disillusioned by the failure of their efforts to attain either economic well-being or economic and political equality, many workers began to ques-

---

[4] Selig Perlman and Philip Taft, *History of Labour in the United States, 1896–1932* (New York: Macmillan, 1935), IV, p. 3.

tion the system itself. In this state of mind, workers, along with other groups, became easy prey for the preachers of social change who proliferated in the late 1830s and the 1840s. The labor movement became overshadowed by the preachments of the apostles of utopian reform and an idealized society. This became the heyday of the intellectual, whose ideas on social and economic change filtered down, and, more than in any other period in our history, these ideas were superimposed upon the labor movement. The *Documentary History of the Labor Movement* catches the almost frenzied activity of the period:

> The forties far outran other periods . . . in its unbounded loquacity. The columns of advertisements in a newspaper might announce for Monday nights a meeting of the antislavery society; Tuesday night, the temperance society; Wednesday night, the graham bread society; Thursday night, a phrenological lecture; Friday night, an address against capital punishment; Saturday night, the Association for Universal Reform. There were all the missionary societies, the women's rights societies, the society for the diffusion of bloomers, the seances of spiritualists, the associationists, the land reformers . . . colonies of idealists . . . a world's convention . . . where a dozen plans of social reorganization—individualistic, communistic, incomprehensible—were submitted in all solemnity. It was the golden age of the talk-fest, the lyceum, the brotherhood of man—the "hot air" period of American history.[5]

With the end of the depression in 1852, workers, concerned more with bread and butter than with the "isms" of the intellectuals and turned off by the lack of practical accomplishments of the idealistic schemes of the 1840s, became more convinced than ever that traditional trade unionism and immediate objectives were the answer. Economic action became once again the means, with bread and butter the objectives, dominating labor's thinking as it turned in the early 1850s to reforming its ranks and experimentally moving to national trade unionism.

What seemed a solid movement to a "pure and simple" trade unionism was delayed by panic and depression in the latter half of the 1850s and, after the Civil War, by the confusion of more panics, depressions, and most of all, the confusion in social and economic life brought on by the impact of the rapidly developing Industrial Revolution.

> The period was, like that of the thirties and forties, one of contradictions and contrasts, working themselves out in a wider competitive area and on a bigger scale of prosperity and depression. Everything seemed pro-

[5] John R. Commons et al., eds., *A Documentary History of American Industrial Society* (Cleveland, O.: Arthur H. Clark Co., 1910), VII, p. 29.

nounced yet nothing very clear-cut. Trade unionism, demoralized though it was by the depressions of the 1870's, became on the whole increasingly vigorous and assertive, but it was interwoven—more closely and more inextricably than in the forties—with the imposing "isms" of the day. . . .

The confusion of the labor movement during this period was, however, only a manifestation of the confusion of American economic and social life.[6]

Worker involvement for the next twenty years—1866–1886—ranged over a wide spectrum, from the "left" to the "right." "Utopianism and job-consciousness," "German Socialism and American trade unionism," black international "anarchism" and the Knights' "religiosity," the violence of the Molly Maguires, troops squelching labor disturbances, trade union instigation of bitter strikes and trade union deprecation of strikes, "wage-earner support of private property and schemes to draw the fangs of capitalism," the pragmatism of Samuel Gompers and concepts of free land, free silver, consumer's cooperation, producer's cooperation, and the 8-hour day, and demands for labor legislation and "tirades against the political state"—all these illustrate well the involved and confused state to which experimentation with ends and means had deteriorated.[7] Yet with the hindsight of historical perspective, it is now quite clear that this confusion veiled a selective weeding-out process of those modes of operation or philosophical bases that were incompatible with the overpowering and rapidly emerging American industrial capitalism. While the incompatible approaches were being eliminated by force or lack of support, some trade union leaders, such as Strasser, McDonnell, McGuire, and Gompers, came to realize from observation and experience that dabbling with groups hostile to American capitalism only concentrated all the hostility and force of society against the labor movement. Being pragmatists, as they became "more deeply absorbed in the practical problems of the everyday struggle of the wage earners . . . the socialistic portion of their original philosophy kept receding . . . into the background until they arrived at pure trade unionism."[8] The pure and simple trade unionism of these leaders was adopted by the new national trade unions, was from them transmitted to the American Federation of Labor, and then became the guiding philosophy of the American labor movement. In essence, this was an opportunistic, day-to-day, bread-and-butter unionism. The American system of capitalism was

[6] Harry A. Millis and Royal E. Montgomery, *Organized Labor* (New York and London: McGraw-Hill, 1945), pp. 46–47.

[7] *Ibid.*, p. 47.

[8] John R. Commons et al., *History of Labour in the United States* (New York: Macmillan, 1918), II, p. 308.

accepted, and labor organized to expand its position within the system. It also involved an aloofness from movements hostile to the capitalistic system and from labor-party political action.

American labor had arrived by 1886 at a consensus on both its organizational structure and the philosophy that would guide its activities as to ends and means. This accomplishment had direct bearing upon the future of not only the progress of American trade unionism but the practice of collective bargaining and the trade agreement system.

Collective Bargaining

By 1825, in a few trades and communities, the practice of unilateral imposition of terms had "given way to one of bilateral negotiation and the drafting on one-sided terms of surrender had in some instances been replaced by two-party agreements." However, "ultimatum rather than conferences was the prevailing practice of both unions and associated employers."[9]

Twenty-five years later, although instances of genuine negotiation between employers and unions were "only straws in the wind," more union officials and employers had gained experience in negotiation, and a few had even become advocates of collective bargaining as a policy of union–employer relations. The idea of collective bargaining was spreading. However, the panic of 1857 brought a temporary halt to both unionism and collective bargaining.

The end of the Civil War witnessed a renewal of union activity, this time at the national as well as the local level. As union activity intensified, interest in collective bargaining revived, although the development must be characterized as slight, and not the customary relationship between management and labor. But however slight it was in terms of overall union–management relations, there was a qualitative difference that had great portent for the future of collective bargaining. First, by 1890, three trades had been able to establish permanent systems of local trade agreements: the railway-operating brotherhoods, the Amalgamated Association of Iron and Steel Workers, and the bricklayers of Chicago. Second, the verbal agreements of earlier years were being replaced by written agreements. Jensen points to a third, less obtrusive trend but one of importance in the development of collective bargaining: the frequent espousal by unions and union leaders of arbitration or conciliation. Jensen indicates that more often than not, since the term *collective bargaining* had not yet come into use, what the parties meant was not arbitration or conciliation in the formal sense, but "a conciliatory rather than a belligerent approach to securing their demands," or a "joint meeting

[9] Chamberlain, *Collective Bargaining*, p. 14.

of workers and employers."[10] Jensen notes, "It is obvious that the term arbitration was used broadly enough, if no more or less synonymously, to include bargaining as well as intervention of third parties." He concludes, "Even so, the practice of this type of arbitration [third-party adjudication] was very limited."[11]

Thus, by 1890, the idea and the practice of collective bargaining as evidenced by written agreements, even though not the customary relationship, were not only gaining ground in both thought and deed but were sufficiently well established to constitute a springboard for future development.

A selective chronology of the recorded instances of collective bargaining negotiations is illustrative of the progress made.

1799   The Journeymen Cordwainers of Philadelphia were locked out for refusing a decrease in wages. It was not long until the journeymen sued for peace. "A deputation from the society waited upon the employers with *an offer of compromise,* and they said they would consider it, and appointed a time for a committee of theirs to meet" with the journeymen. "*They carried on negotiations,* the masters apparently in the end *agreeing to the compromise.*"[12]

1809   An excerpt from a verbatim of negotiations between the journeymen and master printers of New York City reads:

> Minor changes were again made in the new bill of prices on October 7th, and finally . . . adopted as a whole and forwarded to the employers.
>
> Upon receipt of the notification from the journeymen's society the master printers convened. . . . The meeting adopted *a counter proposal* . . . to submit to the union.
>
> The Typographical Society met in general session on October 28th and received a report . . . "that the master printers . . . requested that a committee of the society might be appointed to confer with their committee in order, if possible, to *effect an accommodation.*"
>
> The committeemen . . . "reported that they had waited on committee of master printers . . . who met them with a frankness which was highly creditable to themselves and pleasing to the committee. They had *made many concessions,* and the committee, desirous of putting a speedy termination to our differences, has also consented to advocate some trifling *concession on our part.*" . . .[13]

[10] Jensen, "Notes on the Beginnings of Collective Bargaining," p. 229.
[11] *Ibid.,* p. 231.
[12] Commons et al., *History of Labour in the United States* (1926), I, p. 122. (Italics added.)
[13] Adapted from Chamberlain, *Collective Bargaining,* p. 10. (Italics added.)

The points at issue were then adjusted satisfactorily through further conferences with the employers.

1827   In the conspiracy trial of the Philadelphia Journeymen Tailors, there is another, although less elaborate, account of a bargaining relationship:

> In September, 1825, a bill of prices was agreed upon by the journeymen tailors of this city. . . . It was submitted to several of the master tailors. . . . Such was this bill of prices, being really a *compromise between two conflicting interests,* by which *each party surrendered something and received a satisfactory equivalent.*[14]

1847   Robert MacFarlane, editor for the *Mechanic's Mirror,* declared: "It has always appeared to me . . . that a plain, friendly relationship and statement of facts on both sides would have reconciled both parties, *with a little concession by each.*"[15]

1850s   Horace Greeley actively promoted collective bargaining. Greeley's statement of "principles underlying the joint union–management trade agreement system . . . stands as a landmark in the history of the development of Collective Bargaining in the United States."[16] A few excerpts make this quite clear:

> 3. We believe employers have rights as well as journeymen —that they too should hold meetings and form societies or appoint delegates to confer with like delegates on the part of the journeymen; and that by the *joint action of these conferrers,* fair rates of wages in each calling should be established and maintained. . . .
>
> 5. We believe that strikes, or refusals of journeymen to work at such wages as they can command, are seldom necessary— that *proper representations and conciliatory action* on the part of journeymen would secure all requisite modifications. . . .
>
> 6. . . . If journeymen alone regulate the prices of labor, they will be likely to fix them too high; if employers alone fix them . . . they will as naturally fix them too low; but *let the journeymen and employers in each trade unite in framing,* upholding and from time to time modifying their scale, and it will usually be just about right.[17]

[14] Commons et al., eds., *A Documentary History of American Industrial Society,* IV, pp. 142–143. (Italics added.)

[15] *Ibid.,* VIII, p. 261. (Italics added.)

[16] Chamberlain, *Collective Bargaining,* p. 26.

[17] *Ibid.,* adapted from pp. 27–28. (Italics added.) From the *New York Daily Tribune,* April 13, 1853. This statement will be found in George A. Stevens, New

1869   The printers' union of New York attempted a unilateral promulgation of a wage increase. The employers then complained that they had had no chance to respond before the printers struck. The strike continued for eight weeks.

> Then informal and private conferences were called between leaders of both groups, and it was reported that "*a spirit of mutual concession*" prevailed. Finally, after eleven weeks, a *settlement was jointly reached and incorporated in a written agreement,* which among other provisions included the following: "This scale shall not be altered except by a call for a *mutual conference between a joint committee of employers and journeymen,* and no alterations shall take effect except upon one month's notice by either party to the other unless by *mutual consent.*"[18]

1866 &   The Amalgamated Association of Iron and Steel Workers was a
1876   pioneer in the evolution of collective bargaining and the trade agreement. In the iron industry, an amalgamation took place in 1876 of three heretofore separate craft organizations—the United Sons of Vulcan (puddlers), the Associated Brotherhood of Iron and Steel Heaters (roughers, rollers, and catchers), and the Iron and Steel Hands—under the name of the Amalgamated Association of Iron and Steel Workers. "*The puddlers had had a trade agreement with the employers* upon the sliding scale principle since 1866— *the first national trade agreement in American labour history. . . .* So effective was this organization that *its pioneer trade agreement of 1866* was continued in most of the mills for a quarter of a century, and in a few of the remaining iron mills continues even down to the present time."[19]

1870–   In 1870, the Anthracite Board of Trade (representing coal opera-
1871   tors) proposed a substantial cut in wages for the following year. The miners (anthracite), represented by the Workingmen's Benevolent Association, struck. Franklin B. Gowan, president of the Philadelphia and Reading Railroad, was asked to settle the differences. Through his services, *a compromise* (the "Gowan Compromise") *was reached between the parties.* The next year, further difficulties arose after a drop in coal prices. On July 29, 1870, the two groups *signed the first written agreement in the coal industry.*[20]

York Typographical Union No. 6, New York State Department of Labor, Annual Report of the Bureau of Labor Statistics, 1911, part I, pp. 621–22.

[18] *Ibid.,* pp. 32–33. (Italics added.) From Stevens, *New York Typographical Union,* p. 303.

[19] Commons et al., *History of Labour in the United States* (1918), II, p. 179. (Italics added.)

[20] Philip Taft, *Organized Labor in American History* (New York: Harper & Row, 1964), pp. 71–72.

Later, negotiations took place over an agreement for the next year (1871) without success, and the miners resorted to arbitration. This settled all differences with the exception of wages. The wage issue was settled by further arbitration and agreements. Some changes were made without incident through 1874. Significantly for collective bargaining, the 1871 agreement included an arrangement for settlement of nonwage disputes without resort to a strike:

> All questions of disagreement in any district, excepting wages, which cannot be settled by the parties directly interested shall be referred to a district board of arbitration, to consist of three members on each side, with power in case of disagreement to select an umpire whose decision shall be final. No colliery or district to stop work pending such arbitration.[21]

1870   Jensen notes that an example of early joint relations in the shoe industry had been described as an early example of arbitration but, through the loose use of terms prevalent then, was really more akin to collective bargaining. The arrangement

> . . . at first, consisted of a committee of five from the union . . . and five from the employers, set up to meet . . . and *talk over matters in an amicable manner; so that if possible, some agreement might be reached which would be mutually satisfactory.* In 1870 the *two committees worked out an agreement,* and the men were jubilant, and considered they had gained a point in being recognized by employers as a body to be negotiated with on equal terms.[22]

1875   Only two groups were able to develop a permanent system of trade agreements prior to 1887: the railway organizations, and the iron and steel workers.

All too little attention has been given historically to the tremendous contribution of the railroad-operating brotherhoods to the development of collective bargaining and of protective labor legislation. In both areas, the railroad brotherhoods were pioneers and exercised an influence far beyond their numbers. In the 1880s, they were the aristocracy of the trade union movement. Because of their strategic position in transportation, it is easy to understand why collective bargaining, written agreements, and favorable legislation came earlier to the operating brotherhoods than to most of the labor movement.

[21] Carroll D. Wright, *Industrial Conciliation and Arbitration* (Boston: Rand, Abery & Co., 1881), pp. 138–40.
[22] Jensen, "Notes on the Beginnings of Collective Bargaining," p. 233. From *Eighth Annual Report of the Bureau of Labor Statistics,* Massachusetts, 1877, pp. 27, 30. (Italics added.)

Perhaps because of their traditional independence and aloofness from entangling alliances with the rest of the labor movement, writers have tended to neglect the example set by railway-operating unions for other labor organizations not only in the establishment of collective bargaining but also in the rapidity with which their agreements expanded and matured in content. Indeed, by 1920 these railway organizations had achieved contracts as mature in terms of subject matter as were most agreements of a much later date.

The first agreement on record was between the engineers and the New York Central Railroad in 1875. Since it was only one page long and involved only seven short sections, it is reproduced in its entirety:[23]

New York Central and Hudson River Railroad
                              Grand Central Depot
                              New York, Jan. 26, 1875

The established rate of pay for locomotive engineers of this company as agreed upon this day, to take effect on the 1st day of February, 1872, is as follows:

1. For all passenger and freight engineers 3 cents per mile run, actual mileage, excepting the run is under 100 miles for which $3.50 per day will be paid.

2. For all engineers of switch and work trains $3.50 per day, including Sunday, and when required to report for duty.

3. It is understood that the number of engineers are to be kept down to the lowest possible number necessary to perform the work of the company, and in case engineers are dropped from the service of the company by reason of falling off in business, the youngest enginers in the service of the company are to be taken first.

4. This abolishes all pay for Sundays when not actually running, and all lay-over, shop, and extra days.

5. When engines in actual service become disabled and are put in the shop for repairs, then the master mechanic shall furnish engineers running such engines with engines to take their place.

6. The time and mileage of engineers shall be computed and and carried out separately for each day's work.

[23] Report of the Eight-Hour Commission (1918), pp. 352–354, Brotherhood of Locomotive Engineers, *Official Report of Agreements Made between Officials of the Roads Represented and Committees Representing the Engineers Employed Thereon* (April 1, 1894), pp. 2–3. See also Reed C. Richardson, *The Locomotive Engineers, 1863–1963* (Ann Arbor: Bureau of Industrial Relations, University of Michigan, 1963), pp. 196–97.

7. This shall take the place of all existing agreements.

WM. H. VANDERBILT,
PRESIDENT
J. P. CHAMBERS,
FOR VICE PRESIDENT

M. J. RICKETT, *FOR ENGINEERS*

1830–
1886

By way of further illustrating the extent to which railroad collective bargaining developed during the seventies and eighties, Chart 1–2 gives a chronology of work practices and unilaterally established rules prior to collective bargaining (broken bar) and work rules negotiated (solid bar) from 1830 to 1886. The chronological appearance of the various rules bears no relationship to their general importance. Some rules involved little financial outlay or concession on the part of the carriers and were therefore easily obtained. Other rules of greater importance involved substantial concessions on the part of the carrier and as a result provided grounds for stiffer resistance. The chart does not indicate the extent to which railroads had incorporated any of the rules into their contracts. Its main purpose is to show approximately when the various rules were first incorporated into written contracts and the extensive areas already covered by collective bargaining agreements on some railroads in 1886—a year when most other unions were still fighting for their existence and the general labor movement was passing through the "Great Upheaval."[24]

Environment

Environment is considered to be all those forces outside the collective bargaining process that by their impact have influenced the character and development of collective bargaining. Collective bargaining is an institutional process given birth by the presence and interaction of two organized institutional groups: labor and management. Whatever tends to affect these two institutional groups in their relations with each other may also have an impact on their collective bargaining relationship. The status and character of collective bargaining as an institutional process at any given time is a function of the intermix of broad economic, social, and political forces as they affect society, and through society its institutions, and through these institutions processes such as collective bargaining. To attempt to picture the evolution of collective bargaining without considering the influence of environment would be to see the evolution only as a series of steps without understanding why the steps occurred.

Three points are clear in the description of collective bargaining in

[24] Richardson, *The Locomotive Engineer*, p. 234.

CHART 1–2   Chronology of Work Rules, 1830–1886

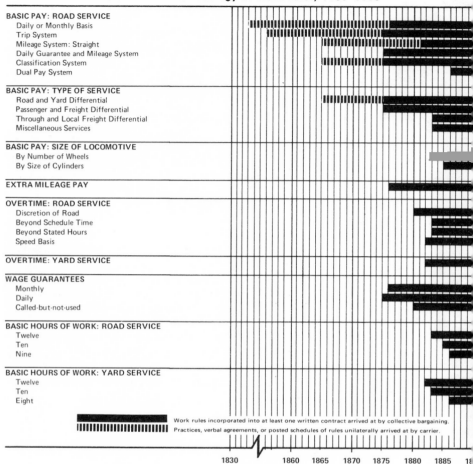

BASIC PAY: ROAD SERVICE
Daily or Monthly Basis
Trip System
Mileage System: Straight
Daily Guarantee and Mileage System
Classification System
Dual Pay System

BASIC PAY: TYPE OF SERVICE
Road and Yard Differential
Passenger and Freight Differential
Through and Local Freight Differential
Miscellaneous Services

BASIC PAY: SIZE OF LOCOMOTIVE
By Number of Wheels
By Size of Cylinders

EXTRA MILEAGE PAY

OVERTIME: ROAD SERVICE
Discretion of Road
Beyond Schedule Time
Beyond Stated Hours
Speed Basis

OVERTIME: YARD SERVICE

WAGE GUARANTEES
Monthly
Daily
Called-but-not-used

BASIC HOURS OF WORK: ROAD SERVICE
Twelve
Ten
Nine

BASIC HOURS OF WORK: YARD SERVICE
Twelve
Ten
Eight

Work rules incorporated into at least one written contract arrived at by collective bargaining.
Practices, verbal agreements, or posted schedules of rules unilaterally arrived at by carrier.

1830   1860   1865   1870   1875   1880   1885   18

18

CHART 1–2 Chronology of Work Rules, 1830–1886 (Continued)

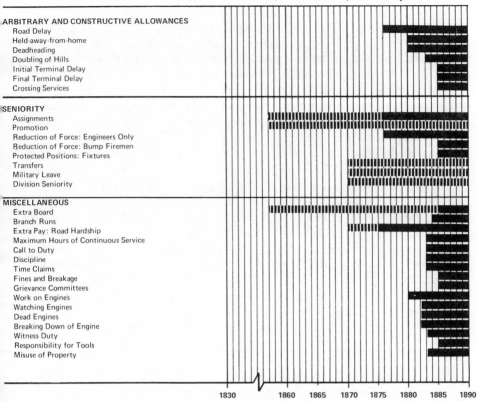

ARBITRARY AND CONSTRUCTIVE ALLOWANCES
  Road Delay
  Held-away-from-home
  Deadheading
  Doubling of Hills
  Initial Terminal Delay
  Final Terminal Delay
  Crossing Services

SENIORITY
  Assignments
  Promotion
  Reduction of Force: Engineers Only
  Reduction of Force: Bump Firemen
  Protected Positions: Fixtures
  Transfers
  Military Leave
  Division Seniority

MISCELLANEOUS
  Extra Board
  Branch Runs
  Extra Pay: Road Hardship
  Maximum Hours of Continuous Service
  Call to Duty
  Discipline
  Time Claims
  Fines and Breakage
  Grievance Committees
  Work on Engines
  Watching Engines
  Dead Engines
  Breaking Down of Engine
  Witness Duty
  Responsibility for Tools
  Misuse of Property

1830   1860   1865   1870   1875   1880   1885   1890

the first century: (1) Collective bargaining was not the customary means by which labor and management reconciled their differences. (2) Its growth was not coextensive with the growth of the labor movement. (3) In spite of its minor role in labor–management relations of the period, the idea had taken hold, and the practice of collective bargaining had evolved sufficiently to provide a sound foundation for future expansion.

The fact that collective bargaining did develop in some instances is probably accounted for by the chance combination of circumstances even though the overall environment was hostile. First, a basic step had been taken toward joint negotiations between labor and management simply with the emergence of labor organizations. This established a natural drive toward such negotiations, since the purpose of the labor organization was to represent its members with the employers. Second, given union organizations, wherever the labor organization and the employer found themselves evenly balanced in power, there was a natural impetus to consider breaking the stalemate through negotiation rather than force. Third, since collective bargaining is essentially a "moderate, businesslike process," whenever a particular labor organization and employer were inclined toward moderation and a businesslike approach to their problems, it was probable that a form of collective bargaining would emerge.

Most union–management situations in the nineteenth century were not characterized by collective bargaining relationships. It follows, therefore, that other environmental factors must have acted to retard the development of the process.

The nature of labor organizations until the latter part of the nineteenth century was often an obstacle in and of itself to the development of collective bargaining. The solid development of collective bargaining is in part a function of stable organization and continuity of relationships between the employer and the labor organization. It would be difficult to characterize the labor organizations of the nineteenth century as stable, since they seemed highly susceptible to destruction by depression and recession. Unions in this period have been described as experiencing "great difficulty . . . in staying organized for any purpose," and as being "highly unstable," and "mowed down and swept out of existence"[25] in every industrial crisis. Union membership in the period prior to the 1890s parallels the business cycle, periodically being weakened or destroyed by such recessions as those of 1817–1820, 1837–1852, 1857–1862, 1873, and 1887. As long as unionism itself was highly unstable, there was not much of a chance, except in a few instances, that collective bargaining and negotiated contractual agreements could develop with any continuity.

[25] Commons et al., *History of Labour in the United States* (1926), I, pp. 159–61.

Along with instability, a second characteristic of labor organizations delayed the development of collective bargaining. This was the lack of a unified approach to their common problems by labor organizations as a group. The type of unionism most conducive to the growth of collective bargaining is business unionism. Collective bargaining itself, as a moderate, businesslike process, thrives best in an atmosphere where the activities of both parties are based on a businesslike approach to problems. Although business unionism was evident in a few instances and seemed about to emerge on a broader scale at times, the full development and formalization of this concept did not emerge until the middle eighties. The typical picture of organized labor's activities during the period was constant experimentation in search of workable goals and the best means to achieve those goals. This led workers into experimenting with economic action, political action, and social reform, the scene shifting from period to period as one particular type of action seemed more enticing than the others. At times, worker organizations appeared bent on turning into hybrid groups where they were at one and the same time espousing the concepts of Marxism, the goals and activities of the uplift groups such as the Knights of Labor, and the "pure and simple trade unionism" of the right. This mixed and changing bag of activities and objectives merely evinced the confusion and turmoil of a highly experimental period of labor. It is no small wonder that as a result, the attention of workers' groups was more often than not turned in directions and to activities that were not favorable to the development of collective bargaining. Cooperation, political action, abolishment of the wage system, and achievement of the 8-hour day were often more high-sounding and alluring concepts than the slow, grinding process of economic pressure and collective negotiation typical of business unionism.

Attitudinal barriers to the emergence of collective bargaining were also significant during the trade union movement's first century. America in this period was slowly emerging from the hold and influence of past customs and traditions in which the relationship between employer or master and employee was fixed—where the employer's role, fixed by the master–servant doctrines of past centuries, was an authoritarian role —a paternalistic relationship, in which the employee was not to know why nor to question, but to do. It underscored what was considered as not only a God-given right and obligation to rule, but the responsibility of the master to guide his employees in their conduct both on and off the job. It was a doctrine that was as demeaning to the position and rights of the employee as it was ennobling to the position and rights of the master or employer.

Therefore, as workers began to apply pressure for a voice in determining their employment relationship, it was a foregone conclusion that they would receive a negative response from their employers. Two aspects of the situation emphasize the importance of custom and tradition. First, the demands of the employees were initially couched in polite and respectful terms, conveying their hesitancy at breaking with old and customary relationships. The employer made it clear, by direct reference or inference, that he considered this pressure an effrontery to him and to all that the employees also should hold sacred. However, as workers' organizations became more active, and as the passage of time and changing events began to whittle away at the rigidity of old customs, the temerity over breaking with the past gradually began to disappear. Individual examples can always be cited of enlightened employers, even from the earliest days of union organization, but for a substantial group, custom and tradition continued to play an important part in these employers' opposition to unions. This employer hostility was somewhat different from that of later periods, when collective bargaining was making rapid progress. The hostility of the nineteenth-century employer to unionism was inextricably interwoven with the social fabric of a society based strongly on custom and tradition, instead of a simple economic conflict between two competitive groups.

Several illustrations might serve as examples of the nature of this social as well as economic cleavage between employers and the employed. In 1825, the Boston house carpenters, 600 strong, struck for a 10-hour day—a strike in which, interestingly enough, they also raised the concept of overtime, working a longer time per day for a proportional equivalent. The response of the master carpenters, as well as that of "gentlemen engaged in building," well illustrates the attitudinal problem facing incipient labor groups. The masters' resolution read:

> RESOLVED, that we learn with surprize and regret, that a large number of those who are employed as Journeymen in this city, have entered into a combination for the purpose of altering the time of commencing and terminating their daily labor, from that which has been customary from *time immemorial*, thereby lessening the amount of labor each day in a very considerable degree.
>
> RESOLVED, that we consider such a combination as unworthy of that useful and industrious class of the community who are engaged in it; that it is fraught with numerous and pernicious evils, not only as respects their employers, but the public at large, and especially themselves. . . .
>
> RESOLVED. . . . that it will expose the Journeymen themselves to many temptations and improvident practices from which they are happily secure, while they attend to that wise and salutary maxim of Mechanics, "Mind Your Business."[26]

[26] Commons et al., eds., *A Documentary History of American Industrial Society*, VI, p. 77.

The "gentlemen of the building industry" followed with their own statement, which read:

RESOLVED, that these proceedings are a departure from the salutary and steady usages which have prevailed in this city and all New England, from *time immemorial* . . . that if this confederacy should be countenanced . . . it must of consequence extend to and embrace all Working Classes in every department in Town and Country, thereby effecting a most injurious change in all the modes of business, and in the operations of agriculture and commerce, opening a wide door for idleness and vice, and finally commuting the present condition of the Mechanical Classes, made happy and prosperous by *frugal, orderly and ancient habits,* for that degraded state, by which in other countries many of these classes are obliged to leave their homes. . . .[27]

In later periods, working rules were posted in establishments throughout the country that, while they might serve as a humorous respite to a dull lecture by a professor, do impart considerable insight into attitudinal problems still existing among employers concerning the status of their employees. No attempt is made to generalize from the examples presented. These rules reflect a continuing carryover of old attitudes and relationships indicative of an atmosphere within which it would be hard to visualize collective bargaining thriving. To say the least, these work rules are indicative of a patronizing attitude and wide social barriers between employer and employee. They underscore the lack of faith of the employer in the ability of the worker to constructively order or determine his own life, on or off the job, and even more so to dictate terms of employment to the employer.

To illustrate, employees were told that their honesty and integrity would be suspect if it were found that they were "in the habit of smoking Spanish Cigars, being shaved at the barber's, going to dances and other places of amusement," using "liquor in any form," or frequenting "pool or public halls." They were further ordered to pay "not less than five dollars per year to the church" or to pay their "tithes," and they "must" or were "expected" to "attend Sunday school regularly." Other work rules covered retirement: "Every employee should lay aside from each pay a goodly sum of his earnings for his benefits during his declining years, so that he will not become a burden upon the charity of his betters."[28] The subject of courting was not beyond employers: "Men employees will be

---

[27] *Ibid.*, p. 79.
[28] Sources used include Store Working Rules, Carson, Pirie Scott and Co. (1857); Mount Cory Carriage and Wagon Work (1872); Sterling Furniture Co. (1872). From the author's personal file.

given an evening off each week for courting purposes, or two evenings a week if they go regularly to church" or "to the prayer meeting."[29]
Wage increases were not overlooked:

> The employee who has performed his labors faithfully and without fault for a period of five years in my service, and who has been thrifty and attentive to his religious duties, and is looked upon by his fellow men as a substantial and law abiding citizen, will be given an increase of five cents per day in his pay, providing a just return in profits from the business.[30]

Instability of union organizations, lack of solidarity as to purpose, confusion, experimentation as to means and ends, and attitudinal obstacles that were social (custom and tradition) as well as economic—all enter into the environmental forces hostile to the rapid growth of collective bargaining in the first century of the labor movement.

SELECTED REFERENCES

INTRODUCTION TO ANNOTATED REFERENCES. The annotated references appended to each chapter are not meant to cover exhaustively all references to the subject matter of the chapter. Rather, I have selected basic readings that for most purposes will adequately cover the reader's quest for additional information. If the reader wishes to pursue any particular subject area in further depth, the readings chosen will provide references to additional reading materials.

Chamberlain, Neil W., *Collective Bargaining*. New York: McGraw-Hill, 1951.
Professor Chamberlain's interpretation of the historical evolution of collective bargaining is basic reading for the interested student. No other writings before or since have analyzed the adaptation of collective bargaining to the changing social environment of which it is a part. Looking ahead from 1950, Chamberlain fully expected collective bargaining to continue to develop as a part of the process of social ferment.

Commons, John R., and associates, eds., *A Documentary History of American Industrial Society*. Cleveland, O.: Arthur H. Clark Co., 1910.
For the serious student of labor history, this series of ten volumes reproduces many documents vital to an understanding of the evolution of industrial society. The series covers a period from the plantation system to 1880.

Commons, John R. et al., *History of Labour in the United States*, Vols. I and II. New York: Macmillan, 1918.

[29] *Ibid.*
[30] *Ibid.*

Few labor historians would quarrel with the notion that the Commons series is the *sine qua non* source for any serious study of unionism and labor–management relations from colonial times to 1932. Volumes I and II provide a rich source of basic information on the development of labor relations to the end of the nineteenth century.

Dulles, Foster Rhea, *Labor in America.* New York: Thomas Y. Crowell, 1966.

For an easily read history of the American labor movement, this book is recommended to the reader. It serves as good background reading.

Jensen, Vernon H., "Notes on the Beginnings of Collective Bargaining," *Industrial and Labor Relations Review*, 9, No. 2 (January 1956), 225–34.

Professor Jensen holds to the idea that in contrast to the traditional view that the early years of unionism were characterized by intense conflict, the real picture was one of the development of collective bargaining as "a moderate, conservative process."

Millis, Harry A., and Royal E. Montgomery, *Organized Labor,* Vol. III. New York: McGraw-Hill, 1945.

This book, in Chapters 2–4, still remains one of the best-structured accounts of the rise of unions from the 1790s to the 1930s.

Sloane, Arthur A., and Fred Witney, *Labor Relations,* 3rd ed. Englewood Cliffs, N.J.: Prentice-Hall, 1976.

This is an excellent source for additional background reading before turning to the simulation exercise using CBO.

Taft, Philip, *The Structure and Government of Labor Unions.* Cambridge, Mass.: Harvard University Press, 1954.

Professor Taft deals with aspects of trade unions that he felt were sadly neglected. As a consequence, this book is concerned with a study of what goes on inside unions, how they conduct their affairs, to what extent there is competition for office, what they collect in dues, what they pay their officers.

Ulman, Lloyd, *American Trade Unionism—Past and Present: 1. The Development of Trades and Labor Unions,* Reprint No. 157, Institute of Industrial Relations, University of California, Berkeley, 1961.

In this study, Lloyd Ulman discusses the development of some of the "major institutional forms that have characterized organized labor in the United States." In discussing these forms, the author relates them to "the objectives they were designed to further" and to some of the "environmental characteristics with which they were designed to cope."

————, *The Rise of the National Trade Union—The Development and Significance of Its Structure, Governing Institutions, and Economic Policies.* Cambridge, Mass.: Harvard University Press, 1955.

Although some studies have been made of individual unions, it was left to Ulman to bring together into a comprehensive study the facts about the development of union government and policies and to show how the present national unions evolved into what they are.

Evolution of Collective Bargaining— 1890-1945

CHAPTER 2

FROM UNILATERALISM TO COLLECTIVE BARGAINING—1890–1930

Labor–management relations moved into the dawn of a new era with the emergence of the twentieth century. Unilateral dealings by each side were replaced by collective bargaining, and the era of the trade agreement emerged. Collective bargaining became coextensive with the trade union movement wherever stable relationships were established between management and labor. The headway made and the acceptance achieved by collective bargaining signified that the "idea of joint partnership between organised labour and organised capital, which, even since the fifties, had been struggling for acceptance, finally came to fruition."[1] In like manner, the clarification of the concept of the trade agreement led "the way from an industrial system which was alternately either despotism or anarchy to a constitutional form of government in industry."[2] However, all was not quiet on the labor front. On the contrary, the successful establishment of collective bargaining and the trade agreement resulted from many hard-fought battles, some successful and some resulting in bitter defeat.

The Labor Movement

Aside from a minor threat by the Industrial Workers of the World, this period reflects the progress of the constituent unions affiliated with the newly organized American Federation of Labor. With formation of the AFL in 1886 from the old structure of the Federation of Organized

[1] John R. Commons et al., *History of Labour in the United States* (New York: Macmillan, 1918), II, p. 524.
[2] *Ibid.*, p. 520.

Trades and Labor Organizations in the United States and Canada, and the decline and demise of labor organizations (Knights of Labor) dedicated to social change and idealism, the period belongs to those unions espousing the new trade union philosophy of business unionism. It was a period during which unions achieved a large measure of stability through better management and through the centralized strength and influence of national organizations. Treasuries, although small by today's standards, were more adequate than in the past. The unions themselves, confined to narrower parameters in both philosophy and organization, were able to exercise greater withholding power in their dealings with employers. It was a period in which a few significant breakthroughs for collective bargaining in the stove, mining, and clothing industries not only served as a pattern for other groups to follow but made it clear that breakthroughs were possible and therefore raised the expectations of others. It was a period also in which organized labor was able to establish continuity of existence even though subjected to the frontal attacks of individual employers, the legal and economic pressures of the "open shop" movements, and the more insidious and damaging effects of scientific management and the introduction of personnel and human relations management by employers. The durability and stability of the labor movement was nowhere better exemplified than in its continuing will and ability to exist in the face of a double threat: The courts, by interpretation, strengthened the hands of the employers in their attempts to contain and destroy unions and at the same time gave full approval to those employer activities aimed at destroying the workingman's right to organize.

In more specific terms, the period witnessed, with the emergence of the AFL and its constituent organizations, a degree of stability and permanence of character that neither the onslaught of depression in 1893 nor the severe defeats at Homestead and Pullman in 1892 and 1894 respectively could appreciably damage. With the return to prosperity in the later nineties, the stage was set for solid advancement.

The wage-earning class was permanently separated from the middle class. Wage consciousness permanently displaced middle-class panaceas, such as productive co-operation, currency, and land reform. The separation from the outside was accompanied by a closing up of the ranks within. Yet the new solidarity was not the emotional solidarity of the Knights of Labor, but a solidarity expressing itself in the co-operation of the national trades unions within the federation and with the growing industrial unionism.[3]

Between 1897 and 1904, a phenomenal growth in union membership

[3] Commons et al., *History of Labour in the United States,* p. 519.

occurred, from 447,000 to 2,072,000. The growth was at a more rapid pace than the increase in population or in the gainfully employed. Viewed in terms of permanence of achievement, this growth found no counterpart in any earlier period of history. Although heavily concentrated in transportation, building construction, and mining, the growth was significant for its extension into "heretofore untouched trades and amongst the unskilled, as well as branching out into new geographical regions, the South and the West."[4]

From 1904 to 1910, there was practically no increase in membership. This was primarily a result of the efforts of employers' groups to contain and destroy unionism by promotion of the open shop. The open-shop campaigns were conducted via direct economic pressure on individual unions, a combination of employer financial resources that could outlast, wear down, and finally break union organizational drives, publicity, and court action under the antitrust laws. Some notable success was achieved in breaking the back of unionism in steel, meat-packing, and some teamsters' and seamen's unions. But the very fact that organized labor was able to maintain its total membership in the face of five critical years of employers' attacks on the industrial, legislative, and judicial fronts bespeaks a newfound strength and stability unlike that in any earlier period of its history.

From 1910 to 1914, the upward movement in membership was resumed, but without the pronounced impetus of the earlier years. This period was followed by wartime years of rapid growth under the patronage of government bodies and edicts that deliberately worked to organized labor's benefit in order to encourage maximum support of workers engaged in the wartime productive effort. Even though the greater part of this membership increase was lost in the next decade, the more positive intervention of government in labor–management relations established a precedent that was to be revived in the 1930s, with the government assuming a permanent role in those relations.

The twenties were years of contrasts and contradictions for organized labor, years in which the opposition was at one and the same time direct, as in the past, but also more subtly involving forces aimed at weakening the American trade union movement. The direct opposition was once again a frontal onslaught against unions in the form of an open-shop campaign, this time accompanied by an appeal to patriotism, called the "American Plan." The more subtle influences that were probably the most effective in reducing the wartime gains in membership were, first, the introduction by employers of personnel management and employee representation plans as a substitute for unionism, and second, the gradual increase in real wages that made unionism on economic grounds less

[4] *Ibid.*, p. 522.

appealing to workers. Between these two influences, organized labor gradually lost most of its wartime gains, and membership returned to a level of 3,442,000 in 1929—just slightly above the pre—World War I period. This was quite contrary to the usual rise in union membership during periods of prosperity.

The subtle impact of personnel management is aptly described:

> The labor policy of Welfare Capitalism, operating as personnel management, and buttressed by psychological researches of both the laboratory and the "what's on the worker's mind" varieties, attempted to treat the worker as a human being and to approach his problems from his own point of view. . . . Thus it substituted direct guarantees for those indirectly secured by the Union's restrictive rules. . . . This general policy of substitution was crowned by the instrumental substitution of the "company union" for historically evolved unionism, carrying out unreservedly the fundamental idea of Welfare Capitalism that the only solidarity natural in industry is the solidarity which unites all those in the same business establishment, whether employer or employee.[5]

Collective Bargaining

The historical record shows that collective bargaining made headway beginning with the 1890s to the point where it was no longer a novel process. It was not long until it was instituted in "numerous individual establishments, in a number of industries on a local basis (such as the building trades and printing), and in ten or twelve industries on a national basis."[6] Although there were some major defeats for both union organization and collective bargaining in such industries as steel and meat-packing, these were more than outweighed, in terms of the continuity of collective bargaining and the firm establishment of the trade agreement system, by the successes in such industries as mining, construction, transportation, printing, and clothing. Perhaps the most effective way to show the form and substance of collective bargaining and the trade agreements in this period is to look at some of the specific success stories.

The era of trade agreements, according to Commons, was launched by the epochal stove molders' agreement of 1891.[7] This agreement capped three turbulent, discontented decades replete with strikes and

---

[5] Selig Perlman and Philip Taft, *History of Labour in the United States, 1896–1932* (New York: Macmillan, 1935), IV, pp. 580–81.

[6] Neil W. Chamberlain, *Collective Bargaining* (New York: McGraw-Hill, 1951), p. 33.

[7] Commons et al., *History of Labour in the United States*, II, p. 480. Commons notes that the iron- and steelworkers had a trade agreement as early as 1866, but the trade was so strong "that its example had no power to make other trades aspire with confidence towards the same." (P. 480.)

lockouts, in which the atmosphere was so highly charged that almost any issue might be a cause for war, and in which the two parties fought each other to a standstill! It is small wonder that the agreement of 1891 was considered a landmark in the evolution of collective bargaining. The friction and unstable relations of the past were replaced by the principle of peaceful settlement of disputes. Under the agreement, when disputes arose, the parties were to attempt settlement directly. If this failed, then the dispute was to be submitted to a conference committee of six, three from each side. The decision of the conference committee was to be binding for one year. While the dispute was being processed, no change in the status quo was to be permitted. For the next eight years, the stove molders' agreement was a "lone road-post pointing the way and acting as an incentive for other industries to follow."[8]

Pointing in the same direction and also epochal in its impact was the so-called "interstate agreement" resulting from the bituminous-coal strike of 1898 in the central competitive bituminous-coal district:

> . . . [T]he outcome of the contest was a great victory for the union and unionism. On the eve of the strike, the union's treasury was empty and its membership at the lowest point in history. Nevertheless, its call was answered by tens of thousands. . . . Besides the stabilizing influence on the miners' organization, the 1897 strike had a most inspiring effect upon the general labor movement. Here was a source of hope: a demoralized union challenging powerful national interests and winning the most important labor victory of a decade. The 1897 strike also encouraged and developed the agreement system. In all it was a notable victory for labor. . . .[9]

Statesmanlike conduct by union president John Mitchell during the anthracite-coal strike in 1902 gave further support to the enthusiasm generated by the bituminous-coal workers' success of 1898. Mitchell, despite the heaviest of pressure, refused to sanction a sympathetic strike by bituminous-coal miners in aid of the anthracite strikers. The ground for his refusal was that the bituminous miners were under an agreement, and to strike would be a breach of faith with the employers signator to that agreement. His stand placed the onus for prolongation of the strike upon the anthracite operators and, most important, encouraged a much more sympathetic public attitude toward labor.

Building-trade unions in the meantime were experiencing significant advances. Comprising almost two dozen unions, the crafts expanded their hold in the building-construction industry from an initial 68,000 members going into the second century, to over 391,000 in 1904 and over 500,000

---

[8] *Ibid.,* p. 524.
[9] Perlman and Taft, *History of Labour in the United States,* IV, p. 25

by World War I. Taft notes that the most stable unions in the United States were in the building-construction industry.[10]

Just as epochal in their impact upon the development of trade agreements were the agreements secured by the Ladies' Garment Workers Union and the Clothing Workers Union. An agreement resulting from the settlement of the Cloakmakers' strike of 1910 established, among a number of other important provisions, a board of arbitration, one representative from each side and attorneys from the two groups. The board was charged with considering and settling all grievances, and rulings of the board were to be final and binding. This brought to an industry "hitherto considered hopelessly anarchial" a form of industrial government. The success and "its highly constructive outcome put the immigrant workers in the forefront of the American labor movement . . . sixty thousand of these workers had demonstrated a capacity for self-discipline and organization unsuspected even by their warmest friends."[11]

Not to be outdone, the railroad brotherhoods had also continued to build upon the sound foundation of collective bargaining and trade agreements established before the turn of the century. For example, the Locomotive Engineers had succeeded by 1920 in enlarging and extending written contracts to about 100 pages and to almost all the railroad systems of the country. By 1902, 118 carriers were covered by written contracts; by 1912, 243 carriers; and by 1916, 348 carriers.[12] The role of these railroad brotherhoods in the extension of collective agreements is graphically illustrated by Chart 2–1, which portrays the chronology of work rules or agreement coverage up to 1920.[13]

Environment

Even though collective bargaining was faced with the restraints of intense employer opposition and adverse court decisions, the environment within which it had to develop, beginning with the 1890s, was much more favorable and conducive to positive results than in earlier periods.

In the first place, unions had developed some permanence and continuity not known in earlier days. This was evinced in two ways. No longer were unions characterized by spasms of union activity during prosperity phases of business cycles, followed by periods of disorganization and decline during depression that in some instances completely destroyed union organizations. But the stability was more than the ability to maintain organization and membership in the face of economic fluctu-

---

[10] Philip Taft, *Organized Labor in American History* (New York: Harper & Row, 1964), p. 203.

[11] Perlman and Taft, *History of Labour in the United States*, IV, p. 300.

[12] Reed C. Richardson, *The Locomotive Engineer, 1863–1963* (Ann Arbor: Bureau of Industrial Relations, University of Michigan, 1963), p. 363.

[13] *Ibid.*, pp. 367–69.

CHART 2–1   Brotherhood of Locomotive Engineers
Chronology of Work Rules, 1830–1920

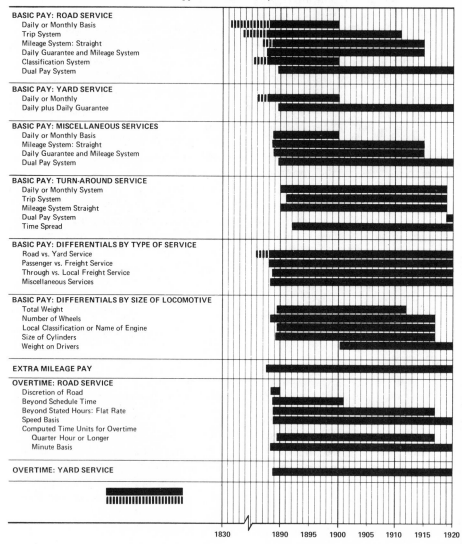

BASIC PAY: ROAD SERVICE
Daily or Monthly Basis
Trip System
Mileage System: Straight
Daily Guarantee and Mileage System
Classification System
Dual Pay System

BASIC PAY: YARD SERVICE
Daily or Monthly
Daily plus Daily Guarantee

BASIC PAY: MISCELLANEOUS SERVICES
Daily or Monthly Basis
Mileage System: Straight
Daily Guarantee and Mileage System
Dual Pay System

BASIC PAY: TURN-AROUND SERVICE
Daily or Monthly System
Trip System
Mileage System Straight
Dual Pay System
Time Spread

BASIC PAY: DIFFERENTIALS BY TYPE OF SERVICE
Road vs. Yard Service
Passenger vs. Freight Service
Through vs. Local Freight Service
Miscellaneous Services

BASIC PAY: DIFFERENTIALS BY SIZE OF LOCOMOTIVE
Total Weight
Number of Wheels
Local Classification or Name of Engine
Size of Cylinders
Weight on Drivers

EXTRA MILEAGE PAY

OVERTIME: ROAD SERVICE
Discretion of Road
Beyond Schedule Time
Beyond Stated Hours: Flat Rate
Speed Basis
Computed Time Units for Overtime
  Quarter Hour or Longer
  Minute Basis

OVERTIME: YARD SERVICE

1830   1890 1895 1900 1905 1910 1915 1920

CHART 2–1   Brotherhood of Locomotive Engineers
Chronology of Work Rules, 1830–1920 (Continued)

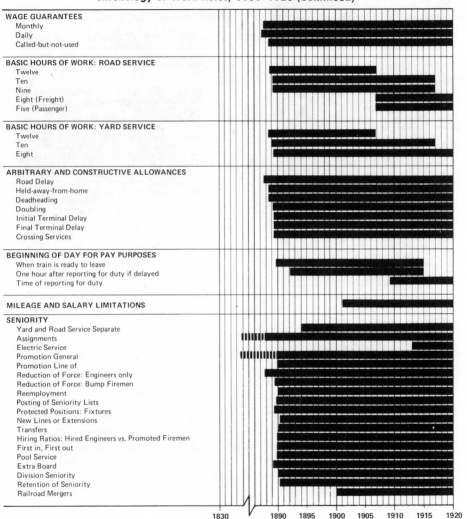

WAGE GUARANTEES
  Monthly
  Daily
  Called-but-not-used

BASIC HOURS OF WORK: ROAD SERVICE
  Twelve
  Ten
  Nine
  Eight (Freight)
  Five (Passenger)

BASIC HOURS OF WORK: YARD SERVICE
  Twelve
  Ten
  Eight

ARBITRARY AND CONSTRUCTIVE ALLOWANCES
  Road Delay
  Held-away-from-home
  Deadheading
  Doubling
  Initial Terminal Delay
  Final Terminal Delay
  Crossing Services

BEGINNING OF DAY FOR PAY PURPOSES
  When train is ready to leave
  One hour after reporting for duty if delayed
  Time of reporting for duty

MILEAGE AND SALARY LIMITATIONS

SENIORITY
  Yard and Road Service Separate
  Assignments
  Electric Service
  Promotion General
  Promotion Line of
  Reduction of Force: Engineers only
  Reduction of Force: Bump Firemen
  Reemployment
  Posting of Seniority Lists
  Protected Positions: Fixtures
  New Lines or Extensions
  Transfers
  Hiring Ratios: Hired Engineers vs. Promoted Firemen
  First in, First out
  Pool Service
  Extra Board
  Division Seniority
  Retention of Seniority
  Railroad Mergers

1830   1890   1895   1900   1905   1910   1915   1920

CHART 2–1   Brotherhood of Locomotive Engineers
Chronology of Work Rules, 1830–1920 (Continued)

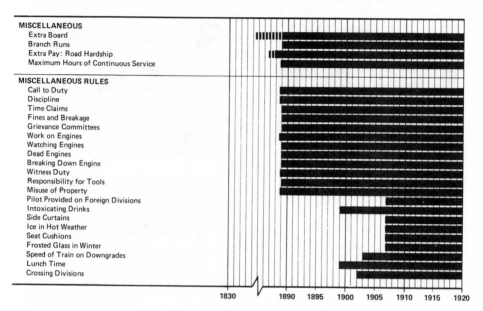

ations. It was also a stability of purpose and goals, born of the unity brought on by the adoption of the new trade unionism philosophy. Now, in good times and bad, instead of alternating between economic or trade union action on the one hand and panaceas and politics on the other, the union movement held steadily to its business unionism mode of operation. This stability of both organization and mode of operation introduced a positive factor in the drive for collective bargaining and trade agreements.

Second, business unionism by its very nature gave a positive thrust to the drive for collective bargaining. It has been pointed out that collective bargaining is a conservative and businesslike process. It is easy, therefore, to conclude that with the adoption of the business unionism philosophy by the trade union movement, the "trade agreement" became the *sine qua non* of American trade unionism and brought with it a natural and positive emphasis upon developing collective bargaining relationships.

Third, nothing succeeds like success. And success is more easily achieved in an atmosphere where the developments taking place are understood, not novel. As a result of developments in iron, transportation, and shoes in the seventies and eighties, and the rapid spread of the trade agreement both geographically and by trade in the 1890s, neither the trade agreement nor collective bargaining was foreign to the American mind. Consequently, with the notable and successful formalization by the stove molders, miners, railroad men, and garment workers of collective bargaining and the trade agreement in their industries, it raised the anticipation and hopes of other workers that they too could accomplish the same results. Both the penetration of these significant industries and the model trade agreements that resulted were certainly an impetus and example for others to follow.

Fourth, not only was the trade agreement no longer novel and therefore more easily accepted by the public, but the nature of developments in the economy created a more favorable, if not at times sympathetic, public attitude toward organized labor and its goals. A "clear gauge" of attitudinal change is shown by the McNamara dynamite case:

> What difference between the attitude of the public toward this case of extreme and premeditated violence and its attitude toward the suspected Chicago anarchists! In 1886, bloody revenge and suppression [Haymarket] were violently demanded. In 1912, nothing more drastic was heard than a demand for an impartial investigation of the causes of labour unrest, with a view to the prevention of future conflicts, and scarcely any call for revenge or any disaster to the labour movement as a whole.[14]

Other indications of attitudinal changes are numerous. In the bituminous-coal strike of 1897, "A great deal of public support had been won by the peaceful attitude of the strikers," and in August of 1897, "the Governor of Indiana publicly expressed his approval of the walkout and urged the citizens of his state to aid the strikers."[15] Mitchell's statesmanship in the anthracite-coal strike of 1902 not only came "as a pleasant surprise to a public which had little inkling that labor unions considered their contractual obligations as binding under all circumstances,"[16] but provoked discussion and publicity to the point where "the public at large became accustomed to view the labour question in a matter-of-course, nonhysterical light."[17] Taft observes:

[14] Commons et al., *History of Labour in the United States*, II, p. 528.
[15] Perlman and Taft, *History of Labour in the United States*, IV, p. 24.
[16] *Ibid.*, p. 48.
[17] Commons et al., *History of Labour in the United States*, II, p. 528.

Prolonged unemployment, with its accompanying destitution and suffering, tarnished the reputation of business, and the public regarded, at least for a time, the workers' quest for greater security and higher pay as justifiable. Exposures of corporate derelictions made the demands of labor for some countervailing power appear reasonable. The friendlier public attitude toward labor was written into federal and state legislation.[18]

Finally, although the court system, imbued with the sacredness of private property rights, was restrictive in its decisions, the federal government itself assumed a more neutral stance. Laissez faire, the less government intervention the better, became the order of the day. Only one industry experienced government intervention—the railroads.

It should be remembered that the brotherhoods, because of their strategic position in the country's transportation system, were involved in frontier developments in labor–management legislation that, even though immediately confined to transportation, were to establish a pattern for much of the labor legislation dealing with collective bargaining enacted after 1932. The philosophy of government intervention in the affairs of the railroad industry, because of the high degree of public interest involved (illustrated by the Interstate Commerce Act of 1887), led directly to a parallel line of reasoning with respect to labor–management relations in the industry. If the railroad industry needed regulation in order to protect the public interest, then labor–management relations might likewise require government supervision in order to ensure uninterrupted service. Thus, the government set about establishing machinery to minimize labor disputes.

But the government did not inject itself into the field of railway labor relations as a regulatory force. Its approach was to provide machinery to facilitate, not force, a solution in disputes that the parties were unable to settle by private negotiation. Three acts were passed between 1888 and 1913, providing variously for the use of arbitration, mediation, and fact-finding boards as instruments to solve disputes. The importance of these acts lay not in their practical accomplishment but in the precedent they set for government intervention in labor relations. Eventually, this led to the passage of the Railway Labor Act of 1926, which for many years was known as the "model act" because of its influence on the National Labor Relations Act and other legislation of the thirties. But beyond its serving as a model, it should be noted that the passage of the Railway Labor Act was a great landmark in the development of collective bargaining because, although confined to a single industry—transportation—the act enunciated for the first time public policy with respect to

[18] Taft, *Organized Labor in American History*, p. 162.

labor–management relations. Employees in an industry were for the first time guaranteed by legislation the right to organize and bargain collectively through representatives of their own choosing. Carriers and their employees were required to exert every reasonable effort to make and maintain agreements concerning rates of pay, rules, and working conditions, and to settle disputes, whether they arose from the application of the agreements or otherwise. Finally, clear recognition was given to the need for a difference in the methods of handling disputes arising over the terms of the agreement, and methods in disputes arising over interpretation of those terms. This marked the zenith of the contributions of both the railroad industry and the railroad brotherhoods to the development of collective bargaining. The brotherhoods, once known as the "aristocracy of the labor movement," and the senior brotherhood, the Locomotive Engineers—described by newspapers in the 1880s as the "most powerful labor organization in the country"—contributed much to the founding period of collective bargaining but now were soon to be eclipsed by the decline of their own industry and their overshadowing by unions in other industries.

COLLECTIVE BARGAINING AND PUBLIC POLICY—1930–1945

Introduction

No previous period in the history of American trade unionism, other than the Great Upheaval of 1886, matched the epochal importance of the 1930s in the development of collective bargaining and industrial self-government for the workingman. With the passage of the National Industrial Recovery Act in 1933, followed in 1935 by the National Labor Relations Act, collective bargaining received a degree of public respectability that a century and a half of private efforts had been unable to achieve. The impact on the organizing and collective bargaining activities of the trade union movement was nothing short of phenomenal.

The Labor Movement

The intent of Congress in the passage of the National Labor Relations Act of 1935 was unmistakably clear. Workers were now, by law, to have the right to organize, to choose their own representatives, and to engage in activities in the pursuit of this right. What a difference this was to make for the millions of unskilled and semiskilled workers who, despite two major attempts in the past, had never been able to gain recognition of their right to representation on any permanent basis! Private efforts to gain such recognition had, for the most part, been successful only among the skilled workers, who had sufficient leverage, through the threat to withdraw their labors, to bring the employers to term. Now, the industrial worker whose ranks had been swelled by the technological changes of the Industrial Revolution, and especially the movement toward mass-production methods of the 1920s, had the leverage of the law in his pursuit of the right to be represented.

The impact of these developments upon the organizing efforts of existing unions and the unorganized was immediate and dramatic. Thousands upon thousands of workers in the basic industries where the proponents of the "open shop" and the opponents of trade unionism had been centered began knocking on the doors of the trade unions. Caught unprepared for the onslaught, the American Federation of Labor first attempted to house the flood of new members by establishing temporary structures where there was nowhere else for the new members to go. These, known as federal unions, were designed to provide a home only until a way could be worked out to absorb the new adherents in the traditional and long-standing craft unions of the trade union movement. The nature of events that followed showed that neither the American Federation of Labor nor its traditional craft union constituency was prepared philosophically to meet the task. Its craft union orientation was simply too narrow to accommodate workers who could not easily be identified as to type of work other than on an industrial basis. There were those, however, in the trade union movement—a minority, to be sure— who saw in the acceptance of the principle of industrial unionism along with craft unionism the only viable solution. This group, led by John L. Lewis and his industrially organized Mine Workers Union, and bolstered by the rapidly expanding membership of federal unions, first introduced the principle of industrial union organization in 1934 at a convention of the AFL. In a resolution approved by the convention, the supporters of the industrial union concept thought they had gained acceptance of the principle. Events that followed showed that the apparent victory was nothing more than political sop thrown to them by the dominant craft majority and was a paper victory only. The next year, the matter was faced head on by Lewis and the advocates of industrial unionism. A resolution was introduced that, if passed, would have placed the AFL's organizing activities unmistakably on a dual basis of both craft and industrial unionism. The resolution failed to receive a majority of votes, although the growing strength of the industrial union advocates was evinced by their receiving more than one-third of the delegate vote.

The next step was for the advocates of industrial unionism, still under the leadership of John L. Lewis and growing in strength, to form a Committee for Industrial Organization (CIO) within the AFL to promote their industrial union advocacy. In the eyes of the craft union majority, this was the commission of the unpardonable sin, "dualism." Without lengthy details, the course of events was then (1) an order from the AFL leadership to disband, (2) suspension upon refusal of the industrial union advocates to obey the order, and (3) expulsion from the AFL in 1938. The former committee was now formally organized into the Congress of Industrial Organization (CIO), a rival federation of the AFL. Dualism had been created in the labor movement.

> The defeat of the industrial union forces at the 1935 convention of the American Federation of Labor marked a new epoch in American labor history. The establishment of the Committee for Industrial Organization heralded a split in the forces of labor deeper and more permanent than anything in the past. For two decades, the factories, the press, and the legislative halls of the nation were to resound with strife between the contesting groups, each attempting to secure the allegiance of workers and to enroll them within its ranks. Seldom, even where political ideological factors separated segments of a national labor movement, has interunion warfare been more bitter and more violent than that which characterized the American scene beginning in 1935.[19]

The impact of dualism was not only to broaden the organizational base but to engender an intense rivalry between the two federations that, coupled with the protection of the right to organize that was extended by the NLRA, brought an era of membership expansion unrivaled in history. From a low of 2,689,000 organized workers in 1933, membership increased to 8,717,000 by 1940, 10,489,000 in 1941, and 14,796,000 in 1945. Even more dramatic than the absolute number of members is the fact that from 1930 to 1945, union membership as a percentage of the labor force grew from 7 to 22 percent. The major sources of gain were the basic industries—automobiles, steel, coal, and so on.

Such a rapid transformation could not help but have reverberations throughout the power structure of society. Now organized labor became a major institutional power group and a political force to be reckoned with by dint of its new legal status and the very rapid accretion of numbers. Not only was the growth in total numbers and therefore power significant, but the extension of unionism into the industrial areas of the economy was of equal significance. Twice before, there had been attempts to extend union organization into the ranks of the semiskilled and unskilled industrial workers—the Knights of Labor and the Industrial Workers of the World—but in both instances, conditions were not ripe for the emergence of permanent organizations in these areas.

The significance of the growth and transformation of the American labor movement in the 1930s is considered by Prof. Arthur M. Schlesinger

---

[19] Walter Galenson, *The CIO Challenge to the AFL* (Cambridge, Mass.: Harvard University Press, 1960), p. 3.

of Harvard to be one of the ten outstanding developments of the first half of the twentieth century, sharing the distinction with such tremendous events as the two world wars, the Great Depression, and the harnessing of atomic energy. Galenson states, "Few episodes in our history have been as dramatic as the upward thrust of American labor, suddenly breaking the bonds of constraint which had checked it for half a century."[20]

Collective Bargaining

The impact of the New Deal on labor's bargaining efforts was not only dramatic but, in many ways, the single most epochal development in the evolution of collective bargaining.

> Within a brief span of six years, American workers in the basic industrial sector of the nation witnessed the transformation of their bargaining organizations from relatively impotent bodies into equal partners in the industrial system.[21]

Not only had union organizing activities been raised by law to a respectability not known in the past, but collective bargaining and the trade agreement had now also achieved the same respectability.

It should be emphasized that by the enactment of the National Labor Relations Act, and through it, guarantee of the "full freedom of association, self-organization, and designation of representatives of their choosing," Congress was establishing the *means* to an *end*. The end or goal that Congress hoped to achieve through guarantee of the right of workers to organize was twofold: (1) an antidepression measure, and (2) the establishment of a system of industrial government through collective bargaining. The lack of the latter, said Congress, was to injure, impair, or interrupt commerce and to aggravate recurrent business depressions. Therefore, as a matter of public policy, Congress stated:

> It is hereby declared to be the policy of the United States to eliminate the causes of certain substantial obstructions to the free flow of commerce and to mitigate and eliminate these obstructions when they have occurred by encouraging the practice and procedure of collective bargaining and by protecting the exercise by workers of full freedom of association . . . for the purpose of negotiating the terms and conditions of their employment or other mutual aid or protection.[22]

The solid evidence of the spread of collective bargaining and trade agreements is found both in numbers and in the nature of the industries

---

[20] Galenson, *The CIO Challenge,* p. xvii.
[21] *Ibid.*
[22] National Labor Relations Act, Section 1.

in which industrial government was established. The increase in membership of unions to almost 15 million by 1945 also meant that some 12 million more workers were covered and constituted an increase of 500 percent, not an insignificant change. Not available is the number of trade agreements in 1933, but in 1945 there were well over 100,000 different trade agreements in operation at one time. The establishment of agreements in the steel and automobile industries reflects well the nature of change going on in individual industries:

> If there is any single series of events in the labor history of this period which may be characterized as of momentous import, it is the organization of the steel industry . . . a crushing defeat by the United States Steel Corporation in 1901. . . . Yet by March, 1937, the United States Steel Corporation, long a symbol of anti-unionism, had signed a collective contract with an outside union, an action that had repercussions throughout American industry.[23]

> By entirely stopping production of all General Motors cars in January and February and obtaining recognition in the first written and signed agreement on a national scale which that great citadel of the open shop had ever granted to a labor union, the CIO . . . opened the way for the remarkable upsurge in sentiment for union organization which is now going on in many sections of the country. . . .[24]

Environment

Basically, the changes in the 1930s that were of such significance for trade unions and the spread of collective bargaining were not changes unrelated to the past. As with most significant historical changes, the process was one of slow evolution, a gathering of forces for change reaching back, in some instances, a considerable period of time. Eventually in the course of time, there is juxtaposition of these underlying forces for change and a catalyst of sufficient power to effect the desired changes. So it was with the tremendous ideological shifts of both the public and the government in the 1930s. Industrial unionism was not new. Labor legislation was not new. The need for social change that would recognize the rights of human beings relative to property was not new. Collective bargaining and the trade agreement were not new. But in the past, the full recognition of these needs was hindered by an environment that was generally hostile and obstructive. Now, in the 1930s, the juxtaposition of needs and historical events occurred. The catalyst was the crash of 1929 and the ensuing Great Depression. The impetus to change was a significant shift in public and governmental

---

[23] Galenson, *The CIO Challenge*, p. 75.
[24] *Ibid.*, p. 141. From Russel B. Porter in the *New York Times*, April 4, 1937, IV, p. 10.

attitudes arising out of the economic and humanitarian needs of this unique, deep, and lengthy period of distress.

The Great Depression was not only the most severe depression in the history of the United States, but it caused a complete economic collapse, cutting across all economic classes and groups: "Great fortunes and the widow's mite together disappeared."[25] It was more shocking in its effect than past depressions had been: "Leaders in all walks of life, including economists, were dumbfounded at the speed with which the glittering structure of prosperity had collapsed like a house of cards."[26] It raised real questions about the applicability of the shibboleths of the past to a modern industrial world:

> In 1928 they had been promised "a chicken in every pot and two cars in every garage," if they elected Hoover. In 1932, when the owner of a garage felt himself lucky to have a roof on it and a chicken to relieve its emptiness, he had ceased to reverence the old shibboleths of "rugged individualism" and the "immutable laws of economics."[27]

The individual stresses of the moment created a state of mind not only more oriented to human needs but susceptible to change. "No language is graphic enough to picture the want that stalked through the land as economic conditions became worse . . . no mind sufficiently keen to measure the human losses that resulted."[28]

It was thus in this atmosphere of doubts about the ideology of the past, and of intense pressures upon the government to find solutions to the economic stress and the primacy of human needs, that the great social legislation of the 1930s in the field of labor was made possible, although it must be admitted that the AFL was more the recipient than the initiator of change.

SELECTED REFERENCES

Brody, David, ed., *The American Labor Movement*. New York: Harper & Row, 1971.

   A series of essays on the American labor movement, with an integrative theme. The editor was charged with the responsibility of selecting some of what he considered the best, most persuasive writings bearing on the

---

[25] James A. Barnes, *Wealth of the American People* (Englewood Cliffs, N.J.: Prentice-Hall, 1949), p. 68.

[26] Harold W. Faulkner, *American Economic History*, 8th ed. (New York: Harper & Row, 1954), p. 651.

[27] Fred O. Shannon, *America's Economic Growth* (New York: Macmillan, 1940), p. 744.

[28] Barnes, *Wealth of the American People*, p. 681.

American labor movement. For a penetrating look at some of the significant aspects of American labor in the late nineteenth century and early twentieth century, this book earns high marks.

Chamberlain, Neil W., *Collective Bargaining*. New York: McGraw-Hill, 1951.

See annotated reference to Chamberlain in Chapter 1.

Derber, Milton, and Edwin Young, eds., *Labor and the New Deal*. Madison: University of Wisconsin Press, 1957.

A definitive work on the rise of organized labor under the New Deal.

Galenson, Walter, *The CIO Challenge to the AFL*. Cambridge, Mass.: Harvard University Press, 1960.

An excellent and highly recommended study of the emergence and rise to power of the CIO.

Gross, James A., *The Makings of the National Labor Relations Board*, Vol. I. Albany: State University of New York Press, 1974.

The author notes the ever-increasing importance of administrative agencies as vital and pervasive forces in our society and the need for a major study of such groups. This study looks into the events of 1933–1937 leading to and following the establishment of the NLRB.

Taft, Philip, *The A. F. of L. in the Time of Gompers*. New York: Harper & Row, 1957.

The first to receive full access to AFL files and records, Professor Taft makes a notable contribution to the information about the rise of the AFL and its activities to the death of Gompers in 1924.

Taft, Philip, *The A. F. of L. From the Death of Gomper to the Merger*. New York: Harper & Row, 1959.

This constitutes the second phase of Professor Taft's study of the AFL. While not addressed directly to collective bargaining during the period, it does provide a useful framework through which a better understanding of the union movement and, with it, collective bargaining can be obtained.

Taft, Philip, *Organized Labor in American History*. New York: Harper & Row, 1964.

A good general history of organized labor, with considerable information about the growth of collective bargaining and the trade agreement.

Perlman, Selig, and Philip Taft, *History of Labour in the United States, 1896–1932*, Vol. IV. New York: Macmillan, 1935.

Continuing in the mold of the other three volumes of the Commons series on labor history, the Perlman and Taft volume provides a wealth of detailed and well-documented materials on the development of labor relations from the depression of the 1890s to the early 1930s. An outstanding feature of the book is the first chapter's "Conclusions from Past Experimentation."

Taylor, Benjamin J., and Fred Witney, *Labor Relations Law*, 2nd ed., Chapters 1–11. Englewood Cliffs, N.J.: Prentice-Hall, 1975.

Excellent coverage of the evolution of the law of collective bargaining from the early stages when, more often than not, the law was a hindrance to the growth of collective bargaining, to the emergence of public policy intended to encourage collective bargaining.

Evolution of Collective Bargaining— 1945-Present

CHAPTER 3

EMPLOYER ACCEPTANCE—1945–1962

One fact became clear in the postwar period: Collective bargaining had come of age. Initially, the move toward collective bargaining had been motivated by the need of workers, threatened by the increasing size and impersonal nature of the modern industrial organization, to make themselves heard through representation lest they be engulfed and lose their identity. The vehicle through which they gained representation and the hope for a collective bargaining relationship came with the formation of the labor organization. Over a century and a half, the growth of employee representation through collective bargaining was the chief beneficiary of the continuity and expansion of the trade union movement. Further progress was made when, in the 1930s, collective bargaining was given public respectability through a policy statement: "It is hereby declared to be the policy of the United States . . . by encouraging the practice and procedure of collective bargaining. . . ."[1] It remained for the postwar period to witness a final step—acceptance of collective bargaining as a permanent institutional process in American society. Finally, the entire evolution was nurtured to respectability through the instrumentality of an environment based on democracy.

No longer faced with the need to devote time and efforts to establishing the principle of collective bargaining, labor and management could turn their efforts toward improvement of it. The result was increasingly to professionalize the practice of collective bargaining. It was well established by this time that collective bargaining included two impor-

[1] National Labor Relations Act, Findings and Policy, Sec. 1.

tant elements: negotiation and contract administration. Moreover, the labor agreement became a more complex and technical document.

Finally, as forces of dramatic change began to affect the social and economic fabric of society, workers' lives and their needs were also affected and became more complex. As more complex matters became involved in labor–management relations, the viability and effectiveness of collective bargaining as a means of solving modern labor–management problems came increasingly under question and even attack.

Labor Movement

Dualism in the trade union movement introduced livelier activity through the competition of the AFL and the CIO. Structurally and philosophically, the advent of the CIO introduced no basic changes, if structure is to be interpreted as the traditional pyramid of federation/national union/local union. Functionally, the CIO did broaden organized labor's approach to unionizing workers by introducing the industrial in contrast to the traditional craft method of organizing. Nor did industrial unionism stray from the traditional concept of business unionism, although there were some who hoped that the CIO would lead the way to a more social-consciousness labor movement rather than the traditional job-conscious unionism.

In 1955, after almost twenty years of dualism, the two federations joined ranks into one federation, the American Federation of Labor and Congress of Industrial Organizations. Time heals most wounds, and such was the reason for ending dualism. Old ideological conflicts over craft versus industrial unionism had been lessened by the fact that affiliates in both organizations had gradually taken on more of the characteristics of mixed unions—craft groups organizing industrial workers, and industrial unions organizing craft workers—rather than holding strictly to their respective forms of organization. Leadership conflict was also resolved, with the demise of the old leaders and the emergence of new leaders who were more conciliatory.

With rapid expansion of unions to power and affluence, they became more businesslike in their operations. No longer was it possible to operate out of the pocket. Staffs of larger unions became more and more like large corporate staffs, with the hiring of professional administrators in such areas as education, public relations, legal matters, and insurance and pension funds. These were not elected officials, nor was it required that they be union members. Unionism was big business and needed expertise in the same way that its counterparts did. With increases in size, unions began to take on the bureaucratic features of big business and big government, with all the inflexibilities that such a development implies. Finally, as the financial affairs of the international unions became more involved, with the advent of larger treasuries, the administration of insurance and pension funds, and the investment of their money in real estate, radio and TV stations, banks, and other holdings, they took on more and more of the characteristics of the old labor capitalism that they had tried and shed in the 1920s.

Organized labor also faced, during most of the period, a fairly hostile climate of public opinion that derived from two different sources.

The first period of hostility was immediately after World War II. Organized labor did not fare so well legislatively. Having been prevented from taking strike action by wartime controls, labor reacted strongly once the war was over and controls were removed. Perhaps *overreacted* is the word, if the response of the public and of Congress is any criterion. September 1945 marked the beginning of a 12-month period of labor–management conflicts unmatched for their "scope and intensity" in any other comparable period. Involved were 4.9 million workers in 4,630 work stoppages. Refinery, automobile, agricultural-implement, coal, electrical manufacturing, and meat-packing workers, longshoremen, railroad and steel workers—all were involved in the frenzy of strike activity. The biggest of the strikes were in the coal, railroading, and automobile industries, but most of the basic industries were involved at one time or another.

To a public deprived of many items because of wartime rationing and scarcities, with money in its pocket and a backlog of pent-up demand, this was an affront and an outrage regardless of the right or wrong of the issues involved. Public hostility to organized labor grew rapidly. Taking advantage of this convenient situation, groups who had smarted ever since 1935 under what they considered one-sided legislation now renewed their efforts to bring about changes in the Wagner Act. Aided by a Republican-dominated Congress that also reflected the public disenchantment with organized labor, the advocates of legislative change were able to push through the Labor Management Relations Act of 1947. More popularly known as the Taft-Hartley Act, this law both amended and added to the NLRA of 1935. Its purpose was to bring organized labor to responsibility by law in the same way that employers had been treated in 1935, specifically singling out certain activities of unions for regulation and establishing additional procedures for the resolution of labor–management conflict. A mark of the pressure of public hostility was that the law was passed over a presidential veto.

In 1959, organized labor once again ran into legislative problems, this time from a different direction. A congressional investigation into the internal affairs of some unions revealed misuse of funds and abuse of power. The revelations of the McClelland Committee resulted in a rising sentiment for additional legislative controls over unions. The result was the Labor Management Reporting and Disclosures Act of 1959, more popularly know as Landrum-Griffin. Under this legislation, unions were now held accountable both for upholding democratic procedures internally and for publicly accounting for the use of funds. The image of corruption was not easily shaken off by the unions, even though the AFL-CIO had taken direct action to expel unions indicted by the congressional hearings.

Meanwhile in the background, another influence was evolving that was to have even greater influence on the development of unionism, and of some unions in particular. This was the impact of rapid technological change upon industry. Repercussions were felt by labor organizations because of not only shifts in total employment by industries, but relative shifts between industries and within occupational groups. The most serious problem resulted from relative shifts in employment from those areas that had traditionally been much easier to organize, to those types of employment where union organizing had experienced great difficulty. For example, in 1956, white-collar employment for the first time exceeded blue-collar employment. Ninety-seven percent of the increase in employment between 1947 and 1962 was accounted for by the professional, managerial, clerical, and sales fields. Likewise, the shift in employment from goods-producing to service-producing industries that had been under way for many years accelerated after 1957, with 58 percent of workers occupying jobs in the service-producing industries by 1962. Government employment, which was not a great source of union membership until after 1962, was the fastest-growing job sector of all. And if this were not enough, increases in employment from year to year were not keeping pace with the increasing numbers of people seeking work; unemployment problems were becoming serious and intractable.

The consequences of these changes were felt by the trade union movement as a whole, but particularly by those unions with members heavily concentrated in industries hardest hit by structural changes in employment—steel, automobiles, railroading, coal mining, and meat-packing, to name a few. Total membership in unions dropped from 25.2 percent of the labor force in 1953 to 22 percent by 1961, and in absolute terms from peak of 18,477,000 members in 1956 to 17,328,000 in 1961. Shifts in employment patterns also show up in the record of unions in NLRB elections. Unions won certification in 72 percent of the elections in 1952, but only 56 percent in 1961.

The tragedy of unionism as it moved into the 1960s was that its membership was largely concentrated in the declining areas of the economy, coupled with its inability or unwillingness to move with dispatch to change old ways to adapt to the new problems at hand.

Collective Bargaining

For collective bargaining, the events of 1945–1962 were somewhat disparate in impact. There were encouraging developments while, at the same time, there were some clouds on the horizon.

One encouraging result of the 1935–1945 expansion of both the trade union movement and collective bargaining was the broadening and deepening impact on the latter. Union organization not only extended collective bargaining to the major industrial employers of the country and through this brought larger numbers of workers under the trade agreement system, but also extended the role of collective bargaining geographically and occupationally. By the very nature of the widening and deepening process, collective bargaining became more and more firmly rooted in America's system.

The metamorphosis from unilateralism to acceptance of collective bargaining in principle was completed. The government had already accepted collective bargaining as necessary; the courts had made an abrupt turnabout from the obstructionist doctrine of individual freedom of contract to the primacy of the collective bargaining contract; the public no longer questioned collective bargaining or trade agreements; it remained only for the last bastion of resistance to the acceptance of collective bargaining to fall—that is, the employer. Within a few years after World War II, it became clear that employers had accepted collective bargaining and the trade agreement as more or less permanent fixtures of the American way of life.

This fact can be illustrated by two events between 1945 and 1950. One clear example of the change occurred in the bargaining relationships in the automobile industry. In 1937, members of the UAW had occupied the premises of the General Motors Corporation and were engaged in a sit-down strike there. The reaction of GM was to request that Governor Murphy send in National Guard troops to expel the strikers and protect company property. In 1950, in contrast, the two former antagonists signed a now-famous agreement, the "Treaty of Detroit," in which they agreed to a labor contract of five years' duration with a no-reopening clause. Also illustrative is the contrast between the issues and the attitudes they reflect of the postwar labor–management conferences called by Wilson and Truman respectively after World Wars I and II. The World War I conference broke up over the unwillingness of the employers to accept unionism and, with it, collective bargaining as the sole vehicle for handling employee–employer problems. The employers felt that employees should freely be able to choose the nemesis of unions, the company representation plan, if they so desired. In contrast, the major issue in the second postwar conference was not over the right of unions to represent workers nor over their right to negotiate collective bargaining agreements. The issue debated most vigorously by the employers, and their major concern, was the scope and coverage of collective bargaining. The acceptability of the process of collective bargaining was not the issue, only how far it was to be allowed to encroach on what employers considered areas of management prerogatives.

A second development in collective bargaining occurred as a result of wartime wage controls. The War Labor Board, which was given the responsibility for controlling wage increases, had allowed unions to negotiate certain noncash benefits. The reasoning was that these benefits, since they were "at the fringe" of wages, would not have a direct and immediate impact on employee spending and therefore were not inflationary in character. The unions, finding an opening through which they could assuage their members' complaints, took vigorous action to keep the door open and to widen it. This then became the platform from which the so-called fringe-benefit movement was launched, destined to play such an important part, in time and in substance, during the negotiations of ensuing years. The impact of fringe items on collective bargaining varied, but there is no doubt that, overall, it introduced a rapidly expanding list of bargaining items to the negotiating table, greatly expanded the length and complexity of labor agreements, and required a greater need for professional expertise on the part of negotiators. Most of the mandatory bargaining items added to negotiations over the years were a result of NLRB or court decisions on disputed fringe items. Illustrative of the extent to which fringe items increased in numbers is the list of 101 of them compiled by Dale Yoder, admittedly only a partial list, under four general categories: (1) For Employment Security, (2) For Health Protection, (3) For Old Age and Retirement, and (4) For Personal Identification, Participation, and On-the-Job Motivation.[2]

The one dark cloud looming on the horizon was the question being raised by more complex benefits and the technological and social problems of the late fifties concerning the viability of the collective bargaining process. There were those who felt that collective bargaining was simply not capable of dealing effectively with the broad national and international economic and social problems emerging at the end of the 1950s. Willard Wirtz, the secretary of labor, raised the challenge in a speech at the International Trade Fair in Chicago in 1961:

> In a world that has shrunk overnight and a national economy in which each part now depends on every other part and on the health of the whole, the continuation of private collective bargaining as the important force in the future it has been in the past, depends on the decision of

[2] Dale Yoder, *Personnel Management and Industrial Relations,* 6th ed. (Englewood Cliffs, N.J.: Prentice-Hall, 1970), pp. 656–57.

the bargainers to exercise, or not to exercise, responsibility for the concerns that affect the whole economy. . . . The future of collective bargaining depends on whether its motive power and its procedures can be adjusted and revised to permit a large recognition and reflection of the common national interests. . . .[3]

An independent CED committee, appointed to look into the matter of the effectiveness of collective bargaining in resolving the matters of the day, reported:

In the quarter century that has elapsed since the mid-thirties, this form of industrial relations has been widely accepted in principle, but is now being criticized more and more in practice. In recent years particularly, collective bargaining has been a target in a cross-fire of mounting complaints about its past and present consequences and of increasing reservation about its future serviceability. Indeed, the fashion today in many quarters is to point to a crisis in Collective Bargaining and to dispense policy prescriptions for drastic change.[4]

Environment

The environment of the late forties and the fifties was mixed. On the one side, it was a nation adjusting from war to peace—a catch-up period for consumer groups deprived of many items during the wartime period, for workers seeking to catch up on wages and other benefits, for industry that was changing over to peace time production but was also considerably affected by advances in technology resulting from wartime technical and scientific progress. It was a period of contrasts in public attitudes, reflecting the pain of adjustment to all groups resulting from the inevitable crosscurrents and conflicts generated by interest groups, each seeking to maximize its own position. Also, there were the beginnings of a closer examination of values—by individuals and groups, ranging from economic to human worth—that were to have such portent for the upheaval in values and relationships of the 1960s. Perhaps the most continuous and basic underlying influence, with widespread repercussions on economic, social, cultural, and human values, was the significant and rapidly changing technology of the nation. True, the basis for the technological changes was laid in the past. However, the rate of change in application of new technology—the technology of the computer and the space age—was what separates this period from others. The rapid rate of change brought to all of American society widespread repercussions,

---

[3] W. Willard Wirtz, "The Future of Collective Bargaining," address delivered at the International Trade Fair, Chicago, August 3, 1961, *Monthly Labor Review*, Vol. 84, No. 11, 1206.

[4] An Independent Study Group, *The Public Interest in National Labor Policy* (New York: Committee for Economic Development, 1961), p. 7.

many of which were not to be really felt until later. In a way, the impact for the modern world of the 1950s was much like the impact of the Industrial Revolution in the late nineteenth century, except that society was a little, but not much, better prepared to adapt to the change in the 1950s. Even so, those living in any such period are too close to the scene to be aware of the full implication of such major changes in technology and the disruption they bring to economic and social relationships and patterns. While the adaptation may not be as dramatic as in the past, it is still painful in many ways. It is in this kind of a changing atmosphere—(1) rapid technological change, (2) a questioning attitude about unions and collective bargaining, and (3) a society in the throes of major change in attitudes and in institutional and personal relationships—that trade unionism and collective bargaining moved from the 1950s into the changing and new world of the 1960s and 1970s.

COLLECTIVE BARGAINING, AN INSTITUTION—1962 TO THE PRESENT

There was no sharp break between the world of 1945–1962 and the world after 1962. Changes took place in a constantly evolving process. Indeed, there was a significant carryover of problems and questions of importance to trade unionism and collective bargaining from the 1950s to the present period. However, there are also several marked differences between the two periods with respect to the evolution of collective bargaining.

One difference of major significance was the extension of union organization and collective bargaining to the public sectors of the economy—federal, state, and local.

Second, in the last decade, the statement that *collective bargaining is an institution in its own right* takes on real and unmistakable meaning.

Third, the doubting Thomases who questioned the effectiveness of collective bargaining in dealing with new and more complex social and economic issues and predicted its imminent demise have been answered, at least in part, by the new viability of the process in the last decade. Contrasting collective bargaining today to the rather questionable and gloomy way its future was viewed at the end of the 1950s gives heart to those who all along have considered it the most effective means among the alternatives available of resolving labor–management problems in a free democratic society. As an institution, it is by its very nature both a product and an integral and functioning part of such a society.

Labor Movement

Had not a major impetus been given to unionization of public-sector employees by the executive order of President Kennedy in 1962 and subsequent state legislation, the present membership of American trade unions would be markedly different.

At the end of the preceding period, 1945–1962, because of industrial and occupational shifts in employment, membership of unions had not only failed to keep pace with the expansion of the labor force but had suffered several years of absolute decline. In contrast, from 1962 to 1972, total union membership increased from just over 16 million to almost 19 million. But union membership as a percentage of the labor force did not increase accordingly; it leveled off at just over 22 percent through 1971 and dropped to slightly below 22 percent in 1972. At the same time, reflecting the occupational changes in employment, union members from the public sector increased in that period from 7.0 percent to 11.8 percent, women members from 18.6 percent to 21.7 percent, and white-collar members from 12.0 percent to 16.5 percent of total union membership. Moreover, as an indication of a new thrust in employee organizations, membership in non-union professional and state associations reached 2.2 million by 1972. Also, unionization of federal employees proceeded on a dramatic scale after the 1962 executive order, and after one decade had reached a level of about 50 percent of total eligible employees. In contrast, the general trade union movement after 150 years had reached only 25.2 percent at its highest point.

The problems facing the movement as it looks to the future are complex. They are a compound of many developments and circumstances, some of labor's own making, some beyond its control. At the base of the difficulties are the changes, social and economic, that have taken place in the world of work and in the mores of society as the "new age" of the last decade has emerged.

Technology has eroded the central industrial base of trade union membership through its impact upon the industrial and occupational mix of the job market. The sustained unemployment of the late 1950s, coupled with the civil-rights movement, raised human-resource problems from a dependency status in public-policy decision making to a key independent status. The result for the 1960s was a period of social experimentation, unmatched historically, characterized by a greater sensitivity to old problems of human distress seen in a new light. The nation was faced with the embarrassing anomaly of a substantial part of the population—20 to 30 million—who, because of discrimination, lack of education, or lack of skills, could not find employment or, if employed, could not find remunerative enough employment to rise above poverty levels. These were the disadvantaged, the hidden poor among the labor force—an embarrassment to a so-called affluent nation. How was trade unionism, with its middle-class orientation, to relate to the social and economic needs of this part of the laboring population?

Changes were also occurring in the membership composition of trade unions. An increasing generation gap was evolving, with firmly ensconced older and older leadership on the one hand, and an inflow in increasing numbers of younger and better-educated members. Also, the changing composition of the membership gradually began to erode the dominance of the blue-collar industrial and craft membership base of unions. Increasing numbers of members were being drawn from among the ranks of female workers, of professional, technical, and clerical white-collar workers, and of workers from the public sector. The needs of these members were not necessarily met by policies and programs oriented primarily to the needs of blue-collar workers.

Add to these the Pandora's box of problems of the 1970s—inflation, unemployment, energy shortages, the environment, foreign competition, and international tensions, for example—and it is self-evident that the challenge to the trade union movement and its leaders transcends that of any previous era in its complexity.

Collective Bargaining

Interestingly enough, even though the decade of the sixties began with doubts being raised about the effectiveness of collective bargaining to meet many of the complex problems of the new age of technology facing the trade union movement, collective bargaining emerged at the end of the sixties with increased status and importance.

Collective bargaining in the past had been synonymous with union organization. In terms of number of contracts negotiated, this is still the most common form of negotiation, with somewhere around 150,000 contracts in effect between unions and employers. However, in recent years a new dimension has been added to the scene. This is the advent of the professional or state association as negotiator of collective bargaining agreements for its members. District, state, and federal associations of teachers are examples. While avoiding the name of unionism or formal affiliations with the union movement, these associations have taken on many of the trappings of unions, not the least of which is the negotiation of the terms and conditions of employment for their members. As a result, while union membership increases have been leveling off as a percentage of the labor force, the number of collective bargaining agreements has been increasing dramatically. For example, in 1972, union membership was estimated as approximately 19.8 million in the United States. Collective bargaining agreements, including both union and association, were estimated to cover about 23 million workers—and this is probably a conservative estimate of total coverage. In addition, it is estimated that total agreements established through collective bargaining by unions and associations in the United States number over 160,000.

The increasing acceptance of collective bargaining is a result not only of its spread beyond the union movement but also of its extension by presidential executive order and state legislation to federal, state, and municipal workers. These official moves by federal and state governments brought whole new areas of employers and employees under the umbrella of collective bargaining agreements, and in so doing, widened the coverage and acceptability of collective bargaining. Of equal import, for the first time, the government extended organizing and bargaining rights to its own employees. This it had failed or refused to do when extending the same rights to employees in the private sector more than 25 years earlier. Both federal and state governments now placed themselves squarely behind the process of collective bargaining; such a commitment to public employees could not help but raise the practice to a more prestigious status. Indeed, in very quick order, the federal and state governments effected more change in public employer–employee relations than in any comparable period in the past.

Because of the prestigious role in labor–management relations achieved in the last decade, collective bargaining has, in its own right, assumed a position of major importance among the institutions of our society. Although there remains the question as to whether unions, as such, are viable enough to meet the broad and complex problems emerging, such does not seem to be the case with collective bargaining. As a result of the willingness of many groups to experiment with new methods, collective bargaining remains vital and operative. Some issues and situations are not amenable to crisis bargaining or frequent strikes. Such issues are finding their answer more and more in innovative changes in bargaining procedures (see Part IV, "Resolution of Conflict"). Less attention is being given today to alternatives and substitutes and more to innovative methods of improving the effectiveness of collective bargaining.

Environment

Inasmuch as the so-called new age is in the process of evolving, it is difficult to describe it fully with any perspective. Certainly, one of the greatest forces influencing the changing nature of the collective bargaining environment is technology. Both World War II and the Korean War were instrumental, with their scientific developments, in accelerating a changing technology. It has been described as the computer age, the television age, or the space age. All are descriptive of the vastly changing world.

It has also been an age in which there has been a new assertiveness expressed by many groups. This has had tremendous impact on relationships of people and institutions: for example, the civil-rights movement; the student movements; young people's questioning the generational virtues and values of their elders; the increased vocalness and activity of women's-rights groups; a new assertiveness of groups caught up in the rights issue over representation, such as teachers, policemen, firemen, and other public employees; and a liberalized Supreme Court handing down decisions that have contradicted old concepts in the fields of civil rights, education, justice, and capital punishment. What all this adds up to is a society in the process of convulsive social changes just as dramatic as—perhaps even more so than—in any previous period in history.

SELECTED REFERENCES

Barkin, Solomon, *The Decline of the Labor Movement*. Santa Barbara, Calif.: Center for the Study of Democratic Institutions, 1961.

Written as a contemporary account by a knowledgeable witness of the labor movement's travail at the end of the 1950s.

Beirne, Joseph A., *Challenge to Labor*. Englewood Cliffs, N.J.: Prentice-Hall, 1969.

A labor leader articulates the responsibility of the labor movement to serve as an effective spokesman not only for union members but for all workers in the pluralistic balances of forces in American society. He sees the labor movement's role in preserving and fortifying American "pluralism" as vital to our democratic processes.

Bowen, William C., and Orley Ashenfelter, eds., *Labor and the National Economy,* rev. ed. New York: Norton, 1975.

The editors note that there has been more and more of a recognition by all groups over the last two decades of the extent to which the success of our economic system depends on the workings of labor markets. The essays included in this pamphlet address themselves to the labor markets and such issues as efficiency, labor problems of minorities and women, and inflation and unemployment.

Brooks, Thomas R., *Walls Come Tumbling Down—A History of the Civil Rights Movement, 1940–1970*. Englewood Cliffs, N.J.: Prentice-Hall, 1974.

While no single development accounts for major changes in the social framework and attitudes of society, certainly there is justification in pointing to the civil-rights movement as one of the catalysts that induced the changes of the 1960s in people's attitudes and relationships.

Chamberlain, Neil W., *Collective Bargaining*. New York: McGraw-Hill, 1951.

Chapter 20 examines the role of collective bargaining in American society. Chamberlain raises the question of the need for synthesis between the group activity or cooperative approach of collective bargaining and the old systematic reliance on individual competition.

Fleming, Robin W., "Collective Bargaining Revisited," in John T. Dunlop and Neil W. Chamberlain, eds., *Frontiers of Collective Bargaining*. New York: Harper & Row, 1967.

A thoughtful and careful coverage of the evolution of collective bargaining from the thirties to the mid-sixties. Discussed are such subjects as structural problems, bargaining in the public sector, the new context for bargaining in the private sector, and interest-dispute handling.

Ulman, Lloyd, *American Trade Unionism—Past and Present: 1. The Development of Trades and Labor Unions; 2. Unionism and Collective Bargaining in the Modern Period,* Reprint No. 157, Institute of Industrial Relations, University of California, Berkeley, 1961.

Professor Ulman brings to the reader a penetrating and informative look at the union movement and collective bargaining in the decade and a half following World War II.

Collective Bargaining Theories

CHAPTER 4

Presumably, theories are developed with three products in mind: (1) explanation, (2) prediction, and (3) control. Moreover, theories may also be identified as general or partial, or as conceptual or operational. Surveying the many theoretical attempts to explain collective bargaining is indeed a mind-taxing task and rather like trying to find one's way through a maze.

Space does not permit, nor does common sense dictate, a detailed analysis or even a description of the wide gamut of theoretical explanations of the collective bargaining process and the forces affecting its nature and results. A few of the theories will suffice to illustrate the directions taken and will draw attention to some of the ways in which collective bargaining theories may be pertinent to the development of a positive approach to collective bargaining negotiations.

Some theories look at the broader framework within which collective bargaining occurs. Illustrative is the "industrial relations systems" approach of John Dunlop.[1] Dunlop emphasizes the environmental construct in which industrial relations is viewed as one of several subsystems operating within a total social system encompassing the entire nation. In Dunlop's system three sets of actors are recognized: the workers and their organizations; a hierarchy of managers and their organizations; and a group of government agencies directly involved in labor–management relations. These actors interact with three related environmental contexts of the industrial relations system—the technology, the market or budgetary constraints, and the power relations in the larger community —to determine the "web of rules" that govern the workplace.

[1] John T. Dunlop, *Industrial Relations Systems* (New York: Holt, Rinehart & Winston, 1958).

An even more inclusive approach has been advanced by Somers.[2] The Somers theory focuses on an overall integrative approach in which consideration is given to both external and internal forces, to both externalists (economics, law, and politics) and internalists or behaviorists (psychology and sociology), and to both conceptual systems and operational systems. Somers advances a theory of exchange as the causal force in which the unifying focus is the interaction of the workers' and managers' jobs at the workplace.

Other theories emphasize the internal or operational aspects of collective bargaining negotiations. Here the concern is with the exchange, but exchange as a social process. Walton and McKersie have brought into one framework the ideas of a number of behaviorists.[3] They view labor negotiations as a fruitful setting for the study of the larger field of social negotiations: "a deliberate interaction of two or more complex social units which are attempting to define or redefine the terms of their interdependence."[4] This analytical framework identifies four constructs (subprocesses) in labor negotiations (in fact, in all social negotiations)—"each with its own function for the interacting parties, its own internal logics, and its own identifiable set of instrumental acts or tactics."[5] These subprocesses are (1) distributive bargaining, where the objectives of the parties on particular issues are in conflict; (2) integrative bargaining, where the objectives of the parties on particular issues are not in fundamental conflict; (3) attitudinal structuring, where the objective of the bargaining actions is to influence the relationships between the parties; and (4) intraorganizational bargaining, where the objective is to obtain consensus within the negotiator's own organization on the bargaining issues.

Other writers concern themselves with particular aspects of the bargaining process, no doubt influenced by their own backgrounds and personal predilections. Thus, some writers consider collective bargaining negotiations as a form of bilateral monopoly or a function of market forces,[6] others as a "form of industrial government [in which] sovereignty in the work place is shared by management and workers' representatives,"[7] and still others as "a form of management method or

[2] Gerald G. Somers, "Bargaining Power and Industrial Relations Theory," in Gerald G. Somers, ed., *Essays in Industrial Relations Theory* (Ames: Iowa State University Press, 1969), pp. 39–53. See also Herbert G. Heneman, Jr., "Toward a General Conceptual System of Industrial Relations: How Do We Get There?" in *ibid.*

[3] Richard E. Walton and Robert E. McKersie, *A Behavioral Theory of Labor Negotiations* (New York: McGraw-Hill, 1965).

[4] *Ibid.*, p. 3.

[5] *Ibid.*, p. 4.

[6] Bevars D. Mabry, *Labor Relations and Collective Bargaining* (New York: Ronald Press, 1966), p. 189.

[7] Meyer S. Ryder, Charles M. Rehmus, and Sanford Cohen, *Management Preparation for Collective Bargaining* (Homewood, Ill.: Dow Jones-Irwin, 1966), p. 145.

procedure for making business decisions—a sharing of management."[8]

In any overall evaluation of the present state of collective bargaining theory, one must conclude that *little progress has been made beyond the explanation state*. Predictive and control aspects of collective bargaining theory are singularly absent. But as an explanation of the bargaining process, viewed from different angles, collective bargaining theory does provide valuable clues for the negotiator by way of greater insight into the essential elements of the negotiation process.

SELECTED REFERENCES

Atherton, Wallace N., *Theory of Union Bargaining Goals*. Princeton, N.J.: Princeton University Press, 1973.

As the author indicates, this book is not about bargaining theory. It is concerned with the union's application of theory to the formulation of goals, which it will then try to achieve "by bargaining with and putting economic pressure on the employer." The author treats the contributions of such writers as Reder, Berkowitz, Dunlop, Fellner, Carter, Ross, Mason, and Higgins and then proceeds to treat two elements: (1) the role of expected strike lengths as determinants of a union's goals, and (2) the task a union faces in trying to find a compromise sufficiently satisfactory to all or most of its members to keep the union together.

Bartos, Otomar J., *Process and Outcome of Negotiations*. New York: Columbia University Press, 1974.

The author states that the purpose of the book is to describe, justify, and test various theories of negotiation. Although labor–management relations are included, the negotiation process is viewed in a broader setting. The author first looks at some theories and hypotheses of negotiation and then experiments in negotiation. He then proceeds to the process of negotiation (models and tests of models) and the strategic aspects of negotiation (models of outcome, tests of the models, and toughness and outcome). Finally, he moves to a comprehensive view of negotiation and notes that any such model should be future-oriented as well as past-oriented—i.e., the model should not only provide a base from which to predict what negotiators will do but also advise them what they ought to do. He concludes that because it is impossible to build a symmetric model of negotiation, it is also impossible to build a faultless normative model.

Burtt, Everett Johnson, Jr., *Labor Markets, Unions, and Government Policies*. New York: St Martin's Press, 1963.

Brief but good coverage of the traditional views of economists over the years with respect to wage determination. These views include the subsistence theory, wage-fund theory, marginal-productivity theory, Marshall's emphasis upon the general interdependence of supply and demand forces,

[8] *Ibid.*, p. 146.

bargaining theories, and modern theories of wage determination that approach influencing factors such as macro and micro, long and short run, and market structures in a much more sophisticated manner.

Chamberlain, Neil W., *Collective Bargaining*. New York: McGraw-Hill, 1951. In Chapter 6, Chamberlain reduces the nature of the bargaining process to three basic theoretical types: (1) the marketing theory, (2) the government theory, and (3) the managerial theory. Chapter 10 contains an excellent examination of the meaning and the role of bargaining power in determining negotiation results. Chamberlain discusses bargaining power from the standpoint of both the union's ability to cause disagreement to be costly to the employer and the employer's ability to cause disagreement to be costly to the union. In the process, he examines the contributions of such stalwarts as Pigou, Commons, Simons, Slichter, Dunlop, Lindblom, and Hicks, but the main contribution of Chapter 10 is Chamberlain's own penetrating analysis of the facts and fallacies of bargaining power. Indeed, he points out that bargaining power is not always measured in terms of the cost it imposes on the other party; it may also be viewed in terms of reducing the cost to the other party of agreeing with the first party.

Cross, John G., *The Economics of Bargaining*. New York: Basic Books, 1969. Believing that intensive work must be done in many allied disciplines individually before the "theory of bargaining" emerges, Cross makes it clear in his title that he is concerned only with the economic aspects of bargaining. The basic premise of the author is that it is possible to treat the bargaining process in terms of economic variables and to come out with a determinate and useful theory.

de Menil, George, *Bargaining: Monopoly Power versus Union Power*. Cambridge, Mass.: M.I.T. Press, 1971. The author points out that markets that do not fit the standard economic models are difficult subjects for economic analysis. The labor market is a case in point. The purpose of the book is to develop a bargaining theory of wage determination. The author discusses other bargaining theories and chooses the Nash model for development of his own theory.

Dunlop, John T., *Industrial Relations Systems*. New York: Holt, Rinehart & Winston, 1958. A must for any reader interested in delving more deeply into industrial relations theory. John Dunlop is concerned with a theoretical construct for industrial relations systems. All industrial relations systems have certain common properties and structures and respond to specified influences.

Heneman, H.G., Jr., and Dale Yoder, *Labor Economics*. Cincinnati, O.: South-Western Publishing, 1965), pp. 628–34. Yoder and Heneman summarize current collective bargaining theory: identification of ranges or bands of possible compromise, union and employer preference functions, and schedules that reflect the comparative costs of agreement and disagreement.

Hutt, W.H., *The Theory of Collective Bargaining.* New York: Free Press, 1954.

A history, analysis, and criticism of the principal theories that have sought to explain the effects of trade unions and employers' associations upon the distribution of products of industry. Of special concern to the author is the thesis of economists from Adam Smith on, and of spokesmen for unions, that unions can raise wages above the market level without harm to anyone except the exploiters. He concludes with the comment that the rate of wages that is best for the workers as a whole is that which is determined in the free market.

Kochan, Thomas A., and Hoyt N. Wheeler, "Municipal Collective Bargaining: A Model and Analysis of Bargaining Outcomes," *Industrial and Labor Relations Review,* 29, No. 1 (October 1975), 46–66.

Kochan and Wheeler report on the result of an attempt to formulate and operate a model of collective bargaining outcomes.

Mabry, Bevars D., *Labor Relations and Collective Bargaining.* New York: Ronald Press, 1966.

Professor Mabry includes an informative treatment of the theory of collective bargaining in Part II. He touches not only on the nature of collective bargaining but also on the pure theory of bargaining, bargaining models, and the economics of bargaining at both the micro and macro levels.

McClean, Alan A., "Personnel Policy Formulation and Psychiatry," *Reprint Series No. 129,* New York State School of Industrial and Labor Relations, 1962.

Collective bargaining, according to the psychiatrist, involves demands that may symbolize needs quite different from their apparent meanings or objectives.

McGregor, Douglas, *The Professional Manager,* pp. 186–87. New York: McGraw-Hill, 1967.

McGregor advances a synthesized behavioral-science approach to collective bargaining theory. He outlines three possible strategies for dealing with conflict: "divide and rule," "the suppression of differences," and "the working through of differences."

Marshall, Howard D., and Natalie J. Marshall, *Collective Bargaining.* New York: Random House, 1971.

An informative discussion of bargaining theory, borrowing from such writers as Nash, Hicks, Morgenstern, and Neumann and the authors' own analysis (Chapter 5).

Perlman, Selig, *A Theory of the Labor Movement.* New York: August M. Kelley, 1949. Mark Perlman, *Labor Union Theories in America, Background and Development.* Evanston, Ill.: Row, Peterson and Co., 1958.

Separate father-and-son considerations of the controlling factors determining the emergence of unionism and the nature and form unionism takes.

Somers, Gerald G., ed., *Essays in Industrial Relations Theory.* Ames: Iowa State University Press, 1969.

Professor Somers sums up the approach of the book by noting that each chapter is directed to a significant theoretical aspect of the industrial relations field, and the combination of all the chapters contributes to the development of the conceptual framework envisaged by the industrial relations theoreticians.

Thompson, Arthur A., and Irwin Weinstock, "Facing the Crisis in Collective Bargaining," *MSU Business Topics,* Vol. 16, No. 3 (Summer 1968), 37–43.

Thompson and Weinstock have developed a model of employer and union strategies in which employers follow the McGregor Theory Y and union representatives are Theory-X-oriented.

Walton, Richard E., and Robert B. McKersie, *A Behavioral Theory of Labor Negotiations.* New York: McGraw-Hill, 1967.

The authors are concerned in this book about labor negotiations in particular and social negotiations in general. Four sets of activities are identified that the authors believe account for almost all the behavior in negotiations and constitute the framework for their theory of labor negotiations. The activities identified are called "distributive bargaining," "integrative bargaining," "attitudinal structuring," and "intraorganizational bargaining."

Legal Framework of Collective Bargaining— An Overview

CHAPTER 5

The purpose of this chapter is to outline the general framework of law that sets the legal boundaries and rules of the game for collective bargaining negotiations at the federal, state, and local levels and in the private and public sectors.

The legal framework of collective bargaining negotiations may be found in the Railway Labor Act, for railroad workers and airline employees; the National Labor Relations Act, covering all other areas of the private economy subject to federal law;[1] Executive Order 11491, cover-

---

[1] The Railway Labor Act covers railroad and airline workers and was initially passed in 1926. It has been amended several times since.

The National Labor Relations Act (Wagner Act) was enacted in 1935 at the demise of the National Industrial Recovery Act of 1933 (NIRA). The NLRA has been amended and supplemented by additional legislation—the Labor Management Relations Act of 1947 (Taft-Hartley), the Labor Management Reporting and Disclosure Act of 1959 (Landrum-Griffin), and, more recently, Public Law 93–360 (Health Care Industry) in 1974.

Excluded prior to 1974, all private health-care institutions, whether or not operated for a profit, have been brought under the NLRA. Government-operated health facilities such as federal, state, county, and city hospitals are still excluded. Under this new legislation, private health-care institutions are covered in the same manner as other private concerns, except for special provisions to minimize work stoppages because of the critical nature of the services rendered by these institutions. Special procedures established by the amendment are covered in Part IV of this book, "Resolution of Conflict." Private health-care institutions include hospitals, convalescent hospitals, health-maintenance organizations, health clinics, nursing homes, extended-care facilities, or other institutions devoted to the care of sick, infirm, or aged persons.

Hereinafter, the term "NLRA" will be used to identify the National Labor Relations Act as amended in 1947, 1959, and 1974. Where "Taft-Hartley" is used, it will be to identify portions of the 1947 law adding new titles to the labor relations statutes.

ing federal employees;[2] and various state laws covering employer–employee activities in both private and public employment not subject to federal law.[3] These statutes are a product of a long period of evolution reaching back almost 200 years. The most recent antecedents and those having the most direct bearing on the statutes of the present day are found in the legislation of the late nineteenth and early twentieth century in the railway labor field. These legislative acts served as a basis of experience and a language model for the labor legislation of the last four decades.

Beginning with the Arbitration Act of 1888, the use of arbitration and investigative boards in work stoppages was introduced. Mediation and conciliation were added by the Erdman Act of 1898. The Newlands Act followed in 1913, continuing both arbitration and mediation, and then was succeeded by the Transportation Act of 1920, which established a Railway Labor Board empowered to investigate and report the facts of disputes. Railway labor legislation reached heights it has never capped in the Railway Labor Act of 1926. The Railway Labor Act, still operative, was for many years considered the model for emerging legislation on employer–employee matters. The most notable feature of the act was the legal right it gave to railway workers to organize, choose representatives. and engage in collective bargaining without "interference, influence or coercion." This was to serve as the cornerstone philosophy of the National Labor Relations Act in 1935 and subsequent legislation in both private and public areas.

LEGAL FRAMEWORK—NATIONAL LEVEL

Although a more detailed examination of the law in both private and public sectors will be made at appropriate points in later chapters, it may be useful here to mention some of the major areas covered by statutes, orders, or regulations that establish the overall legal framework for collective bargaining. Attention is confined initially to those employees covered by the National Labor Relations Act as amended and Executive Order 11491 as amended. It is well to emphasize that this legal framework reflects essentially the same philosophy as that covering

---

[2] Executive Order 11491, issued in 1969 (hereinafter identified as "EO," or "the order"), is an amended version of the original Executive Order 10492, issued by President Kennedy in 1962. EO 11491 has since been amended by EOs 11616, 11636, and, most recently, 11838 in February 1975.

[3] States with labor relations laws patterned after the Wagner and Taft-Hartley Acts number twelve. In the public sector, 40 states and the District of Columbia had, by 1976, extended collective bargaining coverage to public employees.

railway and airline workers under the Railway Labor Act. Seven areas are chosen to illustrate. In each area, the initial coverage will be based on collective bargaining in the private sector covered by the National Labor Relations Act. This is followed by the way or ways that treatment of collective bargaining for public employees under Executive Order 11491 is similar or different. That for public and private employees under state statutes and orders, while similar to the national sector in many respects, will be treated separately for purposes of clarity.

PUBLIC POLICY. It should be recognized that *encouragement of collective bargaining* is a matter of public policy. Section I, Findings and Policies, of the National Labor Relations Act, states:

> It is hereby declared to be the public policy of the United States to eliminate the causes of certain substantial obstructions to the free flow of commerce and to mitigate and eliminate these obstructions when they have occurred by *encouraging the practice and procedure of collective bargaining* and by protecting the exercise by workers of full freedom of association, self-organization, and designation of representatives of their own choosing, *for the purpose of negotiating the terms and conditions of their employment* or other mutual aid or protection. [Italics added.]

Executive Order 11491 is not as direct a statement, but the same charge is given in effect. Combining three parts, the same meaning is clarified:

> WHEREAS the well-being of employees and efficient administration of the Government are benefited by providing employees an opportunity to participate in the formulation and implementation of personnel policies and practices affecting the conditions of their employment;
>
> . . . as President of the United States, I hereby direct that the following policies shall govern officers and agencies of the executive branch of the Government in all dealings with Federal employees and organizations representing such employees. . . .
>
> Sec. 11. Negotiation of Agreements. (a) An agency and a labor organization that has been accorded exclusive recognition . . . shall meet at reasonable times and confer in good faith with respect to personnel policies and practices and matters affecting working conditions. . . . They may negotiate an agreement . . . to assist in such negotiation; and execute a written agreement. . . .

PARTIES TO COLLECTIVE BARGAINING. The primary parties involved in collective bargaining and subject to the NLRA are identified and their rights and obligations specified. Included are employers (and their agents) affecting commerce but excluding public employers, employers with nonprofit corporations or associations, and employers subject to the

Railway Labor Act; employees working for these employers; and employee representatives (usually unions) established for the purpose of dealing with employers "concerning grievances, labor disputes, wages, rates of pay, hours of employment, or conditions of work,"[4] and in which employees participate.

In the public sector, *employer* means an agency. *Agency* means an executive department, a government corporation, or an independent establishment. *Executive department* refers to the departments of State, Treasury, Defense, Justice, Housing and Urban Development, Transportation, and so on. *Government corporation* means a corporation owned or controlled by the government of the United States, such as the TVA or the Atomic Energy Commission. *Independent agencies* refers to the Federal Communications Commission, Federal Trade Commission, Civil Aeronautics Board, or National Labor Relations Board, for example.

Employee refers to an employee of any of the agencies mentioned above but in most instances excludes supervisors. (Exceptions are mentioned in Section 24 of Executive Order 11491.) *Labor organization* refers to a lawful organization of any kind in which employees participate and that exists for the purpose, in whole or in part, of dealing with agencies concerning grievances, personnel policies and practices, or other matters affecting the working conditions of their employees. Excluded are labor organizations that consist of management officials or supervisors, and those that assist or participate in a strike against the government, advocate overthrow of the constitutional form of government, or discriminate with regard to the terms or conditions of membership because of race, color, creed, sex, age, or national origin.[5]

EMPLOYEE RIGHTS. The basic objective of the NLRA is the protection of employee rights, although as an offshoot, both employer and employee representatives are enjoined against certain types of actions directed at each other. Employee rights include the

> . . . right to self-organization, to form, join or assist labor organizations, to bargain collectively through representatives of their own choosing, and to engage in other concerted activities for the purpose of collective bargaining or other mutual aid or protection, and the right to refrain from such activities except where limited by a legally established union security arrangement.[6]

"Employee rights" are stated more simply under the executive order. Each employee "has the right, freely and without fear of penalty or

---

[4] NLRA, Section 2 (5).
[5] EO 11491, Section 2 (b and e).
[6] NLRA, Section 7.

reprisal, to form, join and assist a labor organization or to refrain from any such activity, and each employee shall be protected in the exercise of this right."[7] It should be noted, however, that the EO rights above do not include, as does the NLRA, the right "to engage in other concerted activities [work stoppages]."

UNFAIR LABOR PRACTICES. Under the NLRA, in order to protect employee rights, both employers and employee representatives are placed under certain restrictions in regard to unfair labor practices. Employers are restrained from interfering with the formulation or administration of any labor organization, from discriminating in order to encourage or discourage membership in any labor organization, from refusing to bargain in good faith with the authorized employee representative, from recognizing any employee representative other than the one certified or legally recognized, from resorting to lockout or modification in the contract during the 60-day notice period prior to contract termination or modification, and from violating a valid collective bargaining agreement between the parties. Labor organizations and their representatives are required to bargain in good faith with the employer and to uphold their contractual commitments, and they are enjoined from interfering with an employer's selection of his bargaining representatives, from causing an employer to discriminate against an employee for other than non-payment of dues and fees, from engaging in illegal strikes, boycotts, or picketing, and from forcing the employer to recognize any but the duly authorized bargaining representatives.

In addition to the unfair labor practices enunciated above for the private sector, employers in the public sector may not refuse to accord appropriate recognition to a labor organization qualified for such recognition. Labor organizations are additionally required to refrain from coercing, attempting to coerce, or fining or taking economic sanction against a member as punishment or for the purpose of hindering work performance or discharge of duties; from calling or engaging in a strike, work stoppage, or slowdown, or picketing or condoning any such activity by failing to take affirmative action to prevent it; and from discriminating against an employee with regard to the terms or conditions of membership because of race, color, creed, sex, age, or national origin.[8]

It is important to reemphasize for the purposes of this book that regulations in both the private and public sectors emphatically declare it an unfair labor practice for either party to refuse "to bargain collectively" or "to consult, confer or negotiate."

THE COLLECTIVE BARGAINING REPRESENTATIVE. The designation of an

[7] EO 11491, Section 1.
[8] Ibid., Section 19.

official bargaining representative for a defined group of workers (see the next section, on the appropriate bargaining unit) is the end product of a successful union-organizing campaign culminating either in employer recognition of the union as the bargaining representative for a group of his employees or in an NLRB-conducted election in which the union successfully receives a majority of the votes cast.

The legal basis for the designation of bargaining representative is the NLRA injunction of Section 7, "Employees shall have the right to self-organization . . . to bargain collectively through representatives of their own choosing." The executive order covering federal employees states essentially the same right in Section 10 (a), "Exclusive Recognition": "An agency shall accord exclusive recognition to a labor organization when the organization has been selected, in a secret ballot election, by a majority of the employees in an appropriate unit as their representative."

Now, what is the meaning of exclusive bargaining representative? Section 9 (a) of the NLRA states:

> Representatives designated or selected for the purposes of collective bargaining by a majority of the employees in a unit appropriate for such purposes shall be the exclusive representatives of all the employees in such unit for the purposes of collective bargaining in respect to rates of pay, wages, hours of employment, or other conditions of employment. . . .

For the public sector, Executive Order 11491, Section 10 (3), reads similarly: "When a labor organization has been accorded exclusive recognition, it is the exclusive representative of employees in the unit and is entitled to act for and to negotiate an agreement covering all employees in the unit."

Two additional points are important to the exclusive-representative status of the bargaining representative. First, the union as the bargaining representative must represent *all* the employees in the unit for which it has been designated as representative. Executive Order 11491, Section 10 (e), states that the bargaining representative must represent "the interests of all the employees in the unit without discrimination and without regard to labor organization membership." Section 9 (a) of the NLRA states similarly that the bargaining representative "shall be the exclusive representative of all the employees in such a unit." Second, employees in a unit represented by a bargaining representative may process their own grievances, but in doing so, they may not make any settlements or agreements that violate or are inconsistent with the agreement negotiated by their bargaining representative. Section 9 (a) of the NLRA states that individuals or groups of employees may present their own grievances and have them adjusted "as long as the adjustment is not inconsistent with the terms of a collective-bargaining contract or agreement then in effect." Section 13 (a) of the executive order also allows any employee or group of employees to process their own grievances as long as "the adjustment is not inconsistent with the terms of the agreement."

Up to this point, attention has been given to the designation of the bargaining representative, whom the bargaining representative represents, and the legal authority of the bargaining representative. Before turning to the meaning of the "appropriate bargaining unit," the tenure or limitations upon the tenure of the bargaining agent should be mentioned. Under both the NLRA and the executive order, once a bargaining representative has been selected by a majority vote of the employees of the appropriate bargaining unit, exclusive tenure is assured to such representative until the employees in the bargaining unit reverse the process. For employees to rid themselves of a union they no longer support as their bargaining representative, a petition must be filed with the NLRB requesting a decertification election. If 30 percent of the employees evince support for the petition and a valid election has not been held within the unit within the preceding twelve months, the board will order a decertification election. If a majority of the employees vote for decertification, the union ceases to be the legal representative of the unit of employees. Also, the employer is relieved from all responsibility to bargain with any union for at least twelve months, or longer if there is no subsequent union certified by a valid election as the bargaining representative. The executive order does not spell out decertification procedures as does the NLRA, but the process is provided for in Section 7 (a), under which a union may be dropped if it ceases to meet the "requirements of this Order applicable to . . . recognition."

APPROPRIATE BARGAINING UNIT.   The appropriate bargaining unit is directly linked to collective bargaining activities, since it defines the employees for which the bargaining representative negotiates an agreement and it is the unit of employees to which the contract or labor agreement applies in the contract-administration process. The bargaining-unit designation is interwoven with the process by which the bargaining agent is determined. When a union has reached the point of suing for recognition, it then becomes necessary, either by agreement of the union and the employer or by designation by the NLRB, to determine the unit of employees that will have the right to vote for or against the union seeking to become bargaining representative. In the designation of the appropriate bargaining unit, the NLRB, which has final authority on the matter, uses several criteria to try and arrive at a unit that will afford proper representation to all the employees within the unit. The criteria used by the NLRB are (1) the history, extent, and type of organization of employees in a plant; (2) the history of their collective bargaining; (3)

the history, extent, and type of organization and the collective bargaining of employees in other plants of the same employer, or of other employers in the same industry; (4) the skill, wages, work, and working conditions of employees; (5) the desires of employees; (6) the eligibility of employees for membership in the union or unions involved in the election proceedings and in other labor organizations; and (7) the relationship between the unit or units proposed and the employer's organization, management, and operation of the plant.[9]

COVERAGE. Whether the employer is a private or a public-sector employer, whether the employees in either case are covered by a labor law, and if so, by which law or laws—these are questions that can be answered only by checking each employer's status against several criteria:

1. Is the employer engaged in interstate or intrastate commerce? If the former, the employer is covered by federal law; if the latter, by state law. One exception should be noted, since it vitally affects an employee's labor relations rights and protection. If the employee is in a right-to-work state, the right-to-work law of the state is universally applied whether or not, for other purposes, the employee comes under federal or under state law exclusively.

2. Is the employer in private industry, in transportation (railroads and airlines), or in the public sector? If the employer is in interstate commerce and outside the railroad and airlines industries, then the NLRA applies; if in railroads or airlines, the RLA applies. If the employer is a public employer at the federal level, then Executive Order 11491 applies; if at the state or municipal level, then state public-employee laws apply. If the employer is in intrastate commerce and a private employer, then appropriate state labor relations laws apply. Again, state right-to-work laws apply to all employers regardless of the distinctions above.

3. Other criteria determining an employer's status under the law would be the distinction between industrial employers and agricultural (extractive) employers (the latter not covered by labor laws); and the distinction between union and association representation of employees, the latter recognized by some state laws but not by federal law, and the former recognized by both state and federal laws.

LEGAL FRAMEWORK—STATE AND LOCAL

Although a few states (twelve) have labor relations laws comparable to either the Wagner Act or Taft-Hartley, or both, the real focus of action is with the state statutes, orders, and regulations extending bargaining

---

[9] NLRB, *Fourth Annual Report* (1939). In the public sector, certification of federal-employee bargaining units is under the assistant secretary of labor.

rights to public employees. By 1976, forty states and the District of Columbia had extended bargaining rights to public employees. Only ten states have no bargaining rights by law, regulation, or order for public employees, although in most of these same states some bargaining does occur.

The legal framework for public-employee bargaining at the state level is generally comparable to the Wagner Act, and at the federal level, to EO. Rather than attempting to condense the approach of the forty states and the District of Columbia to present their approach to collective bargaining matters, I shall use three states widely spread geographically (Hawaii, Minnesota, and New York) and illustrate the general features of their comprehensive public-employee bargaining laws.

PUBLIC POLICY.   The Taylor Act in New York is illustrative of a public policy approach at the state level:

> Sec. 179.61. Public policy.—It is the public policy of this state . . . to promote orderly and constructive relationships between all public employers and their employees, subject however, to the paramount right of the citizens of this state to keep inviolate the guarantees for their health, education, safety and welfare.

The Hawaiian public-employees statute reads similarly:

> The legislature declares that it is the public policy of the State to promote harmonious and cooperative relations between government and its employees and to protect the public by assuring effective and orderly operations of government. These policies are best effectuated by (1) recognizing the right of public employees to organize for the purpose of collective bargaining, (2) requiring the public employers to negotiate with and enter into written agreements with exclusive representatives on matters of wages, hours, and other terms and conditions of employment, while, at the same time, (3) maintaining merit principles and the principle of equal pay for equal work among state and county employees . . . and (4) creating a public employment relations board to administer the provisions of this chapter.

PARTIES TO COLLECTIVE BARGAINING.   Definition of the parties (employers and employees) is tailored in two ways: (1) the types of employers and employees found in state and local government units, and (2) the employer units covered by state law or order. Illustrative of state coverage:

> The term "government" or "public employer" means (i) the state of New York, (ii) a county, city, town, village or any other political subdivision or civil division of the state, (iii) a school district or any governmental

entity operating a public school, college or university, (iv) a public improvement or special district, (v) a public authority, commission, or public benefit corporation, or (vi) any other public corporation, agency or instrumentality or unit of government which exercises governmental powers under the laws of the state.

The term "employee organization" means an organization of any kind having as its primary purpose the improvement of terms and conditions of employment of public employees [can include associations].

The term "public employee" means any person holding a position by appointment or employment in the service of a public employer, excluding . . . persons holding positions by appointment or employment in the organized militia of the state and persons who may reasonably be designated from time to time as managerial or confidential. . . .

EMPLOYEE RIGHTS. Employee rights of self-organization, or of forming, joining, or assisting any organization and of bargaining collectively are the same as those at the federal level. However, in contrast to the private sector, the legal framework of most of the states prohibits public employees the right to strike and in the remainder allows the strike only under special rules. The Minnesota law illustrates a prohibition against work stoppages:

Sec. 179.64. Strikes: (1) No person holding a position by appointment or employment in the government of the state of Minnesota, or in the government of any one or more of the political subdivisions thereof, or in the service of the public schools, or of the state university, or in the service of any authority, commission or board or any other branch of the public service . . . may engage in a strike. . . .

The Hawaiian statute provides the right to strike under certain conditions:

Sec. 89–12. (a) Participation in a strike shall be unlawful for any employee who (1) is not included in an appropriate bargaining unit for which an exclusive representative has been certified . . . , or (2) is included in an appropriate bargaining unit for which process for resolution of a dispute is by referral to final and binding arbitration.

(b) It shall be lawful for an employee, who is not prohibited from striking under paragraph (a) and who is in the appropriate bargaining unit involved in an impasse, to participate in a strike after (1) requirements . . . relating to the resolution of disputes have been complied with in good faith, (2) the proceedings for the prevention of any prohibited practice have been exhausted, (3) sixty days have elapsed since the factfinding board has made public its findings and any recommendations, (4) the exclusive representative has given a ten-day notice of intent to strike to the board and to the employer.

(c) Where the strike occurring, or about to occur, endangers the public health or safety, the public employer concerned may petition the board to make an investigation. If the board finds that there is imminent or present danger to the health and safety of the public, the board shall set requirements that must be complied with to avoid or remove any such imminent or present danger.

UNFAIR LABOR PRACTICES. In addition to those included in federal law, the New York statute lists other unfair labor practices: refusal to comply with the grievance procedures, distribution of blacklists, refusal to abide by a valid decision of an arbitrator, refusal to provide information on the budget, seizure or occupation of public property, and, of course, work stoppage.

COLLECTIVE BARGAINING REPRESENTATIVE. State laws delegate the same authority to the duly constituted representative of employees in an appropriate bargaining unit but, in addition, recognize public-employee associations as legitimate representatives along with unions.

APPROPRIATE BARGAINING UNIT. As in federal laws, the procedures for establishing the appropriate bargaining unit as well as the bargaining representative are spelled out. The Hawaiian statute is interesting because it designates the appropriate bargaining units in some detail:

Sec. 89–6 (a). All employees throughout the State within any of the following categories shall constitute an appropriate bargaining unit:
(1) Nonsupervisory employees in blue collar positions;
(2) Supervisory employees in blue collar positions;
(3) Nonsupervisory employees in white collar positions;
(4) Supervisory employees in white collar positions;
(5) Teachers and other personnel of the department of education under the same salary schedule;
(6) Educational officers and other personnel of the department of education under the same salary schedule;
(7) Faculty of the University of Hawaii and the Community College system;
(8) Personnel of the University of Hawaii and the Community College system, other than faculty;
(9) Registered professional nurses;
(10) Nonprofessional hospital and institutional workers;
(11) Firemen;
(12) Policemen; and
(13) Professional and scientific employees, other than registered professional nurses.

COVERAGE. The type of coverage of public employees statute or order varies among the states. Ten states provide no coverage for public employees; 21 extend bargaining rights to state employees, municipal employees, firemen, policemen, and teachers; 4 extend bargaining rights to four of the preceding categories; 6, including the District of Columbia, to three of the groups of employees; 3 to two groups; and 7 states extend bargaining rights to only one group of employees. Looked at in another way, 28 states extend bargaining rights to state employees; 35, including the District of Columbia, to municipal employees; 39, including the District of Columbia, to firemen; 31, including the District of Columbia, to policemen; and 30 to teachers.

The states in their statutes and orders have been much more active and detailed in their approaches to impasse-settlement procedures. They include traditional use and also various combinations in the use of mediation, fact-finding, and arbitration. (See Part IV.)

SUBSTANTIVE FEATURES OF THE AGREEMENT AND OTHER STATUTES

By mandate, restriction, and exclusion, the statutes discussed up to this point have established a legal framework within which the process of negotiating an agreement must function. Other statutes, many of them products of the social and human-rights movements of the 1960s, add another dimension to the negotiation of the agreement. Rather than influencing the process itself, these statutes have influenced the substantive features, the subject matter, of the agreement.

Representative of these statutes and the negotiation matters they affect are (1) the Fair Labor Standards Act of 1938, as amended, covering wage and hour limitations; (2) the Civil Rights Act of 1969, concerning discrimination in employment because of race, color, religion, or national origin; (3) the Equal Opportunity Act of 1972, applying to all personnel actions affecting employees or applicants for employment and their right to be free from any discrimination based on race, color, religion, sex, or national origin; (4) the Equal Pay Act of 1963, prohibiting discrimination in the payment of wages on the basis of sex for equal work on jobs whose performance requires equal skill, effort, and responsibility and that are performed under similar working conditions; (5) the Occupational Safety and Health Act, 1970, requiring that the employment and place of employment be free from recognized hazards that are likely to cause death or serious physical harm to employees; (6) the Employee Retirement Income Security Act of 1974, which establishes regulations covering retirement plans and minimum vesting and funding standards; and (7) the Veterans' Re-Employment Rights Act, 1975, which requires reemployment of veterans meeting certain requirements of their former positions and, if they are qualified, restoration of seniority or to a position of like seniority, status, and pay.

SELECTED REFERENCES

Employment Practices. New York: Commerce Clearing House, Inc.

An excellent source of information on federal and state laws banning discrimination in employment on account of race, color, religion, sex, national origin, and age. Equal-pay rules are covered in detail. This is a continuing and up-to-date service.

Fair Employment Practices. Washington, D.C.: Bureau of National Affairs, Inc.

This continuing series provides comprehensive coverage of federal and state laws that prohibit discrimination in employment based on race, color, religion, national origin, sex, and age.

Federal Wages–Hours. New York: Commerce Clearing House, Inc.

An up-to-date and continuing service concerning rules, statutes, regulations, and forms; government-contract wage–hour rules; administrative and court decisions; and current comment on wage–hour developments.

Industrial Relations Guide. Englewood Cliffs, N.J.: Prentice-Hall, Inc.

Bi-weekly reports in this continuing series explain the impact of new developments and new trends in collective bargaining and arbitration. The basic text of the looseleaf volume, updated periodically, includes a complete explanation of the nature of labor arbitration, plus descriptions of past awards and thousands of sample contract clauses. "New Ideas" articles are written by outside experts in the field on subjects of interest to management and labor alike.

Labor Cases. New York: Commerce Clearing House, Inc.

A continuing service that includes full-text federal and state court decisions on labor law.

Labor Relations. Washington, D.C.: Bureau of National Affairs, Inc.

This is a continuing series covering the problems arising under federal and state labor laws. Here, the numerous rulings of the National Labor Relations Board, state boards, and the courts have been combed, sorted, and put into nonlegal language. Provisions and procedures of the Occupational Safety and Health Act are also included.

Labor Relations Guide. Englewood Cliffs, N.J.: Prentice-Hall, Inc.

This service, updated weekly, is particularly useful for business executives, lawyers, personnel managers, and consultants who want information that quickly and easily answers day-to-day labor-relations questions. Important decisions of the National Labor Relations Board, the Equal Employment Opportunity Commission, the Occupational Safety and Health Administration, and the courts are reported promptly in easy-to-understand language.

The service includes an explanation of labor laws—Wage-Hour, the NLRA, the Civil Rights Act, Age Discrimination, Reemployment of Veterans, OSHA, garnishment, state labor laws, and others—and provides the full texts of federal laws and executive orders.

Law of Labor Relations. Washington, D.C.: Bureau of National Affairs, Inc.

A comprehensive series that provides a current account of court opinions and decisions of the National Labor Relations Board.

Levine, Marvin J., *Comparative Labor Relations Law.* Morristown, N.J.: General Learning Press, 1975.

Most readers would relate the title of this book to an intercountry comparison. Instead, and in a timely way, the author's concern is between the two major sectors of labor relations activity in America—the private and public sectors. This unique text "examines the extent to which private industry labor law standards and precedents are applied to federal, state, and local governmental level."

Morris, Charles J., ed., *The Developing Labor Law.* Washington, D.C.: Bureau of National Affairs, Inc., 1971.

This book, a product of a diverse group composing the section of labor relations law of the American Bar Association, is outstanding as a chronicle of the developments of the law under the National Labor Relations Act. It is the product of some 60 prominent specialists in labor relations law and will be kept current by annual supplements.

NLRB Decisions. New York: Commerce Clearing House, Inc.

A continuing service that includes comprehensive digests of new NLRB decisions.

Public Personnel Administration: Labor-Management Relations. Englewood Cliffs, N.J.: Prentice-Hall, Inc.

Focusing on public-sector collective bargaining, this service explains laws, methods, rulings, clauses, and established precedents (including summaries of arbitration awards). Bi-weekly reports provide news of developments in this complex area. Sections of the basic text include "New Ideas," "Collective Bargaining Problems and Answers," "Annotated Public Employment Relations Laws and Regulations," "Union Contract Clauses," and "Arbitration Awards Analyzed."

Smith, Arthur B., Jr., "The Impact on Collective Bargaining of Equal Employment Opportunity Remedies," *Industial and Labor Relations Review,* 28, No. 3 (April 1975), 376–94.

The author discusses the seniority-system cases under Title VII and the impact this has on the substantive features of collective bargaining.

State Labor Laws. Washington, D.C.: Bureau of National Affairs, Inc.

A comprehensive and up-to-date compilation of state laws dealing with the fields of labor relations, employment regulations, and wages, hours, and child labor. In addition, there is included a directory of the agencies that administer and enforce the laws.

Taylor, Benjamin J., and Fred Witney, *Labor Relations Law*, 2nd ed. Englewood Cliffs, N.J.: Prentice-Hall, 1975.

A most readable coverage of the legal framework within which collective bargaining operates. A significant contribution of the book is that it assumes that the law of labor relations will have little meaning to the reader if he cannot see it against the dynamics of labor unions and collective bargaining—i.e., the labor relations environment within which the legal structure operates. Hence, the book strikes a balance between the law of collective bargaining and current problems of labor relations. Both the private and public sectors of collective bargaining are covered.

Wages and Hours. Washington, D.C.: Bureau of National Affairs, Inc.

A continuing series that deals with the application of the federal and state wage–hour laws to business enterprise.

Wage-Hour Guide. Englewood Cliffs, N.J.: Prentice-Hall, Inc.

This volume includes the texts of both the Equal Pay Law and the Wage-Hour Law. Information is provided on who is covered, who is exempt, wages and overtime, child labor restrictions, records-investigations, enforcement methods, government contracts, and related topics. A regular report explains current developments. A "Current Matter" section contains administrative opinions and digests of court decisions.

Players in
Collective Bargaining

CHAPTER 6

By the *players* in collective bargaining negotiations is meant those individuals, groups, agencies, or boards that may play a role at one point or another in the negotiation process. This includes the main players—employers and employee representatives—plus others such as the national and state labor relations boards, mediators, arbitrators, fact-finders, and, in the public sector, the assistant secretary of labor–management relations, the Federal Labor Relations Council, and the Federal Service Impasses Panel. There are still others, such as the courts, the legislatures, and various agencies dealing with employment or human rights. But these groups are usually less directly related to the negotiation process as such, although they may have an important influence on the legal environment and particular substantive features of the negotiated labor agreement.

EMPLOYER

With respect to collective bargaining negotiations, the term *employer* may refer to an employer bargaining on a single-firm basis, a single employer bargaining on a multiple-plant basis, a single employer negotiating on a companywide basis, or a group of employers bargaining on an association basis. The employer may likewise be negotiating on an areawide, regional, industrywide or nationwide basis. Public-sector employers may organize for negotiations on a plant or installation, craft, function, or other basis at the federal level. At the state level, *public employer* may mean a state or political subdivision, including a town, city, borough, district, board of regents, school board, public or quasi-public corporation, housing authority, or other authority established by law.

EMPLOYEE REPRESENTATIVE

The union or *employee representative* organized for negotiations might mean a local union, an international union, or joint or multiunion bargaining by local or international unions negotiating at the local, regional, or national level. Employee associations also perform these functions in many states, some protected and some not protected by labor laws. However, the bargaining process and objectives are essentially similar in both associations and unions.

From the foregoing it can be seen that the way labor and management combine for collective bargaining varies considerably over a wide variety of arrangements, such as negotiations between (1) a local, one-plant company and a local union; (2) a division of a company and a local union; (3) a single plant of a company and a local union; (4) an employers' council or association of employers and a local union; (5) a single company and/or joint council or coalition of local unions; (6) an association of employers and a joint council or coalition of local unions; (7) employers in a region (such as trucking) and all local unions of an international union within the region (Teamsters' Master Agreement); (8) a company representing a number of plants and an international union; (9) a single company and a coalition of international unions; (10) a single employer, separately with each of a number of local unions; (11) a coalition of companies on an industrywide basis and a single international union; (12) a government installation and a union or unions; (13) a state government and a state employees' association or union: (14) a municipal government and one or more associations or unions of its employees, such as policemen, firemen, sanitation workers, or office employees; or (15) a school board and a teachers' association.[1]

This does not exhaust all the combinations, but it does illustrate the variety collective bargaining combinations may take. The form used by labor or management in any particular situation reflects in part historical circumstances but most certainly is a product of the needs of the parties to fit their bargaining and their contract to the nature of their own industry, firm, agency, and employee-representative situation.

[1] In 1967, it was estimated that 1.2 percent of collective bargaining agreements covered units of 1,000 or more employees but 50 percent of all covered workers; 98.8 percent of contracts were for units of less than 1,000 workers; 36 percent of contracts were on a multiplant–single-employer basis; 28 percent on a single-employer–single-plant basis; and 36 percent on a multiemployer basis. Lloyd Ulman, ed., *Challenges to Collective Bargaining* (Englewood Cliffs, N.J.: Prentice-Hall, 1967), p. 25.

THIRD PARTIES

National Labor Relations Board

To protect the rights prescribed by the NLRA and to remedy unfair labor practices, Congress established the National Labor Relations Board (NLRB). The NLRB is organized into two major divisions, the five-member board itself and the office of the General Counsel. The five members of the board, appointed by the President with the approval of Congress, hear and decide unfair labor practice cases prosecuted by the General Counsel that have not been settled at earlier steps of the complaint procedure. In addition, the board determines questions concerning representation elections that are referred to it from the regional offices. The board function is primarily a judicial function. The office of General Counsel was established in 1947 to separate the prosecuting function (earlier under the board) from the judicial function. The General Counsel and his staff, who investigate, have the sole discretion to prosecute, and do prosecute all unfair labor practice cases. The General Counsel's staff also conducts representation elections to determine whether a union is to be certified as the bargaining agent for a unit of employees. The regional offices of the NLRB are under the general supervision of the General Counsel. It is with him and his staff, especially in the regional offices, that the most public contacts with the NLRB are made.

Most of the day-to-day work of investigating and processing unfair labor practice charges and conducting representation elections devolve upon the regional offices located in 28 major cities throughout the country under authority granted them by the NLRB and the General Counsel.

If, during the collective bargaining negotiations, any individual or organization feels that the law has been violated, an unfair labor practice charge may be filed against the offending party, alleging a violation of the NLRA.[2] This complaint is filed with the regional office of the NLRB. The charge is then investigated by an agent from the regional office, and upon completion of this investigation, the regional director decides whether a formal complaint is warranted. If there is substance to the charge, an informal settlement may be agreed upon. Failing this, the regional director issues a formal complaint. A formal hearing is then held before a board trial examiner, who issues a decision and a recommended order based on his findings of fact in the case. Appeals from this decision may be made to the NLRB, and from there, matters of enforcement or appeal go to the circuit court of appeals. It must be em-

---

[2] Kenneth C. McGuiness, *How to Take a Case before the National Labor Relations Board*, 3rd ed. (Washington, D.C.: Bureau of National Affairs, 1967). See also the annual reports of the NLRB.

phasized that the interpretative function of the board, even though the board has no direct enforcement powers itself, plays an extremely important role in what the parties may or may not do during the bargaining process and the scope of their bargaining activities. In some areas, such as the meaning of "other concerted activities for the purpose of collective bargaining or other mutual aid or protection," or "confer in good faith with respect to wage, hours, and other terms and conditions of employment,"[3] the board, through its interpretations, has expanded significantly the role of collective bargaining.

Executive Order 11491

In the public sector, the counterpart of the NLRB is a function of two groups, the assistant secretary of labor for labor–management relations and the Federal Labor Relations Council.[4] The assistant secretary has primary responsibility for operational functions. Included are determining the appropriate bargaining unit, supervising and certifying the results of representative elections, deciding questions on national consultation rights of labor organizations, adjudging unfair labor practice complaints and violations of standards of conduct for labor organizations, deciding questions as to whether a grievance is subject to a negotiated grievance procedure or to arbitration under an agreement, and issuing cease-and-desist and affirmative-action orders. The FLRC, consisting of the chairman of the Civil Service Commission, the secretary of labor, the director of the Office of Management and Budget, and any other officials designated by the president, has final authority in administering and interpreting the executive order, deciding major policy issues, prescribing regulations, and making recommendations to the president. In these functions as final adjudicator and interpreter of policy, its functions are similar to those of the National Labor Relations Board. As the person responsible for operational matters, the assistant secretary and his staff are somewhat comparable to the regional directors of the NLRB. The public sector has no direct counterpart to the general counsel of the private sector. In addition, EO 11491 provides for a Federal Service Impasses Council to assist in the resolution of negotiation impasses.

State Labor Relations Boards

Most states also have agencies established to adminster state labor laws.[5]

---

[3] Section 8 (d), Labor Management Relations Act of 1947.

[4] Write to Federal Labor Relations Council, Assistant Secretary of Labor-Management Relations, Federal Service Impasses Panel, or the Civil Service Commission, Washington, D.C. for more detailed information.

[5] See sections in the Prentice-Hall, Commerce Clearing House, and Bureau of National Affairs services covering state labor relations laws or the states directly. The University of Hawaii, Industrial Relations Center, has published some excellent material on public-sector bargaining at the state and local levels.

These agencies come under a number of titles, but essentially they are to the state what the National Labor Relations Board is to the federal sector. For example, in Colorado, the Industrial Commission administers state labor laws; in Connecticut, it is the State Board of Labor Relations (which administers laws covering both public and private sectors); Hawaii has an Employment Board; and New York operates through a Labor Relations Board. For the public sector, the responsibility for administration varies: There is no state board in California, but there are Employee Relations Boards to administer local labor relations in the city of Los Angeles and Los Angeles County. In Kansas, a new Public Employee Relations Board administers public-sector labor relations.

Federal Mediation and Conciliation Service

The FMCS is an administrative arm of the executive branch of the federal government.[6] Through it, the parties may obtain the services of a federal mediator (located in regions throughout the country) to assist them in resolving differences and breaking impasses.

A long-standing concept, but one that has taken on added meaning in recent years, is "preventive mediation." Under this concept, the mediator maintains a continuing dialogue with the parties in order to smooth relations and put out fires before, rather than after the fact.

It should be noted that the mediator does not serve a judicial function; he cannot adjudicate or decide or impose a decision on the parties. His sole function is to use his good offices as a representative of the government, acting in a neutral capacity, and his expertise in labor relations to aid the parties in reconciling their differences and arriving at an amicable settlement of their contract. As William E. Simkin, former director of the FMSC, notes, the mediator "may cajole, he may recommend, but the parties always have the right to say 'no,' even on most procedural matters."[7] Simkin describes the mediator as one who performs "a continuum of possible functions of an impartial person in the collective bargaining relationship beginning with the common notions about conciliation and going across the scale to, but not including, arbitration."[8] Mediators come from a variety of backgrounds in labor relations—union, management, and education—but have one thing in common: They enter the service from a broad base of practical experience.

The Federal Mediation and Conciliation Service is also available in the resolution of negotiation disputes in the public sector, since no comparable body was established under Executive Order 11491. However, when voluntary efforts such as mediation fail to resolve a negotiation

---

[6] William E. Simkin, *Mediation and the Dynamics of Collective Bargaining* (Washington, D.C.: Bureau of National Affairs, 1971). See also annual reports of FMCS.
[7] *Ibid.*, p. 28.
[8] *Ibid.*, p. 27.

impasse, either party may request that the matter be considered by the Federal Service Impasses Panel, a new body established under the executive order. The panel, at its discretion, may consider the matter and recommend a way of resolving it or may settle the impasse by appropriate action. Arbitration or fact-finding by a third party may be turned to by the parties if such action is authorized or directed by the panel.

Arbitration

The nation's arbitrators are private individuals whose main function is to arbitrate appealed grievances (rights disputes) rather than disputes arising from collective bargaining negotiations (interest disputes). Occasionally, an arbitrator will be brought in on a contract-negotiation problem, but both parties shy clear, for the most part, of using an arbitrator on such problems, because it means a third party imposing on them the terms that will be incorporated in their contracts. Arbitration is a judicial process and, as such, is more appropriate to situations where an interpretation of existing language is needed that could not be decided by the parties through their normal grievance procedures. The arbitrator—after being selected from names secured from the Federal Mediation and Conciliation Service, the American Arbitration Association, various state agencies, or direct contact with private individuals—holds hearings, takes testimony, hears arguments of both parties over a specified issue, and then after study renders a decision, interpreting the clause or clauses in question or the action of the party under a particular clause of the contract. The decision of the arbitrator is final and binding on the parties, may be enforced through appeal to the courts, and may be overturned by court action only if it involves a misuse of authority. The courts do not inquire into the reasoning of the arbitrator on the facts presented, nor into the decision based on that reasoning, except where there is evidence that the arbitrator has exceeded his authority or has been guilty of procedural error. The Supreme Court reasons:

> The refusal of courts to review the merits of an arbitration award is the proper approach to arbitration under collective bargaining agreements. . . . an arbitrator is confined to interpretation and application of the collective bargaining agreement: . . . when the arbitrator's words manifest an infidelity to this obligation, courts have no choice but to refuse enforcement of the award.[9]

In addition to providing for arbitration in negotiation disputes with the approval of the Federal Service Impasses Panel, the executive order

[9] *U.S. Steel Workers of America* v. *Enterprise Wheel and Car Company,* 363 U.S. 593 (1960).

also allows a negotiated procedure in the labor agreement for the arbitration of grievances over the interpretation or application of the agreement if invoked by either party to the agreement. Departing from private-sector practice in the use of arbitration, the order allows either party to file exceptions to an arbitrator's award with the Federal Labor Relations Council for final determination.[10]

Fact-finding

Fact-finding involves the introduction of a third party of neutrals or disinterested parties to a dispute situation. Their responsibility under rules established either by the parties or by statute is to investigate, ascertain the facts, determine positions of the parties, and report their findings with or without a recommended settlement. The rationale in the use of the fact-finders is that it somehow introduces the public interest, brings the facts to light, establishes a basis either for the parties to continue negotiations or for the marshalling of public pressures on the parties to settle, or serves as a basis for a public body to order a settlement on the basis of facts gathered by disinterested parties. The use of the fact-finding technique is fully covered in Part IV.

Joint Study Committees

Admittedly, the main parties involved in joint study committees are labor and management themselves. But it should be recognized that in the use of such committees, either on a one-time problem-solving assignment or as a continuously functioning committee, the use of neutrals as members has proved a very effective device in a number of instances. Full coverage of this committee approach with the involvement of neutrals will be found in Part IV.

SELECTED REFERENCES

Baer, Walter E., *Labor Arbitration Guide*. Homewood, Ill.: Dow Jones-Irwin, 1974.

The author brings to the reader a comprehensive account of the basic features of the arbitration process.

Barbash, Jack, *American Unions, Structure, Government and Politics*. New York: Random House, 1967.

An informative and easily read account of unions as a government system. Professor Barbash brings the reader a combined union–government–academic experience in his interpretation of unionism.

[10] Section 13 (b) of EO 11491.

Bloom, Gordon F., and Herbert R. Northrup, *Economics of Labor Relations,* 6th ed. Homewood, Ill.: Richard D. Irwin, 1969.

A readable account of the structure and function of unions in Chapter 3. Chapter 4 contains two sections well worth reading for information concerning the setting of union and management policy for collective bargaining.

Current References and Information Services for Policy Decision-Making in State and Local Government Labor Relations—A Selected Bibliography. U.S. Department of Labor, November 1971.

With the rapidly changing picture in state government collective bargaining activities, publications pointing to sources of information, such as this one, are of vital importance.

Directory of National Unions and Employee Associations. U.S. Department of Labor, 1973; Supplement 2, September 1975.

This publication is updated periodically and includes a listing of national unions, employees' associations, the AFL-CIO, other federations, and state labor organizations. In addition, a summary of developments since the last directory and statistics on the labor movement are included.

A Directory of Public Employee Organizations—A Guide to the Major Organization Representing State and Local Public Employees. U.S. Department of Labor, 1974.

Information is provided on each organization listed as to its headquarters, jurisdiction, type and purpose of organization, organizational structure, membership, supporting groups, work-stoppage policy, publications, conventions, and year of origin.

A Directory of Public Management Organizations. U.S. Department of Labor, November 1971.

This DOL publication includes a guide to national organizations of state and local governments and associations of public officials with an interest in public-employee management relations.

Hardman, J.B.S., and Maurice F. Neufeld, eds., *The House of Labor—Internal Operations of American Unions.* Englewood Cliffs, N.J.: Prentice-Hall, 1951.

Two objectives guided the organization of this book's material: "(1) to acquaint persons outside of organized labor with the 'inside' of the American Labor movement, its performance, and motivation; and (2) to present to the participants in union activity an over-all view of their group activities in the promotion of union objectives."

Maggiolo, Walter A., *Techniques of Mediation in Labor Disputes.* Dobbs Ferry, N.Y.: Oceana Publications, 1971.

A complete picture of the mediator and what he does.

McGuiness, Kenneth C., *Silverberg's How to Take a Case before the National Labor Relations Board.* Washington, D.C.: Bureau of National Affairs, Inc., 1967.

For those engaged in collective bargaining in the private sector, this book constitutes a definitive source on the NLRB and how the parties may use its services.

Morris, Charles J., ed., *The Developing Labor Law*, VII. Washington, D.C.: The Bureau of National Affairs, Inc., 1971.

The chapters included in Part VII give a comprehensive view of the administration of the NLRA by the NLRB and the role of the courts in such administration.

Simkin, William E., *Mediation and the Dynamics of Collective Bargaining*. Washington, D.C.: Bureau of National Affairs, Inc., 1971.

Few people have the credentials to talk about mediation that this author, a former director of the FMCS, has. This is not just a description of the mediation function but a book aimed at understanding and analyzing the mediation process.

State Labor Laws. Washington, D.C.: Bureau of National Affairs, Inc.

A series that is kept up to date on the agencies that administer and enforce the laws, and the laws that establish and define the powers and duties of these agencies.

Yoder, Dale, *Personnel Management and Industrial Relations*, Chapter 16. Englewood Cliffs, N.J.: Prentice-Hall, 1970.

A readable account of union theory, policy, and practice. Understanding the union—how it is organized and functions, and its relationship to management—is vital to an understanding of the collective bargaining relationships of the parties.

Collective Bargaining Process— Negotiation

When we come to the settlement of the terms upon which a new general agreement should be entered into, an entirely different set of considerations is involved. Whether the general level of wages in the trade should be raised or lowered by 10 per cent; whether the number of boys to be engaged by any one employer should be restricted, and if so, by what scale; whether the hours of labor should be reduced, and overtime regulated or prohibited—are not problems which could be solved by the most perfect calculating-machine. Here nothing has been decided, or accepted in advance by both parties, and the fullest possible play is left for the arts of diplomacy. In so far as the issue is left to Collective Bargaining there is not even any question of principle involved. The workmen are frankly striving to get for themselves the best terms that can permanently be extracted from the employers. The employers, on the other hand, are endeavoring, in accordance with business principles, to buy their labor in the cheapest market.

Sidney and Beatrice Webb   *1902*

PART TWO

Introduction to
Part Two

CHAPTER 7

MEANING OF COLLECTIVE BARGAINING

Parts II, III, and IV deal with topics that, while treated separately, are essentially elements of one process: collective bargaining. Beatrice Potter Webb introduced this term in 1891.[1] When the Webbs later popularized the term *collective bargaining* in the great classic, *Industrial Democracy*,[2] it had a more restricted meaning than it has today. Primarily, the Webbs and the American writers of the day were applying the term *collective bargaining* to the negotiation process. The Webbs, in discussing "the method of collective bargaining," noted first the meaning of the term *individual bargain*[3] as applying strictly to a situation between an employer and workingmen individually under which the terms of employment were determined. They then proceeded to describe, in contrast, what they meant by "the method of collective bargaining":

> But if a group of workmen concert together, and send representatives to conduct the bargaining on behalf of the whole body, the position at once changes. Instead of the employer making a series of separate contracts with isolated individuals, he meets with a collective will, and settles, in a single agreement, the principles upon which, for the time being, all workmen of a particular group, or class, or grade, will be engaged.[4]

[1] Beatrice Potter, *The Co-operative Movement in Great Britain* (New York: Scribner's, 1891), pp. 216–17.
[2] Sidney and Beatrice Webb, *Industrial Democracy* (London: Longmans, Green, 1902), p. 173.
[3] *Ibid.*
[4] *Ibid.*

Even though collective bargaining was used initially to describe negotiations, another collective bargaining function that was later to be of equal importance was beginning to emerge. This was the incorporation in the trade agreement of machinery to resolve disputes that might arise during the contract period over the meaning and application of the agreement—the process now known as contract administration. It should be recognized that yet a third collective bargaining function has also been developing. This third element involves the use of techniques and devices outside the regular negotiation and contract-administration procedures aimed at strengthening both processes—techniques such as mediation, arbitration, fact-finding, and continuous bargaining. Insofar as these supplementary aids are aimed at facilitating and strengthening collective bargaining and are not considered as substitutes, they should be recognized as formal elements of what we call collective bargaining. This is the reasoning behind the three-way division of materials that follows: Part II, "Negotiation"; Part III, "Contract Administration"; Part IV, "Resolution of Conflict."

NEGOTIATION AND THE COLLECTIVE BARGAINING AGREEMENT

Of immediate concern is the negotiation stage of collective bargaining. As background, it is understood that collective bargaining negotiation is a multifaceted process that takes on somewhat the coloration of the time, place, and participants involved. This is why there are many variations in the contract results from one bargaining situation to another, even where the same union is involved but with different firms, or where the locals of the same international are dealing with essentially similar firms but in different geographic areas. Other differences are related to community, economic, political, and social influence; in the way the employer is organized; in production methods and technology; in the nature of the product; in the industry environment (manufacturing, transportation, service, construction, and government, and their subcategories); in historical circumstances; in the legal atmosphere (legislation, court decisions, arbitration decisions, grievance settlements); and not least, in the personalities and predilections of negotiators from one bargaining situation to another. All these are a part of the forces influencing the specific nature of the trade agreement and language that results from any particular collective bargaining negotiation. In sum, collective bargaining negotiation is not an easily described process nor does it lend itself to being reduced to what one might describe as a typical situation. It is the product of many environmental forces that shape its nature, some general and some unique to the particular negotiation.

COLLECTIVE BARGAINING BY OBJECTIVES

In the arrangement of material for this book, highest priority has been given to the practical matter of bridging the gap between information and use. Part II, Chapters 8–14, presents information vital to an understanding of collective bargaining negotiation. In addition, the reader is introduced to a methodology for bargaining, a step-by-step way of preparing for and carrying on collective bargaining negotiations. The result is to bridge the gap between information and use and to provide a more positive thrust to the entire negotiation procedure, increasing the effectiveness of the negotiator, experienced or inexperienced. The key to this methodology is that the ordinary tasks that must be completed in any negotiation situation are placed within an easily followed framework. This methodology not only provides a systematic sequence for bargaining but, by its discipline, forces the negotiator in advance of negotiation to adequately familiarize himself with the subjects to be bargained and to approach negotiations in a more positive frame of mind. This methodology is termed *collective bargaining by objectives* (CBO) and is an adaptation of management by objectives (MBO) to the collective bargaining negotiation process.

SELECTED REFERENCES

Bloom, Gordon F., and Herbert R. Northrup, *Economics of Labor Relations,* 6th ed. Homewood, Ill.: Richard D. Irwin, 1969.

Chapter 4 contains excellent sections on the economic and social settings of collective bargaining.

Davey, Harold W., *Contemporary Collective Bargaining*, 3rd ed. Englewood Cliffs, N.J.: Prentice-Hall, 1972.

Professor Davey brings to the reader a remarkable blending of the academician and the practitioner, having been a leading arbitrator for over three decades. The reader will find the material not only understandable but down to earth. I have used the Davey book often in conjunction with the objectives and learning-experience approach to collective bargaining training.

Hildebrand, George H., "The Public Sector," in John T. Dunlop and Neil W. Chamberlain, eds., *Frontiers of Collective Bargaining*. New York: Harper & Row, 1967.

The author raises and discusses many of the issues relative to bargaining in the public sector, such as special features of public-sector bargaining, what to do about impasses, and the question of relative bargaining power.

Kassalow, Everett M., *Trade Unions and Industrial Relations: An International Comparison*. New York: Random House, 1969.

The author is convinced that the comparative method provides new insights for social scientists examining American industrial relations. This is an excellent examination of industrial relations—trade unions and collective bargaining—on a comparative basis between Europe and America. He addresses such collective bargaining topics as the agreement, scope of bargaining, legislation, bargaining methods, and union security.

Levinson, Harold M. et al., *Collective Bargaining and Technological Change in American Transportation.* Evanston, Ill.: The Transportation Center at Northwestern University, 1971.

A magnificent study of omnibus proportions of the technological developments and the economic and social aspects of one of America's most vital industries. Included for the first time in one study are trucking, the railroad industry, the maritime industry, and the airline industry. The study not only covers the background developments of each industry but through analysis arrives at important policy recommendations.

Moskow, Michael H., J. Joseph Loewenberg, and Edward Clifford Koziara, *Collective Bargaining in Public Employment.* New York: Random House, 1970.

A good basic source not only on the collective bargaining process in public employment but with special attention to the federal, state, and municipal sectors and to teachers, police, and fire fighters.

Peters, Edward, *Strategy and Tactics in Labor Negotiations,* 3rd ed., pp. 7–20. Swarthmore, Pa.: Personnel Journal, 1966.

An excellent source for obtaining the feel of negotiating; we accompany an accomplished and experienced practitioner through situation after situation while he illustrates the practice of negotiation. In this section, he delves into the question of bargaining characteristics and practices as they vary from one union to another and one industry to another.

Pezdek, Robert V., "Public Employment Bibliography," *Bibliography Series No. 11,* New York School of Industrial and Labor Relations, 1973.

An excellent source of materials on collective bargaining for public employees at all levels and for specific groups of public employees.

Rehmus, Charles M., ed., *Public Employment Labor Relations: An Overview of Eleven Nations.* Ann Arbor: Institute of Industrial Relations, University of Michigan/Wayne State University, 1975.

This study provides greater insight into our own labor relations issues and developments in the public sector by means of a comparison with Canada, Japan, England, France, the Republic of Germany, Austria, and the Nordic countries.

Ryder, Meyer S., Charles M. Rehmus, and Sanford Cohen, *Management Preparation for Collective Bargaining.* Homewood, Ill.: Dow Jones-Irwin, 1966.

This study was motivated by the apparent lack of writings on management preparation for collective bargaining. It is based on an extensive survey of practices of firms and is most detailed about the preparation process.

Slichter, Sumner H., James J. Healy, and E. Robert Livernash, *The Impact of Collective Bargaining on Management*. Washington, D.C.: The Brookings Institution, 1960.

Almost two decades later, this study still stands out as one of the penetrating looks at the impact of collective bargaining upon management policy and practice represented by a cross section of 150 companies, 25 industry associations, and 40 unions. The book is divided according to substantive areas of management policy and practice, such as hiring, training and apprenticeship, seniority, work-sharing and layoff, and promotion, to name a few.

Stanley, David T., with the assistance of Carole L. Cooper, *Managing Local Government under Union Pressure*. Washington, D.C.: The Brookings Institution, 1972.

This volume concentrates on the influence of unions on administrative practices at the municipal level of government.

Stieber, Jack, *Public Employee Unionism: Structure, Growth, Policy*. (Washington, D.C.: The Brookings Institution, 1973.

Professor Stieber examines the various types of unions and associations representing employees in state and local sectors of government, exclusive of schoolteachers and transit employees. The study is concerned with the impact of the structure, growth patterns and policies upon collective bargaining. Included are topics such as the organization of employees in public service, conflict and cooperation, collective bargaining, the strike issue, and emerging patterns.

Walsh, Robert E., ed., *Sorry . . . No Government Today—Unions vs. City Hall*. Boston: Beacon Press, 1969.

This book is in the form of an anthology of collective bargaining in public employment at the municipal level, containing pieces by a large number of authors. Coverage is broad.

Warner, Kenneth O., and Mary L. Hennessy, *Public Management at the Bargaining Table*. Chicago: Public Personnel Association, 1967.

The authors effectively cover three aspects of the newly emerged sector of public-employee bargaining: the dynamics of collective bargaining for public employees, the bargaining process for public employees, and the future of public-employee collective bargaining. Comparisons are made with Canada.

Weber, Arnold R., ed., *The Structure of Collective Bargaining*. New York: Free Press, 1961.

An excellent look at the role of collective bargaining in the decision-making process of our economic system. The focus of the book is on trends and problems in the structure of collective bargaining, covering such topics as the size and scope of bargaining units and the power function between managements and unions in the making of decisions. Industries covered are steel, chemical, airline, construction, and farm equipment.

Wellington, Harry H., and Ralph K. Winter, Jr., *The Unions and the Cities*. Washington, D.C.: The Brookings Institution, 1971.

This book in the Brookings Institution series on local level collective bargaining concentrates on the legal problems arising from the importation of collective bargaining into the public sector.

Wolfbein, Seymour L., ed., *Emerging Sectors of Collective Bargaining.* Braintree, Mass: D. H. Mark, 1970.

The last two decades have been one of the most momentous periods in the evolution of collective bargaining. This book, which includes names such as Dunlop, Taylor, Ross, and Moskow, looks at the emerging sectors of collective bargaining and the new internal structures and responses resulting.

Worman, Max S., Jr., *Critical Issues in Labor.* New York: Macmillan, 1969.

A useful source of background information concerning the changing character and challenges of the labor management developing issues, experimental techniques, behavioral approaches, and changing attitudes related to collective bargaining, and what all this means for labor in a free society.

Yoder, Dale, and Herbert G. Heneman, Jr., eds., "Employee and Labor Relations," in *ASPA Handbook of Personnel and Industrial Relations.* Washington, D.C.: Bureau of National Affairs, Inc., 1976.

Arvid Anderson of the Office of Collective Bargaining, New York City, brings to the reader an up-to-date practitioner's view of labor relations in the public service.

Zagoria, Sam, ed., *Public Workers and Public Unions.* Englewood Cliffs, N.J.: Prentice-Hall, 1972.

From a broader approach to the role, development, and structure of public-sector bargaining, this study then turns more specific with articles on the municipal employer, the school board, the union leader, and the budget director. The book concludes with the problem areas of impasses, strikes, politics at the bargaining table, and race relations.

The Collective Bargaining Agreement

CHAPTER 8

The collective bargaining agreement is included at this point to aid the reader in developing a better understanding and perspective of the chapters that follow concerning the negotiation process. The agreement is the objective and result of the negotiation process. With a fuller understanding of the end product, the agreement, each step in the negotiation process as it unfolds takes on new meaning because it is judged against the foreknowledge of the final product.

The collective bargaining agreement may be described in a number of ways. It is a compromise between the self-interests of the two parties that they have agreed upon as a guide to their relationships on certain matters for a specified period of time. In this sense, it is a form of constitutional government introduced into the work relationship. Justice Douglas, in delivering the majority opinion in the *Steelworkers* v. *Warrior Navigation Co.* segment of the "Trilogy,"[1] addressed himself to the significance of the collective agreement:

> It is a more than a contract; it is a generalized code to govern a myriad of cases which the draftsmen cannot wholly anticipate.
>
> [It] is an effort to erect a system of industrial self-government.
>
> [It is a choice] between having that relationship governed by an agreed upon rule or law or leaving each and every matter subject to a temporary resolution dependent solely upon the relative strength of any given movement, of the contending forces.

[1] On June 20, 1960, the U.S. Supreme Court handed down three decisions of great import to the arbitration process. The three cases, each involving the United Steelworkers of America, have come to be known as the "Trilogy" cases. They include: Warrior & Gulf Navigation, American Manufacturing, and Enterprise Wheel & Car Corporation cases.

It calls into being a new common law—the common law of a particular industry of a particular plant. [363 U.S. 574 (1960)]

The Webbs would call it the introduction of industrial democracy to the workplace, since it represents the joint voice of labor and management as to how their relationship should be governed. More specifically, its substantive terms not only define such basic matters as wages and hours but include a whole myriad of complex rules regulating almost every aspect of the employment relationship—even to maternity leave, garnishment of wages, location of plant, patent rights, and political activity. When signed, the collective agreement constitutes a contract between the parties—the employer, the union, and the employees within the bargaining unit.

A LEGAL CONTRACT

That Congress viewed the collective agreement as a legally enforceable contract is attested to by Section 301 (a) of the Labor Management Relations Act of 1947:

> Suits for violation of *contracts* between an *employer* and a *labor organization representing employees* in an industry affecting commerce as defined in this Act, or between any such labor organizations, may be brought in any district court of the United States having jurisdiction of the parties, without respect to the amount in controversy or without regard to the citizenship of the parties. [Italics added.]

Regardless of the nitpicking that some writers engage in when trying to distinguish between the nature of a collective agreement and that of commercial agreements, the fact remains that Congress makes it clear that the collective agreement is a contract and is between two parties—"an employer and a labor organization representing employees." The agreement signed by the parties remains legally binding upon all three —the employer, the union, and the employees—unless within their legal rights they remove themselves from its coverage. In the case of the union, this would mean, for example, that the union was decertified and was no longer the bargaining agent for the employees of a designated appropriate bargaining unit, or that upon renegotiation of the agreement, the parties failed to reach a settlement. In the latter instance, the contract, and with it, legal responsibility, would then cease to exist. In the case of employees who belong to the designated appropriate bargaining unit, whether they belong to the union or not, there is a legal responsibility to comply with the provisions of the collective agreement as long as they continue as employees. They may, of course, remove themselves from legal responsibility by quitting or severing their employment relationship.

Congress intended that there also be a clear relationship between the union and the employees in a bargaining unit relative to the collective agreement, by stating in Section 9 (a):

> Representatives designated or selected for the purpose of collective bargaining by the majority of the employees in a unit appropriate for such purposes, shall be the exclusive representatives of all the employees in such a unit for the purpose of collective bargaining in respect to rates of pay, wages, hours of employment, or other conditions of employment. . . .

As long as the union has met the requirements of the law as to certification as bargaining representative and, upon the completion of the negotiations, has met its own requirements of ratification by its membership, the collective agreement so signed is a binding contract on both the union and the employees in the bargaining unit. The inviolate nature of this representation is further emphasized by the later language of Section 9 (a), in which employees within the bargaining unit are granted the right to individually process their own grievances if they so desire, without the participation of the union, as long as any settlement does not violate the terms of the collective agreement of which the union as their signator is a party.

ENFORCEMENT OF THE COLLECTIVE AGREEMENT

It is clear by both practice and legal decisions that the collective agreement is a legal contract enforceable by law. Several avenues of recourse are provided, either by the parties or by legislation. The most frequent method of enforcement of provisions of the agreement is through grievance arbitration. This is a method that usually uses an outside third party as the sole judge, or a combination of an arbitration board made up of representatives of the two parties plus an outside neutral. In most instances, this amounts to little difference from the single-arbitrator approach, since the outside neutral arbitrator in effect hears the case, writes it up, and makes a decision. However, the point is that this method of enforcement of the contract is a legal recourse established under the contract or agreement itself. About 94 percent of collective agreements provide for arbitration of grievances not settled by the parties themselves. Ninety-nine percent of these provide that arbitration shall follow automatically if the grievance process has been exhausted, and/or that it may be invoked by either party. Sample arbitration clauses may illustrate the process:

> . . . if the above [grievance] procedure in its entirety does not result in a satisfactory adjustment of any grievance arising under this Agreement, the grievance may be submitted to arbitration at the instance of either party. . . .

The binding nature of the arbitrator's decision is also usually stated in the agreement:

> The decision of the arbitrator shall be final and conclusive and binding upon employees, the Company and the Union: subject to the right of the Company or the Union to judicial review, any lawful decision of the arbitrator shall forthwith place into effect. . . .

Although it has been stated earlier, it is important to emphasize that the arbitrator's decision is final and binding upon the parties, may be enforced through appeal to the courts, and may be overturned by court action only if it involves a misuse of authority. The courts do not inquire into the reasoning of the arbitrator as he reviews the facts presented, nor into the decision based on that reasoning, except where there is evidence that the arbitrator has misused or exceeded his authority substantively or procedurally.

The courts have also held that under certain circumstances, the National Labor Relations Board may, ancillary to its main function of enforcing the law against unfair labor practices, rule on matters related to a violation of the collective agreement that would normally be subject to the arbitration procedure. For example, the board was involved in a case where the charge was refusal to sign a contract (an unfair labor practice). In making a decision on this charge, the board also ruled on an ancillary payment of certain benefits that if not made would have constituted a breach of contract by the employer (the defendant). Other than these special instances, primacy is given to the arbitration procedure internally to enforce the agreement.[2]

Finally, Section 301 makes it clear that final recourse may be had to the courts to enforce the collective agreement. Either party may resort directly to the courts when violation of the agreement does not involve arbitration or, for example, when a party refuses to go to arbitration under an arbitration clause of the contract. Damages caused by an unlawful strike (no-strike clause in contract) may be resolved in the court also. Finally, appeal to the courts may be resorted to in order to enforce arbitration awards.

[2] See Benjamin J. Taylor and Fred W. Witney, *Labor Relations Law*, 2nd ed. (Englewood Cliffs, N.J.: Prentice-Hall, 1975), p. 659.

Under Section 301, collective agreements are enforceable in both federal and state courts, although primacy in enforcement and the issuance of injunctions is given under the law to the federal district courts.

CONTENTS OF THE COLLECTIVE AGREEMENT

Some agreements run only twenty or thirty pages; others are well over 100 pages. To describe the agreement in detail is an impossible task within the confines of a chapter. However, a good idea of the agreement can be gained by looking at the main items and types of provisions. This approach will serve to acquaint the reader with the general content. More details will follow in the chapters on negotiation and contract administration, but an in-depth understanding can come only through becoming involved in negotiations and contract administration. Aside from examining collective agreements individually, comprehension of the various items of bargaining may be gained through the excellent, detailed, and up-to-date services published by the Bureau of National Affairs, Commerce Clearing House, and Prentice-Hall. These are most objective and exhaustive in their coverage.

Beal and Wickersham assert that the agreement serves four primary functions, and "no matter what the number of pages or clauses, or the order of presentation, every complete union agreement shows this pattern."[3] It is the fundamental pattern of collective bargaining in the United States. The four areas are union security and management rights, the wage and effect bargain, individual security, and administration.

Dale Yoder gives the major areas of a collective agreement as:[4]

Preamble and purpose	Union label or shop card
Term, life, duration	Holidays
Bargaining unit	Vacations
Recognition (form, type)	Leaves
Union security (form)	Reporting, call-in, etc.
Management rights	Shift differentials
Wages	Discharge
Reopening	Benefits
Hours	Safety
Grievances	Apprenticeship
Strikes, lockouts	Amendment

[3] Edwin F. Beal and Edward D. Wickersham, *The Practice of Collective Bargaining*, rev. ed. (Homewood, Ill.: Richard D. Irwin, 1963), p. 320.

[4] Dale Yoder, *Personnel Management and Industrial Relations*, 6th ed. (Englewood Cliffs, N.J.: Prentice-Hall, 1970), p. 440.

An even more detailed picture of the myriad of subjects and their variations found in agreements can be obtained by scanning the main topical division of the "Contract Clause Finder" that accompanies the BNA Service on Collective Bargaining Negotiations and Contracts:[5]

Absence from work
Accidents and illness
Accidents within plant
Admission of members to union
Admission of union reps.
Age limitations
Agency shop
Amendment and duration
Annual wage
Apprenticeship
Arbitration
Assignability of contract
Automatic increases
Automatic renewal of contract
Back pay
Bargaining agent
Bargaining unit
Bonuses
Boycotts
Bulletin boards
Bumping
Call-in pay
Change in hours
Check-off
Classification of employees
Clean-up time
Closed shop
Coercion
Company rules
Contracting work out
Cooperation between union & mgt.
Coverage of contract
Damaged goods
Damages—breach of contract
Dangerous work
Death in family leave
Deductions from wages
Demotion
Differentials in wages

Disabled employees
Discharge, discipline
Disciplinary action
Discounts to employees
Discrimination
Dismissal compensation
Disputes
Dues to collect
Duration of contract
Early retirement
Employer associations
Encouragement of union membership
Enforcement of contract
Expenses incidental to work
Firing
Foremen
Funeral leave
Garnishment of wages
Get-ready time
Government regulations
Grievances and arbitration
Handicapped workers
Hazardous work
Health and sanitation
Health & welfare plans
Hiring halls
Hiring—new employees
Holiday
Hours guarantees
Hours and overtime
Illness
Incentive systems
Income maintenance
Injury on job
Insurance
Job evaluation
Jury duty
Layoff, rehiring, work sharing

[5] *Collective Bargaining Negotiations and Contracts* (Washington, D.C.: Bureau of National Affairs, Inc., Service Current), pp. 32:11–32:16.

Leave of absence
Legal services
Limitations on production
Living quarters
Loans to employees
Location of plant
Lockouts
Lunch periods
Maintenance of membership
Make-up time
Management & union rights
Maternity leave
Meal allowance
Mediation
Medical service
Membership in union
Military service
Minimum wage guarantees
Modification of agreement
Modified union shop
"Most favored employer" clauses
Negotiations
New employees
Night work
Non-union goods
Notice of amendment & termination
Occupational sickness & accident
"Open shop"
Overtime
Parties to contract
Patent rights
Pay guarantees
Payroll data
Pensions
Physical examination
Picketing
Piece work
Plant removal
Plant rules
Political activity
Posting information
Preferential hiring
Premium pay
Probationary employees
Production standards
Profit-sharing plans
Promotion, demotion, transfer

Recall from layoff
Recognition
Regular rate of pay
Rehiring
Reinstatement
Relief periods
Relocation of business
Renewal of agreement
Reopenings
Resignation of employees
Rest periods
Restrictions on conduct of business
Retirement plans
Retroactive pay
Retroactivity
Return to work
Rules
Runaway shop
Safety
Sale of business
Saving provisions
Scheduling hours or production
Security for performance of agreement
Security risks
Seniority
Severance pay
Sharing of work
Shifts of work
Shop stewards & committeemen
Sick leave
Spoiled work
Standby time
Strikes and lockouts
Subcontracting
Superseniority
Supplement unemployment pay
Supervisory employees
Technological displacement
Temporary employees
Termination
Time studies
Tools
Training and apprenticeship
Travel time
Transfers
Trial periods
Unemployment benefits

Uniforms and tools	Violation of contract
Union activity on company time and property	Visits by union representatives
	Voting time
Union label	Wages
Union–management cooperation	Waiting time
Union representatives	Waivers of bargaining rights
Union rights and responsibilities	Warnings to employees
Union security	Welfare plans
Union shop	Work by employer
Unit for bargaining	Work permits
Vacations	Working conditions
Vesting	Work sharing
Veterans	Workweek

It is also important to remember that the contents of the collective bargaining agreement vary between the private and public sectors because of the more restrictive approach of the public sector to what is a bargainable subject. Illustrative of the types of items that may not be negotiated into the provisions of public-sector agreements (although they, or parallel items, may be included in those of the private sector) are:

1. Pay scale (not bargainable in the federal sector—varies in the state and local sectors)

2. Mission of an agency

3. Budget of an agency

4. Organization of an agency

5. Number of employees

6. Numbers, types, and grades of positions or employees assigned to an organizational unit, work project, or tour of duty

7. The technology of performing a government agency's work

8. Internal security practices

9. Any item in conflict with existing or future laws and the regulations of appropriate authorities, including policies set forth in the *Federal Personnel Manual;* published agency policies and regulations in existence at time of approval of agreement; and subsequently published agency policies and regulations required by law or by the regulations of appropriate authorities, or authorized by the terms of controlling agreement at a higher agency level

10. Any item in conflict with the right of officials of an agency to direct employees; to hire, promote, transfer, assign, retain, suspend, demote, discharge, and discipline employees; to reduce force; to maintain efficiency; to determine methods, means, and personnel to do whatever is necessary to carry out the mission of the agency

11. Retirement benefits
12. Any provisions inconsistent with merit principles[6]

SELECTED REFERENCES

Feller, David E., *A General Theory of the Collective Bargaining Agreement.* Reprint No. 372, Institute of Industrial Relations, University of California, Los Angeles, 1973.

Professor Feller notes that a definitive theory of the rights created by the collective bargaining agreement has never developed in American law. There have been analogies drawn from time to time, and particular answers have been provided in suits between unions, employers, and employees, but nowhere has a unified theory been developed that attempts to relate these particular answers to each other in a coherent manner. In this article, the author sets himself to the task of developing just such a theory.

Livernash, E. Robert, "Special and Local Negotiations," in John T. Dunlop and Neil W. Chamberlain, eds., *Frontiers of Collective Bargaining.* New York: Harper & Row, 1967.

Professor Livernash deals with negotiation situations involving more than a single agreement between the parties: special supplemental agreements (pensions, benefit plans) and local agreements under a master agreement.

Morris, Charles J., ed., *The Developing Labor Law,* Chapter 17. Washington, D.C.: Bureau of National Affairs, Inc., 1971.

The legal enforceability of the collective bargaining agreement and the relationship of the NLRB to the court system are dealt with here.

Taylor, Benjamin J., and Fred Witney, *Labor Relations Law,* 2nd ed., Chapter 15. Englewood Cliffs, N.J.: Prentice-Hall, 1975.

This is good coverage of the legal status of the labor agreement and the internal enforcement procedures that are usually included in labor agreements.

---

[6] Items 1–10 are from EO 11491 and included in most state statutes; 11–12 from Hawaii statute.

Collective Bargaining by Objectives— An Overview

CHAPTER 9

Let me emphasize that the main thrust of the objectives approach is upon a *methodology for bargaining*. It is not claimed that this methodology will by itself develop in the negotiator those personal qualities of preparedness, knowledgeability, sensitivity, timing, analytical abilities, coolness, and patience that are so important to his becoming skilled and effective. These qualities develop as a result of observation, conscious individual effort, and experience. On the other hand, it *is* maintained that the methodology outlined here does provide a meaningful framework within which these skills may be more easily developed and, as they develop, a framework to further enhance the effectiveness and positiveness of their applications. Let me also emphasize that the positive results claimed are in direct relationship to the willingness of the negotiator *to adhere completely to the methodology* outlined. This requires a high degree of self-discipline on the part of the negotiator, combined with a desire and a willingness to put forth the effort and time to do the job right. The lazy negotiator, the seat-of-the-pants negotiator, or the negotiator who leaves results to chance will find little comfort in the discipline and orderliness that this methodology requires.

At this point, only an overview of the objectives approach to collective bargaining negotiations is presented. This is shown in Form 9–1. A more detailed explanation is deferred to sections that follow.

OVERVIEW

Column 1, *Bargaining Items*, is for the listing of all those items or contractual subjects, whether introduced by the employee or the employer

FORM 9-1

COLLECTIVE BARGAINING BY OBJECTIVES

(A GUIDE FOR DATA PREPARATION, STRATEGY, AND EVALUATION OF BARGAINING RESULTS)

BARGAINING * ITEMS	PRIORITIES **	RANGE OF BARGAINING OBJECTIVES			INITIAL *** BARGAINING POSITION	EVALUATION RESULTS		
		PESSIMISTIC	REALISTIC	OPTIMISTIC		P	R	O

*   Classify Items in Two Groups: Financial and Non-financial.

**   Relative Priority of each Bargaining Item to all Bargaining Items.

*** Actual Visible Position taken Iat Opening of Negotiation (Union Initial Proposal or Company Response or Counter Offer) representative, that the parties will consider during the course of the collective bargaining negotiations—wages, vacations, holiday, promotions, seniority, insurance, and so on. These bargaining items should be separated into two listings—one for all cost or financial items, the other for noncost or nonfinancial items. As many objectives sheets should be used as are necessary for a complete listing of the bargaining items.

Priorities, column 2, refers to the relative importance of each bargaining item in the system of priorities of the party concerned. For every item, a priority rating is determined based on its value or importance relative to all other items on the bargaining agenda.

Columns 3, 4, and 5, *Range of Bargaining Objectives,* are for the purpose of establishing a range of actual objectives for each bargaining item listed in column 1. The range includes columns for realistic (column 4), optimistic (column 5), and pessimistic (column 3) objectives. This range should constitute, in the best judgment of the party, an actual, not hypothetical or theoretical, *settlement range.* For example, objectives entered in column 4 for each item are those that the party believes realistically can be achieved. This is the negotiator's *realistic* goal—not what he hopes or guesses will be achieved, but what he fully expects will be the most probable final settlement on that particular bargaining item.

The *optimistic* goal for the particular item would be what the negotiator thinks can be achieved, as a real and preferred possibility, but whose odds are not as favorable as those for the realistic objective. The *pessimistic* goal would be a possible outcome if everything did not go as well as expected—not as favorable as either the realistic or optimistic, but definitely within the acceptance range of the party. It is important to emphasize that the range represented by the pessimistic, realistic, and optimistic positions is a preconceived and acceptable bargaining settlement range, not an impasse range or a strike or lockout range, although, as a result of the give-and-take of bargaining, any of these may occur. Above all, these objectives are a strictly confidential part of the negotiator's blueprint of goals and objectives and should be treated as such and never revealed to the opposing bargaining representative.

Initial Bargaining Position, column 6, is the visible stance (the initial proposal or counterpropsal) that the negotiator presents to the other party at the outset of negotiations on each item, whether it is an item the negotiator introduced or one the other party introduced. This must not be confused with the range of objectives mentioned above (columns 3, 4, and 5), which must be confidential to the party concerned if its strategy is to be successful.

Columns 7, 8, and 9, *Evaluation Results,* are a checklist, to be used after negotiations have been concluded, to compare results achieved (pessimistic, realistic, or optimistic) with original objectives set for each bargaining item. This may be used for other useful purposes also, such as assessment of effectiveness of strategy and tactics relative to each item during the negotiations just concluded. This will be explained later.

POSITIVE COLLECTIVE BARGAINING

It will be noted that the elements identified in the form are commonsense elements of bargaining. How the objectives approach influences negotiating effectiveness is not in the identification of the commonsense elements. These are known. *The difference is in placing what is common sense within a methodology that provides a systematic framework* for approaching collective bargaining negotiations. The formalizing or structuring outlined here is not at the expense of flexibility in strategy and tactics so vital to negotiation. This approach continues to allow flexibility, albeit within a more tangible framework and set of goals. But it does introduce discipline and system to the negotiator's actions. The following positive advantages to collective bargaining negotiations result from the use of the CBO methodology:

1. While structuring the approach to collective bargaining negotiations, the objectives approach is not at the expense of the flexibility so necessary to the give-and-take of negotiations.

2. It gives the negotiating team a real sense of direction and tangible goals (objectives) by which team members may measure their progress during negotiations.

3. It provides a more meaningful basis for data preparation, because positions and goals are specifically identified.

4. The range of bargaining objectives is in reality a settlement area toward which the negotiating team works, rather than the range, so often described by writers of the field, whose minimum and maximum represent conflict or breakdown. The latter introduces negativism into the approach of the bargaining team, whereas the objectives approach effects a positive tone and thrust.

5. The team has a ready-reference, easy-to-scan blueprint that provides a confidential guide to strategy and tactics for all cost and noncost bargaining items, individually and/or collectively.

6. The identification of not just one goal but a range of possible settlement goals on each bargaining item requires by its very nature a more detailed and careful analysis.

7. Limiting the objectives approach to methodology makes it equally applicable and useful to private-sector bargaining, public-sector bargaining, or, for that matter, any type of bargaining situation.

8. Nothing is introduced into the methodology that is foreign to the normal bargaining situation.

9. It provides a better means of evaluating past negotiations as a useful experience base from which to launch a more effective plan for the next round of negotiations.

10. It may be used equally well as an effective tool for actual negotiations or as a simulation device to train negotiators.

11. It provides (a) the parties individually with a safe and effective mechanism (agreed-upon settlement range) for delegating authority to their bargaining teams, and (b) a built-in means of establishing a rewards system for successful negotiators.

SELECTED REFERENCES

Odiorne, George S., *Management by Objectives*. New York: Pitman, 1969.

George S. Odiorne is well known as a leading advocate of the system known as management by objectives. Not only has he been an effective proponent of MBO on the lecture circuit, in the classroom, and as a leading consultant to business corporations, but he has actively involved himself in the installation of MBO systems. It was through a close association with Dean Odiorne that I saw the potential of adapting the system of MBO to the process of collective bargaining (CBO).

Preparing
for Negotiations—
Bargaining Items

CHAPTER 10

Column 1 of the bargaining-by-objectives form requires a listing of all items that have been introduced by either the employer or the union for negotiation: wages, overtime, sick leave, vacations, promotion, discipline, insurance, management rights, and so on.

For its maximum usefulness as a confidential guide to negotiation, all economic or financial items should be listed in one major grouping. This would include all those items for which a recurring money outlay can be identified, such as wages, vacations, and holidays. All noncost items should be listed in a separate but contiguous grouping. These would include such items as seniority, grievance procedure, and management rights.

Differences and similarities between private-sector and public-sector bargaining items will be identified where appropriate in the material that follows.

PRELIMINARY AND FINAL IDENTIFICATION OF BARGAINING ITEMS

Usually, the union takes the initiative in introducing items for negotiations, although there is nothing in the law that requires this to be the procedure. The union introduction of the items is most often in the form of an initial request for contract modification sixty days or more prior to the termination of the existing agreement. The bargaining items could also be introduced as part of a first-time contract demand if there had been no prior collective bargaining agreement between the parties. Demands of the union might be in the form of additions, deletions, clarifications, or other changes in the expiring agreement.

When the company responds to these initial demands of the union, the full agenda of items to be considered at the bargaining table is established. The company response may be merely a counterproposal or response to the specific items introduced by the union, or may include this response plus additional items the company feels should be considered. There is nothing in collective bargaining law or practice that prevents the company from introducing items of its own that it wants considered at the bargaining table, or even taking the initiative by giving the initial 60-day notice to the union.

It can readily be seen that there are two preliminary steps before the listing of bargaining items becomes final for either of the parties. Step 1 for the union is accomplished when it presents its initial demands to the company. Step 2, completing the union's list of any additional items to be considered at the bargaining table, is accomplished when the union receives

FORM 10–1

COLLECTIVE BARGAINING BY OBJECTIVES

(A GUIDE FOR DATA PREPARATION, STRATEGY, AND EVALUATION OF BARGAINING RESULTS)

BARGAINING * ITEMS
Holidays
Wages
--
--
--
--
--
--
Union Security
Probationary Period
--
--
--

(Financial Items)

(Nonfinancial Items)

management's response. Similarly, step 1 for management is taken when the union position is formalized and all the items the union wishes to consider have been introduced. Step 2, completing the company's list of items to be considered, is taken after the company has made its formal response to the union. At this point, the listing of items for bargaining, but *only* that listing, will be identical for both parties. From this point on, the information on the bargaining form will differ for the two parties in line with their separate and confidential priorities and objectives. It is essential that every item or subitem that is to be a subject for bargaining be listed on the bargaining form within one of the two general categories, financial or nonfinancial. By way of illustration, Form 10–1 shows a few items of what the first column of the bargaining form might include.

APPLICATION OF LAW TO BARGAINING ITEMS

Private Sector

The law has a direct bearing on the negotiation items that the parties put on the bargaining table. Three categories relative to subjects or items for bargaining are recognized:

1. Mandatory bargaining items
2. Voluntary bargaining items
3. Illegal bargaining items

The last two may be disposed of with less discussion than the first. Voluntary or permissive bargaining items refer to those middle-range items that are neither mandatory nor illegal.[1] Crucial to an understanding of voluntary items and collective bargaining is the fact that these become a part of negotiations only through the joint agreement of both parties. Neither party can be compelled against its wishes to negotiate over voluntary items, nor can the signing of a contract be held up as a result of one party's refusal to bargain on a voluntary item. Moreover, adamant refusal to bargain about a voluntary subject or to include it in the final agreement is not illegal. Finally, either party may propose a voluntary item for bargaining, the parties may bargain in good faith on the item, and if both parties agree, they may include the item in the final contract.

Illegal bargaining items are those that are forbidden by law. A closed

---

[1] *Primer of Labor Relations*, 18th ed. (Washington, D.C.: Bureau of National Affairs, Inc., 1971), pp. 424–34.

shop, a hot-cargo clause, a hiring hall giving preference to union members, or a union security clause in a right-to-work state are examples of illegal subjects for bargaining.

Mandatory bargaining items are those over which the parties must bargain if they are introduced to the bargaining table by either party through the demand and/or counteroffer process. The number of mandatory bargaining items has been constantly expanding over the past forty years as more and more subjects have been declared by the NLRB and the courts to come within the meaning of the National Labor Relations Act's definitions of wages, hours, and other conditions of employment.

Court and NLRB decisions have declared some seventy basic items as mandatory for bargaining purposes. It is obvious that the list would be many times as long if all the subcategories of these items were listed. Included are nineteen classified under "wages," three under "hours," and the remainder under "other terms and conditions of employment." The items are as follows:

Wages	Work assignments and transfers
Hours	No-strike clause
Discharge	Piece rates
Arbitration	Stock-purchase plan
Holidays—paid	Work loads
Vacations—paid	Change of employee status to independent contractors
Duration of agreement	Management-rights clause
Grievance procedure	Cancellation of seniority upon relocation of plant
Layoff plan	
Reinstatement of economic strikers	Discounts on company products
Change of payment from hourly base to salary base	Shift differentials
Union security and checkoff	Contract clause providing for supervisors' keeping seniority in unit
Work rules	
Merit wage increase	Procedures for income tax withholding
Work schedule	
Lunch periods	Severance pay
Rest periods	Nondiscriminatory hiring hall
Pension plan	Plant rules
Retirement age	Safety
Bonus payments	Prohibition against supervisor's doing unit work
Price of meals provided by company	Superseniority for union stewards
Group insurance—health, accident, life	Checkoff
	Partial plant closing
Promotions	Hunting on employer forest reserve where previously granted
Seniority	
Layoffs	Plant closedown and relocation
Transfers	

Change in operations resulting in reclassifying workers from incentive to straight time, or cut work force, or installation of cost-saving machine

Plant closing

Job-posting procedures

Plant reopening

Employee physical examination

Union security

Bargaining over "Bar List"

Truck rentals—minimum rental to be paid by carriers to employee-owned vehicles

Musician price list

Arrangement for negotiation

Change in insurance carrier and benefits

Profit-sharing plan

Motor-carrier—union agreement providing that carriers use own equipment before leasing outside equipment

Overtime pay

Agency shop

Sick leave

Employer's insistence on clause giving arbitrator right to enforce award

Company houses

Subcontracting

Discriminatory racial policies

Production ceiling imposed by union

Most-favored-nation clause

Public Sector

The National Labor Relations Act's statement of general policy concerning employee rights reads, "Employees shall have the right to self-organization, to form, join, or assist labor organizations." Similar rights are also extended to federal employees by Executive Order 11491, which states, "Each employee of the executive branch of the Federal Government has the right, freely and without fear of penalty or reprisal, to form, join, and assist a labor organization." Both directives protect the right to bargain collectively through representatives of the employees' own choosing. The NLRA states, "Employees shall have the right to . . . bargain collectively through representatives of their own choosing. . . ." In the words of the executive order, "An agency and a labor organization that has been accorded exclusive recognition through appropriate representatives, shall meet at reasonable times and confer in good faith."

Up to this point, the treatment of employee rights and bargaining is somewhat the same for the private and public sectors. It is in the implementation of these rights that differences of treatment under the regulations begin to appear. Attention is confined to differences that affect the collective bargaining process between the public and private areas. The particular focus is the ways in which the NLRA and the executive order differ as to the items that are the subject matter of collective bargaining negotiations.

The preceding section examined in some detail the items for bargaining in the private sector—mandatory, permissive, and prohibited. Bargaining subject matter in the private area has evolved through NLRB and court interpretation of Section 8 (c) of the NLRA, which states, "to bargain collectively is the performance of the mutual obligation of the employer and the representatives of the employees to meet at reasonable times and confer in good faith with respect to wages, hours, and other terms and conditions of employment." What "wages, hours, and other terms and conditions of employment" constitute has already been discussed.

In the federal sector, the executive order treats the bargainable subjects in a somewhat more restricted manner. Part of this results from a desire to prevent conflict with other, already established laws and regulations affecting employer–employee relations; part of it relates to the question of sovereignty and the functioning of government bodies under the law; and part of it results from the less flexible nature or ability of government, compared to the private sector, in responding to demands of employees. At any rate, and for whatever reason, definite restrictions are placed upon the parties to collective bargaining in the public sector as to what they may bargain over. These items fall into two categories. Included in the first are those matters over which the parties may not bargain either because they are covered elsewhere or because they are not proper matters for public-sector bargaining. The second includes those items the government considers are the rights of management and are to be expressly stated in the contract but are not bargainable subjects.

With respect to the first group, Section 11 (a) states:

> An agency and a labor organization . . . shall . . . confer in good faith with respect to personnel policies and practices and matters affecting working conditions, *so far as may be appropriate* under applicable laws and regulations, including policies and regulations, a national or other controlling agreement at a higher level in the agency, and this Order. [Italics added.]

Note that, in contrast to the private sector, the language above does not include wages.

Section 11 (b) is even more specific in its restrictions on bargainable subjects:

> . . . the obligation to meet and confer does not include matters with respect to the mission of an agency; its budget; its organization; the number of employees; and the numbers, types, and grades of positions or employees assigned to an organizational unit, work project or tour of duty; the technology of performing its work; or its internal security practices.

Section 13 (a) places limitations upon a negotiated grievance procedure by stating that it "may not cover any other matters, including matters for which statutory appeals procedures exist."

Also, Section 13 (b) states that a negotiated grievance procedure may "provide for arbitration of grievances over the interpretation and application of the agreement, but not over any other matters," and, "Either party may file exception to an arbitrator's award" with the Federal Labor Relations Council.

The second group of limitations on bargainable items results from the tendency of government statutes and orders to reserve rather inclusive management rights rather than leaving them to the negotiation process. This is illustrated by Section 12 (b), and (c) which states that management officials of the agency have the right:

(1) to direct employees of the agency;

(2) to hire, promote, transfer, assign, and retain employees in positions within the agency, and to suspend, demote, discharge, or take other disciplinary action against employees;

(3) to relieve employees from duties because of lack of work or for other legitimate reasons;

(4) to maintain the efficiency of the Government operations entrusted to them;

(5) to determine the methods, means, and personnel by which such operations are to be conducted; and

(6) to take whatever actions may be necessary to carry out the mission of the agency in situations of emergency; and

(c) nothing in the agreement shall require an employee to become or to remain a member of a labor organization, or by payment to the organization except pursuant to a voluntary, written authorization by a member for the payment of dues through payroll deductions.

The requirements of this section shall be expressly stated in the initial or basic agreement and apply to all supplemental, implementing, subsidiary, or informal agreements between the agency and the organization.

The limitations on the scope of bargaining continue to be carried over from the federal to the state and local sectors. It should be observed, however, that between the two sectors of public-employee bargaining, the federal is the more restricted in its scope. For the most part, at either federal or state and local levels of public-employee bargaining, sufficient time has not elapsed to allow as definitive a list of mandatory and prohibited bargaining items to develop as have done so in the forty years of private-sector bargaining under the NLRA. Nevertheless, one state, Nevada, has chosen not to wait for interpretive decisions on bargaining scope; it has specifically spelled out the scope of mandatory bargaining and those subject matters that are not within the scope of mandatory bargaining but are reserved to the local-government employer. Nevada's Local Government Employee–Management Relations Act, Section 288. 150 (2), "The Scope of Mandatory Bargaining," is limited to:

(a) Salary or wage rates or other forms of direct monetary compensation,

(b) Sick leave,

(c) Vacation leave,

(d) Holidays,

(e) Other paid or nonpaid leaves of absence,

(f) Insurance benefits,

(g) Total hours of work required of an employee on each workday or workweek,

(h) Total number of days' work required of an employee in a workyear,

(i) Discharge and disciplinary procedures,

(j) Recognition clause,

(k) The method used to classify employees in the negotiating unit,

(l) Deduction of dues for the recognized employee organization,

(m) Protection of employees in the negotiating unit from discrimination because of participation in recognized employee organizations consistent with the provisions of this chapter,

(n) No-strike provisions consistent with the provisions of this chapter,

(o) Grievance and arbitration procedures for resolution of disputes relating to interpretation or application of collective agreements,

(p) General savings clauses,

(q) Duration of collective bargaining agreements,

(r) Safety,

(s) Teacher preparation time,

(t) Procedures for reduction in work force.

Section 288.150 (3) lists those matters that are not a subject of mandatory bargaining as:

(a) The right to hire, direct, assign or transfer an employee, but excluding the right to assign or transfer an employee as a form of discipline,

(b) The right to reduce in force or lay off any employee because of lack of work or lack of funds, subject to paragraph (t) of subsection 2,

(c) The right to determine:

   (1) Appropriate staffing levels and work performance standards except for safety considerations;

(2) The content of the workday including without limitation work-load factors, except for safety considerations;

(3) The quality and quantity of services to be offered to the public; and

(4) The means and methods of offering those services.

As in the private sector, it is assumed that subjects not identified within the mandatory or the prohibited items are within the permissive subjects for bargaining and may be introduced only upon the agreement of both the parties.

SOURCES IN THE DEVELOPMENT OF BARGAINING ITEMS

The items or subjects over which the parties negotiate are formally introduced to the bargaining table through the initial demand and counter-proposal process of the two parties. Inasmuch as changes in the collective bargaining agreement can be made only periodically (usually when the agreement terminates or is up for renewal), it is extremely important to both parties that all subject areas under the agreement needing revision be introduced. If an item is overlooked, there might be a wait for a period of one, two, or three years, or maybe longer, before another opportunity to negotiate changes or new terms in the agreement appears again. Failure to negotiate timely modifications to the agreement can prove costly to one or both parties, in the form of either poor management–employee relations or excessive costs, or both.

It is important, then, as a first step in preparing for negotiations, to be aware of the major sources from which the items for negotiation originate. These will be discussed as internal and external sources. It is also important to know the best sources of information to support or defend one's position once the bargaining items are known and positions of the parties taken. Knowing the sources of bargaining items and of information to support any position on these items is crucial to the negotiating success of a party, either as a means of supporting its position on an item of its own introduction or as a line of defense against demands made on it by the other group. Sources of supportive data, although quite similar to sources of bargaining items for purposes of clarity and emphasis, are discussed separately in a later section.

Internal Sources

The most obvious internal source from which the subjects or items for negotiation are derived is the front-line experience of labor and management with each other. Employees and supervisors are in close daily contact. For the company to operate effectively, this must be an essentially cooperative relationship. Unfortunately, human relations do not always run smoothly, and differences do occur, especially when the parties are living under a collectively bargained agreement. It is in these day-to-day relations that the agreement negotiated by the parties is tested. Most suggestions for financial items originate with the staff, while rules changes originate from the line. Where the testing indicates weaknesses in the agreement because of poor wording, or because clauses have proved inoperative, or because some area of employer–employee relations is not adequately covered, it becomes evident that the contract will have to be modified when negotiation time arrives. Of course, weaknesses in the contract do not always have equal impact upon the parties. As a result, some desired changes may be to the advantage of only one party and will be resisted at negotiations by the other party. However, in some cases, a desired change may be advocated by both parties.

These inadequacies of the agreement in covering day-to-day employer–employee matters, which lead to requests for modification at negotiation time, become evident at three different levels internal to the firm and should be observed with great care.

The first level is less visible than the others, since there may be little or no formal record, but this does not reduce its importance as a source of bargaining items. This includes those employer–employee relations problems that arise daily but are not sufficiently important at the time or do not lead to a formal grievance or require an entry in the employee records. Any kind of supervisor–employee conflict should be considered a danger signal and should be considered carefully in the light of the agreement. If it is an occurrence that results from inadequacies of the agreement or that could be corrected by changes in the agreement, then the matter should be formally noted as something to consider at the next negotiations. Because these kinds of matters stop short of formal grievances, the employer must rely heavily on supervisors and foremen, and the union on shop stewards and union members, to channel the information to those concerned with negotiations and contract matters. Too much emphasis cannot be placed upon the vital role the supervisor or union representative can and may play in determining subjects for bargaining and the posture that management or the union might take on bargaining subjects introduced. It is important in this respect that the supervisor or union representative not only clearly understand the contract and the importance of his role in contract matters, but have a clearly defined channel through which to communicate useful information to upper management or union officials.

The second level internal to the firm or agency from which bargaining subject matter may be derived is a highly visible level. As soon as a contract is signed, the testing process begins as the contract moves into the administrative phase of collective bargaining. The union is now faced with the responsibility of making the contract a viable device to protect the rights of its members. Every time an employee within the bargaining unit is disciplined, becomes disgruntled over a promotion or assignment, is not paid properly, or feels that he is not being treated fairly in any way under the contract, the union is obligated to be his defender, and the contract becomes the basis for such defense. Regardless of the unanimity at the bargaining table, once the contract is signed, that phase of the relationship is a thing of the past. At this point, the union, in serving its constituents, looks with new eyes upon the agreement after any incident affecting the rights of employees. It is now under obligation to do everything within its power to make the contract language mean whatever will protect best the rights of its clients. The company or agency, in turn, once the contract is signed, is compelled to guard its own interests by making the contract protective of them as cases emerge for interpretation. The grievance procedure becomes a testing ground for the meaning of the contract. It is a matter of utmost importance that all weaknesses or difficulties of the contract that are revealed under the test of grievances be carefully recorded, analyzed, and then introduced by the concerned party at the next negotiations. Here again, supervisors and foremen are a vital link in accumulating a list of such items in anticipation of the next negotiations.

Arbitration, which is really an extension of the grievance procedure, is a third level, internal to the firm or agency, from which bargaining items are derived. Arbitration is separated here from the grievance procedure proper primarily for emphasis and because an external party is introduced, effecting a step somewhat apart from the previous steps of the grievance procedure. Generally, grievances are referred to an impartial arbitrator for adjudication when the parties are at an impasse over a matter of contract interpretation and have taken all other steps of the grievance procedure. The impasse may result from a genuine difference between the parties over the interpretation of a particular area of the contract as it applies to a particular grievance, or it may result from other reasons, such as the union's unwillingness to face up to a member who feels he has a justifiable grievance, even if he has not, or an employer's unwillingness to acknowledge that a supervisor has exceeded his authority or acted unwisely. In these situations, face-saving or in-group politics sometimes dictate that weak cases be carried to arbitration, where an adverse decision can be blamed on the arbitrator, and the union or company can escape responsibility for it. Attention to arbitration issues and decisions can be a meaningful source from which bargaining items may be drawn, because these cases usually involve difficulties under the contract that the party may want to correct at the next negotiation. More about grievance arbitration will appear in Chapter 17.

If grievances and arbitrations are important sources from which needed changes in the agreement may be drawn, it follows that record keeping and analyses of grievances and arbitration cases are of vital concern in properly identifying items for negotiation. These records may be kept in a number of ways. Some companies and unions keep careful, well-organized files and combine them with bargaining books at negotiation time. Others do little in a formal way, preferring to rush around, sixty or ninety days before contract termination, to locate and assemble grievance and arbitration materials from their files. The latter method is obviously open to difficulties. A systematic way of keeping records on grievance and arbitration decisions will be found in Chapter 18, "Contract Administration and Collective Bargaining by Objectives."

External Sources

Many developments external to the firm also influence the choice of bargaining items or subjects to be introduced at negotiations. Such external sources include contract settlements in the industry, settlements within the community (especially with firms competitive to the firm in question), settlements by the union with other firms, pattern-setting agreements on a regional or national basis, changes in legislation, market conditions, and economic conditions generally, to name some of the more important. Here again, it is to the advantage of the company, agency, or union to keep a current file on all materials relevant to these areas.

SOURCES OF SUPPORTING DATA

Nothing can substitute for adequate preparation. A vital part of that preparation is *establishment of definite goals* and objectives relative to each item to be negotiated. This is discussed in Chapter 12. Another vital key to success is the *expertise* with which the party negotiates, which is also discussed later. But neither identification of goals nor expertise can entirely substitute for *proper supporting data.* Supporting data, along with defined goals and bargaining expertise, are necessary elements to a complete and successful approach to bargaining.

Internal

The *most immediate source* of data to support a bargaining position is found in the firm's, agency's, or union's own files and records. Knowing the subjects to be considered at negotiation, the firm or agency should make capital out of its ready access to such facts as grievance records, arbitration awards, employee records, and financial and production data. Under the law, the union must likewise be given access to company records and data relevant to the negotiations.

External

There are a number of reliable information sources outside the firm or agency. These include the following:

1. Department of Labor (Bureau of Labor Statistics) publications and services. Among these are regular publications, such as the *Monthly Labor Review, Employment and Earnings, Occupational Outlook Quarterly,* and *Current Wage Development,* plus many special studies on specific areas and industries covering wages, employment, prices and productivity, and collective bargaining.

2. Agencies and professional associations involved directly in collective bargaining activities or in administering statutes and orders covering labor–management relations:
   a. The National Labor Relations Board
   b. The Federal Mediation and Conciliation Service
   c. The Federal Labor Relations Council
   d. The assistant secretary of labor for labor–management relations
   e. The Federal Service Impasses Panel
   f. The Civil Service Commission
   g. Various state agencies, boards, and associations. A good primary source from which to find such groups at the state level is *A Directory of Public Employment Relations Boards and Agencies,* U.S. Department of Labor, Management Services Administration, November 1971.

3. Highly recommended are the publications of the Bureau of National Affairs, Commerce Clearing House, Prentice-Hall, and other, similar types of published services on labor–management relations. These organizations provide a variety of vital information, such as national trends in contract settlements identified by specific bargaining items, guidance to the negotiator on contract language and trends, useful background information on bargaining strategy and techniques, current bargaining issues and settlements, and National Labor Relations Board and court decisions.[2]

4. Publications of trade associations.

5. Labor relations journals, such as the *Industrial and Labor Relations Review* of Cornell, the AAA's *Arbitration Journal,* and the *Industrial*

---

[2] These services are sometimes too expensive for the small employer or union. They may usually be found in a university library, law school library, employer-association office, or the libraries of the larger unions.

Relations Journal of Berkeley, plus many individual studies published by the universities. The University of Hawaii has a series of excellent studies on both the federal and state sectors.

6. Various labor-law journals.

7. Magazines and newspapers, such as *Time, Newsweek, U.S. News & World Report, Fortune,* and *The Wall Street Journal.*

8. Information issued by local and area employers' councils or local labor groups on local or area bargaining development, wages, and employment.

9. Publications of international unions, the AFL-CIO, and state and city federations.

If in doubt as to where to find any of the sources of information above, consult the universities (especially those with a bureau or institute of industrial relations or labor relations, or a law school). The federal mediator in your area is also an excellent source.

It should be evident that time spent in researching is well spent, both to support one's own position in bargaining negotiations and to counter arguments of the opposite party. Marshalling of arguments, based not on rhetoric but on facts and logic, is an integral component of what has been referred to as bargaining expertise. Its importance should never be taken lightly in any step of the process, from the identifying of subjects for bargaining to developing priorities and goals, and finally to the actual negotiation process.

SELECTED REFERENCES

Campo, Arnold F., "Entering into Negotiations," in LeRoy Marceau, *Dealing with a Union,* pp. 86–99. New York: American Management Association, Inc., 1969.

Contains information sources and advice on preparing for negotiations for both labor and management.

Collective Bargaining Negotiations & Contracts. Washington, D.C.: Bureau of National Affairs, Inc.

A current and continuing service that provides information on bargaining trends and techniques, current settlements, basic patterns in union contracts, and facts for bargaining. An invaluable source for the negotiator who needs information on trends in contract settlements or the language of specific provisions of union contracts. Along with this major service, the BNA also issues a condensed account of *Basic Patterns in Union Contracts* in pamphlet form (8th ed., 1975).

Contract Clause Manual. St. Louis Region, U.S. Civil Service Commission, February 1975.

Useful information concerning various types of contract clauses that have been incorporated into federal-sector collective bargaining contracts.

Davey, Harold W., *Contemporary Collective Bargaining*, 3rd ed. Englewood Cliffs, N.J.: Prentice-Hall, 1972.

Chapter 5 provides sound advice on the need for professionalism in collective bargaining and the value of sound preparation. The author notes that "negotiation of contracts today is a job for professionals, not amateurs," and "effectiveness in negotiations is in direct relationship to the thoroughness and far-sightedness of their preparation."

Government Employee Relations Report. Washington, D.C.: Bureau of National Affairs, Inc.

BNA provides in this service a weekly reporting for subscribers on federal, state, and local developments, including union demands for recognition; bargaining-unit determination; contract negotiations; new clauses in public-sector contracts; grievance settlements; arbitration awards; statistical data on earnings, hours of work, cost of living, and employment in the public sector; and federal and state legislation affecting public employees.

Labor–Management Relations in the Federal Service. U.S. Federal Labor Relations Council, Washington, D.C., 1975.

Among those involved in federal-sector labor relations, this is a useful and informative publication. Included are the EOs applying to federal-sector labor relations, and reports and recommendations that have led to changes in these laws. Thoroughly informative.

LAIRS, Labor Agreement Information Retrieval System. Office of Labor–Management Relations of the U.S. Civil Service Commission.

The file is composed of data, in various forms, extracted from federal labor agreements, third-party determinations, and statistical reports submitted regularly by federal agencies.

Marting, Elizabeth, ed., "A Step-by-Step Guide to the Preparatory Process," in *Understanding Collective Bargaining*, pp. 96–109. New York: American Management Association, Inc., 1958.

A basic discussion of what must be done to prepare for negotiations, covering advance preparations, facts required for bargaining, contract termination notice, reviewing the union's proposals, company proposals and final preparation.

————, ed., "Getting Ready to Talk Contract," in *Ibid.*, Part II.

An older but excellent discussion of the negotiation process. Part II is a combination of articles by both practitioners and academicians. Selwyn H. Torff, Clive B. McKee, Fred D. Hunter, Hjalmar Rosen, R.A.H. Rosen, and Monroe Berkowitz blend their efforts in bringing to the reader a down-to-earth approach to adequate preparation, a key to effective bargaining, the negotiating teams, and a step-by-step guide to preparatory process.

Morris, Charles J., ed., *The Developing Labor Law*, Chaps. 14–16. Washington, D.C.: Bureau of National Affairs, Inc., 1971.

These sections contain a comprehensive coverage of the subjects of bargaining—mandatory, permissive, and illegal. For the negotiator, the knowledge of what subjects, if raised, he must bargain over, what subjects he may not bargain over because of prohibitions in the law, and what subjects he may, but choose not to, bargain over is basic to his bargaining success.

Peters, Edward, *Strategy and Tactics in Labor Negotiations,* 3rd ed., pp. 90–98, 108–14. Swarthmore, Pa.: Personnel Journal, 1966.

For years a mediator, Mr. Peters brings his practical experience and ability to articulate the nuances of collective bargaining to bear on negotiable issues and fringe issues.

Public Personal Administration: Labor-Management Relations. Englewood Cliffs, N.J.: Prentice-Hall, Inc.

Focusing on public-sector collective bargaining, this service explains laws, methods, rulings, clauses, and established precedents (including summaries of arbitration awards). Bi-weekly reports provide news of developments in this complex area. Sections of the basic text include "New Ideas," "Collective Bargaining Problems and Answers," "Annotated Public Employment Relations Laws and Regulations," "Union Contract Clauses," and Arbitration Awards Analyzed."

Ryder, Meyer S., Charles M. Rehmus, and Sanford Cohen, *Management Preparation for Collective Bargaining.* Homewood, Ill.: Dow Jones-Irwin, 1966.

Excellent coverage of practices of firms surveyed, covering such subjects as final preparation, subjects, strategic aspects of preparation, intercompany cooperation, and joint union-management preparation.

Taylor, Benjamin, and Fred Witney, *Labor Relations Law,* Chapter 14. Englewood Cliffs, N.J.: Prentice-Hall, 1975.

Excellent coverage of the subject of bargaining as controlled by law and agency decisions.

Union Contracts, Arbitration. New York: Commerce Clearing House, Inc.

A continuing service that includes specimen contracts, arbitration procedures, and current information on contract terms being negotiated.

U.S. Department of Labor publications.

The publications of DOL are a gold mine of information for the negotiator in both the public and private sectors. Included are such publications as *Characteristics of Construction Agreements,* 1972–73 (BLS Bulletin 1819), 1974; *Collective Bargaining Agreements in the Federal Service, Late 1971* (BLS Bulletin 1789), 1973; *Municipal Collective Bargaining Agreements in Large Cities* (BLS Bulletin 1759), 1972; *Negotiation Impasse, Grievance, and Arbitration in Federal Agreements* (BLS Bulletin 1661), 1970; *Grievance Procedures* (BLS Bulletin 1425–1), 1964; *Calendar of Major Contract Expirations and Reopenings* (December or January issues of the MLR); *Wages Calendars* (a yearly bulletin); *Work Stoppages* (a yearly bulletin); *Collective Bargaining Summary* (industry summaries); *A Directory of Public Employment Relations Boards and Agencies* (November 1971); *Scope of*

Bargaining in the Public Sector (1972); *Arbitration Procedures* (Bulletin No. 1425–6), 1966; *Grievance and Arbitration Procedures in State and Local Agreements*, 1975; *Characteristics of Major Collective Bargaining Agreements*, July 1, 1974; and *Understanding Grievance Arbitration in the Public Sector*, 1974.

Preparing for
Negotiations–Priorities

CHAPTER 11

Column 2 of Form 9–1, "Bargaining by Objectives," requires the negotiating party to think out carefully and identify by number or some other form of ranking the importance to that party of each bargaining item in relation to all others on the agenda. Priority does not necessarily relate directly to whether the item is introduced by the company or the union, or whether it is a cost or noncost item. It may be of higher priority to the company in terms of its objectives, financial and otherwise, to resist a particular demand introduced by the union, or to achieve a settlement on the item below the union position, than to achieve settlement on another item that the company itself introduced but that has less impact on the company operation. The priority given to the bargaining items need not be a consecutive listing. Some items might have about the same relative priority as others. Ranking the items by relative priority or importance to the bargaining party, therefore, might be done consecutively, with no two items the same, or by groups of items. The key is to establish an identification method that is easily followed, but most of all *to establish the priorities*, whatever the method used. Both the identification of priorities that is so extremely important for strategy considerations and the thinking process necessary to establish a relative priority system are positive steps for successful negotiations.

The *how* of setting priorities must be related to the individual party's value system. Criteria that might be considered are the importance of the bargaining goals established for each individual bargaining item as they relate to such measures as cost or income, continuing relations of the union and the company, continuing employer–employee relations, ease of implementation and administration, precedent established for future negotiation, and personal prestige of the parties. Establishing relative priorities on all items on the bargaining agenda is an individual matter and, therefore, requires that each party (1) know its own goals and/or value structure, and (2) be able to relate each item on the bargaining agenda specifically to such goals and value structure.

When one considers that initial demands and counteroffers, setting of bargaining goals, strategy and tactics, trade and compromise—in fact, the entire give-and-take of the collective bargaining negotiation process—are all inextricably connected with a priority system, it is hard to avoid the conclusion that establishing priorities is of vital importance to negotiation success. The key element in the objectives approach is that these priority values are pinned down and *known prior to negotiation;* otherwise, there can be only one result for the bargaining party: confusion

FORM 11–1

COLLECTIVE BARGAINING BY OBJECTIVES

(A GUIDE FOR DATA PREPARATION, STRATEGY, AND EVALUATION OF BARGAINING RESULTS)

	BARGAINING * ITEMS	PRIORITIES **
(Financial Items)	Holidays	8
	Wages	1
	--	
	--	
	--	
	--	
	--	
	--	
(Nonfinancial Items)	Union Security	12
	Probationary Period	20
	--	
	--	
	--	
	--	

*   Classify Items in Two Groups: Financial and Non-financial.
** Relative Priority of each Bargaining Item to all Bargaining Items.

and fumbling, during both the preparatory process and the actual negotiations.

Attempting to ascertain the priority system of the other party before and during negotiations is equally important and a part of the goal of any successful negotiator, but this is more logically discussed later, in the section on the formal negotiation process. It should not be necessary to point out that each party's priority system should be kept highly confidential to that party, since it is so closely related to bargaining strategy.

Determining the relative priority of each bargaining item completes the second stage of the objectives approach. To illustrate, priorities might appear as in Form 11–1 for an employer, whereas the union, in contrast, might consider union security its number 1 priority item and holidays a number 3 or 4 item. The thinking process necessary to establish priorities is just as important to successful bargaining as is the system of priorities itself. The more that representatives of each party have to think through the relative importance they want to place on each item under consideration, the better their understanding and the more positive their approach to negotiating on that item will become.

Preparing for Negotiations–Range of Bargaining Objectives

CHAPTER 12

It must be reemphasized that the range of objectives (columns 3, 4, and 5) referred to in Form 12–1 is (1) a potentially acceptable settlement range; (2) a range starting from the most desirable (optimistic) to the least desirable (pessimistic) type of settlement, which constitutes an actual set of goals toward which the company or the union negotiates positively; and (3) an unchanging set of goals, once negotiations begin, unless there is a change in the basic assumptions on which the goals were first established. The positiveness with which the party negotiates is as closely linked to unwavering goals as to any other factor influencing bargaining success.

REALISTIC BARGAINING OBJECTIVE

It is easiest and most efficient for the party to start out by first establishing the realistic objective or bargaining goal (expected final settlement) for each bargaining item listed in column 1. This realistic objective is established by assessing all the factors and forces that it is anticipated will enter into a final settlement on that particular item, including patterns and trends in pertinent local, regional, and national settlements and the extent to which the party feels it can defend its position. Another force is the bargaining climate—that is, relations between the parties. These relations result from the position of the union relative to its membership, the guidelines being set by the local union or its parent international, the personalities involved at the bargaining table, economic and political conditions within the union and the company and in the community and the nation, the relative bargaining strength of the two parties, employee attitudes, community attitudes, and any other factor that it is felt might affect the bargaining outcome on that particular item.

What a party estimates that the objectives of the other party will be is a consideration. For example, suppose the present contract provides for six holidays. The union has made an initial demand for nine holidays—three additional. In assessing the situation, the company estimates, looking at the matter practically and realistically, that the final settlement on the bargaining item will most likely be one additional holiday, or seven in all. Seven holidays then becomes the realistic bargaining objective or settlement that the company sets its sights on in the negotiations. Form 12–1 illustrates this step with the entry, "7 days," in column 4. The same procedure would be followed by the union in setting up a realistic bargaining objective concerning holidays. The union might consider "8 days," as its realistic objective. The entry, as will be shown later, is what the union (or the company) expects the settlement outcome will be, not what the union asks or makes visible, or the company makes visible in its initial counterproposals, during the early stages of negotiations. The bargaining objectives established must be kept confidential by the party setting them.

OPTIMISTIC BARGAINING OBJECTIVE

The establishment of an optimistic bargaining objective essentially derives from the study and setting of the realistic objective. The optimistic bargaining objective is merely looking on the brighter side of settlement possibilities relative to each bargaining item—the frosting-on-the-cake concept. The chance of achieving the optimistic objective is not as great as that of achieving the realistic objective but is still a distinct and attainable possibility. It is crucial to the establishment of the bargaining-objective approach that the party clearly understand that the optimistic goal *must be* a distinct possibility—within the range of possible bargaining settlements, according to the best judgment of the party. For example, as shown in Form 12–1, column 5, using the previous example concerning holidays, the company might establish its optimistic settlement goal as no change from the old contract on holidays—that is, holidays remain at six a year, a distinct possibility according to company analysis. The union, on the other hand, in setting *its* optimistic goal, might consider nine holidays, an addition of three, a distinctly obtainable objective if everything goes better than expected at the bargaining table.

PESSIMISTIC BARGAINING OBJECTIVE

The pessimistic bargaining objective for any bargaining item must also be an objective that is a distinct possibility, even though less probable than the realistic objective. It, too, is most easily derived from the con-

COLLECTIVE BARGAINING BY OBJECTIVES
(A GUIDE FOR DATA PREPARATION, STRATEGY, AND EVALUATION OF BARGAINING RESULTS)

BARGAINING * ITEMS	PRIORITIES **	RANGE OF BARGAINING OBJECTIVES		
		PESSIMISTIC	REALISTIC	OPTIMISTIC
Holidays	8	8 days	7 days	6 days
Wages	1	10¢ 1st yr. 10¢ 2nd yr. 5¢ 3rd yr.	5¢ 1st yr. 10¢ 2nd yr. 10¢ 3rd yr.	5¢ 1st yr. 10¢ 2nd yr. 5¢ 3rd yr.
--				
--				
--				
--				
--				
--				
Union Security	12	Union Shop	Modified Union Shop	Agency Shop
Probationary Period	20	30 days	60 days	90 days
--				
--				
--				
--				

(Financial Items) — (Nonfinancial Items)

*   Classify Items in Two Groups: Financial and Non-financial.
** Relative Priority of each Bargaining Item to all Bargaining Items.

siderations that gave rise to the establishment of the realistic goal for a particular item. It is simply a lesser settlement that the party may have to accept, if reluctantly, if all does not go quite as planned in the negotiations. Using the previous example of holidays, the pessimistic objective for the company might be a settlement at eight holidays, or an increase of two over the old contract, as in Form 12–1, column 3. The union might consider seven holidays as its pessimistic objective, one that is less desirable but nevertheless within the range of possibilities for which it might settle.

COSTING CONTRACT CHANGES

Determining the cost of changes in contract conditions is an absolutely essential ingredient in determining bargaining objectives. For the company, it is added costs; for the employees, it is added income. Eventually, both parties in renegotiating a contract come to a point where the cost of the package becomes crucial to reaching an agreement. Several types of cost factors are recognized in this costing-out process: (1) direct payroll costs (cost of work and nonwork paid time), (2) changes in costs that are a direct function of changes in the direct wage rate, (3) nonpayroll costs, and (4) nonwork paid time. Nonwork paid time is included in (1) but separated out in (4) because of the importance of knowing the difference between increases in cost attributable to productive effort and increases resulting from nonwork paid time.

In single accounting form, the following illustrates the kinds of considerations and computations that need to be made. More detailed advice and information should be secured from qualified accountants or from such excellent sources as Granof's *How to Cost Your Labor Contract*[1] or Morse's *How to Negotiate the Labor Agreement*.[2]

Changes in Costs

I. Direct Payroll—Annual
Straight-time earnings—36¢ per hour general increase
   100 employees
   100 × 2,080 hrs. × 36¢ =

Premium earnings, second-shift established differential—10¢ per hour
   30 employees involved
   30 × 2,080 hrs. × 10¢ =

Overtime: Overtime costs increased by increased straight-time rate, average straight-time rate increase 36¢
   36¢ × 12,000 overtime hrs. × .5 overtime rate =

Bonus—none

Other direct payroll cost increases
   Total Increase in Direct Payroll Costs =

II. Added Costs Directly Resulting from Higher Payroll Costs—Annual
F.I.C.A.—5.85% times increase in average straight-time earnings below $14,200 annually, 100 employees
   100 × 36¢ × 5.85% × 2,080 =

Federal and state unemployment insurance tax
   Number of employees × 4,200 × tax rate (2.5%) =

Workmen's compensation
   (Total cost or estimate)

---

[1] Michael H. Granof, *How to Cost Your Labor Contract* (Washington, D.C.: BNA, 1973). The author carries "costing-out" beyond the simple example illustrated and discusses the cost impact of adjustment in overall operations to contract changes.

[2] Bruce Morse, *How to Negotiate the Labor Agreement* (Detroit: Trends Publishing Company, 1971).

Other

Total Additional Direct Payroll Costs =

III. Nonpayroll Costs—Annual

Insurance—company portion
   Health insurance, no change
   Dental insurance, none
   Eye care, none
   Life insurance—added employer contribution
      $100 per year
      $100 × 100 employees =

Pension Costs
   Fully vested pension reduced from 25 years and age 65 to 20 years and age 62
   Estimated additional cost per year =

Miscellaneous
   Tuition reimbursemnts
   Service rewards
   Suggestion awards
   Loss on employee cafeteria
   Overtime meals
   Cost of parking lots
   Company parties
   Personal tools
   Personal safety equipment
   Personal wearing apparel

Profit sharing

Other

Total Additional Nonpayroll Costs, Annual =

IV. Changes in Nonwork Paid Time

Holidays—2 new holidays added to 6 already in contract
   100 employees × 8 hrs. × 2 holidays × Average new wage ($3.96) =

Vacation, new category added—4 weeks (160 hours annual vacation) with 20 or more years service; former top was 3 weeks after 15; average number of employees affected annually, 15
   15 × 40 × Average new wage ($3.96) =

Paid lunchtime—paid ½ lunchtime added to contract
   100 employees × ½ hr. × days worked yearly (236) × Average new wage ($3.96) =

Paid washup time, none

Coffee breaks, no change

Paid time off for union activity—new, one hour per week per shop steward
   10 shop stewards × Average new wage shop stewards ($4.20) × 1 hr. × 52 weeks =

Paid sick leave

Paid time off over and above workmen's compensation paid time, none

Jury-service time off, no change

Funeral-leave time off, no change

Paid time off for safety or training, no change

Other

> Total change in hours paid for but not worked, annual =

V. Financial Data Derived from Costing Out

Total increase in contract costs
> I + II + III

Average total increase in contract costs per employee payroll hour
> I + II + III ÷ 2,080 hours

Average total increase in direct payroll costs per man-hour
> I + II ÷ 2,080 hours ÷ 100 employees

Average total increase in nonpayroll costs per payroll-hour, per employee
> III ÷ 2,080 hours ÷ 100 employees

Average total increase in nonwork paid time per payroll-hour per employee
> IV ÷ 2,080 hours ÷ 100 employees

Average total increase in direct payroll costs per prod. (worked) hour (per employee)
> I + II ÷ 1,888 hours ÷ 100 employees

Average total increase in nonpayroll costs per prod. (worked) hour (per employee)
> III ÷ 1,888 hours ÷ 100 employees

Average total increase in nonwork paid time per prod. (worked) hour (per employee)
> IV ÷ 1,888 hours ÷ 100 employees

SOME OBSERVATIONS

1. Of vital importance in using the objectives approach is the confidentiality of the information concerning priorities and especially objectives. This becomes the focal point from which all the actions of the parties in the negotiations emanate, and the bargaining-by-objectives form becomes a ready reference from which to determine position, tactics, and progress being made. Grouping all financial items, as explained earlier, on either an hourly or a total-cost basis provides a ready source for the company or the union to determine the money impact of trades and compromises on money items and the effect on the total money package. By tying this initially to its own range of bargaining objectives, each party will have done some preparatory work and thinking prior to negotiation.

2. The identification of objectives becomes the basis for a more organized and careful approach to gathering and assembling data to support the party's bargaining position. It should really enhance the usefulness of data whether organized in bargaining books or some other way. Because the party must consider a range of bargaining objectives (possible settlements), the objectives approach enhances and broadens the whole process of preparation for bargaining. The party is forced to do more positive thinking and is, therefore, better prepared and has more clearly in mind where it expects and wants to go than by any other approach to bargaining.

3. The establishment of objectives as definitive as required under the objectives approach, offers a safe and effective way for management or the union to delegate authority to its bargaining team. Of great importance is that the authority is a flexible authority—the bargaining range of objectives —which is so necessary to effective strategy and negotiating. All the party must do is take the time to sit down with its bargaining team, agree on the range of objectives for each individual bargaining item, and then delegate authority to its team to settle within the range, except where too many of the settlements are falling in the pessimistic range. In this case, there should be further assessment by the party in authority and the bargaining team, because the assumptions on which the original goals were established may have changed, or perhaps there is a decided weakness in the bargaining team itself. Nothing is more frustrating to the negotiating process than for a party to have to sit across the bargaining table and attempt to bargain with a party that lacks bargaining authority. It is an exercise in futility.

4. It is recognized that by nature, not all items lend themselves to a three-way range of objectives. This is particularly true with some of the noncost bargaining items. Where this is the case, the party should at least establish two positions for the bargaining item, either a realistic–pessimistic range or an optimistic–realistic range. This is crucial both in terms of having positive objectives in mind while negotiating, and in terms of the way in which such prior consideration and thought of the particular bargaining item enhances preparation prior to negotiations.

5. Objectives should not be altered unless assumptions change—firmness and clarity are a strength.

6. Concerning the meaning of the bargaining-objectives range, it is well to point out that this range has no particular meaning with respect to strike or lockout points. Introducing strike or lockout considerations into the methodology would introduce a negativism that would undermine the overall usefulness of the objectives approach. The emphasis and focus of bargaining by objectives is to approach negotiations with positive and attainable goals and to relegate decisions on strikes, lockouts, and such considerations to strategy and tactics that might result from the actual negotiation process rather than being a major factor in the establishing of objectives. The objectives approach, while not ignoring pressure tactics, is based primarily on the achievement of goals through sound preparation and a careful, systematic approach to negotiation.

CONCLUSION

The very process required by the objectives approach—identifying the bargaining items, establishing priorities, and deciding on a range of achievable objectives—introduces positiveness because it not only systematizes what must be done but also *requires* a high degree of thought, analysis, and preparation before negotiations. There is nothing theoretical about the methodology. It is a practical and workable concept based on what must be done. The negotiator, through this methodology, enters negotiations knowing what he is doing, where he is going, and how strong his position is—not just generally, but relative to each item on the agenda. He is not "flying by the seat of his pants."

Finally, it must be emphasized that the objectives approach introduces a methodology or systematic way of negotiating that is useful in any negotiation. It may be and has been used for such collective bargaining activities as negotiating government contracts, budgets, insurance claims, and purchase of real estate, to name a few.

SELECTED REFERENCES

Burtt, Everett Johnson, Jr., *Labor Markets, Unions, and Government Policies.* New York: St. Martin's Press, 1963.

Good background reading for the objectives of unions in collective bargaining (Chapters 11–12).

Granof, Michael H., *How to Cost Your Labor Contract.* Washington, D.C.: Bureau of National Affairs, Inc., 1973.

Professor Granof, an accountant, fills a long-delayed need in addressing himself to the cost implications of the labor contract. He feels that the cost implications are too important to be left to the labor relations specialist. Yet the book is not a "how-to-do-it" manual. Instead, it approaches contract evaluation from the premise that there must be an explicit integration of plans relative to collective bargaining with those pertaining to other functions of the company.

McKee, Clive B., "Climate-Key to Effective Bargaining," in Elizabeth Marting, ed., *Understanding Collective Bargaining,* pp. 73–74. New York: American Management Association, Inc., 1958.

Emphasizes the importance of management's bargaining objectives being carefully discussed and definite targets set before negotiation begins.

Morse, Bruce, *How to Negotiate the Labor Agreement.* Detroit: Trends Publishing Co., 1971.

The author discusses the development of an employer's objectives and relates these to the final proposals.

Peters, Edward, *Strategy and Tactics in Labor Negotiations*, 3rd ed., pp. 31–54. Swarthmore, Pa.: Personnel Journal, 1966.

Here the author is concerned with two topics: setting a realistic goal and criteria for a realistic goal. From his years of experience in negotiations as a leading mediator on the West Coast, the author ties goal setting to his experience on the firing line.

Preparing for Negotiations–Initial Bargaining Positions

CHAPTER 13

As stated earlier, the initial bargaining positions of the parties are the visible position each takes at the outset of negotiations that is reflected in the initial demands of the union and the response or counteroffer of the employer. These are not the same as the range of bargaining objectives recorded in columns 3, 4, and 5 of the objectives form. The range of objectives, to reiterate, constitutes the confidential goals that the party actually expects to achieve in the final settlement. Under no circumstances should these be made visible to the other party, since this knowledge would destroy the bargaining leverage and the strategy based on these final goals.

A number of approaches are evident from observation of negotiations throughout the country. In some situations, the initial bargaining position (demand and response) may be close to what the parties have set as their objectives and expect to settle for finally. This approach creates the distinct possibility of a narrower negotiating range between the parties, although this may not be true without exception. This is more akin to the Boulware approach. In other instances, the parties' initial positions are based on the philosophy that the more the union asks for, the more there is to be gained, and the less offered by the company, the less will have to be given. This may result in a wide negotiating gap between what have been set as objectives and what the union and the employer demand and offer respectively. Other situations are characterized by combinations of these two approaches, sometimes differing according to the particular bargaining item.

The only general kind of guide for the negotiator is to very carefully examine each item for which objectives have been established, and from this examination determine where the first visible position on each item must be in order for the party to have a good chance to achieve the optimistic objective, a strong possibility of settling at the realistic-objective level, and a reasonable possibility that the settlement will not be at the pessimistic-objective level. Establishing the initial bargaining position is such an individual matter that more specific advice than this is not very useful. I do contend, however, that having gone to the trouble of accomplishing the spadework necessary to establish bargaining objectives, and having gone through the careful thought process required to establish such objectives, a party is in the best position possible to establish a logical and meaningful initial or visible position on each item to present to the other party at the start of negotiations. The objectives process minimizes the uncertainty in determining the initial bargaining position, and at the same time relates this initial posture more meaningfully to final attainable goals.

The initial bargaining position may be illustrated as in column 6 of

FORM 13–1

COLLECTIVE BARGAINING BY OBJECTIVES

(A GUIDE FOR DATA PREPARATION, STRATEGY, AND EVALUATION OF BARGAINING RESULTS)

BARGAINING * ITEMS	PRIORITIES **	RANGE OF BARGAINING OBJECTIVES			INITIAL *** BARGAINING POSITION
		PESSIMISTIC	REALISTIC	OPTIMISTIC	
Holidays	8	8 days	7 days	6 days	6 days
Wages	1	10¢ 1st yr. 10¢ 2nd yr. 5¢ 3rd yr.	5¢ 1st yr. 10¢ 2nd yr. 10¢ 3rd yr.	5¢ 1st yr. 10¢ 2nd yr. 5¢ 3rd yr.	12¢ over three years
--					
--					
--					
--					
--					
--					
ion Security	12	Union Shop	Modified Union Shop	Agency Shop	Agency Shop
robationary Period	20	30 days	60 days	90 days	120 days
--					
--					
--					
--					

Classify Items in Two Groups: Financial and Non-financial.
Relative Priority of each Bargaining Item to all Bargaining Items.
Actual Visible Position taken at Opening of Negotiation (Union Initial Proposal or Company Response or Counter Offer)

Form 13–1 (the company, in this instance). The union's initial demand on holidays might be for nine, as indicated earlier, or if the union representatives expect a hard time in securing their objectives relative to holidays, they might very well set their initial position at ten or eleven. The visible position that either party takes relative to any particular item then depends upon how difficult the parties estimate the negotiation will be in reaching, most preferably, their optimistic goal, and more probably, their realistic goal. It is this estimate of the amount of "haggling" or "horse trading" they must go through to achieve their objectives that determines whether their initial position (demand or counterproposal) is identical to their optimistic objective (the other party would not know this, since the objectives are confidential to the party) or to some position close to or wide of the optimistic. Of course, one party should not normally assume a position that is ridiculous on its face, because the other party will treat it for what it is worth, and serious negotiations will not proceed until the position is brought somewhere within the realm of reality.

SELECTED REFERENCES

Bloom, Gordon F., and Herbert R. Northrup, *Economics of Labor Relations,* 6th ed. Homewood, Ill.: Richard D. Irwin, 1969.

This includes a short but useful section on the union's formulation of demands.

Dunlop, John T., and James J. Healy, *Collective Bargaining—Principles and Cases,* pp. 54–57. Homewood, Ill.: Richard D. Irwin, 1955.

A short but informative discussion of the relationship of the initial positions of the parties to each other.

Marting, Elizabeth, ed., "A Step-by-Step Guide to the Preparatory Process," in *Understanding Collective Bargaining,* pp. 106–8. New York: American Management Association, Inc., 1958.

Brief but important material on union and management proposals.

Collective Bargaining
Process—Negotiation

CHAPTER 14

All the foregoing discussions have focused on obtaining background knowledge, preparing basic data, developing expertise, and using a sound methodology as a foundation for the actual negotiations at the bargaining table.

With this as background, attention is now focused on the actual negotiation process, using the tools already developed. Three aspects of the process are delineated: (1) the legal framework for negotiation; (2) bargaining format and procedures; and (3) the negotiation process.

LEGAL FRAMEWORK

Central to the legal framework governing the negotiation process is the injunction that the parties must bargain in good faith, as per Sections 8 (a) (5), 8 (b) (3), and 8 (d) of the National Labor Relations Act as amended.

As defined by Section 8 (d), this requirement means:

> For the purposes of this section, to bargain collectively is the performance of the mutual obligation of the employer and the representative of the employees to meet at reasonable times and confer in good faith with respect to wages, hours, and terms and conditions of employment, or the negotiation of an agreement, or any question arising thereunder, and the execution of a written contract incorporating any agreement reached if requested by either party, but such obligation does not compel either party to agree to a proposal or require the making of a concession.

Since the passage of the Taft-Hartley Act in 1947, there has been no major federal legislation that affects bargaining in good faith; rather, it has been up to the National Labor Relations Board and the courts to interpret the meaning of the law and decide when an employer or employees' representative has acted in good or bad faith. However, neither the board nor the courts have spelled out in precise language the criteria they use for this determination. Instead, there is a large body of decisions rendered over the years that collectively identify some informal guidelines. It must quickly be added, however, that a very large grey area has cropped up as the result of court and board interpretations.

Generally, the courts and the board have established that the totality of bargaining is taken into consideration when determining good faith. In other words, one violation or one charge of an unfair labor practice will not necessarily constitute a refusal to bargain, but a series of charges or violations might. Based on decisions to date, it is usually the employer upon whom rests the burden of proof. He is the one who most frequently has to justify good-faith intentions.

As interpreted by the NLRB and the courts, determining a violation of Section 8 (d), good-faith bargaining, includes consideration of the following types of bargaining behavior:

1. *Surface Bargaining.* This involves merely going through the motions of bargaining, without any real intent of completing a formal agreement.

2. *Concessions.* Even though Section 8(d) does not require the making of a concession, the court and board definitions of good faith suggest that willingness to compromise is an essential ingredient.

3. *Proposals and Demands.* The board will consider the advancement of proposals as a factor in determining overall good faith.

4. *Dilatory Tactics.* The law requires that the parties meet and "confer at reasonable times and intervals." Obviously, refusal to meet at all with the union does not satisfy the positive duty imposed on the employer.

5. *Imposing Conditions.* Attempts to impose conditions that are so onerous or unreasonable as to indicate bad faith will be scrutinized by the board.

6. *Unilateral Changes in Conditions.* This is viewed as a strong indication that the employer is not bargaining with the required intent of reaching an agreement.

7. *Bypassing the Representative.* An employer violates his duty to bargain when he refuses to negotiate with the union representative. The duty of management to bargain in good faith involves, at a minimum, recognition that the statutory representative is the one

with whom the employer must deal in conducting bargaining negotiations.

8. *Commission of Unfair Labor Practices during Negotiations.* Such action may reflect upon the good faith of the guilty party.

9. *Providing Information.* Information must be supplied to the union, upon request, to enable it to understand and intelligently discuss the issues raised in bargaining.

10. *Bargaining Items.* Refusal to bargain on a mandatory item or insistence on a permissive item to an impasse is usually viewed as bad-faith bargaining.[1]

Under Executive Order 11491, there is also an injunction that, once exclusive recognition has been accorded, an agency and a labor organization, through appropriate representatives, are to "meet at reasonable times and confer in good faith with respect to personnel policies and practices and matters affecting working conditions." No further explanation of the meaning of good-faith bargaining is given except to explicitly exclude from the obligation to meet and confer such matters as the mission of the agency, its budget, organization, number of employees, positions and assignments of employees, technology, and internal security matters; matters contrary to existing or future laws and the regulations of appropriate authorities, including policies set forth in the *Federal Personnel Manual;* and matters that are contrary to the right of officials of the agency to direct its employees, or to hire, promote, transfer, assign, retain, suspend, demote, or discharge employees, to reduce force for lack of work or other legitimate reasons, to maintain efficiency, to determine the methods, means, and personnel for conducting operations, and to take whatever actions are needed to carry out the mission of the agency in time of emergency.

One modification of these exclusions that is important to note was made in the 1975 amendments to Section 11 (a). Under this amendment, only those published policies and regulations for which a "compelling need exists" may bar their inclusion in contract negotiations. To bar negotiations concerning agency policy or regulations, the "compelling need" must (1) be "at the agency headquarters level or at the level of a primary national subdivision," and (2) meet "compelling need criteria" established by the Federal Labor Relations Council. The purpose behind the amendment was to remove unnecessary constriction of "meaningful negotiations at the local level on personnel policies and practices and matters affecting working conditions," to "permit a wider scope of nego-

---

[1] Adapted from Charles J. Morris, ed., *The Developing Labor Law* (Washington, D.C.: Bureau of National Affairs, Inc., 1971), pp. 271–310.

tiations," and to avoid the issuance of "overprescriptive" higher-level agency regulations that are "not critical to effective agency management or the public interest."[2]

Bargaining in good faith in the state and municipal sectors is not treated differently enough from EO 11491 to merit additional discussion.

It would be logical to assume that except for these restrictions and directions to the parties, the meaning of bargaining in good faith will be guided primarily by the large body of reasoning already available in the private sector.

From the material above it can be seen that the legal framework is a vital force in negotiation and should not be overlooked by the negotiator in either the private or the public sector.

BARGAINING FORMAT AND PROCEDURES

There is no foolproof prescription for the procedure a party should follow in negotiations. The choice of procedure needs to be flexible to fit the bargaining situation. Moreover, it should be recognized that procedure is a negotiable item. Each party in successive negotiations tends to develop its own particular approach and pattern of bargaining. Some guidelines might be suggested from bargaining experience, but only in a very general sense if flexibility is to be maintained.

The first step beyond the preparatory work of establishing bargaining items, priorities, and objectives (columns 1 through 5 of the objectives approach) is the presentation of the initial bargaining positions of the parties. This is a visible step, as stated before (column 6). The step may be accomplished at a prenegotiation session or as a part of the first stage of the negotiation process. The parties' presentation or exchange of positions through demand and counteroffer or response brings into focus, pinpoints, and completes the list of bargaining items to be negotiated (column 1). It has been customary for the union to take the initiative by presenting to the company its proposal for changes in the contract. It must be emphasized that this is not a legal requirement. There is nothing to prevent the employer from taking the initiative and making the first move. Whether an employer should or should not do this depends upon the particular strategy the employer chooses to follow. The union presentation may be formal or informal, in detailed language, or by bargaining items only. This is followed by a company response or counteroffer in which the company, at its option, may make a formal counteroffer, re-

---

2 *Labor–Management Relations in the Federal Service* (Washington, D.C.: U.S. Federal Labor Relations Council, 1975), p. 38.

spond in general to the union, and demand and/or make proposals of its own in addition to the bargaining items raised by the union.

At this point, the parties *must* be sure that the bargaining priorities and objectives on each negotiation item are fully firmed up in their own minds *before* actual negotiations begin.

The next step of importance, either as a part of the prenegotiation meetings or as a part of the formal negotiation process, is the establishment of rules and procedures for the negotiations: time and place of meeting, length of meetings, rules concerning conduct of meetings, and, last but certainly not least, the order of presentation of the bargaining items, procedures in dealing with each item, method of approval of items, and other matters of purely procedural nature. At this stage in the bargaining it is also important that the parties reach an understanding as to whether additional bargaining items may be introduced during the negotiations, except by joint agreement. As a matter of practical necessity, not of law, the parties have usually followed the practice of not allowing new items to be introduced during the negotiations unless both parties agree. This is to avoid the chaos and disruption to negotiations that such a practice might create.

NEGOTIATING

Once the bargaining items to be considered have been established and procedural guidelines have been agreed upon, the parties are ready for the actual negotiations. As long as the negotiations fall within the 60-day notice period, the parties in the private sector must "continue in full force and effect, without resorting to strike and lock-out, all the terms and conditions of the existing contract. . . ."[3] In the public sector, the same status quo is effected by Executive Order 11491, Section 19 (b) (4), under which the labor organization is enjoined from calling or engaging in a strike, work stoppage, slowdown, or picketing of an agency, or causing any such activity. Although state public-employee statutes are not so explicit about notice periods, they do, in effect, accomplish the same result. Most of the states with such statutes prohibit strikes, and those with a limited right to strike have alternative impasse procedures that delay strike action while efforts are made to settle the dispute.

The actual process during the weeks or months from start of negotiations to ultimate resolution, signified by a signed agreement, varies considerably in detail and in the emotional level at which it is conducted. The differences in the negotiation process are products of the personalities of those involved, the labor–management situation at the outset of

[3] Sec. 8 (d) (4), NLRA.

negotiations, outside events, bargaining techniques and strategy followed, and the relative power positions of the parties. However, most negotiations have the following common elements: (1) a settling-in stage, (2) a consolidation stage, (3) a finalization stage, and (4) a mopping-up stage.

SETTLING-IN STAGE. During the initial phases of the negotiations, the parties do a great deal of jockeying for position, acquainting themselves with the issues, and testing out the bargaining climate. All this is done without either party's committing itself too far until it fixes on the other party's position. Quite often, this involves discussing the items, with only minor commitments forthcoming, frequent caucusing to assess and analyze moves being contemplated, and a general tightening up on support for positions.

CONSOLIDATION STAGE. From the first stage, the parties then move to more detailed discussion of items, some agreements and trade-offs on items of lesser priority to both parties (mainly noneconomic items), and the beginning moves toward packaging economic or financial items. Again, one witnesses joint discussions at the bargaining table, parties caucusing on items under discussion, meeting together again to further move toward agreement, further caucusing, and finally agreement and sign-off of items or setting items aside for later consideration.

FINALIZATION STAGE. In this stage, the range of negotiation items has been significantly reduced, fewer but higher-priority items are being dealt with, the parties settle in to harder bargaining, the feeling of impending impasse or final settlement is much more pervasive, and packaging the remaining items becomes more and more dominant. It is also at this point that the parties begin to opt for other types of pressure or intervention in order to effect a final settlement and avoid an impasse. It is in this stage that a union may (although there is an increasing tendency not to do so) threaten a strike deadline. It is also at this stage that a federal mediator or other outside intervention may be called in or, if the situation is governed by statutes, be called upon to head off any sort of work stoppage (by mediation, fact-finding, arbitration).

Although strikes do take place during negotiations, and even though crisis bargaining is still in evidence in many situations, the whole climate of collective bargaining seems to be changing with regard to these types of bargaining and bargaining pressures. More and more, the parties are seeing the futility of the strike except in very special circumstances and are moving to alternative approaches such as early bargaining, joint study committees, mediation–arbitration, and voluntary arbitration of unresolved issues (see Part IV). More and more, the statutory procedures are looking to alternative ways of resolving conflict without resort to the strike. Although there is an element of compulsion in the statutory procedures, the intent seems to be not compulsion, but a real desire to find viable alternatives to work stoppages. Except in instances of danger to health, safety, or national welfare, all these alternatives are aimed not at denying the *right* to strike, but at reducing or eliminating the *need* to strike.

MOPPING-UP STAGE. The agreement has been reached. The parties heave a big sigh of relief. The frustrations and the tedious time-consuming work of negotiation are over. Yet, the work is not completely over if the parties want to be spared grief in the coming months during which they will be living under the agreement. The final stage is to be sure that what they have agreed upon is put in language that conveys the intent of their agreement on each bargaining item and will not elicit grievances because of its sloppy construction.[4]

Conduct of Negotiations

The conduct of the actual negotiations by either party is certainly enhanced and firmed up by the objectives approach described earlier. The negotiator, through this methodology, is provided with a positive and known framework within which to develop strategy and techniques. However, there is no single formula or guide from which the negotiator may draw, other than experience and observation, that tells him what to do in each specific situation. The negotiator is required to be at one and the same time a poker player, a master at timing, an expert at divining the other party's intent and visualizing his own moves far ahead, a master at persuading and, where needed, applying pressure, and finally, a professional in labor relations who sees the consequences of what happens at the bargaining table in both the legal sense and the labor relations sense. In short, collective bargaining has evolved from the older, table-pounding trial of economic strength into both an art and a profession. The effective negotiator is indeed a professional in his field.

Even experience cannot guarantee that a basically inept person will do a good job. But for the individual who has the potential of developing the personal qualities of a good negotiator, experience can mean the difference between success and lack of success. In the meantime, the negotiator should be wary of neatly capsulized packages or formulas on strategy and tactics supposedly guaranteeing success at the bargaining table. The human factor in negotiating, complicated by all other factors affecting the situation, is too variable to lend itself to such neat packaging. Rather, the best advice must be cautionary in nature. Such advice,

---

[4] LeRoy Marceau, *Drafting a Union Contract* (Boston: Little Brown, 1965). Drafting the language of the contract is one of the most crucial parts of negotiation and should never be relegated to a secondary position out of relief that an agreement has been reached.

when bolstered by experience and guided or strengthened by the systematic and logical approach to bargaining suggested herein, is the best assurance that the negotiator, inexperienced or experienced, will be doing the best job for his party that he can under the conditions within which he must operate. Perhaps the best way to describe these cautionary bits of advice is to call them "bargaining homilies."

BARGAINING HOMILIES

Be sure that you have set *clear objectives* on every bargaining item and that you understand on what ground the objectives were established.

Do not hurry.

When in doubt, *caucus.*

Be *well prepared* with firm data support for clearly identified objectives.

Always strive to keep some flexibility in your position—don't get yourself out on a limb.

Do not concern yourself with only what the other party says and does—*find out why.* Remember that economic motivation is not the only explanation for the other party's conduct and actions.

Respect the importance of *face saving* for the other party.

Constantly be alert to the *real intents* of the other party—with respect not only to goals, but also to priorities.

Be a good *listener.*

Build a reputation for being *fair* but *firm.*

Learn to control your *emotions*—don't panic. Use emotions as a tool, not an obstacle.

Be sure as you make each bargaining move that you know its *relationship* to all other moves.

Measure each move against your *objectives.*

Pay close attention to the *wording* of every clause negotiated; words and phrases are often the source of grievances.

Remember that collective bargaining negotiations are by their very nature part of a *compromise* process. There is no such thing as having all the pie.

Learn to *understand* people and their personalities—it may mean a payoff during negotiations.

Consider the *impact* of *present negotiations* on negotiations in *future* years.

EVALUATION OF BARGAINING RESULTS

The last columns (7, 8, and 9) of bargaining by objectives provide a systematic way of evaluating bargaining experience.

FORM 14—1

COLLECTIVE BARGAINING BY OBJECTIVES

(A GUIDE FOR DATA PREPARATION, STRATEGY, AND EVALUATION OF BARGAINING RESULTS)

BARGAINING ITEMS *	PRIORITIES **	RANGE OF BARGAINING OBJECTIVES			INITIAL *** BARGAINING POSITION	EVALUATION RESULTS		
		PESSIMISTIC	REALISTIC	OPTIMISTIC		P	R	O
(Financial Items)								
Holidays	8	8 days	7 days	6 days	6 days	X		
Wages	1	10¢ 1st yr. 10¢ 2nd yr. 5¢ 3rd yr.	5¢ 1st yr. 10¢ 2nd yr. 10¢ 3rd yr.	5¢ 1st yr. 10¢ 2nd yr. 5¢ 3rd yr.	12¢ over three years		X	
--								
--								
--								
--								
--								
(Nonfinancial Items)								
Union Security	12	Union Shop	Modified Union Shop	Agency Shop	Agency Shop			
Probationary Period	20	30 days	60 days	90 days	120 days		X	X
--								
--								
--								
--								

*   Classify Items in Two Groups: Financial and Non-financial.
**   Relative Priority of each Bargaining Item to all Bargaining Items.
*** Actual Visible Position taken at Opening of Negotiation (Union Initial Proposal or Company Response or Counter Offer)

For each bargaining item indicated in the appropriate column—P (pessimistic), R (realistic), or O (optimistic)—the final settlement is compared to the original bargaining objective established for that item. If the settlement achieved was the realistic one, then check column 8; if optimistic, check column 9; if pessimistic, check column 7. Form 14–1 is an example of an employer's objectives and results. Based on its own objectives, the union would probably come up with a different picture of results after checking columns 7, 8, and 9. It should be noted that on some items settled at the realistic level, the results might be the same for both parties if they had established identical realistic objectives originally.

Then, for each item determine why the end result was P, R, or O. If on a particular item the optimistic objective was achieved, what happened during negotiations to bring about such a result? Analysis of bargaining results at the R and P levels for any particular item should also be carried through the same procedure. From this exercise, the party should be able to determine the kinds of strategies and tactics that proved succesful in negotiations and those that did not. Notes should be taken to serve as a basis for doing a better job at the next negotiations. Furthermore, if the analysis is accomplished immediately after the negotiations have concluded and while recall is still at a maximum, the benefits to be derived by the party will be much greater and more useful when negotiation ensues.

As a spinoff from using the objectives approach, this final comparison of bargaining results to bargaining objectives can, if used with care, serve as a basis for a rewards system for successful negotiators.

CONCLUSION

The primary aim of the foregoing has been to present the practitioner with a working methodology for collective bargaining negotiations. The bargaining methodology described has equal usefulness in both private- and public-sector bargaining. It is also applicable to any negotiation situation. The objectives method has many advantages for negotiators, experienced or inexperienced, in providing a systematic and purposeful approach to negotiations, where the goals are identified and progress at the bargaining table is measurable. The bargaining methodology illustrated by the objectives approach is not a complete answer to positive and successful negotiation at the bargaining table but, combined with personal expertise, provides the most efficient framework within which to ensure success.

SELECTED REFERENCES

Burtt, Everett Johnson, Jr., *Labor Markets, Unions, and Government Policies.* New York: St. Martin's Press, 1963.

A good discussion of contract negotiations and bargaining power (pp. 194–200) in terms of economic pressure, the political process, and negotiation tactics.

Chamberlain, Neil W., *Collective Bargaining.* New York: McGraw-Hill, 1951.

See Chapter 4, "Selected References."

Dunlop, John T., and James J. Healy, *Collective Bargaining—Principles and Cases,* Chapter IV. Homewood, Ill.: Richard D. Irwin, 1955.

Chapter IV contains a good discussion of the bargaining process in a step-by-step account.

Fischer, Harry C., *The Uses of Accounting in Collective Bargaining.* Institute of Industrial Relations, University of California, Los Angeles, 1969.

Rightfully, the author points to the importance of accounting to negotiations, where so much of the subject matter is concerned with cost items. The author notes that language in which the employer's ability to pay is expressed is accounting. This pamphlet is intended as an introduction to that language.

Gilroy, Thomas P., et al., *Educator's Guide to Collective Negotiations.* Columbus, O.: Charles E. Merrill, 1969.

The authors have directed this book to the needs of the local school district and the parties involved in negotiation sessions. It provides a good background and some down-to-earth information about the process of negotiation in education.

Karrass, Chester L., *Give and Take: The Complete Guide to Negotiating Strategies and Tactics.* New York: Thomas Y. Crowell, 1974.

The author includes 200 strategies and tactics as a guide to negotiation. He notes that this is the first complete guide to practical negotiating strategies, tactics, and countermeasures. As director of the Center for Effective Negotiating, the author responds to what he considers is the most frequently asked question: "What works at the table?"

Knee, Robert C., and Robert C. Knee, Jr., *Collective Bargaining Clauses.* Cincinnati, O.: W. H. Anderson, 1975.

The authors provide a practical guide to the negotiator by selection of clauses that they feel are either standard or realistic approaches to the area of negotiations.

Levin, Noel Arnold, *Successful Labor Relations—An Employer's Guide.* New York: Fairchild Publications, 1967.

David Cole's comment in the introduction epitomizes the reason for including this book. Cole states, "Arnold Levin is realistic and rational, and his book reflects this. While he has good practical advice for management representatives, he does not neglect the philosophical and long-range implications and objectives." Written as advice for management, the author's excellent coverage of the negotiation process and his practical suggestions can also be used by unions.

McMahon, Edward J., "The Negotiation Process," in LeRoy Marceau, *Dealing with a Union*. New York: American Management Association, Inc., 1969.

An informative discussion of the steps and strategies of the negotiation process.

Marceau, LeRoy, *Drafting a Union Contract*. Boston: Little, Brown, 1965.

The author properly notes that there are many books written about ways to facilitate agreements but a real dearth of information on how to draft a union contract properly. Marceau notes that the function of the draftsman is to "prevent rather than to resolve labor disputes." This book offers an excellent step-by-step approach to drafting the contract.

Marshall, Howard D., and Natalie J. Marshall, *Collective Bargaining*. New York: Random House, 1971.

A thorough study in Chapter 5 of the strategies of collective bargaining.

Marting, Elizabeth, ed., "At the Bargaining Table," in *Understanding Collective Bargaining*, Part III. New York: American Management Association, Inc., 1958.

Excellent down-to-earth discussion of the techniques of bargaining, pitfalls for the unwary, blueprint for the bargaining sessions, and how to handle crisis bargaining.

Morris, Charles J., ed., *The Developing Labor Law*, Chapter 11. Washington, D.C.: Bureau of National Affairs, Inc., 1971.

Chapter 11 provides a complete examination of the injunction of the NLRA that the parties have a duty to bargain in good faith. The explanation is in terms of both the evolution of the good-faith bargaining concept and the current state of the law with respect to indicia of good- and bad-faith bargaining.

Morse, Bruce, *How to Negotiate the Labor Agreement*. Detroit: Trends Publishing Co., 1971.

Morse provides brief (83 pages) and practical advice on preparing for bargaining, organizing negotiations, and conducting negotiations.

Peters, Edward, *Strategy and Tactics in Labor Negotiations*, 3rd ed. Swarthmore, Pa.: Personnel Journal, 1966.

One would be hard put not to recommend the entire book, it is so full of on-the-firing-line types of information from an experienced practitioner. For the actual negotiations, the reader is referred to the chapters on "Collective Bargaining: A Science or an Art?"; "The Essential Nature and

Purpose of Negotiations"; "From Bargaining Position to Final Offer"; "Prestige, Power, and Paternalism"; "Sign Language"; "Settlement"; "Bargaining in Good Faith"; and "Strike Negotiations."

P-H Industrial Relations Guide. Englewood Cliffs, N.J.: Prentice-Hall.

This service of Prentice-Hall offers a complete guide that is updated continually and provides vital information to the negotiator or IR representative on arbitration awards, union contract clauses, useful information concerning negotiating a contract, and new developments in the field.

Prentice-Hall Editorial Staff, *Manual for Drafting Union Contracts.* Englewood Cliffs, N.J.: Prentice-Hall, 1968.

P-H fulfills a vital need with this handy guide to drafting a union contract. Not only is the importance of a carefully written contract emphasized, but P-H takes the reader step by step through the areas of the contract, such as union recognition and parties, union security and representation, grievance, arbitration and strikes, wages and working time, seniority, and working conditions and benefits.

Repas, Bob F., *Collective Bargaining in Federal Employment,* 2nd ed. Industrial Relations Center, University of Hawaii, August 1973.

The publication was especially crafted for the use of the union that seeks recognition and subsequent negotiation of an agreement with an agency of the federal government. Repas includes a wealth of information plus practical advice to the prospective negotiator.

Rothenberg, Herbert, and Steven B. Silverman, *Labor Unions—How To: Avert Them, Beat Them, Out-Negotiate Them, Live with Them, Unload Them.* Elkins Park, Pa.: Management Relations, Inc., 1973.

The authors, whose days are fully occupied representing the interests of management in their labor relations problems, make no apology for the title of their book. It is frankly written out of an impatience of the authors, both attorneys, with the attitude of many firms of "not rocking the boat" and of "quiet surrender and acceptance" in their dealings with labor organizations. In their own words, the scope and the purpose of the book "is to demonstrate not only that it is possible to successfully stand up against a labor union, but how to avoid those mistakes and miscalculations which frequently result in the employer's loss of a dispute which could otherwise have been won."

Stevens, Carl M., *Strategy and Collective Bargaining Negotiation.* New York: McGraw-Hill, 1963.

A volume that significantly contributes to collective bargaining literature by applying theoretical tools to the negotiation process. Provides a way to interpret the strategy of the parties and their tactics at all stages of the contract negotiation process.

Summers, Clyde W., "Ratification of Agreements," in John T. Dunlop and Neil W. Chamberlain, eds., *Frontiers of Collective Bargaining.* New York: Harper & Row, 1967.

A thorough discussion of the function and problems of ratification of the agreement.

Weisberger, June, *Examples of Language and Interpretation in Public Sector Collective Bargaining Agreements: A Guide for Public Officials and Other Interested Parties.* IPE Monograph No. 3, Institute of Public Employment, New York State School of Industrial and Labor Relations, February 1975.

The author has brought together some useful information. The title is self-explanatory.

Collective Bargaining Process— Contract Administration

Finally, we see the whole machinery for collective bargaining seriously hampered, except in two or three trades, by the failure to make the vital distinction between interpreting an existing wage contract, and negotiating the terms upon which a new general agreement should be entered into.

Sidney and Beatrice Webb   *1902*

PART THREE

Contract Administration— The Grievance

CHAPTER 15

The introduction of industrial democracy to the workplace, so highly heralded by the Webbs, was the primary result of the rise of unionism and the subsequent development of collective bargaining relationships. Collective bargaining introduced a process of *joint determination of the rules* under which the employer–employee relationship would be governed. But the determination of the rules only would have resulted in the establishment of the structure of industrial government without the viability that such government requires to be fully effective on a day-by-day basis. Consequently, to the negotiated terms under which the parties would be governed was added a second process, more interpretive in nature: the *right to grieve* through machinery established in the collective bargaining agreement. The right to grieve created the means by which the terms negotiated could prove viable under the stresses and strains of everyday application. The point to be made, then, is that an operative type of industrial democracy between employers and employees depends not only upon jointly determined rules governing the relationship, but equally so upon *a process by which differences over the interpretations of the terms may be verbalized and jointly settled.* Without the right to grieve, the concept of industrial democracy would have been only partially realized. Supreme Court Justice Douglas stated that the grievance machinery under a collective bargaining agreement "is at the heart of the system of industrial self-government."[1]

A grievance may be broadly defined as a real or imagined wrong or cause for complaint. As used within the framework of collective bargaining contract administration, the cause for complaint requiring an adjust-

---

[1] *Labor Arbitration Reports* (Washington, D.C.: Bureau of National Affairs, Inc., 1961), Vol. 34 LA 563.

ment between the parties is a real or imagined violation of the rights of a party—employer, employee, or union—as stipulated by the terms of the collective agreement or by past practice. The *primary focus* of the grievance process is upon the protection of the rights of the employee. However, it also provides an avenue through which either the union may grieve on its own behalf or for the bargaining-unit employees, or the employer may grieve if he feels that his rights under the agreement are being violated.

In order to give maximum exposure to the legal nature of the grievance, the sources from which grievances arise, and some types of grievances, this chapter confines itself to the grievance and nothing more. Ensuing chapters will deal with the machinery established to expedite the resolution of grievance questions.

THE GRIEVANCE—LAW AND POLICY

The right of an employee or group of employees to grieve matters related to their employment is strongly supported by both the NLRA and Executive Order 11491 for private- and public-sector employees respectively. Protecting the right to grieve as a basic right, grievance procedure or no grievance procedure, is clearly enunciated.

The right of "any individual employee or a group of employees . . . to present grievances to their employers" was established first by the National Labor Relations Act of 1935.[2] While this established a legal pattern for recognition of the right to grieve, it was rather too general. It did not give enough recognition to (1) the status of the majority union as the sole representative of workers in the bargaining unit, and (2) the binding nature of the labor agreement on the employees in the bargaining unit, on the union, and on the employer. By interpretation, the National Labor Relations Board was trying to enforce both principles, but this was a poor substitute for a clear statement through the law. Congress, in the Taft-Hartley amendments of 1947, attempted to make both the language and the intent of the law clear. The amendments nullified the old NLRB doctrine dealing with the presentation and adjustment of grievances and in its place established two standards for all grievance-procedure structures: (1) The individual worker must still be allowed to present his grievance on an individual basis if he so chooses. (2) The employer must be allowed to make an adjustment of a grievance so presented, provided the adjustment is not inconsistent with the terms of the collective bargaining agreement covering the bargaining unit. The sec-

---

[2] Benjamin Taylor and Fred Witney, *Labor Relations* (Englewood Cliffs, N.J.: Prentice-Hall, 1975), p. 366.

ond point constitutes the major shift in the old NLRB doctrine. Originally, the employer had to invite the representative of the employee to be present for both the presentation and the adjustment of the grievance. Under the Taft-Hartley amendments, the bargaining unit representative does not have to be present during the adjustment but must be given the opportunity to be present during the proceedings. But, to reiterate, the individual employee and the employer may not agree to an adjustment of the grievance *that is not consistent with the labor agreement.*

In the newer field of public-sector policy, it is also clear that by Executive Order 11491 (as amended by 11616 in 1971), the right of the employee to grieve must be made a part of the labor–management relationship. The revised order (11616) requires that a negotiated agreement between a public agency and federal-employee representatives for an inclusive unit must include a grievance procedure. The revised order also provides that employees may present their grievances directly rather than through their bargaining representative. If the grievance matter is not covered by the labor agreement, it may not be presented through the negotiated grievance procedure but must be processed through any other available system.

The same sort of reasoning found in the NLRA and EO 11491 is carried over in the state laws with respect to the right of an employee to grieve. Most of the state laws grant the right to grieve to an employee within a bargaining unit with or without utilizing the bargaining representative. As with the NLRA and EO 11491, if the employee chooses to grieve directly without use of his bargaining representative, he cannot make any settlement that contravenes the labor agreement then in effect.

For example, Minnesota's Employment Relations Act provides in Section 179.65:

Nothing . . . shall be construed to limit, impair or affect the right of any public employee or his representative to the expression or communication of a view, grievance, complaint or opinion on any matter related to the conditions or compensation of public employment.

Connecticut's Municipal Employee Relations Act, in Section 7.468 (d), also provides:

An individual employee at any time may present a grievance to his employer and have the grievance adjusted, without intervention of an employee organization, provided the adjustment shall not be inconsistent with the terms of a collective bargaining agreement then in effect. The employee organization certified or recognized as the exclusive representative shall be given prompt notice of the adjustment.

The important point to remember is that in both the public and private sectors, either by legislation or executive order, *the right to grieve is clearly enunciated and protected.*

THE BASIS AND NATURE OF GRIEVANCES

The situations out of which grievances arise and the nature of the grievances themselves are of such a great variety and involve such a multiplicity of considerations that they defy tabulation. They are limited only by the variety of circumstances that might arise in the employment relationship and by the real or imagined grievances arising therefrom. In order at least to give the reader some flavor for the sources and the nature of grievances, a number of grievance situations broadly illustrative are presented. Again, these examples are illustrative only, not exhaustive of all grievances.[3]

Absenteeism

- An employer fired an employee for excessive absences. The employee filed a grievance stating that there had been no previous warnings or discipline related to excessive absences.

- An employer fired an employee for excessive absences. The employee disputed the discharge and brought evidence that absences were related to a shop injury suffered earlier and that his personal physician had notified the employer that the date of return to work was unascertainable.

- As a result of failure to report to work following a holiday, coupled with a poor work attendance record, the employer discharged an employee. The employee contested the discharge on a just-cause basis.

Appearance

- A truck driver was discharged for wearing a beard. He filed a grievance charging discrimination and lack of just cause.

- An employee was disciplined for wearing a wig in a meat-packing plant in disregard of a plant rule banning wigs for sanitary and safety reasons. The employee grieved the disciplinary action as unreasonable and in conflict with the Department of Agriculture minimal rules.

- A bus ticket agent was discharged for refusing to trim his hair. The employer based the discharge on a plant rule that required male employees to trim hair covering the ears and extending below the collar line. The employee grieved contending lack of just cause.

[3] From my own arbitration cases over a 20-year period, and *Labor Arbitration Reports,* BNA, variously. For more illustrations of past grievances, see Prentice-Hall's Industrial Relations Guide.

Assignment

- The employer assigned the fabrication and installation of a support structure for a whirlpool bath to millwrights in his employ. As a result, employees who were pipefitters filed a grievance claiming that they should have been assigned the work.

- A laborer partway into his shift was assigned some work of a higher-paying classification. When he received his weekly paycheck, he noticed that he had been paid at the laborer rate for the hours worked in the higher classification. He filed a grievance when the employer refused to adjust his pay.

- The employer assigned the dismantling, repair, and assembling of valves to instrument mechanics in his employ. Machinists in his employ filed a grievance claiming that the work should have been theirs, based on custom and practice.

- It had been the practice to assign work of vacationing helpers to other helpers. The employer assigned a journeyman machinist to fill the position of a machinist helper while the latter was on vacation. A grievance was filed on behalf of the helpers affected, protesting the action of the employer.

- A detective sergeant was temporarily assigned to the job of assistant detective chief. His next paycheck revealed no change in pay to that of the high-paying position. He filed a grievance when informed by his employer that he would not receive the higher pay.

Bargaining Unit

- An employee voted in an NLRB-conducted election in which the union was certified as the bargaining representative. Later, this same employee was promoted to "acting reservations manager." Soon after, the company fired him. He filed a grievance claiming the protection afforded bargaining-unit employees under the labor agreement and protesting his discharge.

Behavior

- A male employee used foul language to a female employee and was discharged. The employee filed a grievance claiming that discharge was not based on just cause, since foremen set the tone for employees by using similar language in the presence of female employees.

- An employee in a plant where horseplay was widespread squirted a fellow employee with a fire extinguisher. The employer fired him for violation of a plant rule. The employee filed a complaint.

- A 20-year employee who had not been warned before was fired for drinking beer on the job. The employee filed a grievance claiming lack of just cause.

- An employee who had an altercation with another employee was discharged, while the other employee was not disciplined. The employer based his action on the discharged employee's being the aggressor in the altercation. The employee filed the grievance charging unequal treatment.

- An employee posted unauthorized inflammatory notices pertaining to the employer on the union bulletin board in violation of company orders. After repeated warnings from the employer concerning other notices posted by the grievant, he was discharged. The employee disputed discharge.

- An employee of long-time service in the company went into what was described as a screaming temper tantrum upon being denied two weeks' leave after returning from his annual vacation. He was terminated as a voluntary quit. He then filed a grievance stating the action of company was precipitous and premature.

- The company had a plant rule requiring inspection of female employee's large purses. An employee of long seniority refused to allow this inspection of her purse. As a result, she was discharged. She filed a grievance stating that the discharge was unwarranted and unreasonable.

- An employee was apprehended stealing company property and was discharged forthwith. The employee filed a grievance claiming too-severe discipline and lack of progressive discipline before discharge.

Call-out–Call-in

- The contract called for a four-hour guarantee at an overtime rate for call-outs. An employee was called to work at 6:00 A.M. He worked to 8.00 A.M. and then continued through the regular 8:00 A.M. to 4:30 P.M. work shift. The employer paid the employee two hours at the overtime rate for call-out plus his regular eight-hour pay. The employee filed a grievance for the four-hour guarantee for call-out plus his regular-shift pay.

- An employee was called from his home, after finishing his regular shift, to load a trailer. He completed the loading work in 38 minutes and then submitted a claim for the call-in guarantee of four hours' pay at the overtime rate. This was disallowed by the employer and a grievance ensued.

- Three employees were required to make emergency repairs during their lunch break. They submitted a claim for call-in pay. The employer denied the request. A grievance was filed.

- As a result of a computer breakdown, employees came to pick up paychecks on a holiday rather than at the scheduled payday. The employees filed for extra pay under a call-in clause requiring call-in pay for employees reporting to "work" and finding none. The employer refused. A grievance resulted.

Classification

- An employer required a cleaning-room foreman to perform minor clerical duties incidental to his other duties. The foreman filed a grievance claiming that this required that he be placed in the clerk classification for the clerical duties.

- Employees in a job that underwent a new job description, resulting in a change of job classification with a pay rate of 10 cents an hour below their current rate, filed a grievance when the employer refused to red-circle their current pay rate.

- The employer established the wage for a new job of operating an EDM machine, which produces dies for die makers, at a lower rate than the wage for skilled die makers. Employees hired into the new job filed a grievance claiming a skilled die maker's pay rate.

- Employees classified as "production layout artists" claimed they had the ability to do work of the higher classification of "creative artists." As a result, they asked to be reclassified at the higher classification. This was refused by the employer. The employees filed a grievance.

Contract

- Under the contract, unless 60-day notice is given prior to the termination date of the contract, the contract is automatically renewed. In this particular instance, the union failed to give the 60-day notice prior to the reopener date. The employer then assumed that the contract was automatically renewed and refused to negotiate changes with the union. The union went out on strike. The employer, on the assumption that the no-strike clause of the contract had been automatically renewed, filed a grievance against the union claiming violation of the contract.

Damages

- A union steward called an unauthorized strike at a construction site. The company presented the union with a statement of damages caused by the strike, claiming that the union was responsible for the act of its agent, the union steward. The union disclaimed responsibility and took the matter to the grievance procedure.

Days of Work

- The employer was required to place an employee in the job to which he is entitled within a maximum of ten days. Interpreting this as ten working days, the employer, on the tenth working day but the twelfth calendar day, placed an employee in the required job. The employee grieved stating it should have been within ten calendar days and requesting compensation for the two days' delay.

Discrimination

- An employer refused to withdraw written reprimands from an employee's file. The reprimands were imposed for failure of the employee to improve on his attendance record as required by the probationary agreement. The employee filed a grievance charging racial discrimination.

- A black employee was given a 45-day disciplinary layoff for violation of plant rules. The employee filed a grievance charging discrimination, since white employees guilty of the same rules violations were never given more than two weeks' layoff.

- An employer had separate lines of male and female progression. As a result, a job was awarded to a male applicant who had the qualifications instead of to a senior female applicant who had potential ability to perform the work. The female applicant filed a grievance charging sex discrimination in promotions.

Falsifying

- An employee who was almost blind in one eye had not stated the fact on his application. Subsequently, after employing the man, the employer found out about the blindness. The man was discharged for failure to disclose the condition on his employment application and as a hazard to other employees. The employee filed a grievance claiming that he could perform his work adequately.

Gratuities

- In the past, the employer had provided on his own an annual gratuity to his employees in the form of a family picnic outing. For economic reasons, he unilaterally discontinued the annual outing. His employees brought a grievance protesting this unilateral action.

- For a number of years, the employer allowed hunting privileges to employees on company-owned surplus lands. The employer then unilaterally discontinued the hunting privileges, and the employees affected filed a grievance protesting the action.

- For twenty years, employees had been bringing radios on the job. The contract contained the clause, "past practice shall not be binding on either party." The employer unilaterally banned use of radios on the job. Employees grieved, stating that the employer could not unilaterally take such action.

Habits

- It was found by the employer that an employee involved in the use of machinery smoked marijuana. The employer fired the employee on the assumption that he constituted a danger to the safety of other employees who were working on the same machinery. A grievance was filed maintaining just cause had not been shown.

Health and Welfare

- The contract specifically stated that employees would pay a specified amount as their contribution toward dependent coverage. The premium was increased on dependent coverage. The employer increased the deduction from employees for dependent coverage by a pro rata amount of the overall increase in the premium. The employees grieved stating that the employer should pay the entire increase in the premium rate for dependents.

- The teachers and the board of education had a contract provision that required the district to provide the teachers full family health-care insurance, with the options as they become available. A pharmaceutical rider became available, but the board failed to add this to the insurance package. The teacher organization filed a grievance.

- The company had had a pension plan under which a number of employees had already retired. At the most recent negotiations, an agreement was reached on an increase in the pension benefits. The employer interpreted this as applying only to subsequent retirements. Retirees filed a grievance arguing that the increase was for all, past and present.

- An employer had a management right under the labor agreement to determine types and classes of insurance policies to be sold. He used this right to unilaterally eliminate several insurance policies. The Insurance Workers' Union filed a grievance claiming this was an abuse of management rights.

- Through an error, the clause on hospitalization insurance benefits was omitted from the labor agreement. An employee filed for the benefits and was denied by the employer on the basis that the contract contained no provision for them. The employee filed a grievance.

Holidays

- Christmas and New Year's are official holidays. In this incident, both holidays fell on Saturdays, a regular day off for shop employees. The employer refused to pay the holiday pay for the two holidays, since they fell on nonworking days. The shop employees, through their union, grieved the employer's decision.

- The employer's plant was partially burned down a week before the Thanksgiving holiday. The employer received permission from the insurance company to use some of the employees to do special clean-up work extending through the last scheduled workday before and after the holiday. When these employees filed for holiday pay for Thanksgiving, the employer refused to pay on the basis that the employees had not worked on a regular scheduled workday before and after the holiday. The employees filed a grievance claiming the holiday pay.

- Three employees worked on Washington's Birthday. The employer paid them regular overtime instead of premium holiday pay. They filed a grievance for the extra pay.

- The company refused to pay an employee holiday pay for July 4, which fell within his vacation period. The employee grieved, claiming holiday pay.

- The contract called for payment of holidays worked at time and a half plus holiday pay. An employee worked a shift from 12:01 A.M. to 8:00 A.M.

on the holiday and claimed holiday pay plus time and a half for the hours worked. The employer denied the claim, arguing that the workday was 7:00 A.M. to 7:00 A.M., and therefore, for pay purposes the holiday began at 7:00 A.M. and not at 12:01 A.M. A grievance was filed.

• The employer is required to pay holiday pay to all "regular full-time employees and part-time employees." A probationary employee who was denied holiday pay filed a grievance.

• A wildcat strike took place on the last scheduled shift prior to a Memorial Day holiday. As a result, employees were not able to work the shift. The employer therefore did not pay them holiday pay, because they had failed to work the day prior to the holiday. The employees filed a grievance.

• The employer scheduled observance of a Memorial Day holiday falling on Saturday on the following Monday. The contract called for double time for working on holidays. Two employees worked on the Saturday. The employer paid them regular overtime rather than double time. The employees, claiming they should have received double time for working on the official holiday and not the employer-designated holiday, filed a grievance.

Hours of Work

• In the past, employees had frequently left work before the end of a shift without permission. Under a lax supervision, this had never been questioned. The employer then instituted a strict policy requiring the service manager's permission to leave prior to the end of a shift. Several months after this change of policy, three employees left without permission and were given a one-day suspension. These employees grieved the suspension on the basis of long-established past practice.

• The labor agreement established a 7½-hour workday. It had been the practice to allow workers to quit a half-hour early. The employer issued an order requiring employees, effective the date of the order, to begin working a full 7½-hour day. The employees grieved this unilateral action.

• Machinists worked the Sunday midnight shift but, because of a time change, actually worked only seven hours. They claimed a full eight hours' pay, claiming that by the clock, there was eight hours' difference between the times of reporting and finishing the shift. The employer refused the eight hours' request. A grievance was filed.

• The employees on the first shift, upon reporting to work, found the plant door locked. They returned home and the next day applied for reporting pay. This was refused by the employer on the basis that the supervisor had overslept but was there to open the plant within half an hour of starting time. A grievance ensued.

Incentive

• A new incentive standard was unilaterally established by the employer. The union grieved the unilateral action.

Inefficiency

- A head mixer in a bakery was discharged for omitting essential ingredients in a batch of cookie dough. He filed a grievance claiming that, in terms of his past record, the disciplinary action was too severe.

- An employee was discharged because of poor work, which was linked also to a negative attitude toward work, customer complaints about inadequate performance, and several prior warnings by the employer. The employee filed a grievance claiming the evidence was not sufficient to warrant discharge.

Insubordination

- A leadman refused to heed the supervisor's order to drill holes for fixtures in a "picture boat," and allegedly told the supervisor thereafter that he had changed his mind about going home so that he could whip the supervisor that afternoon. He was discharged. The leadman filed a grievance asserting lack of just cause.

- An employee refused to follow a work order that departed from specifications and was discharged. The employee filed a grievance claiming there was not just cause for disciplinary action, since he was following reasonably good judgment.

- An employee was given a legitimate order to mount a decal publicizing the union–employer status on a company car. The employee failed to comply with the order and was given a 10-day suspension. The employee filed a grievance stating that he felt the suspension was an excessive penalty.

- In order to perform repair work to a tachometer generator located in a box atop a hot strip mill, it was necessary for the employer to require that a motor inspector stand on an extension ladder. Because of the height, the motor inspector refused and was disciplined. He filed a grievance claiming that the employer had not shown just cause.

- An employee on two occasions refused to obey a supervisor's order to meet with him, unless a union representative was present at the meeting. As a result, the employee was discharged and subsequently filed a grievance protesting discharge.

- An employee of 31 years' seniority was suspended for his adamant refusal to obey an order of his foreman to return to work. At the time of the incident, the employer refused to let the employee have the assistance of his chief steward. The employee filed a grievance claiming improper suspension.

- A driver refused to allow a dispatcher to drive his truck, although ordered to do so by his superior. There was no question of health, safety, or legality involved. The driver was suspended. He filed a grievance protesting the employer's action.

- The employer scheduled overtime work for several of the employees, including the union steward. The union steward refused to work the overtime, used abusive language toward his supervisor, and instructed other employees not to work overtime. The supervisor directed the union steward to leave the company premises when he refused to work overtime. The union steward refused. The employer then discharged the union steward for insubordination. The union steward filed a grievance claiming he was fired because of his union activity.

Job Participation

- An employer posted a job opening, listing the job involved but not including the classification, wage rate, and shift assignment involved. A request was made that these items be included. The employer refused, claiming no need. The union filed a grievance stating that posted jobs must include characteristics of the position so that the potential bidder would be informed of the exact position he proposed to accept.

Layoff

- A firm became a subsidiary of another company but retained its corporate identity, and the contract it had been operating under with the union remained unchanged. It had been the practice in the past for the employer to continue production during inventory. After becoming a subsidiary, the employer abandoned the practice and put employees not involved in the inventory on temporary layoff. The union, on behalf of the affected employees, filed a grievance stating that the employer did not have the right to unilaterally take such action on the basis of past practice.

Leave

- An employee attended the funeral of his stepfather-in-law on personal leave. He then submitted a claim for funeral-leave pay for attending the funeral of a member of his "immediate family." The pay was refused by the employer. The employee grieved.

- During the time a city fire fighter was on sick leave, he participated briefly in picketing by off-duty fire fighters to protest layoffs of fire-fighting personnel. When he applied for sick-leave pay, the pay was denied by the employer. The employee grieved the employer's action.

- An employee was sentenced to serve a prison term for commission of a felony. Claiming that his leave-of-absence rights had been violated by the company, an authorized member of the union filed a grievance in his behalf. This was denied by the company, based on their claim that only the employee himself could file a grievance. The grievance then became a matter of whether another authorized union member could file a grievance on behalf of a member incarcerated in prison.

- A traffic officer took paid sick-leave time to work for another employer. For this he was discharged. He grieved, claiming lack of just cause.

- An employee called in sick but was later seen by a member of management at a baseball game. The employee was fired for abusing sick leave. The employee then filed a grievance noting that she left the ballgame before it was over because she was sick and that the discipline was excessive.
- An employer failed to pay sick benefits during a strike. The employee affected filed a grievance claim for the sick benefits.
- A teacher was refused paid sick leave by her employer when she was re-hospitalized for postdelivery complications arising from an unwanted pregnancy. She grieved.
- A female teacher who took leave to have a baby wanted the leave applied against her accumulated sick leave. The district denied this claim and applied the leave to maternity leave. The teacher filed a grievance.

Loss

- The tools of an employee, owned by him, were stolen from the company premises. The employee requested replacement by the employer, since the theft had happened on company premises. The employer refused. A grievance was then filed.
- During a strike, several employees lost articles from their lockers through theft. They applied for reimbursement for the lost articles. The employer refused payment, stating that it was not his responsibility. The employees filed a grievance requesting that the employer take the responsibility for what employees considered to be the employer's lack of security precautions.

Lunch Break

- Workers in the plant traveled from work stations to the main plant to eat their lunches. The lunch break had been set at one-half hour. The employer noticed that there was considerable abuse of the half-hour unpaid lunch break and docked workers' time for lateness. A grievance was filed.

Meals

- Under their labor agreement, employees working overtime were given free meals or extra pay. The employer initiated a program in which those working overtime no longer received payments but were provided a free meal cooked in a microwave oven. The employees grieved the employer's unilateral discontinuance of the payment in lieu of a meal.

Notification

- Notification of discharge of an employee was made by the personnel manager, who gave the union president and chief steward a copy of the discharge letter. A grievance was filed protesting the discharge on the grounds that proper notification of the decision to discharge had not been given.

- The contract required a day's notice in lieu of pay in cases of reduction of working force or hours. Without giving proper notice, the company shut down the plant for the Martin Luther King funeral to avoid racial disturbance. The employees claimed pay for the day and grieved when it was not received.

- The contract called for two days' notice of any general layoff. The employer neglected to give the required notice. As a result, the employees affected filed a claim for the two days' pay. The employer denied the claim and a grievance was then filed.

Overtime

- A practice unprotested by the union was to include no more than a maximum of 30 minutes' travel time to a job site for the purpose of computing overtime pay. The actual time involved in traveling to the particular job site was 45 minutes. But based on the unprotested past practice of the union, the employer counted a maximum of only 30 minutes. The employees filed a grievance, claiming the full 45 minutes' travel time.

- An employee felt that another had improperly been given overtime that belonged to him. As a result, the aggrieved employee refused a scheduled overtime assignment. The employer fired the employee under a contract that prohibited strikes, slowdowns, or other interruption of work. The aggrieved employee filed a grievance protesting the discharge.

- Sunday overtime work was discontinued after a department was split. Employees affected filed a grievance protesting loss of the overtime work.

- An employer inadvertently violated the overtime-pay requirements. When it was discovered, he immediately changed the practice to comply. Employees who had not received the proper overtime filed a claim retroactive to the date the mistake was made. The employer refused the claims and paid back to the date the mistake was discovered. The employees filed a grievance.

- A rotation system of assigning overtime was used by the company. An employee failed twice to report for overtime. The employer thereupon refused him overtime the next time his name appeared. The employee grieved.

- City policemen reported for roll call at the beginning of a shift. The union filed a claim for overtime pay for the time involved in the roll call. The city denied the claim. A grievance was filed.

- An employer gave preference to an employee with 889 hours overtime over an employee with 835 hours in a scheduled overtime. The second employee filed a grievance, claiming that the contract required that "low-houred" employees must be given first opportunity.

- An employee repeatedly refused to give a reasonable explanation for refusing to work Sunday overtime. As a result he was given a three-day disciplinary layoff. A grievance was filed protesting mandatory overtime for nonworking days.

Pay

- The union contract calls for compensation of employees while "engaged in meetings with company officials." After an arbitration hearing in which several employees were required as witnesses, the employees requested compensation for lost worktime. The company denied this request, stating that an arbitration is not a "meeting." The employees grieved the situation.
- Union committeemen were paid by the company for time lost from work. When a committeeman filed for pay for committeeman work performed when work was not scheduled, the employer refused to pay. A grievance was filed.
- Several employees at an army installation were engaged in work of a hazardous nature. They were denied hazard pay by their employer. They filed a grievance.
- Employees had to wait for their paychecks several minutes past quitting time. The practice had always been to pay during working hours. The employees filed for extra pay for the time they had to wait. This was denied by the employer, and a grievance was then filed by the employees.
- A teachers' strike was in progress. As a result of weather conditions, the school was closed for two days, during which the teachers continued to strike. At the conclusion of the strike, the teachers requested back pay for the two days the school was closed. The school refused. A grievance was filed.

Plant Rules

- The plant had a posted rule barring employees from eating or drinking during unscheduled breaks. The employees filed a grievance, claiming the rule was arbitrary.
- Company rules relating to safety and conduct had been posted and operative for several years. The company was sold to another interest. Upon assuming control, the new management unilaterally changed the posted rules on safety and conduct. The result was that an employee was suspended for violation of the changed safety rules. The employee filed a grievance stating that the employer did not have the right to unilaterally change the rules and impose disciplinary action without discussion and notice of change to the union.
- An employer made a sudden change in several plant rules relating to disciplinary action. As an immediate result, there was an uneven application of the plant rules. During the process of change, three employees were discharged under the new rules. They filed a grievance stating the discharge was unreasonable and not based on just cause.

Probation

- In computing the probationary period of an employee, the employer excluded Saturday and Sunday work because he claimed this was not part of the basic workweek. The employee filed a grievance claiming the employer should have counted all workdays.
- A probationary employee was fired prior to completion of the probationary period. He filed a grievance disputing the discharge.

Promotion

- A senior employee was disqualified for promotion because of the results of an aptitude test. Since past use of tests had not resulted in junior employees' being promoted over senior employees, he filed a grievance protesting the disqualification.

Rating

- An administrative assistant in the political-science department of a university obtained exceptional ratings in two evaluations. Following the last exceptional evaluation, the assistant was appointed union steward. On the next evaluation, the university employer rated him as average or below average on all value factors of the performance evaluation. The employee charged discrimination.

Reduction of Force

- Contending that it would increase efficiency, an employer gave notice that the company would dissolve two departments and re-form them into a single new department with a reduced number of employees. The union, on behalf of the employees affected, filed a grievance stating that, even though the contract did not specifically prohibit the employer from taking such action, doing so required negotiation with the union on behalf of its members.
- The company found itself with a temporary material shortage and therefore found it necessary to temporarily lay off five employees. The five employees filed a grievance stating that the company could have anticipated delays in delivery of goods and thus prevented the need for the temporary layoff. The five employees asked for pay and allowances to compensate for management's error in not anticipating the shortage.

Reports

- The employer issued an order requiring production workers in the plant to fill out a daily production report. Four employees filed a grievance stating that they were not responsible for such reports under the labor agreement and their job descriptions.

Representation

- An employee was summoned to an office meeting with his foreman. It was alleged that during the course of the meeting, the employee threatened the foreman. As a result, the employee was discharged. The employee then filed a grievance claiming that his grievance representative was not present during the meeting.

Rights

- A teachers' union filed a grievance on its own behalf. The board of education refused to acknowledge the grievance, stating that only grievances on behalf of individual employees could be entertained. The union filed another grievance claiming that the employer had violated the right of the union to grieve over contract violations.

Safety

- Employees at the plant were required to change their footgear to steel-toed safety shoes. These were considerably more expensive, but the employer refused to compensate employees for the extra expense. A grievance protesting the extra cost was filed.

- An employee refused to wear protective equipment in a manner that the company felt proper. He was discharged. He filed a grievance claiming that the company had not shown just cause.

- An employee repeatedly refused to wear a hard hat in the safety-hat area after his supervisor asked, "Where is your hat?" and after he had been given a warning slip. The employer discharged the employee. The employee filed a grievance claiming lack of just cause.

Scheduling

- The employer unilaterally changed the starting time of an engraver etcher from 6 P.M. to 7 P.M. The employee filed a grievance claiming that the employer had failed to comply with notice requirements and priority requirements of the contract.

Seniority

- In taking over a plant, the successor employer reduced the force and, in so doing, laid employees off without regard to seniority. The union, which had the contract with the previous employer, filed a grievance claiming that the new employer was bound by the contract.

- An employee was hired during a strike. He was not able to report to work until the end of the strike and then was not assigned to a specific job until some time later. The employer dated his seniority as of the date of assignment to the specific job. The employee filed a grievance claiming that his seniority in the specific job should have been from the date of hire during the strike.

- A junior employee was hired to fill the position of a laid-off senior employee. The senior employee filed a grievance protesting the action.

- An employee in a bargaining unit was promoted to foreman. At the time, he had accumulated ten years' seniority. Three years after his taking over the foreman's job, there was a reduction of force and he was returned to his old job. The employer dated the employee's seniority at the time of transfer back to the job as if he were a new hire with no accumulation of previous seniority. The employee filed a grievance.

- A strike occurred. After it ended, the employer began to rehire employees without regard to seniority. There was no clause in the contract requiring that seniority be used, but history and conduct supported this. The union filed a grievance.

- A senior employee was on vacation when a new job, that of set-up man, was posted. A junior employee successfully applied for the position. On his return, the senior employee filed a grievance asking that he be given the position on the basis of seniority.

- An employer laid off two mailing employees while retaining employees with lesser seniority. The laid-off employees filed a grievance claiming they had been improperly laid off.

- An employer awarded a job to a junior employee with technical college training instead of a senior employee with less education. The senior employee filed a grievance protesting the action.

- In a reduction in force, the employer allowed a supervisor to return to the bargaining-unit position he had held previously by bumping a less-senior unit employee. The employee bumped filed a grievance claiming improper use of seniority.

Shift

- The company had been operating on a 16-hour schedule with a 7:00 A.M. to 3:00 P.M. day shift and a 3:00 P.M. to 11:00 P.M. evening shift. The company unilaterally changed the schedule to 12 hours, and the shifts to 7:00 A.M. to 3:00 P.M. and 11:00 A.M. to 7:00 P.M. On behalf of the employees in the bargaining unit, the union grieved, stating that the employer did not have the right to change the shift without the approval of the union. The union asked that the schedule and shifts be returned to the earlier arrangement pending negotiations between the union and the company.

- An employer used outside help to perform unit work in the plant. The resulting effect on one employee was to bring about a change in his shift assignment. The employee filed a grievance claiming his shift should not have been changed.

- The employer unilaterally changed a fixed shift based on seniority to a rotation shift for employees. A grievance was filed protesting the elimination of seniority.

Strike

- Employees protesting incentive standards met with their foreman to discuss their grievance. Instead of returning to work after the meeting with the foreman, the employees insisted, over the foreman's direct order to the contrary, upon meeting with the grievance-committee chairman. This was during working hours. The contract had a no-strike clause. The employer discharged the workers for violating the contract. The employees grieved, claiming they had not gone on strike.

- The contract has a no-strike clause. Employees of the company went on strike anyway. Complying with the contract, the union disavowed the strike. The employer suspended the participants of the strike. A grievance was filed stating that the disavowal by the union of the strike was a bar to the employer's suspending employees on strike.

- State law prohibits public employees from striking. A local board of education decided to hold back a projected radio installation in district buses. Subsequently, mass illness was reported by employees. The district took action by disciplining employees for striking within the meaning of the state law. The employees filed a grievance arguing they had not struck in violation of the state law.

Subcontract

- The employer assigned work in the plant that he considered outside the bargaining unit to nonunit employees. The union immediately filed a grievance claiming that the work properly fell within their jurisdiction and therefore should have been performed by the unit employees.

Successor Firm

- The radio and equipment of a taxicab corporation was purchased, but the new owner did not assume the labor contract of the corporation. A dispute occurred involving the old contract, and the new owner refused to recognize the dispute because he felt he was not bound by the old contract. The union filed a grievance claiming that the contract went with the sale of the corporation.

- A business was sold. Under the previous owner, employees had the option of working on holidays at triple time. Under the new employer, employees claimed, they should not be deprived of income previously enjoyed. The new employer refused to be bound by practices of the earlier employer. Affected employees filed a joint grievance.

Surveillance

- The company had installed an incentive system. In order to evaluate the system, the company installed closed-circuit television to study the performance of incentive workers. There was no clause in the contract specifically forbidding such action. The workers being monitored filed a grievance stating that this was not a unilateral right of management under its management-rights clause.

Technical Change

• The employer installed a motorized crane block to technologically improve operation. He also reduced the number of hookers on the operation from two to one. The hooker laid off filed a grievance requesting reinstatement on the grounds that (1) the crane block did not significantly reduce hooker duties, and (2) the increased work load for the remaining hooker required outside assistance.

Time Study

• An employer unilaterally changed the time-study method, resulting in a possible change in earnings. The employees affected filed a grievance protesting the change.

Transfer

• A teacher was removed from a varsity basketball coaching position. The principal stated that this was his prerogative, since the position was outside the labor agreement. The teacher contested this interpretation and filed a grievance.

• The state health department ordered a safety shutdown that resulted in a temporary layoff. The employees laid off were transferred to lower-paying jobs temporarily. They claimed the rate of their regular jobs, which were at a higher rate. The employer denied the claims. A grievance was filed.

Union

• During working hours, an employee asked the union president, who was a fellow employee, for a checkoff card. The employer discharged the union president for improper organizational activities during working hours.

Union Security

• The labor agreement included a union-shop clause. Four members of the union employed in the bargaining unit refused to pay their dues. The union requested that the employer discharge these workers for failure to pay dues. The employer refused. The union brought a charge asking that the company pay the initiation fees and dues of the employees in arrears.

• In a non-right-to-work state, an employer failed to require new employees to join the union within 31 days, although there was a union-shop clause in the labor agreement. The union filed a grievance for compensation for loss of initiation fees and dues resulting from this action.

Vacation

- The contract provides for pro rata vacation benefits during plant shutdowns. Under the past agreements, the former union representative failed to require enforcement of this provision. In the most recent plant shutdown, the plant followed the past practice of ignoring the pro rata vacation-benefit provision. The new union leadership filed a grievance asking that the agreement be upheld under the clear language of the contract.

- An employee voluntarily resigned from his employment. At the time of his resignation, he was assured by a supervisor that he was entitled to pay for unused vacation time even though the contract contained no such guarantee. The employer refused payment of the vacation time. The employee then filed a grievance based on the supervisor's statement.

- The contract required paid vacations. An employee was on his two-week paid vacation when a wage increase took effect. The employer, however, computed the vacation-pay rate at the rate in force at the beginning of his vacation. The employee claimed that the rate increase should have been applied and filed a grievance.

- The contract called for a three-week vacation for 10-year employees. One employee worked nine months of a 12-month fiscal year for 27 years and then worked 12 months each year for four years. The employee was paid for a full 12 months for each of the 31 years. The employee requested the accrued vacation time for the last four years. His employer denied the request. A grievance was filed.

Vending Machines

- As a result of malfunction of vending machines on the employer's premises, several employees lost money to the machines. The employer refused to refund money to employees who claimed they had lost money in the machines. The employees filed a grievance to regain their money.

Wages

- The school board negotiated with the teachers' union a contract that provided for a wage reopener only. At the time the contract was reopened for wages only, the school board contended this meant only annual salaries. The teachers' union contended that "wages only" meant all economic matters— all compensation received by teachers, direct or indirect. A grievance was filed by the union.

- A districtwide labor agreement called for wage rates by established geographic areas. A contractor made an error in his bidding on a job and based it on a wage rate lower than that required for his area. When notified of this by the local business agent, he decided to use workers from his home base. The business agent, in order to maintain the employment for local people, agreed to allow the lower wage rate to be paid for that job. Several months later, the district council of the union, through a complaint by a competitor of the contractor, found out about the wage rate being paid and filed a grievance with the contractors' association requesting that the proper wage be paid retroactively.

Whole, Make Whole

- An employee was improperly terminated. As a consequence of an arbitration decision, he was later reinstated. In making the employee whole for the period of the termination, the employer refused to pay the employee for holiday pay for contract holidays that fell within the termination period. The employee filed a grievance stating that he was not made whole for all back pay and benefits.

Workmen's Compensation

- In computing workmen's-compensation payments to eligible employees, the employer changed the basis of computation from the past policy of using gross earnings to a net-earnings method. This resulted in a reduction of the amount of payments. The employees filed a grievance asking that the former policy be reinstated and retroactive to the time of change of policy.

Workweek

- The boiler workers in the plant were on a rotation shift basis running over a 5-day work schedule. The employer, while maintaining the rotation shift basis, placed the work on a 7-day work schedule. Employees filed a grievance claiming that this was not a reasonable exercise of the employer's rights under the management-rights clause of the labor agreement.
- The employer unilaterally changed the pay week, from Friday through Thursday with one-day-delayed payday, to Monday through Sunday with payday on the following Tuesday. The union claimed this was a negotiable item and filed a grievance.
- The employer unilaterally changed the workweek from Monday through Friday to Tuesday through Saturday. The employees filed a grievance stating that the employer had violated the contract, which required a Monday-through-Friday workweek "wherever possible."

SUMMARY

It can readily be seen that grievances arise from a vast number of circumstances and situations and take on a great variety of forms. Basically, grievances arise because:

1. A particular employee or group of employees has a complaint concerning a problem affecting him or them personally with respect to wages, hours, or other conditions of employment.

2. A union has a complaint that concerns:
   a. All bargaining-unit employees directly and their rights under the labor agreements
   b. The union's and its representatives' status
   c. General matters of contract observance and operation with only an indirect impact on the bargaining-unit employees
   d. Matters of principle vital to the labor–management relationship

3. An employer or association of employers attempts to both protect and en-enforce its rights under the labor agreement.

SELECTED REFERENCES

BNA Editorial Staff, *Grievance Guide*. Washington, D.C.: Bureau of National Affairs, Inc., 1972.

An excellent source of materials on the problems of employers, unions, and workers in the day-to-day business of living under the union contract.

Crane, Bertram R., and Robert M. Hoffman, *Successful Handling of Labor Grievances*. New York: Central Book Company, 1965.

Complete coverage of the various schools of thought as to what constitutes a grievance, methods of classifying and selecting grievance definitions, and what is not a grievance.

Industrial Relations Guide. Englewood Cliffs, N.J.: Prentice-Hall, Inc.

Bi-weekly reports in this continuing series explain the impact of new developments and new trends in collective bargaining and arbitration. The basic text of the looseleaf volume, updated periodically, includes a complete explanation of the nature of labor arbitration, plus descriptions of past awards and thousands of sample contract clauses. "New Ideas" articles are written by outside experts in the field on subjects of interest to management and labor alike.

Labor Relations Guide. Englewood Cliffs, N.J.: Prentice-Hall, Inc.

This service, updated weekly, is particularly useful for business executives, lawyers, personnel managers, and consultants who want information that quickly and easily answers day-to-day labor-relations questions. Important decisions of the National Labor Relations Board, the Equal Employment Opportunity Commission, the Occupational Safety and Health Administration, and the courts are reported promptly in easy-to-understand language. The service includes an explanation of labor laws—Wage-Hour, the NLRA, the Civil Rights Act, Age Discrimination, Reemployment of Veterans, OSHA, garnishment, state labor laws, and others—and provides the full texts of federal laws and executive orders.

Peach, David A., and E. Robert Livernash, *Grievance Initiation and Resolution—A Study in Basic Steel*. Boston: Graduate School of Business Administration, Harvard University, 1974.

An excellent analytical study of the grievance, ranging from environmental influences on problems and their resolution to union influences on the challenge rate and the resolution process, and management influences on the grievance rate and resolution process. The authors conclude with a discussion of interrelationships and their implications for management.

Public Personnel Administration: Labor-Management Relations. Englewood Cliffs, N.J.: Prentice-Hall, Inc.

Focusing on public-sector collective bargaining, this service explains laws, methods, rulings, clauses, and established precedents (including summaries of arbitration awards). Bi-weekly reports provide news of developments in this complex area. Sections of the basic text include "New Ideas," "Collective Bargaining Problems and Answers," "Annotated Public Employment Relations Laws and Regulations," "Union Contract Clauses," and Arbitration Awards Analyzed."

Wage-Hour Guide. Englewood Cliffs, N.J.: Prentice-Hall, Inc.

This volume includes the texts of both the Equal Pay Law and the Wage-Hour Law. Information is provided on who is covered, who is exempt, wages and overtime, child labor restrictions, records-investigations, enforcement methods, government contracts, and related topics. A regular report explains current developments. A "Current Matter" section contains administrative opinions and digests of court decisions.

Contract Administration–
Grievance Procedure

CHAPTER 16

The preceding chapter dealt with the sources and nature of the grievance. This chapter will treat the machinery established to process and resolve grievances, including all the steps short of grievance arbitration. Since grievance arbitration, the last step of the formal grievance procedure, involves a third party and is a judicial rather than a legislative step, it is given separate treatment in Chapter 17.

The main product of collective bargaining as envisioned by the Webbs was the establishment of industrial democracy in the workplace. Labor–management relations would have fallen short of this objective had collective bargaining been confined to the negotiation stage alone; negotiating the terms of the collective bargaining agreement establishes a constitution to guide the parties in their joint relations in the workplace but, as the Webbs recognized, is not enough to fully establish industrial democracy. To be really meaningful, the terms needed to be supplemented with a mechanism by which questions or problems arising in the day-to-day application of the labor agreement may be jointly and peacefully resolved.

In their classic work, *Industrial Democracy*, the Webbs, with their usual foresight, stated:

We must here plunge into a maze of complicated technical detail relating to these industries, each of which has developed its machinery for Collective Bargaining in its own way, and we despair of making the reader understand either our exposition or our criticism unless he will keep constantly in mind one fundamental distinction, which is all important. *This vital distinction is between the making of a new bargain, and the interpreting of the terms of an existing one.* Where the machinery for Collective Bargaining has broken down, we usually discover that this distinction has not been made; and it is only where this fundamental distinction has been clearly maintained that the machinery works without friction or ill-feeling. . . . This, it will be seen, is exclusively an issue of fact, in which both the desires and the tactical strength of the parties directly concerned must be entirely eliminated. For conciliation, compromise, and balancing of expediences, there is absolutely no room. On the other hand, it is indispensable that the ascertainment of facts should attain an almost scientific precision. Moreover, the settlement should be automatic, rapid, and inexpensive. The ideal machinery for this class of cases would, in fact, be a peripatetic calculating-machine endowed with a high degree of technical knowledge, which could accurately register all the factors concerned, and unerringly grind out the arithmetical result.[1] (Italics added)

What the Webbs were talking about has since come to be known as *contract administration.* The vehicle for contract administration is the jointly negotiated grievance procedure.

After a labor agreement has been negotiated and the parties have signified their commitment to its provisions for a specified contract period of one, two, three, or more years, the process of giving meaning to the agreement begins. Management and the bargaining-unit representative *continue, in effect, to bargain collectively on a day-by-day basis* for the length of the contract period. Such bargaining does not involve negotiation of new terms or a new labor agreement, nor is it directed— although by agreement of the parties it can be—at altering the terms already negotiated in the contract. The administration of the agreement on a day-to-day basis is an interpretive process whereby the labor contract is applied, given meaning, and in effect transformed into a "living organism." The grievance procedure is the formal mechanism through which this transition is effected.

Not every day-to-day problem or question that might arise between employees and/or the union and the employer can be anticipated during the period when the terms of the agreement are being negotiated. The complexities of labor–management relations preclude the drawing up of such an all-inclusive, anticipatory labor agreement. Although both parties have sought to anticipate a problem through the negotiation of a particular clause or section of the agreement, they may discover that looking at the same clause or section later, under the pressure of an actual grievance, often results in a shift in their thinking. When negotiating, the parties are motivated by a desire to find an area of compromise in the language of the agreement. As a result, their view of the meaning of a particular clause or phrase or term may not anticipate all the varied

[1] Sidney and Beatrice Webb, *Industrial Democracy* (London: Longmans, Green and Co., 1902), pp. 182–84.

applications to which it might be subject once it is applied. Also, as has been pointed out, the ambiguities in a contract may be deliberate: "The language is purposely indefinite because it is all the negotiators can agree to. Making a section of the agreement ambiguous may represent a decision by the negotiators to 'pass the buck' to those charged with administering the agreement."[2] It is thus that a union representative, responding to a complaint of one of his members, first looks at the particular clause in the agreement in terms of the way or ways it can be used to support the point of view of his aggrieved member. Management will also be looking at the clause in terms of how it may be used to protect its own interests. As a result, what seemed to be a consensus at the time of the joint negotiation may turn into a conflicting interpretation under the pressure of the separate interests and needs of the parties.

The grievance procedure provides management and the union with an institutional mechanism by which to dispose of complaints and charges of contract violation in an orderly and equitable manner. It provides a peaceful means of resolving misunderstandings, permits enforcement of the contract, and minimizes the use of strikes and lockouts. Indeed, industry would be chaotic if the strike or the lockout were the only means available to effect compliance with the contract. As William Whyte succinctly puts it, "If the grievance procedure works, the contract will work. If the grievance procedure does not work, then, of course, the contract does not work, and what you have is really jungle warfare."[3]

Not only is the grievance procedure crucial in vitalizing the agreement through the daily process of contract administration; it also performs an animating role in ensuring industrial democracy in the workplace by means of an open forum through which complaints and grievances may be peacefully resolved. Moreover, as Whyte notes, the grievance procedure

> . . . is a social invention of great importance for our democratic society. . . . Nothing quite like this exists in most countries of the world. On the continent of Europe, for example, unions are organized on a much different basis. They are politically oriented, and the tie of the worker to the local organization, such as it is, is very tenuous indeed. The things we call grievances, if handled at all, are generally handled in other channels. They get out of the plant and into the government sphere. On the other hand, what we have built up here is an essential part of demo-

---

[2] Sumner H. Slichter, James S. Healy, and E. Robert Livernash, *The Impact of Collective Bargaining on Management* (Washington, D.C.: The Brookings Institution, 1960), p. 695.

[3] William F. Whyte, "The Grievance Procedure and Plant Society," in *The Grievance Process,* Proceedings of a Conference (March 23–24, 1956), Labor and Industrial Relations Center, Kellogg Center, Michigan State University, p. 20. (Comment by Ken Bannon.)

cratic society. It is a means whereby the lone individual and the work group can take up their problems, have some means of redress, and furthermore, argue their problems with people who are pretty close to those problems in the plant itself.[4]

Three major areas relative to the grievance procedure are the focus of the remainder of this chapter: (1) the legal framework within which the grievance procedure operates; (2) the substantive features of the grievance procedure—initiator, scope, time limits, steps, costs, and variations; and (3) some helpful hints for successful handling of grievances.

THE GRIEVANCE PROCEDURE AND THE LAW

Private Sector

Although the right to grieve is clearly enunciated in the Taft-Hartley Act, there is no companion provision requiring that the right to grieve be implemented by a formal grievance procedure. Section 201 (c) alludes to such a process but places main emphasis upon a terminal procedure for final adjustment of grievances and/or questions regarding the application or interpretation of agreements. Despite this omission, almost all private-sector labor agreements include formal grievance machinery, owing to the realization by both labor and management that unless they jointly establish a means of internally enforcing the contract terms and an orderly and peaceful means of solving complaints of violations of the agreement, *only chaos and resort to jungle tactics will ensue.* Instead of an instrument of peace, the collective bargaining agreement *deteriorates into an instrument of open war.*

However, while Taft-Hartley does not require the parties to include a negotiated grievance procedure in the labor agreement, it does address itself in other ways to the grievance procedure once such a procedure *is* included in the agreement. Under the terms of Section 9 (a), grievance-procedure structures *must be broad enough* to meet two standards: First, the individual worker must be permitted to present grievances to his employer on an individual basis: "any individual employee or a group of employees shall have the right at any time to present grievances to their employer." Second, any employee has the right

. . . to have such grievances adjusted, without the intervention of the

---

[4] *Ibid.,* p. 11. A.W.J. Thomson also notes that the grievance procedure may perform important secondary functions as a diagnostic device, a medium of communication and consultation, and a means of improving the quality of decision making. A.W.J. Thomson, *The Grievance Procedure in the Private Sector* (New York: New York School of Industrial and Labor Relations, Cornell University, 1947), p. 2.

bargaining representative, as long as the adjustment is not inconsistent with the terms of a collective-bargaining contract or agreement then in effect: Provided further, That the bargaining representative has been given opportunity to be present at such adjustment.

It is sometimes argued that this construction of the law as it relates to the grievance process encourages individual bargaining, provides a vehicle for weakening the practice of collective bargaining, and diminishes the ability of the bargaining agent to act for the entire unit of employees.[5] Offsetting this tendency are several practical considerations that tend to tie the bargaining-unit employee closely to the formal grievance procedure of the agreement and to his union representatives in handling his grievance. First, the majority of employees do not possess the expertise, nor do most employees want to take the time to develop the expertise, to process their own grievances under the terms or language of the contract. Second, there is the peer pressure that belonging to the union brings on bargaining-unit members to show their loyalty by utilizing their own organization to process the grievance. Third, the normal reluctance of the average employee to take on his superiors directly over a violation of the contract is somewhat overcome when he has the union acting as a buffer and an advocate in his behalf. Fourth, if the grievance must be appealed to higher levels of management, with the consequent need for more expert and knowledgeable handling, the union provides greater capability and resources to effectively represent the grievant than the individual employee has using his own resources only. It is for these reasons that, notwithstanding the language of Section 9 (a), most employees with a grievance or complaint will opt to use their collective bargaining representative. Therefore, since the union is a formal party to the negotiated grievance structure of the labor agreement, it follows that most grievances will be processed via the formal grievance procedure of the contract.

Enforcement for most complaints of violations of the agreement proceeds from (1) a settlement of the grievance by the parties at one of the preliminary steps of the grievance procedure, or (2) a settlement through the final step of grievance arbitration. Even though the grievance procedure is in most instances the means used to enforce the terms of the contract, it should be made clear that *the employee is not without alternate means, if needed, to enforce his rights* under the contract. Two other avenues of enforcement are available where the labor agreement has been violated: (1) through the National Labor Relations Board, and (2) through the courts. Where there is no arbitration step in the grievance

[5] Benjamin J. Taylor and Fred Witney, *Labor Relations Law* (Englewood Cliffs, N.J.: Prentice-Hall, 1975), p. 368.

procedure, where an employer tries to force a solution in violation of the contract, or where a union representative refuses to properly represent the employee, *enforcement is possible either through the NLRB by claiming an unfair labor practice, or through the courts by charging a violation of a contractual right.* If a union that holds the position of exclusive bargaining representative of employees declines to process the grievance of a member of the bargaining unit, this is *tantamount to refusing representation,* which constitutes a violation of Section 8 (b) (1) (A) of the National Labor Relations Act.[6] Furthermore, Section 301 of the Taft-Hartley Act allows access to both state and federal courts for suits arising from violations of collective bargaining contracts. This means that "in the absence of an arbitration clause a court can be asked to decide whether to resort to arbitration or to the Courts."[7]

Public Sector

Whereas the NLRA includes no direct injunction requiring a formal grievance procedure in collectively bargained agreements, *there is no such ambivalence under Executive Order 11491.* In EO Section 13 (a), there is the injunction that "an agreement between an agency and a labor organization *shall provide a procedure,* applicable only to the unit, *for the consideration of grievances.*" (Emphasis added.) Section 13 (b) adds grievance arbitration: "A negotiated procedure may provide for the arbitration of grievances."

It should be noted that the grievance procedure of the executive order was not retroactive but was to apply only to new agreements negotiated after August 1971 or to old agreements only when they came up for renegotiation after August 1971.

Although Executive Order 11491 is more forceful in requiring a formal grievance procedure than is the NLRA, it is at the same time more restrictive than the NLRA with respect to the scope of the grievance procedure. In the February 1975 amendments to EO 11491, Section 13 (a) was changed to reflect a recommendation of the FLRC that the coverage and scope of the negotiated grievance procedure be left to the negotiation of the parties except for statutory exclusions. To the original Section 13 (a) was added:

> The coverage and scope of the procedure shall be negotiated by the parties to the agreement with the exception that it may not cover matters for which a statutory appeal procedure exists and so long as it does not otherwise conflict with statute or this Order. It shall be the exclusive

---

[6] Taylor and Witney, *Labor Relations Law,* pp. 368–69.

[7] R.W. Fleming, "Some Observations on Contract Grievances before Courts and Arbitrators," *Stanford Law Review,* Vol. 15, No. 4 (July 1963), 612.

procedure available to the parties and the employees in the unit for resolving grievances which fall within its coverage.

In arriving at this rather flexible approach to the scope of grievance procedures, the emphasis by the FLRC was upon a procedure that would not interfere with the freedom and voluntariness of the bilateral process. The FLRC had considered two alternatives along with this finally approved provision. The first would have changed Section 13 (a) to include grievances arising over agency regulations even though such regulations might be referenced or cited in the agreement. The second would have required that the grievance procedure be the sole procedure available for all grievances, including grievances over agency policies and regulations not included in the agreement, and excluding only those issues subject to statutory appeal procedures. In choosing the more general-language route of the final amendment, which neither includes nor excludes grievances over agency policies and regulations, the FLRC reasoned:

> This would permit the parties to negotiate a grievance procedure with coverage and scope as narrow as that which would be required by the first proposal, or as broad as that which would be required by the second proposal, to revise Section 13. The parties could agree that the negotiated grievance procedure would be the only procedure available for all grievances, including grievances over agency policies and regulations not contained in the agreement, subject only to the explicit limitations of the Order. The parties would be free to expand the negotiated grievance procedure to cover any matters except those which are subject to resolution under statutory appeal procedures.[8]

Other sections of the executive order do circumscribe the matters that might be negotiated upon and incorporated into the agreement. Section 11 (b) provides that

> . . . the obligation to meet and confer does not include matters with respect to the mission of an agency; its budget; its organization; the number of employees; and the numbers, types, and grade of positions or employees assigned to any organizational unit, work project or tour of duty; the technology of performing its work; or its internal security practices.

In addition, Section 11 (a), in setting down the basic collective bargaining responsibility of the parties to meet and confer in good faith, also places a limit on the scope of such bargaining, by adding that the per-

---

[8] U.S. Federal Labor Relations Council, *Labor–Management Relations in the Federal Service* (Washington, D.C.: U.S. Government Printing Office, 1975), p. 42.

sonnel policies and practices and matters affecting working conditions to be considered must be

> . . . appropriate under applicable laws and regulations, including poli-
> cies set forth in the Federal Personnel Manual, published agency
> policies and regulations for which a compelling need exists under criteria
> established by the Federal Labor Relations Council and which are issued
> at the agency headquarters level or at the level of a primary subdivision.
> . . .

Section 12 (a) adds further limitations. It provides that, in the administration of all matters covered by the collective bargaining agreement
between the parties, officials and employees are governed

> . . . by existing or future laws and regulations of appropriate author-
> ities, including policies set forth in the Federal Personnel Manual; by
> published agency policies and regulations in existence at the time the
> agreement was approved; and by subsequently published agency
> policies and regulations required by law or by the regulations of appro-
> priate authorities; or authorized by the terms of a controlling agreement
> at a higher agency level. . . .

What these provisions mean is that, even though the executive order
mandates a negotiated grievance procedure and by the February 1975
amendments has enlarged the possible scope and coverage of such
grievance procedures, EO still falls short of providing one comprehensive procedure for processing all types of grievances, as is the case under
the NLRA. Federal employees are also limited in using the negotiated
grievance procedure by the mandate that certain types of problems
must be pursued through appeal procedures already established by
statute. For example, the negotiated grievance procedure may not provide for grievances "based upon disciplinary actions, because appeals
from 'adverse actions' are subject to Civil Service Commission regulations. Thus, discharge, suspension for more than 30 days, furlough without pay, or reduction in rank or pay cannot be taken through a grievance
procedure negotiated by labor and management."[9]

The following types of problems have been typically dealt with
through separate procedures:

1. Violation of reemployment priority rights—via Civil Service Commission
   and then Board of Review, Civil Service Commission (FPM, Chp. 30:5
   United States Code 3502)

2. Reduction-in-force actions—via Civil Service Commission and then to

[9] William J. Kilberg, Thomas Angelo, and Lawrence Lorber, "Grievance Arbitration Patterns in the Federal Service," *Monthly Labor Review*, November 1972, p. 25.

Board of Appeals and Review, Civil Service Commission (FPM, Chp. 351, 5 USC 3502)

3. Reemployment or reinstatement rights—via Civil Service Commission and then Board of Review, Civil Service Commission (FPM, Chp. 352, 5 USC 2193 [d], 2385 [b])

4. Violation of military restoration rights—via regional director, Civil Service Commission, and then Board of Appeals, Civil Service Commission (FPM, Chp. 353, 5 USC 3551)

5. Performance ratings—via agency review and Board of Review, Civil Service Commission (FPM, Chp. 430, 5 USC 4305)

6. Position classification decisions—via the agency or the Civil Service Commission (FPM, Chp. 511, 5 USC 5112 [b])

7. Denial of within-grade pay increase—via the agency and then the Civil Service Commission (FPM, Chp. 531, 5 USC 5304, 5338)

8. Salary-retention decision—via appeal board of agency if available, to regional director, Civil Service Commission, to Board of Appeals, Civil Service Commission (FPM, Chp. 531, 5 USC 5338)

9. Job-grading decision—via the agency and then the Civil Service Commission (FPM, Chp. 532, 5 USC 5338)

10. Discrimination based on race, color, religion, sex, national origin, or age— via agency director EEO, Board of Appeal of the Civil Service Commission, and review by the Federal District Court (FPM, Chp. 713, Exec. Order 11478, as amended)

11. Discharges or suspension based on national security—via the agency and Civil Service Commission (FPM, Chp. 732, 5 USC 7313, Executive Order 10430)

12. Discharges or suspension based on prohibited political activity—via Civil Service Commission (FPM, Chp. 733, 5 USC 1504, 5, 6, 8)

13. Fitness-for-duty examination—via the agency and then the Civil Service Commission (FPM, Chp. 831, 5 USC 8337)

14. Health-benefits decision—via Bureau of Retirement and Insurance to Civil Service Commission, to Board of Reviews and review, Civil Service Commission (FPM, Chp. 890, 5 USC 8912)

15. Appeals of adverse actions—via agency or Civil Service Commission procedures[10]

Grievance arbitration is also treated somewhat differently in the public sector under Executive Order 11491. Section 13 (b) permits the parties to provide for an arbitration of grievances. Arbitration may be invoked

---

[10] Adapted from Bob E. Repas, *Collective Bargaining in Federal Employment*, 2nd ed. (Industrial Relations Center, University of Hawaii, 1973), pp. 75–89; and Kilberg et al., "Grievance Arbitration Patterns in the Federal Service," p. 30.

only by the agency or the exclusive representative. Either party may file exceptions to an arbitrator's award with the Federal Labor Relations Council, and questions that cannot be resolved by the parties as to whether or not a grievance is on a matter subject to the grievance procedure or grievance arbitration may, by agreement of the parties, be submitted to arbitration or may be referred to the assistant secretary of labor for labor–management relations for decision.

Unfair labor practices also may relate to either the regular statutory appeals procedures or to the negotiated grievance procedure. Section 19 (d) provides that issues that can be properly raised under a regular governmental or statutory appeals procedure may not be raised and processed as regular unfair labor practice complaints. These must be handled through the appeals procedure designated for that type of issue. Unfair labor practice issues that can be raised under the negotiated grievance procedure may, if the aggrieved party so chooses, be raised under that procedure or under the regular unfair labor practice procedure based on Section 19. It is important to remember, however, that if the party chooses one or the other of the two routes—negotiated grievance procedure or the regular unfair labor practice procedure—he may not then appeal through the other procedure. Neither can he use both procedures together. If an issue is processed through a governmental appeals procedure or through the negotiated grievance procedure, the parties may not construe the decision that ensues as an unfair labor practice decision nor as precedent for any other unfair labor practice complaint.

The majority of the states and municipalities, through statutes or orders, have followed the lead of the EO in explicitly authorizing or requiring negotiated grievance procedures. This is in contrast to the NLRA, which is silent on the subject, although by intent it encourages the establishment of grievance procedures. Section 1173-8.0 (f) of New York City's Collective Bargaining Law incorporates the grievance procedure in its statement of policy: "It is hereby declared to be the policy of the City that written collective bargaining agreements with certified or designated employee organizations should contain provisions for grievance procedures." Under the Minnesota state law, Section 179.65 (4), public employees are given the right through their bargaining representative to "meet and negotiate in good faith with their employer regarding grievance procedures and the terms and conditions of employment." Hawaii's Public Employment Relations Act, Section 89-10 (a), states that the negotiated labor agreement "may contain a grievance procedure and an impasse procedure culminating in final and binding arbitration, and shall be valid and enforceable when entered into in accordance with provisions." Finally, it should be noted that many of the state statutes and orders under pressure to find alternatives to strike action have incorporated nontraditional techniques into the grievance procedure. These are treated more fully in Chapter 20.

THE GRIEVANCE PROCEDURE

In 1973, formal grievance procedures were included *in more than 95 percent of private-sector labor agreements,* around 90 percent of the labor agreements covering state and municipal workers, and in excess of 82 percent of the labor agreements covering federal employees. It is fairly safe to assume that as of the present day, close to 100 percent of labor agreements—private, municipal and state, and federal—include formal grievance procedures. Studies show that for the most part, the mechanical aspects of public grievance procedures are found to be similar to those of private procedures. Some areas in which differences have been noted are these: (1) Private- and federal-employee labor agreements have been more specific and more comprehensive than state and municipal agreements; and (2) the scope of the grievance procedure is more limited in the federal, state, and local sectors than in the private sector. Finally, the trend over time has been for grievance procedures, as incorporated into contract language, to become more detailed and formal, not only in the newer agreements of the public sector, "but also in the older established procedures of the private sector."[11] In what follows, the reader is introduced to some of the more common features of grievance procedures by the use of examples from a broad sampling of labor agreements. Where there is a marked difference between public and private grievance procedures, this will be brought out specifically in the illustrations. Otherwise, the examples used are indicative of the common features of grievance procedures, although in detail there are variations, whether in the public or private sector.[12] The illustrations are organized under the following headings: scope, grieving party, steps, expedited procedure, time limitations, recompense for time involved, and variances from standard procedures.

Scope. Provisions establishing the scope or coverage of the grievance procedure fall into two general classifications, limited and unlimited. The BNA notes that the scope of the grievance is included in 68 percent of the labor agreements containing a grievance procedure and that, of these, *81 percent restrict the subject matter of the grievance procedure to the interpretation or application of the contract,* while 18 percent

---

[11] Thomson, *The Grievance Procedure in the Private Sector,* p. 13.

[12] No attempt is made to identify the clauses used as examples of particular contracts. The purpose of the illustrations is to show types of language and procedures, not to personalize the sources. The examples were drawn from a broad cross section of industries plus agreements in the public sector.

allow broad latitude as to what might be appealed to the grievance procedure.

Grievance procedures that are limited in scope usually confine the grievance that might be appealed to specific matters of the labor contract, its interpretation, conflicts between clauses, and the application of the specific terms of the agreement to specific cases. Examples of such a restricted scope are:

- A grievance is a difference of opinion with respect to the meaning and application of the terms of this agreement and/or the respective supplementary agreements.
- The term *grievance* as used herein shall mean disputes arising over the interpretation or application of any of the provisions of this collective agreement, including disputes arising over the termination of the employment of an agent.
- In the event that any difference arises between the company and the union, or any employee, concerning the interpretation, application or compliance with the provisions of this agreement, such differences shall be deemed to be a grievance and shall be settled only in accordance with the grievance procedure set forth herein.
- Grievances, within the meaning of the grievance procedure, shall consist only of disputes about wages, hours of work, and working conditions, as provided in this agreement; about the meaning and application of this agreement; and about alleged violations of this agreement. . . .

Procedures that are less limited in scope allow other types of employee complaints to be processed, such as those conflicts that arise because the contract is silent, or because the issue is too unusual to be covered by the contract, or for any number of other reasons. Illustrations of some of these matters are:

- Grievances pertaining to rates of pay, hours of work, or conditions of employment.
- Any questions or problems which might arise concerning working conditions.
- Should any difference of opinion, controversy, or dispute arise between the parties hereto, such differences of opinion, controversy, or dispute shall constitute a grievance.
- A grievance is a matter of personal concern or dissatisfaction to an employee arising from the terms or conditions of employment, the consideration of which is not covered by other systems for agency review and the resolution of which has not been made at the normal supervisory level. Before a matter of personal concern or dissatisfaction (i.e., a complaint) becomes a grievance within the meaning of this section, the parties hereto encourage attempts at informal resolution as set forth in Section 9 of this article. Employee grievances include, but are not limited to, such matters as:

a. Working conditions and environment.
b. Relationships with supervisors and other employees and officials.
c. Implementation of personnel policies, practices and provisions of this agreement.

- Employee grievances do not include *questions of policy* in the areas itemized above. They may, however, include questions of the application of such policy to an individual employee or to a group of employees.

WHO MAY FILE A GRIEVANCE. It goes without saying that all contracts provide for the initiation of grievances by individual employees or groups of employees. The same privilege is not accorded universally to the management or the union. Sampling of contracts in the private sector by the BNA showed that in 37 percent of the manufacturing-area contracts and 30 percent of the nonmanufacturing-sector contracts, unions were allowed to initiate a grievance. In 26 percent of the manufacturing contracts and 23 percent of the nonmanufacturing, management was allowed to initiate a grievance. Some illustrative clauses are:

- The union and/or any employee or group of employees shall have the right to present a grievance to the company.
- Grievances may be originated by a complaint of an employee or the union.
- Grievances must be initiated by employees (either singly or jointly); *they may not be initiated by the union.* The union may, however, present a grievance on behalf of an employee or employees who request the union to act for them if they are identified by name.
- Grievances may be presented by the company to the local lodge.

STEPS IN THE GRIEVANCE PROCEDURE. Grievance procedures are structured and tailor-made so as to provide a fair hearing for an employee at progressively higher levels of management. Although all procedures are generally similar in this respect, it is obvious that because some firms or agencies are larger, with a more complex management structure, progressive appeal to higher levels of management will involve more steps than the procedures of small and less-complex firms or agencies. Collective bargaining agreements, *while containing many general features in common from one bargaining group to another, must also be tailored in their specific details, primarily work rules, to fit the needs of the specific parties involved.* The same reasoning applies to the specifics of grievance-procedure structure. The number of steps required to achieve the objectives of grievance processing will depend upon such factors as the nature of the bargaining units, past experience in negotiation between the parties, the policies of management and the union, the size of the company and the union, patterns established in similar situations in the industry, the happenstance of personalities and their backgrounds, and any number of other factors that influence the results of a particular contact negotiation. Thus, a perusal of grievance provisions in a wide variety of labor agreements shows anywhere from *two-step procedures to as many as six- or seven-step procedures, if the arbitration step is included. The most common number of steps found in grievance structures is three, and the next most common four.*

The following illustrations of grievance procedures reflect the general features of the step-by-step approach to the resolution of grievance complaints but, of course, do not and are not intended to reflect the specific tailoring of the steps to the needs of each situation. Time requirements at each step are omitted in order to highlight the step sequence to higher levels of appeal.

• Two-Step

If at any time a difference arises between the union and the company regarding the true intent and meaning of a provision of this contract, or a question as to the performance of any obligation hereunder, a conference shall be held between a representative of the union and the company in an attempt to settle said differences. If, after such conferences, the matter is not settled, either party may institute arbitration proceedings.

• Three-Step

Step 1. After the complainant or the union has had an opportunity to become aware of the event complained of, he or the union shall discuss it in person with the appropriate foreman; a member of the workmen's committee may accompany the complainant if he so desires.

Step 2. Present the grievances in writing to the company.

Step 3. Demand arbitration of the grievance if it is arbitrable.

• Four-Step

Step 1. Between the shop steward accompanied by the aggrieved employee, at the employee's discretion, and the overseer of the department.

Step 2. If the grievance is not adjusted after its presentation to the overseer, it shall be reduced to writing, dated and signed by the employee involved and the shop steward. The grievance shall then be discussed between the shop committee for the mill in which the dispute arose and the union business agent on the one side and the representative of the plant (and such assistants as he may desire) on the other side.

Step 3. If the grievance shall not have been adjusted [under Step 2] it shall be taken up between a representative of the union on the one side and representatives of the company on the other side.

Step 4. Any grievance not adjusted may be submitted by either party to arbitration.

• Five-Step

Step 1. The grievance shall be taken up between the employee and his immediate supervisor in an effort to settle the matter. The employee may request his shop committeeman to be present at this time if he so desires.

Step 2. If not adjusted under Step 1, the grievance shall be submitted to the shop steward or to a shop committeeman who shall discuss the matter with the employee's immediate supervisor if either believes the grievance has any merit.

Step 3. If the matter is not thus settled, the grievance shall be reduced to writing and submitted to the plant superintendent, after which it shall be discussed at a meeting of the company and the shop committee where a satisfactory settlement shall be sought.

Step 4. If not adjusted under Step 3, the grievance shall be submitted to higher officials of the company and the union and they shall try to work out a mutually satisfactory settlement.

Step 5. If the grievance is not settled, it shall be submitted to an Arbitration Board.

• Six-Step

Step 1. Between the aggrieved employee and his immediate supervisor, with or without the employee's steward, as the employee elects.

Step 2. Between the aggrieved employee, his steward and the location manager. Upon request of the steward, the Step 2 hearing shall include the representative of the local lodge.

Step 3. Between representatives designated by the local lodge and representatives designated by the district manager. If the company's answer does not resolve the grievance, it shall be reduced to writing by the local lodge.

Step 4. Between representatives designated by the local lodge and representatives designated by the labor relations department of the company.

Step 5. Step 5 may be invoked only at the option of the local lodge which appealed the grievance. Between representatives designated by the grand lodge and representatives designated by the labor relations department of the company.

Step 6. An arbitrable grievance which has not been settled under the above-described procedure may be appealed to arbitration by the grand lodge automotive coordinator or the company.

TIME LIMITATIONS ON APPEAL STEPS. There is considerable variation between grievance procedures as to the time limitations in appealing and receiving answers at each step in the grievance procedure. These range all the way from grievance procedures that incorporate no time limitations or merely state that the grievance should be handled expeditiously at each step, to grievance procedures that are very detailed in stating time limitations at each phase. Then, too, there is considerable variation, even among those agreements with time limitations, as to the length of time established, some extending over a considerable time period and some confining the time sequence to short periods. Four cases are used merely to illustrate the variation one might find among different contracts in the time span from the beginning of the grievance procedure to the final step, if used.

One way of determining time and step sequences in any particular contract situation is to consider two requirements: (1) To gain commitment to final decisions of the parties at lower levels, *the procedures should not be so short as to bypass or ignore important contributors.* (2) *On the other hand, the procedures should not be so long as to make the grievance process unnecessarily cumbersome and time-consuming.* Moreover, while the absence of time limits may have some merit in terms of flexibility and simplicity of the grievance procedure, these are more than offset by the advantages provided by the more timely, systematic, and just treatment of grievances that such time limits help to provide. For illustrative purposes only, several procedures of different lengths are described:

• Example 1

Step 1. No time limit.

Step 2. No time limit.

Step 3. If matter not settled within five (5) days, appeal may then be made to Step 4.

Step 4. Arbitration.

• Example 2

Step 1. Each party recognizes the value of processing grievances promptly.

Step 2. If not settled at Step 1, reduce to writing within twenty-four (24) hours.

Step 3. Appeal to Step 3 may be made if settlement at Step 2 not reached within forty-eight (48) hours. Step 3 grievance meeting to be held within seventy-two (72) hours.

Step 4. If unsettled at Step 3 meeting, then Step 4 meeting to be held within ten (10) days.

Step 5. If unsettled at Step 4, appeal to arbitration must be made within ten (10) days.

• Example 3

Informal—Discuss with foreman within five (5) days of occurrence or knowledge of occurrence.

Step 1. If no satisfactory settlement at informal step within two (2) days, then appealed to Step 1, but no later than three (3) days. Written grievance presented and must be answered within two (2) work days. If unsettled, may be appealed to Step 2 within two (2) days.

Step 2. Must be reviewed by management within four (4) workdays with the union. Company must answer within four (4) workdays of this meeting. If answer unsatisfactory, appeal to Step 3 must be made within four (4) workdays.

Step 3. Parties must meet within ten (10) workdays of appeal. Company must answer within five (5) workdays of meeting. If answer is unsatisfactory, appeal to arbitration must be made within fifteen (15) days.

Step 4. Arbitration.

• Example 4

Step 1. Grievance must be filed within sixty (60) days after it arises. Grievance to be reviewed within fourteen (14) days of submission. Management decision to be made within seven (7) business days of review.

Step 2. If decision unsatisfactory at Step 1, appeal to Step 2 may be made within twenty (20) business days of written notice of management decision at Step 1.

EXPEDITED PROCEDURE. In approximately 74 percent of agreements, there are included special procedures for expediting the handling of the grievance. *Expediting is usually in the form of special time limits, or of starting at a later step in the procedure rather than going through the preliminary steps.* Subjects for which agreements most commonly provide an expedited procedure are *discharges, suspensions, general policy or group grievances, grievances filed by the company, safety or health matters, time study and incentive rates, plantwide or areawide grievances, hiring, issues requiring technical assistance, and benefit plans.* Some illustrations of these special procedures are as follows:

• If the dispute involves a matter of general application, the initial step shall be Step 3. The initial step shall also be Step 3 in any case where the grievance has arisen from the action of an official other than the immediate superior.

• Discharges or disciplinary actions are to be taken to the manufacturing manager. Appeals from his decision are to go directly to Step 3 of the grievance procedure.

- Discharge and discipline matters not settled directly by the manager–industrial relations and the union are to go directly to Step 4.

Costs of Grievance Processing. Fifty-four percent of agreements allow pay for representatives who present, investigate, or handle grievances. Thirteen percent allow pay for time lost by grievants and witnesses during investigation and settlement, including arbitration of grievances. Illustrative of such provisions are the following:

- Where Steps 1 and 2 of the grievance procedure take place during working hours, the company will pay on a straight-line basis for time actually lost by the shop steward, the union committeemen and the employee involved. The company shall not be bound to pay for the time lost in attending Steps 3 and 4 of the grievance procedure.
- Total union group at any [grievance] meeting shall not exceed eight persons. Committee members shall be paid for actual working time while attending such meetings. Time spent in meetings outside working hours shall not be considered as time worked.
- Grievances shall be handled during working hours without loss of pay to the grievance committee, union stewards, or employees involved.

EFFECTIVE GRIEVANCE HANDLING

As with negotiations, the variety of situations that arises in the handling of grievances precludes a formal approach. Each grievance, while similar in some aspects to other grievances, also has its own peculiar characteristics, either as to the details of the problem giving rise to it or as to the personalities involved in it. As a substitute for formulas for effective grievance handling, the reader is given a list of what might be called "grievance-procedure homilies." This list is a composite of the sound kinds of admonition and advice that experience in the field has found essential to successful grievance handling:

Homilies for Management

- Establish clear-cut policies, understood by all supervisors and employees.
- Authority to handle grievances should be given to the supervisor, and the limits of such authority made clear.
- A responsible management representative should provide time for the grievant to tell his/her full story in private and without interruption. Give him/her your full attention. End on a friendly note.
- Show your concern for the grievant's problem by following through promptly on any action required by a settlement.
- No grievance should be considered too trivial for your attention.

Homilies for the Union

- Exercise a firm but fair hand in screening grievances for appeal. A poor grievance results in a lost grievance, a dissatisfied union member, a loss of valuable time, and a waste of union money.
- Take care to distinguish between gripes and grievances.
- Don't let grievances become political issues or let union politics influence your work.
- Level with the grievant on his/her case, and be sure the grievant levels with you. This may save later embarrassment and loss of face.

Homilies for Both Parties

- Be sure information on the grievance is complete and accurate.
- Know your labor agreement; check it often. Remember that it may take on a different meaning when applied to different grievance situations.
- Prepare each grievance as if it were to be appealed and presented before an arbitrator.
- Settlement at the lowest step in the grievance procedure pays off in time, expense, and emotions.
- Keep the grievant fully informed of the course of a grievance.
- Control your emotions. It is not who is right, but what is right. Tantrums, vindictiveness, personal dislikes, provoking the other party, petty jealousies, and high-pressure tactics weaken your case.
- Delay can be costly as well as disruptive. Process grievances with promptness and dispatch.
- Facts! Facts! Facts! Do not base your case on hearsay. Do not allow verbal statements and hearsay testimony to substitute for written proof and first-hand testimony.
- Never horsetrade one grievance for another. Grievance settlements establish precedence. Settlement on grounds other than merit may return to haunt you.
- Accept settlement graciously. Tomorrow you must go back to living with each other.
- Keep adequate written records to ensure consistency and effectiveness.
- Saving face is important to the grievant, the employer, and the union. It can mean the difference between an amicable and a hostile settlement.
- Always use recognized channels. The agreement is your creation. Maintain the integrity of the agreement by religiously following its procedures.
- Remember, the grievance procedure is intended to resolve, not create, conflict.

Remember that these are only checkpoints for grievance handling, generally drawn from the experience of those on the front line; they in no way cover all possible types of problems arising in human relationships. They are indicative of both the nature of the human problems that arise and what seems to work in handling such problems, but it must be remembered that each situation is a combination of different personalities and problems, and no two are exactly alike. The successful handler of grievances must at one and the same time understand contract law and be an expert in human behavior.[13] Too often, those who are in closest contact with the grievance at its origin and have the best chance to solve it at an early stage have neither characteristic, but are in that spot because of technical competence relative to the product or service of the particular business. In these days of comprehensive labor agreements and laws bearing on human rights and dignity, it no longer behooves management to hire supervision for technical competence only. Today's supervisor, besides being technically competent, *must be at least aware of behavioral psychology,* if not a student in the field.

SELECTED REFERENCES

Begin, James P., and Joseph C. Ullman, *Negotiated Grievance Procedures in the Public Sector.* Reprint No. 24, Institute of Management and Labor Relations, Rutgers University, 1971.

> Three articles, two by the authors jointly, including "The Structure and Scope of Appeals Procedures for Public Employees," "The Private Grievance Model in the Public Sector," and "Negotiated Grievance Procedures in Public Employment."

Brandt, Floyd S., and Carroll R. Daugherty, *Conflict and Cooperation.* Homewood, Ill.: Richard D. Irwin, 1967.

> An excellent casebook with major emphasis upon grievance administration. The authors lean heavily upon the many cases in which Professor Daugherty was involved. Provides an excellent format for establishing a learning-experience approach to grievance administration.

Crane, Bertram R., and Roger M. Hoffman, *Successful Handling of Grievances.* New York: Central Book Company, 1965.

> A detailed and thorough coverage of every aspect of grievance handling, from the nature of the grievance to the grievance machinery and labor agreements, and finally ending with the achievement of grievance control and proper grievance handling.

Government Employee Relations Report and *Collective Bargaining Negotiations & Contracts,* by BNA. (See annotated references, Chapter 10.)

---

[13] See Thomson, *The Grievance Procedure in the Private Sector,* pp. 14–19, for a discussion of "What Constitutes a 'Good' Grievance Procedure?" For sample private-sector clauses, complete with the names and locations of the companies and unions that negotiated them, see Prentice-Hall's *Industrial Relations Guide.*

Excellent source material on contract administration in both the private and public sectors.

Industrial Relations Guide. Englewood Cliffs, N.J.: Prentice-Hall, Inc.

Bi-weekly reports in this continuing series explain the impact of new developments and new trends in collective bargaining and arbitration. The basic text of the looseleaf volume, updated periodically, includes a complete explanation of the nature of labor arbitration, plus descriptions of past awards and thousands of sample contract clauses. "New Ideas" articles are written by outside experts in the field on subjects of interest to management and labor alike.

Kuhn, James W., "The Grievance Process," in John T. Dunlop and Neil Chamberlain, eds., *Frontiers of Collective Bargaining.* New York: Harper & Row, 1967.

A thorough discussion of the grievance process as a power base and problems and opportunities in grievance handling.

Labor Relations Guide. Englewood Cliffs, N.J.: Prentice-Hall, Inc.

This service, updated weekly, is particularly useful for business executives, lawyers, personnel managers, and consultants who want information that quickly and easily answers day-to-day labor-relations questions. Important decisions of the National Labor Relations Board, the Equal Employment Opportunity Commission, the Occupational Safety and Health Administration, and the courts are reported promptly in easy-to-understand language. The service includes an explanation of labor laws—Wage-Hour, the NLRA, the Civil Rights Act, Age Discrimination, Reemployment of Veterans, OSHA, garnishment, state labor laws, and others—and provides the full texts of federal laws and executive orders.

Najita, Joyce M., *Guide to Statutory Provisions in Public Sector Collective Bargaining—Grievance Adjustment Procedures.* Industrial Relations Center, University of Hawaii, 1975.

An excellent coverage of grievance-adjustment procedures under state statutes, ordinances, rules, and regulations.

Public Personnel Administration: Labor-Management Relations. Englewood Cliffs, N.J.: Prentice-Hall, Inc.

Focusing on public-sector collective bargaining, this service explains laws, methods, rulings, clauses, and established precedents (including summaries of arbitration awards). Bi-weekly reports provide news of developments in this complex area. Sections of the basic text include "New Ideas," "Collective Bargaining Problems and Answers," "Annotated Public Employment Relations Laws and Regulations," "Union Contract Clauses," and "Arbitration Awards Analyzed."

Rehmus, Charles M., ed., *Developments in American and Foreign Arbitration.* Washington, D.C.: The Bureau of National Affairs, Inc., 1968.

Chapter 1 includes papers delivered at the 1968 meetings of the National Academy of Arbitrators concerning American grievance procedures compared to the British and Canadian.

Taylor, Benjamin J., and Fred Witney, *Labor Relations Law*, 2nd ed., Chap. 15. Englewood Cliffs, N.J.: Prentice-Hall, 1975.

A comprehensive statement of the legal nature of the grievance procedure as it has evolved through the Wagner and Taft-Hartley acts. (See Chapter 21 for the public sector.)

Thomson, A.W.J., *The Grievance Procedure in the Private Sector*. New York: New York State School of Industrial and Labor Relations, Cornell University, 1974.

In pamphlet form, this is a very basic and informative account of the function, development, structure, operation, and problems of the grievance procedure.

U.S. Department of Labor, *Grievance Procedures* (1964) and *Grievance and Arbitration Procedures in State and Local Agreements* (1975). (See annotated references, Chapter 10.)

Wage-Hour Guide. Englewood Cliffs, N.J.: Prentice-Hall, Inc.

This volume includes the text of both the Equal Pay Law and the Wage-Hour Law. Information is provided on who is covered, who is exempt, wages and overtime, child labor restrictions, records-investigations, enforcement methods, government contracts, and related topics. A regular report explains current developments. A "Current Matter" section contains administrative opinions and digests of court decisions.

Werne, Benjamin, *Administration of the Labor Contract*, Chs. 1, 2, and 3. Mundelein, Ill.: Callaghan & Company, 1963.

The author provides a most exhaustive and comprehensive study of arbitral interpretation and application of contract clauses. In his coverage of hundreds of arbitration decisions, the author finds one overriding factor standing out: the importance of precise, clear, and correct language.

Yoder, Dale, and Herbert Heneman, Jr., eds., "Employee and Labor Relations," *ASPA Handbook of Personnel and Industrial Relations, PAIR*. Washington, D.C.: Bureau of National Affairs, Inc., 1976.

An excellent account of the process of contract administration, approached positively by K. L. Sovereign of Hoerner-Waldorf Corporation and Mike Boganno of the University of Minnesota.

Contract Administration–
Grievance Arbitration

CHAPTER 17

In Chapter 3, the point was made that in the last decade, the statement
collective bargaining is an institution in its own right has taken on real
and unmistakable meaning. It now seems appropriate, in view of the last
few years' activity, to add that *grievance arbitration has also come of age.*
A president of the prestigious National Academy of Arbitrators, Bert L.
Luskin, succinctly stated his own point of view:

> Arbitration has come of age and with it have come the carpers, snipers,
> and sensation seekers. With one notable exception, each and every attack
> on the process and those who administer it has come from persons and
> groups who have absolutely no knowledge of the process, its history, its
> purpose, and its aims.
>
> . . . I do not believe, however, that there has been a single proposal
> advanced that can serve as a worthy substitute for honest, effective ad-
> ministration of good grievance procedure or the arbitration process.[1]

Although the coming of age of grievance arbitration received its stim-
ulus under the War Labor Board policy of World War II,[2] requiring the
adoption of grievance-arbitration clauses in labor agreements, this distinctive use of arbitration in concept is not new. The Webbs, as already
noted, recognized early the need for a judicial approach to problems of

---

[1] Bert L. Luskin, *Arbitration Comes of Age* (Amherst: Labor Relations and Research Center, University of Massachusetts, 1967), pp. 1, 8.
[2] For a full account, see Paul Prasow and Edward Peters, *Arbitration and
Collective Bargaining* (New York: McGraw-Hill, 1970), Chap. 1. U.S. Supreme
Court decisions such as the Trilogy also added to the impetus given by the WLB
activities. *Ibid.,* Chap. 13.

contract interpretation. In their monumental study, *Industrial Democracy*, they noted:

> . . . This vital distinction is between the making of a new bargain and the interpreting of the terms of an existing one. Where the machinery for Collective Bargaining has broken down, we usually discover this distinction has not been made. . . . *This, it will be seen, is exclusively an issue of fact, in which both the desires and the tactical strength of the parties directly concerned must be eliminated.* . . . It is indispensable that the ascertainment of facts should attain an almost scientific precision. Moreover, the settlement should be automatic, rapid, and inexpensive.[3] (Emphasis added)

And as related in Chapter 2, an agreement resulting from the settlement of the Cloakmakers' strike of 1910 established, among a number of other important provisions, a board of arbitration, one representative from each side and attorneys from the two groups. The board was charged with considering and settling all grievances, and its rulings were to be final and binding.

Recognition of the need for distinction between the handling of disputes over new contract terms and disputes arising from interpretation of the contract was also recognized early in the railroad industry. The Newlands Act of 1913 first made the distinction. The Transportation Act of 1920 continued the distinction by authorizing a system of regional boards of adjustment on each railroad, to which disputes involving contract interpretation could be referred if unsettled at the local level. Under the Railway Labor Act, as originally established, the twofold division—between disputes over changes in the contracts and disputes involving interpretation of the contract or arising from disciplinary action—was continued. The Railway Labor Act of 1926 included sections authorizing the establishment of boards of adjustment to deal with disputes involving interpretation of the contract. This was followed in 1934 by amendments to the act, which replaced the regional boards of adjustment with a permanent adjudicating agency, the National Railroad Adjustment Board.[4] It was from such a background that the War Labor Board activities of World War II created the impetus for the broad usage of grievance arbitration today.

In this chapter, use of the term *arbitration* is confined to its use in conjunction with the grievance procedure. Thus, the term *grievance arbitration* is used to describe the special function of arbitration as a

---

[3] Sidney and Beatrice Webb, *Industrial Democracy* (London: Longmans, Green and Co., 1902), pp. 182–84.

[4] Reed C. Richardson, *The Locomotive Engineer, 1863–1963* (Ann Arbor: Bureau of Industrial Relations, University of Michigan, 1963), pp. 410–12.

part of the contract-administration process. Moreover, grievance arbitration refers to voluntary rather than compulsory arbitration—that is, the use of arbitration as a final appeal step in the grievance procedure through the voluntary agreement of the parties. This voluntary agreement becomes a part of the language of the negotiated agreement and therefore a contractual obligation of the parties for the term of the agreement. This use is in contrast to *compulsory arbitration,* which is imposed upon the parties rather than resulting from their voluntary agreement. Distinctions will also be made among various constructs of voluntary arbitration, such as *single-arbitrator* arbitrations, *tripartite board* of arbitration, *ad hoc* arbitration, and *permanent* arbitration (single arbitrator or panel of arbitrators).

The use of a quasi-judicial process such as grievance arbitration indicates a recognition by the parties that more is to be gained by a judicial solution to problems of contract interpretation than by resorting to such overt actions as lockouts and strikes. In adopting grievance-arbitration clauses in their contracts, the parties are agreeing under contract that this process will be followed in lieu of the right to lock out or to strike. But it is even more than this. The acceptance of grievance arbitration is an act of support for the concept of self-government in the workplace and an act of faith in the free-enterprise concept, since the probable alternative to self-government is government intervention in the affairs of both parties.

A measure of the broad acceptance of grievance arbitration in matters of contract interpretation and administration may be seen in the usage statistics for both the public and private sectors of the economy. In the private sector, negotiated grievance procedures, including clauses providing for grievance arbitration, are almost universally prevalent. A recent study based on agreements between agencies and unions in the federal sector found, in the LAIRS (Labor Agreement Information Retrieval System) file, that as of May 1, 1975, 90 percent of the agreements, covering 93 percent of the federal employees, contained provisions for grievance arbitration.[5] In the state and local sectors, nine out of ten agreements between government organizations and unions contained provisions for grievance arbitration.[6] The trend in federal-, state-, and local-sector agreements toward duplication of the prevalence of arbitration procedures in private-sector agreements is clear, and further emphasizes the coming of age of grievance arbitration in labor agreements.

It is the purpose of this chapter to complete the discussion that began

---

[5] *Negotiated Grievance Procedures and Arbitration in the Federal Government,* U.S. Civil Service Commission, November 1975, p. 1.

[6] *Grievance and Arbitration Procedures in State and Local Agreements,* U.S. Department of Labor, Bureau of Labor Statistics, Bulletin 1833, 1975, p. 1.

in Chapter 15 with the *grievance* and continued in Chapter 16 with the *grievance procedure,* by considering the nature and mechanics of *grievance arbitration* as the terminal step in the grievance procedure. First to be considered is the legal environment within which grievance arbitration operates in both the private and public sectors. Next, a detailed examination is made of types of language in contracts directed to all aspects of grievance arbitration. The contract must also be considered as a factor in the overall legal environment of grievance arbitration. Finally, as in the chapters on negotiation and grievance procedure, some selected bits of advice in the form of arbitration homilies are noted as a way to be effective in presenting arbitration cases.

LEGAL ENVIRONMENT

The Courts

The legal environment of grievance arbitration is a matter of law resulting from court decisions, from statutes, from executive orders, and from the trade agreement. In the discussion in Chapter 6 of arbitrators as third parties to the collective bargaining process, the legal status of grievance-arbitration decisions was explained. The decision of the arbitrator is not only final and binding by contractual agreement but may be enforced through appeal to the courts. It may be overturned by the courts only if it involves a misuse of authority or procedural error by the arbitrator. The courts do not inquire into the reasoning of the arbitrator or the decision based upon the reasoning. Court inquiry is confined to whether or not the arbitrator has exceeded or abused his authority. Justice William H. Douglas, writing the majority opinion in the "Trilogy" decision of the Supreme Court, clearly stated the case for private arbitration in collective bargaining. The flavor would be lost by any attempt to paraphrase. On the matter of the equity of grievance claims, the Court stated:

> The question is not whether in the mind of a court there is equity in the claim. Arbitration is a stabilizing influence only as it serves as a vehicle for handling every and all disputes that arise under the agreement.
> . . . The function of the court is very limited when the parties have agreed to submit all questions of contract interpretation to the arbitrator. It is then confined to ascertaining whether the party seeking arbitration is making a claim which on its face is governed by the contract. Whether the moving party is right or wrong is a question of contract interpretation for the arbitrator. In these circumstances the moving party should not be deprived of the arbitrator's judgment, when it was his judgment and all that it connotes that was bargained for.

The courts therefore have no business weighing the merits of the grievance, considering whether there is equity in a particular claim, or determining whether there is a particular language in the written instrument which will support the claim. The agreement is to submit all grievances to arbitration, not merely those the court will deem meritorious.[7]

The Court then made clear its refusal to review the merits or equity of an arbitration award:

The refusal of courts to review the merits of an arbitration award is the proper approach to arbitration under collective bargaining agreements. The federal policy of settling labor disputes by arbitration would be undermined if courts had the final say on the merits of awards.
. . . As we there [*American Manufacturing Co.* case] emphasized, the question of interpretation of the collective bargaining agreement is a question for the arbitrator. It is the arbitrator's construction which was bargained for; and so far as the arbitrator's decision concerns construction of the contract, the courts have no business overruling him because their interpretation of the contract is different from his.[8]

Finally, the Court outlined the situation under which it would review an arbitration case:

. . . Nevertheless, an arbitrator is confined to interpretation and application of the collective bargaining agreement; he does not sit to dispense his own brand of industrial justice. . . . When the arbitrator's words manifest an infidelity to this obligation, courts have no choice but to refuse enforcement of the award.[9]

Statutory and Executive Order

It is not only the courts that have addressed themselves to the legal meaning and parameters of grievance arbitration. By statute and executive order also, the use of grievance arbitration has been not merely encouraged but made a part of public policy. This may be witnessed in the Railway Labor Act of 1926, in the provisions of the Labor Manage-

---

[7] *Steelworkers* v. *American Manufacturing Co.*, 363 U.S. 564 (1960).

[8] *Steelworkers* v. *Enterprise Wheel and Car Corporation*, 363 U.S. 593 (1960). Similarly, the National Labor Relations Board, although not going quite so far, has adopted the policy of deferring to arbitration awards involving conduct allegedly consisting of both an unfair labor practice and a violation of contract, if certain specified conditions have been met. See Benjamin Aaron, *Contemporary Issues in the Grievance and Arbitration Process: A Current Evaluation,* reprinted from *Collective Bargaining Today* (Washington, D.C., Bureau of National Affairs, Inc., 1971), p. 163.

[9] *Ibid.*

ment Relations Act of 1947, in Executive Order 11491 of 1969 as amended, and in state statutes.

As noted earlier, adjudication of appealed grievances is a process of long standing in the railway industry. The Railway Labor Act, in Section 3 of Title I, provides for the establishment of a "National Railway Adjustment Board." In Section 3, under Subsection (i), the nature of the work to be handled by the adjustment board is delineated:

> (i) The disputes between an employee or group of employees and a carrier or carriers growing out of grievances or out of the interpretation or application of agreements concerning rates of pay, rules, or working conditions, including cases pending and unadjusted on the date of approval of this Act, shall be handled in the usual manner up to and including the chief operating officer of the carrier designated to handle such disputes; but, failing to reach an adjustment in this manner, the disputes may be referred by petition of the parties or by either party to the appropriate division of the Adjustment Board with a full statement of the facts and all supporting data bearing upon the disputes.

If a deadlock occurs on the board with respect to the settlement of a case, the act provides further that the board shall select a neutral person "to be known as 'referee,' to sit with the division as a member thereof and make an award." The act further provides that the awards of the adjustment board "shall be final and binding upon both parties to the dispute, except insofar as they shall contain a money award" and may be enforced through the district court of the United States, where the findings of the board "shall be prima facie evidence of the facts therein stated. . . ."

In the private sector (excepting Railway Labor Act coverage), the Labor Management Relations Act of 1947 supports a terminal step for grievance appeals as a matter of public policy. As a part of the charge to the Federal Mediation and Conciliation Service, Section 203 (d) states:

> (d) Final adjustment by a method agreed upon by the parties is hereby declared to be the desirable method for settlement of grievance disputes arising over the application or interpretation of an existing collective-bargaining agreement. The [Mediation] Service is directed to make its conciliation and mediation services available in the settlement of such grievance disputes only as a last resort and in exceptional cases.

The LMRA also makes clear that one of the obligations the government assumes in promoting industrial peace is to use its facilities to furnish assistance to employers and the representatives of the employees in "formulating for inclusion within" their agreements provision for "final adjustment of grievances or questions regarding the application or interpretation of such agreements. . . ."[10]

10 LMRA, Title II, Section 201 (c).

Nor has the government failed to encourage the use of a terminal procedure for appealed grievances among federal employees. Executive Order 11491 as amended repealed the previous provision under EO 11491, providing for voluntary use of advisory arbitration in appealed grievance situations, and substituted authority for final and binding arbitration. Section 13 (b) states that a "negotiated procedure may provide for the arbitration of grievances over the interpretation or application of the agreement, but not over any other matters. Arbitration may be invoked only by the agency or the exclusive representative."[11] The result, as noted earlier, was a rapid increase in the incorporation of binding arbitration clauses in negotiated agreements. However, one notable difference in the treatment of grievance arbitration in the private sector should be noted. In the private sector, decisions of arbitrators can be appealed only to the courts, and then only if the arbitrator has exceeded his authority. The executive order parts from this appeal procedure and states that in the federal sector, "Either party may file exceptions to an arbitrator's award with the [Federal Labor Relations] Council, under regulations prescribed by the Council."[12]

LEGAL FRAMEWORK—THE LABOR AGREEMENT

The previous discussion, whether referring to congressional, court, or executive-branch action, has stressed one point: uniform support for a terminal step in the grievance procedure—arbitration—that permits the process to operate with minimal interference from the outside except for matters irrelevant to the contract or where authority under the contract has been abused or exceeded by the arbitrator.

---

[11] Three points added by the 1975 amendments to EO 11491 should be noted: (1) Where arbitration is included as the terminal step, it, along with the other steps, becomes the exclusive procedure available to the parties and the employees in the unit for resolving grievances that fall within its coverage. (2) Questions over whether or not a grievance is on a matter for which a statutory appeal procedure exists are to be referred to the assistant secretary of labor for decision. (3) Other questions as whether or not a grievance is on a matter subject to the grievance procedure in an existing agreement, or is subject to arbitration under that agreement, may by agreement of the parties be submitted to arbitration or may be referred to the assistant secretary for decision. EO 11491, Sections 13 (a) and (d).

[12] For regulations and forms, write the offices directly. Where an appeal from an arbitrator's decision has been made to the FLRC and it appears that the award has violated applicable law, appropriate regulation, or the EO, the Council, under its rules, will grant review of the award. For example, should the Council find that an award violates the provisions of Title 5, *United States Code*, or that an award violates the regulations of the Civil Service Commission, or that an award violates Section 12 (b) of the EO, the Council would modify or set aside the award. *Labor-Management Relations in the Federal Service*, United States Federal Labor Relations Council, FLRC–75–1, 1975, p. 44.

Attention now turns to the collective bargaining agreement and grievance arbitration. The purpose of this section is to inform the reader about the manner and the language by which the agreement, a legal document, incorporates the terminal step of arbitration into the formal grievance procedure. Emphasis is not upon the union or industry where the particular clause originated, but upon the basic language and construction of grievance-arbitration clauses. The illustrations used are ordered somewhat chronologically to the grievance-arbitration procedure, so as to follow step by step through the entire process from the request for arbitration to the final decision of the arbitrator. This outline is not exhaustive of all variations in grievance-arbitration provisions but is indicative of the general language and structure of such provisions.

Time Limits on Request for Arbitration

Following the practice of setting time limits in moving from one step of the grievance procedure to another, most agreements set a definite time limit within which the grieving party must request arbitration. As the following examples indicate, this time limit may vary considerably.

- If the grievance is not settled, either party may, within 15 days after the reply of the Director is due, by written notice to the other, request arbitration.
- If no satisfaction has been reached in the first two steps, then the grievance may be submitted to arbitration upon written notice within thirty days after delivery of the Company's Second Step answer.
- If such efforts fail to produce a mutually satisfactory understanding, the Council [labor organization] may, within six (6) months following the date of the occurrence or situation which is in dispute . . . be referred to arbitration. . . .
- Any grievance which remains unsettled after having been fully processed . . . may be submitted to arbitration . . . provided such request is made within 60 days after the final decision of the Company has been given. . . .
- Within and no later than one (1) year after the Union's notice of intent to arbitrate a grievance has been made . . . the Union may notify the American Arbitration Association to proceed with the selection of an Arbitrator under its Voluntary Labor Arbitration rules; provided the Union shall not be deemed to have forfeited its grievance by reason of its failure to notify the Association. . . .

What May Be Submitted to Arbitration

In most instances, the issues referable to arbitration are identical to issues subject to the grievance procedure or are put in general terms as being matters covered by the contract. In some instances, however, the parties have specifically excluded certain issues from the arbitration procedure.

• The provisions of this Article [Arbitration] shall be applicable only to discipline or termination grievances and to grievances involving disputes concerning the application or interpretation of this contract or the application or the interpretation of the business practices, rules, regulations, now or hereafter in force in accordance with this contract. . . .

• The Umpire shall have no power to . . . establish or change any wage; nor to rule on any dispute . . . regarding Production Standards. The Umpire shall have no power to rule on any issue or dispute arising under the Waiver Section or the Pension Plan, Insurance Program and Supplemental Unemployment Benefit Plan Section, except with respect only to the question of whether a discharged employee should receive a supplemental allowance. . . .

• Grievances not concerning the application of the provisions of this Contract and grievances concerning general rates of pay shall not be arbitrable.

• Any dispute, difference, disagreement or controversy of any nature or character, whether or not a grievance between the Union and Company which has not been satisfactorily adjusted . . . shall be promptly referred to arbitration. . . .

• In the event that parties shall be unable under the Grievance Procedure herein provided, to resolve any dispute growing out of the application or interpretation of any provisions of this Contract, such dispute shall be submitted to arbitration upon the sole issues of interpretation or application. . . .

• [Public sector] It is agreed that arbitration of grievances only applies to the interpretation or application of this agreement. Arbitration does not extend to the interpretation or change of the agency or higher regulations or policy. Arbitration does not extend to grievances filed under agency procedures.

A good indication of the relative numbers of different types of issues appealed to arbitration may be gathered from the FMCS report on numbers of closed arbitration-award cases reported to the service for the fiscal year 1975. Total cases amounted to 5,243.[13]

GENERAL ISSUES
    (Overtime other than pay, Seniority, Union Officers, Strikes and lockout, Working conditions, Discrimination, Management Rights and Work Scheduling.)   26%
ECONOMIC: WAGE RATES & PAY ISSUES
    (Wages issues, Rate of pay, Severance pay, Reporting, Call-in and call back, Holidays, Vacations, Incentive, Overtime.)   14%

[13] Federal Mediation and Conciliation Service, *27th Annual Report, Fiscal Year 1975.*

FRINGE BENEFIT ISSUES	
(Health & Welfare, Pensions, Other.)	3%
DISCHARGE & DISCIPLINARY ISSUES	35%
TECHNICAL ISSUES	
(Job posting and bidding, Job Evaluation.)	5%
SCOPE OF AGREEMENT	
(Subcontracting, Jurisdictional disputes, Foreman, Supervision, Mergers, Consolidations, Other.)	5%
ARBITRABILITY OF GRIEVANCES	
(Procedural, Substantive, Other.)	9%
NOT ELSEWHERE CLASSIFIED	4%

Who May Request Arbitration

Although it may seem a simple matter, agreements do vary as to who—the union, the employer and/or the employee—may initiate arbitration. Employee initiation unilaterally is the exception rather than the rule, for a very simple reason: Arbitration is costly and time-consuming. As a result, the union either retains to itself the right to request arbitration or requires that an employee initiating arbitration have its approval. In a few instances, employees may take the initiative alone.

- No individual employee himself may invoke Step 4 [arbitration].
- . . . such matters thus arising may be submitted to arbitration at the request of either the Agent or Union, or both.
- If the union or the Town is not satisfied with the decision of the Personnel Board, it may . . . submit grievance to arbitration.
- Any and all matters in dispute . . . which have not been adjusted pursuant to the procedure therein provided, shall be referred to arbitration. . . .
- [Public sector] If the employee or union is dissatisfied with such decision, he or the union may request arbitration. . . .

In the federal sector, the question of who may initiate arbitration is established by EO Section 13 (b), "Arbitration may be invoked only by the agency or the exclusive representative."

Selecting the Arbitrator

Agreements vary in two general ways in selection of the arbitrator: (1) the method of selection, and (2) the type of arbitration—ad hoc single arbitrator, permanent arbitrator, tripartite arbitration board, or some other variation.

- The dispute shall then be submitted for final and binding determination to a single arbitrator, who shall be such person as may be mutually agreed upon.

- [Public sector] The question in dispute shall then be referred to an arbitrator selected by the parties from a panel or panels submitted by the American Arbitration Association, provided that the parties may mutually agree on a different method of selecting an arbitrator than that herein set forth.

- The arbitrator shall be agreed upon by the Local Management and the Regional Director. If they cannot agree on an arbitrator . . . the moving party may request the Federal Mediation Service to name seven (7) arbitrators. The arbitrator shall be selected from such list in the following manner:

  (1) Within ten (10) calendar days from receipt of the list of arbitrators the Union or the Company . . . shall strike the names of three (3) on this list of seven (7) arbitrators;

  (2) The other party shall then strike three (3) names within the next ten (10) calendar days; the remaining name shall be the arbitrator.

- The parties shall jointly request the Director of the FMCS to submit a list of five (5) arbitrators. From this list the Grand Lodge Automotive Coordinator shall first strike three names. The Company shall then select the arbitrator from the remaining two names.

- . . . if the parties cannot agree upon any member of such list the Arbitrator shall be designated by the head of said Service [FMCS].

- In the event that the first two arbitrators are unable to agree on the appointment of the third arbitrator, then they will, together, ask the American Arbitration Association for a list of five persons, each fit to act as a neutral arbitrator. The names of these persons shall be arranged in alphabetical order upon two sheets of paper. The Company and the Union shall each take one sheet and cross out not more than two names. The first name not crossed out on both lists shall be the third arbitrator. . . .

- In the event that these two [employer–union-representative board] are unable to reach a decision within seven (7) days, then in that event a third person shall be chosen by the committee to act as an arbitrator and chairman of the committee. This committee shall act as a board of arbitration and the decision of such board shall be final and binding upon the parties to this agreement.

- The parties shall select a permanent arbitrator who shall serve subject to conditions mutually specified by the parties in agreement with the arbitrator.

- The impartial chairman shall have only the functions set forth herein and shall serve for one year from date of appointment provided he continues to be acceptable to both the Union and the Corporation.

- [Public sector] Such arbitration shall be conducted by an arbitrator designated from a standing panel of three (3) arbitrators maintained by the Office of Collective Bargaining in accordance with applicable law, rules, and regulations.

- The third arbitrator [neutral] shall be chosen from the seventeen-man permanent panel agreed to by the parties by alternately striking names until one remains and he shall be immediately notified.

- The question as to which party will strike first shall be determined by the toss of a coin.

In private-sector agreements, both the Federal Mediation and Conciliation Service and the American Arbitration Association are used widely as a source of names of arbitrators who, after being investigated and approved, have been placed on their arbitration panels. In the federal sector, the FMCS is used heavily as a source of arbitrator names; in the state and local sectors, almost 90 percent of the agreements call for use of either state or local labor agencies or the American Arbitration Association. Complete information on the AAA and FMCS may be obtained by writing to these organizations.

Prehearing Presentations

In most instances, the matter of submission of prehearing material or statements is left to the predilection of the parties or the desires of the arbitrator. In some cases, the parties choose to make these a formal contract commitment.

- The parties shall by mutual agreement select an arbitrator and shall execute a submission agreement. If the parties fail to agree on a joint submission each shall submit a separate submission and the arbitrator shall determine the issue or issues to be heard, provided that said issue is arbitrable in accordance with this Section.
- The charging and defending parties shall prepare brief written statements of the grievance which outlines the respective positions of the parties and shall deliver such statements to the Arbitator and the other party at least seven (7) calendar days prior to the arbitration hearing.
- The Union and the Employer shall prepare a written submission agreement which shall be presented to the Board. The submission agreement shall specify the issue in dispute and the section or sections of the Agreement that are involved. In the event that the parties cannot agree on a joint submission agreement, then each party shall make its submission separately and supply the other party with a copy of such separate submission.
- [Public sector] Following selection of the arbitrator and his acceptance, the parties will prepare a joint letter submitting the matter in dispute. The joint letter of submission shall stipulate that the arbitrator, in arriving at his award, shall be limited to the interpretation or application of this agreement or agency policy and regulations; and shall not extend to changes, or proposed changes, in the Agreement, policies or regulations. The letter may contain mutually agreed-upon stipulations of fact and may be accompanied by documents the parties mutually agree should be submitted to the arbitrator prior to the hearing. Either party may submit pre-hearing and/or post-hearing briefs, provided a copy of such briefs is furnished the other party.

Arbitrability

A question that is important from time to time is whether the issue submitted is arbitrable within the agreement or the authority of the arbitrator. This may involve either procedural matters or substantive matters. Procedural matters are usually related to improper procedures through the preceding grievance steps or exceeding the time limits for appeals. Substantive matters usually refer to the type of issue being appealed to arbitration. In the private sector, the only appeal route over a disputed issue of arbitrability is to the courts. In the federal sector, a regular appeal process is established to the assistant secretary of labor. Appeals to the courts in the private sector over an arbitrability issue has resulted more recently in the courts' deferring, at least in the first instance, to the arbitrator himself. The reasoning behind this is "that this issue is itself a dispute between the parties to be resolved through the procedure voluntarily established by them."[14]

- In the event that either party takes the position that a certain matter is not arbitrable, the question of arbitrability shall be submitted to arbitration together with the dispute on the merits of the matter before the arbitrator.
- The arbitrator shall have exclusive authority to determine whether he has jurisdiction over any matter submitted to him for arbitration. Any case appealed to the arbitrator on which he determines he has no power to rule shall be referred back to the parties without decision or recommendation.
- [Public sector] Questions that cannot be resolved by Union or Management as to whether or not a grievance is on a matter subject to arbitration under this Agreement may be referred to the Assistant Secretary of Labor for decision.[15]
- Failure of the charging party to act within the applicable time limit specified for any step in the grievance procedure or the time limit herein above specified [arbitration] will constitute waiver of the charging party's right to further consideration of the case.
- In the absence of a written request for arbitration within 15 days after receipt by the union of the third step answer, the grievance shall be settled in accordance with the company's answer.

The Hearing

In most instances, the time, place, and conduct of the hearing are worked out by the parties and/or the arbitrator. Since the hearing is a quasi-

[14] Arnold Zack, *Understanding Grievance Arbitration in the Public, A Report to the Division of Public Employee Labor Relations,* United States Department of Labor, 1974, p. 9.

[15] Most of the reported cases have been submitted voluntarily to the arbitrator rather than to the assistant secreary of labor.

judicial process, less formal than a regular court session and not confined to the strict rules of procedure and evidence of the courts, the detailing of the hearing in the contract becomes rather difficult and, for good reason, is not often resorted to. One of the advantages of the arbitration process in lieu of court action is its viability and flexibility to respond to the human problems of the work relationship, as well as the contractual and legal problems. At the close of a hearing, the parties do not simply walk away from each other. The next day, they must continue to live with each other. The greater flexibility and procedural permissiveness of the arbitration process allow it to be tailored somewhat in each hearing to both the legal problem and the employer–employee problem, although consideration of the employer–employee problem must be within the allowable parameters of the legal problem.

Each arbitrator has his/her own way of conducting a hearing, but the general procedures are similar. The arbitrator will usually open the hearing for settling of any preliminary issues that need to be attended to, such as agreement on the issue to be arbitrated, permission for publication of the decision, the format to be followed, whether witnesses are to be sworn, and any other procedural matters of importance to the arbitrator or the parties. This is followed by a request that the parties make an initial statement of the issue as they view it and of the general context of their case. Usually, the grieving party will be asked to go first, unless the case involves a discharge or discipline case, in which the burden of proof is upon the employer to show "just cause." In the latter type of case, the arbitrator will usually have the employer start first.

Following the opening statements, the parties, in the same order, are permitted to proceed with their full case, including witnesses and exhibits to be presented in support of their positions. The choice of when to introduce exhibits is a matter of party preference. Some introduce them at the beginning and then refer to the exhibits as witnesses or arguments are presented in sequence of development of the case. Each party has the opportunity of cross-examining witnesses and re-cross-examining if necessary. This is followed in an orderly way, but often, depending on the case, in a rather informal give-and-take manner. The important requirement, from the standpoint of the arbitrator, is that he/she be given adequate information on which to base a well-thought-out and fair decision.

The hearing may last for just a few hours or it may run for several days, depending upon the complexity of the issues and the presentations of the parties. At the conclusion of the presentation of their positions by the parties, there is usually a summing-up orally by each party of the main points on which its case rests; or, in some instances, if there is to be a written posthearing brief submitted by each party, both may forego a formal summation of their arguments. Before the hearing concludes, the arbitrator and the parties, if the contract does not already specify, come to agreement on submission of posthearing briefs. If they are to be submitted, a date for exchange of the briefs must be established. The easiest way I have found is for the parties to submit two copies of their briefs to the arbitrator, to be posted on a given date, and then for the arbitrator to send each party the other party's brief.

- Within 30 days after the filing of statements with the permanent arbitrator, the permanent arbitrator shall hold an oral hearing at which both parties shall have the privilege of being represented and to present oral, documentary, or physical evidence; to present testimony of witnesses and to examine the witnesses of the other party.

- At any time before the commencement of the arbitration hearing, either party may demand that the proceedings be recorded by a court reporter, in which case the arbitrator shall make arrangements to secure the attendance of a court reporter to record all the testimony and all the proceedings. The reporter shall transcribe the notes of the hearing within twenty (20) calendar days from the completion of the hearing and a copy of the transcript shall be furnished the arbitrator and the party requesting the court reporter. . . . The cost of the transcript for the arbitrator and for the party requesting it will be borne by the party requesting the transcript.

- Any hearing by an arbitrator shall start within three (3) scheduled working days after the arbitrator accepts the assignment and such hearing shall not exceed a period of three (3) calendar days.

- The arbitrator shall follow rules of procedure agreed to by the parties, but in the absence of the agreement thereon, the rule of the voluntary labor arbitration tribunal of the American Arbitration Association shall govern.

- Each party to a case submitted to arbitration will do everything in its power to permit early selection of and decision by the Arbitrator. The parties shall cooperate in arranging with the selected Arbitrator for the time and place that, subject to the Arbitrator's convenience, will best serve for the quickest and least costly disposition of the matter.

- The arbitrator shall hear and decide only one grievance in each case. He shall not be bound by formal rules of evidence. He shall be bound by and must comply with all of the terms of this Agreement. He shall have no power to delete or modify in any way any of the provisions of this Agreement. He shall have the power to make appropriate awards.

- [Public sector] The arbitration hearing shall be held between the hours of 0800–1600 hours, Monday through Friday, excluding holidays.

- [Public sector] Hearings are administrative proceedings and not court proceedings. An arbitrator will explain the procedures to be followed by both parties at the outset of the hearing.

    Rules of evidence are not applied strictly, but the arbitrator shall exclude irrelevant or unduly repetitious testimony.

Decisions on admissibility of evidence or testimony will be made by the arbitrator.

The arbitrator will give the parties opportunity to cross-examine witnesses who appear to testify.

The arbitrator may exclude any person from the hearing for contumacious conduct or misbehavior that obstructs the hearing.

There shall be no posthearing submissions to the Arbitrator by either of the parties.

Time Limits on Arbitrator's Decision

- The . . . arbitrator will issue the decision within ten (10) days following the date the oral hearing is scheduled.
- Any decision by the arbitrator shall be handed down within fifteen (15) days after the conclusion of the hearing. The parties may mutually agree to extend any or all of the foregoing time limitations.
- The arbitrator shall, within forty-eight (48) hours of the completion of such hearing, provide the parties with an oral record of his award, to be followed by a written statement of his recommendation as soon as time permits.
- The arbitrator shall render his decision in writing within thirty (30) days after the conclusion of the hearing.
- The arbitrator shall render in writing his or her decision within ninety (90) days after the record of the case is closed.

The Arbitrator's Decision

The importance of the arbitration step in the grievance procedure is the finality and terminal nature of the award or decision. Although this is the implied objective in the parties' invoking arbitration rather than resorting to a strike, lockout, or other overt action or litigation, almost all agreements in the private sector drive the point home by way of specific language. Increasingly, the same pattern is becoming evident in federal, state, and municipal labor agreements. In 1975, approximately 80 percent of federal-sector agreements and 82 percent of state- and municipal-sector agreements with arbitration clauses opted for binding arbitration as the terminal step of the grievance procedure. One significant difference remains, however, between the private- and federal-sector agreements. While appeal to the courts from private-sector arbitration decisions is governed by the rather strict guidelines established by the "Trilogy," it is not certain at this time what the right to file an exception with the Federal Labor Relations Council from arbitration decisions in the federal sector means. It would be hoped that the council will follow the guidelines of the Supreme Court in the "Trilogy" in ruling on exceptions to the arbitration decisions. Among the agreements in which the decision of the arbitrator is not final and binding, the most frequent alternative is arbitration of an advisory nature. It should also be pointed out that agreements such as the National Bituminous Coal Agreement do not part from the binding concept of arbitration, since appeal from a regional panel arbitrator's decision is to another arbitration board at the national level. The bindiag nature of the decision is still preserved in the process.

- The arbitrator's decision shall be final and binding on the Company, the Union, and the employee or employees involved.
- The arbitrator shall have the authority to interpret and apply the provisions of this Agreement, but shall not have the authority to amend or modify this Agreement or to establish new terms and conditions of this Agreement. There shall be no stoppage of work on account of any controversy which may be made the subject of arbitration and the decision of the arbitrator shall be final and binding on the Company, the Union, and the employee.
- An arbitration award shall be final and binding as to all issues involved in the grievance.
- [Public sector] The decision or award of the arbitrator shall be final and binding to the extent permitted by and in accordance with applicable law and this agreement. The arbitrator shall confine himself to the precise issue submitted for arbitration and shall have no authority to determine any other issues not so submitted to him.
- [Public sector] The party requesting arbitration will determine whether the arbitrator's award will be advisory or binding.
- [Public sector] . . . When an issue has been subjected to binding arbitration, either party may file exceptions to any award with the Federal Labor Relations Council, under regulation prescribed by the Council.
- [Public sector] In the event an arbitrator's award is appealed by the Union or management to the Federal Labor Relations Council, then the award shall be stayed pending the Council's final determination.
- Either party to an arbitration, upon receiving a final award by a panel arbitrator, may petition the Arbitration Review Board to appeal the decision of the panel arbitrator.

In a few agreements, provision is made not for review of an arbitrator's decision, but for a request for clarification:

- If clarification of the arbitrator's decision is deemed necessary, either party may request clarification from the arbitrator and a copy of the request shall be given to the other party.
- Any dispute between the parties as to the interpretation or construction to be placed upon the award made . . . shall be submitted to the impartial arbitrator who made the award, who may thereupon construe or interpret the award so far as necessary to clarify the same, but without changing

the substance thereof, and such interpretation or construction shall be binding upon all parties.

Arbitrator and Arbitration Costs

Two types of costs are usually involved in arbitration hearings: (1) the fee and expenses of the impartial arbitrator; and (2) the costs other than for the arbitrator, such as legal counsel, time off from work for witnesses and officials presenting the two sides of the case, and transcripts, to name a few. Although contracts are usually explicit about the method of bearing the cost of the arbitrator, they are not always explicit about how the other costs will be handled, leaving this matter to direct arrangement between the parties or to established practice. Predominantly, the parties split the cost of the arbitrator equally. Payment of lost time for employees whose presence is necessary at the hearing varies. Legal costs and transcription costs are usually the responsibility of the party receiving the service. Some variations of these more common procedures are included below:

- The arbitrator's fee shall be divided equally between the Company and the Union.
- In the event of arbitration each party shall pay the fee of its arbitrator [a tripartite board] and all costs of preparing and presenting its case. The cost of the third arbitrator and all other reasonable costs of the arbitration proceeding shall be shared equally by the parties.
- All expenses and fees incurred by the impartial arbitrator . . . shall be divided equally and paid in equal portions by the Union involved, the contractor or contractors involved, and/or the individual Employer.
- The expenses and fees of the arbitrator shall be paid by the party requesting arbitration if the specific award sought is not granted by the arbitrator; if the specific award sought is granted, such fees and expenses shall be paid by the other party.
- . . . the fees and expenses of said arbitration shall be paid by the party against whom the decision is rendered.
- The costs of arbitration will be borne by the party who requests arbitration.
- [Public sector] The costs of the arbitrators shall be borne equally by the parties up to $1,000 per grievance. Additional costs above $1,000 shall be paid by the city.
- [Municipal level] The costs of arbitration shall be borne as follows: one-third by the employee organization and two-thirds by the County.
- [Public sector] The fees and expenses of the arbitrator shall be borne equally by the Fire Department and employee concerned; provided, if the union is a party to the dispute, such fees and expenses shall be borne equally by the Fire Department and the union.

- [Public sector] One-half of such compensation [arbitrator] shall be paid by the Authority. The other one-half shall be paid by the union, less the sum of $10 for each grievance appeal to the impartial arbitrator by an individual employee, which sum shall be paid by the individual employee.

- Each party shall bear the expenses in respect to its own witnesses. Each party shall pay one-half of the aggrieved employee's time lost from work for appearance at the arbitration proceedings.

- [Public sector] The employee's representative, appellants, and witnesses shall be on a pay status without charge to annual leave while participating in the arbitration proceedings if they are government employees and the hearings are conducted during the regularly scheduled tour of duty.

- Each party shall be responsible for costs of presenting its own case to arbitration.

- If an employee or other witness is called by the company, the company will reimburse him for time lost. If an employee or other witness is called by the union, the union will reimburse him for time lost.

- [Public sector] The employee serving as the Union representative, the aggrieved employee and the employee witnesses who have direct knowledge of the circumstances and factors bearing on the case shall be excused from duty to participate in the arbitration proceedings without loss of pay or charge to annual leave.

Grievance-Arbitration Homilies

In keeping with the pattern established in the chapters on negotiation and grievance procedure, the reader is presented with advice drawn from experience in the field on how to be effective in the handling of arbitration cases. Although not exhaustive, the homilies listed below emphasize some of the more important requirements in the proper presentation and processing of arbitration cases.

- Don't take cases without merit to arbitration.

- Organize well. Prepare well. Facts are what count.

- The person to convince with the merits of your case is the arbitrator, not the other party.

- Be sure that the submission statement or statement of the issue says what you want it to say. The way the issue is worded dictates the kind of consideration the arbitrator must give to the case. An improperly worded issue can result in a decision contrary to what you seek and may be contrary to the weight of evidence or the obvious merits of the case.[16]

- Know your labor agreement and any laws, regulations, or orders that may

[16] For an excellent discussion of the significance of the submission agreement to the outcome of a case, see Prasow and Peters, *Arbitration and Collective Bargaining*, Chap. 2.

be pertinent. Be sure you have firmly in mind their relationshisp to each other.

- Assemble factual support for your case in the form of documents, records, and witnesses for the purpose of hard proof. Don't attempt to "snow" the other party or the arbitrator by the volume of your exhibits and testimony.

- Do not try to influence the arbitrator on any grounds other than the merits of the case.

- Do not overemphasize, exaggerate, make wild claims, engage in personalities, bicker with the other party, withhold facts, distort, belabor points, fail to show respect for the position of the arbitrator, take your case lightly, badger witnesses, or attempt to belittle the other party.

- Be sure you make clear to the arbitrator all the surrounding circumstances pertinent to the case. Remember, until the hearing, the arbitrator must be assumed to be a stranger to the case. He can make a decision based upon only the information the parties provide him. He does not second-guess.

- Even if the arbitrator does not request such information, be sure that he has relevant material in advance, such as a copy of the contract, a statement of the issue, or any other information that is not argumentative but is relevant to an understanding of the case.

- Do not approach the arbitrator with the merits of your case or in any way compromise his position as a neutral prior to the hearing.

- Be sure you have clearly in mind what you have to prove. Next, find facts or reasoning necessary to prove your point. Then organize your arguments and documentations in an orderly way. When you present your case, move smoothly from point to point. This will create a good impression.

- Anticipate the other party's arguments and prepare to counter them.

- Be sure you know what you will ask your witnesses and what their answers will be.

- Do careful research on past practice. It may make the difference between proving and not proving your case. Remember, past practice that is applied equitably and not in violation of the clear language of the contract may be used to give the contract meaning. But when it is a matter of past practice versus the clear meaning of the contract, go with the latter in preparing your case.

- Be sure, in preparing your case from the contract language, that you carefully review the entire contract for relevant material. The arbitrator will undoubtedly go through such a process.

- When arbitrators are treating such terms as "just cause" or "reasonableness," the most common tests they apply are whether the accused party has been arbitrary (not governed by principle), capricious (using unpredictable conduct), and/or discriminatory (not treating all equally).

- Eyewitness and written records are much more substantial forms of proof than hearsay or verbal statements.

- Select your arbitrator carefully. Impartiality, integrity, and experience are the most important points to check. Never let an adverse decision from any particular arbitrator blind you to his competence and impartiality as an arbitrator. Go with impartiality and competence every time. It will pay dividends where you have a substantial case.

- Try to find out in advance how the particular arbitrator conducts the hearing. This will give you a key to the way you should prepare for the hearing.
- Don't go into a hearing with a chip on your shoulder or in fear of the arbitrator.
- Remember that an experienced arbitrator is not impressed with histrionics. He wants the facts, not the embellishments.

CONCLUSION

Voluntary grievance arbitration, by the widespread nature of its use, shows a general acceptance and preference over such alternatives as the strike, lockout, or compulsory settlement. This widespread acceptance and use does not mean that the process of grievance arbitration is without its problems. With the added pressure of increasing numbers of employers and employee groups in the public sector that are turning to grievance arbitration, several aspects of the process have come under close scrutiny and criticism. More and more effort and experimentation have been given to reducing costs, to reducing the time involved in grievance arbitration, and to increasing the number of qualified arbitrators. The efforts being made along these lines will be a part of the discussion of resolution of conflict in Part IV.

SELECTED REFERENCES

Baer, Walter E., *Labor Arbitration Guide.* Homewood, Ill.: Dow Jones-Irwin, 1974.

An excellent guide by an authority on labor contracts, written in everyday language, concerning arbitration principles and procedures, with the main focus on grievance arbitration. Any individual involved or intending to be involved in arbitration matters would benefit by this study.

BNA Editorial Staff, *Grievance Guide.* Washington, D.C.: Bureau of National Affairs, Inc., 1972.

Informative and useful, illustrating general principles of grievance resolution based on a series of examples from arbitration awards. From these examples the reader should secure a good picture of the kinds of points arbitrators consider in handling grievance appeals. Moreover, as the BNA staff emphasizes, care should be taken in attempting to apply the rulings to one situation. No two contracts are exactly alike; therefore, one should carefully check contract language before concluding that any particular ruling would apply.

Carlson, Robert, *Labor Arbitration—What You Need to Know*. New York: American Arbitration Association, 1973.

Short but helpful and includes three chapters: (1) "So You Have a Labor Grievance," (2) "How to Select a Labor Arbitrator," and (3) "Preparing for the Arbitration Hearing." A useful appendix includes "The Jargon of Labor Arbitration," "Court and NLRB Decisions," a bibliography of useful readings, the AAA voluntary labor arbitration rules, AAA's expedited arbitration rules, and the U.S. Arbitration Act.

Davey, Harold W., *Contemporary Collective Bargaining*, 3rd ed. Englewood Cliffs, N.J.: Prentice-Hall, 1972.

A leading arbitrator combines his research and experience to bring to the reader an invaluable description of the arbitration process. An excellent bibliography for further reading is also included.

Dennis, Barbara D., and Gerald G. Somers, eds., *Labor Arbitration at the Quarter-Century Mark*. Washington, D.C.: Bureau of National Affairs, Inc., 1973.

For any party interested in a look backward and a look forward at the arbitration process, this volume of the *Proceedings of the National Academy of Arbitrators for 1972* is required reading. Bringing together some of the most experienced arbitrators in the country, the editors have given the reader the benefit of their views of arbitration as they have evolved and what these portend. In addition, some topics of current concern are the use and abuse of arbitral power, judicial review from the viewpoints of the arbitrator and the parties, changing life-styles and problems of authority in the plant, and advancing the acceptability of arbitrators.

Industrial Relations Guide. Englewood Cliffs, N.J.: Prentice-Hall, N.J.

By providing numerous examples of grievances that reached arbitration, the "Arbitration Awards Analyzed" section of this volume offers a useful reference for anyone who wants to see how arbitrators have handled particular types of grievances in the past. This section can help guide the grievance-handler in the early steps of the grievance procedure or in preparing the case for arbitration. References are footnoted.

Labor Arbitration Awards. New York: Commerce Clearing House, Inc.

A continuing service containing the full texts of current arbitration awards, published weekly.

Labor Arbitration Reports. Washington, D.C.: Bureau of National Affairs, Inc.

Included in the *Labor Arbitration Reports* are awards of arbitrators, reports of fact-finding boards, and court decisions on labor arbitration. This is a continuing service, covering a period from 1946 to the present. Arbitrators are also listed, with biographical sketches.

Prasow, Paul, *The Arbitrator's Role*, Reprint No. 240, Institute of Industrial Relations, University of California, Los Angeles, 1974.

Professor Prasow discusses the role of the arbitrator in grievance-arbitration matters.

Prasow, Paul, and Edward Peters, *Arbitration and Collective Bargaining, Conflict Resolution in Labor Relations.* New York: McGraw-Hill, 1970.

This book represents the effort of the academician-arbitrator and the professional mediator to provide a theoretical basis for understanding the arbitration process. It is based on empirical analysis of the arbitration process, but not to examine the arbitration awards as such. Rather, the analysis is of the reasoning behind the awards, in order to identify criteria that might be translated into a body of common law governing judicial interpretation and enforcement of collective agreements. Prasow and Peters have made a major contribution by cutting through the verbiage of arbitration decisions to extract the common elements that constitute the formative basis of common-law development. Furthermore, the sections dealing with the grievance-arbitration process on such matters as the submission agreement, the semantics of contract language, the role of past practice, and evidence and proof should be required reading for every aspiring participant in arbitration procedures.

Rehmus, Charles M., ed., *Developments in American and Foreign Arbitration.* Washington, D.C.: Bureau of National Affairs, Inc., 1968.

The 1968 annual meeting of the National Academy of Arbitrators delves into such questions as the role of law in decisions based on the language of the negotiated contract, grievance-arbitration matters that are also subject to the remedial processes of the NLRB, the influence, if any, of the arbitrator's need for joint acceptability of his professional services and the arbitration process, and the use and misuse of tripartite boards in grievance arbitration. Luskin and Cole, respectively, address themselves to the increasing acceptability of arbitration and the changing attitudes and increased maturity of labor and management representatives.

Report of the Federal Labor Relations Council, FLRC, Washington, D.C.

The FLRC issues continuing mimeographed reports of its decisions on appeals from the assistant secretary of labor's decisions and from appealed grievance-arbitration decisions. An invaluable source for public-sector parties who are involved in grievance-arbitration matters. Since there is no "common-law" body of decisions in the public sector as in the private sector, the decisions of the FLRC are ground-breaking and precedent-setting in their impact on public-sector labor relations.

Taylor, Benjamin J., and Fred Witney, *Labor Relations Law,* 2nd ed., Chaps. 15, 21. Englewood Cliffs, N.J.: Prentice-Hall, 1975.

An excellent examination of the legal status of grievance arbitration and the role it plays in collective bargaining in both private and public sectors.

U.S. Department of Labor publications. See those annotated in Chapter 10 as *Arbitration Procedures,* 1966; *Grievance and Arbitration Procedures in State and Local Agreements,* 1975; *Understanding Grievance Arbitration in the Public Sector,* 1974; *Negotiation, Impasse, Grievance and Arbitration in Federal Agreements,* 1970.

Updegraff, Clarence M., *Arbitration and Labor Relations,* 3rd ed. Washington, D.C.: Bureau of National Affairs, Inc., 1970.

Chapters III through VIII are especially useful in providing an account of the steps of the arbitration process, from selection of arbitrator to submission of agreement, to legal rules of evidence, to the hearing, and finally to the arbitrator's award. Excellent reference source.

Yaffe, Byron, ed., *The Saul Wallen Papers: A Neutral's Contribution to Industrial Peace.* New York: The New York State School of Industrial and Labor Relations, 1974.

This book is not only to honor a man of great compassion and effectiveness as a neutral in labor–management disputes, but to bring some insight into the views of Mr. Waller to those who are interested in the process of conflict resolution. Two areas of major emphasis are arbitration and mediation.

Contract Administration and Collective Bargaining by Objectives

CHAPTER 18

KEEPING RECORDS

One theme consistently emphasized throughout this book is the value of (1) proper preparation, and (2) an orderly and systematic approach, whether it be at the negotiation table, during the grievance procedure, or before the arbitrator. The purpose of this chapter is to add one more ingredient to the technique of preparing thoroughly and being orderly and systematic, by introducing a method for keeping a running record of grievance and arbitration decisions.

It is apparent that one of the major sources from which the parties draw ideas for proposed changes or alterations to the agreement at negotiation time is their day-by-day experiences in administering the contract. It is during this day-by-day contract administration that the parties learn the weaknesses and the strengths of the contract as a means of governing their relationships. As problems under the contract arise and then take the form of grievances, one or both parties are often made aware of the need to change the contract language. This cannot formally take place until the next negotiations. Because that may be a year, two years, or even three years hence, the need becomes paramount for an ongoing, well-organized way of keeping a record of the needed changes pending the date of the next negotiations. The need for a written record —one that is easy to refer to and use—becomes quite clear when the fallibility of memory is taken into account. Experienced arbitrators early conclude that memory unsupported by written records is far from infallible as to what happened in the past in a particular circumstance. Written records aid in the reconstruction of the meaning of what happened and what the party or parties at the time considered must be done contractually to avoid the same problem in the future.

It is the objective of the following discussion to introduce a method of record keeping that is orderly and systematic, is easily referred to, and generates a blueprint for input into the establishment of objectives for the next negotiations based on contract-administration experience. If followed, this method of record keeping affords a system of discipline for the representative of the union or the employer, ensuring that the full recording of settlements or decisions will be made, with a current assessment of the positive and/or negative impact on the party concerned. At the same time, based on this immediate and first-hand knowledge, there are recorded any recommendations as to needed contract changes for the next round of negotiations. Form 18–1 shows the specific information needed to keep such a record. It can be kept in a looseleaf binder, and sheets added as they are needed. It will be noted that this method of record keeping is formulated in such a way as to serve as a direct link between the experience in applying the contract and establishing objectives for contract changes (CBO) in the next round of negotiations.

The use of Form 18–1 is best illustrated by using an example and following through, as in the CBO chapters, with the specific recording based on the sample case. The case illustrating this method of record keeping involves a recall problem after a market decline caused a substantial reduction in force.

Illustration: Recall to Work after Reduction in Force and Layoffs

In the face of a general slump in sales because of a decline in the market, the XYZ Corporation reduced some of its operations, with a resultant reduction in the number of employees. The labor agreement, Section 14.10, *Lay-Offs Other Than Temporary*, establishes the method and order of reduction of force from the departments involved in the cutback operations:

(a) Reduction, other than on a temporary basis, in the number of employees in a job classification . . . shall first be accomplished on the basis of Departmental seniority, with those employees having the least Departmental seniority on the job involved in the reduction the first to be laid off therefrom.

(b) An employee removed from his job in accordance with paragraph (a) above shall be reassigned (in the reverse order of his line of promotion) to his most recently held permanent job within said Department to which he is entitled on the basis of Departmental seniority. In the event no such job is available, he shall be assigned to replace any employee within said department having less Departmental seniority, provided he has the skill and ability necessary to do the required work efficiently.

(c) In the event of a reduction in the total number of employees within a

FORM 18-1

CONTRACT ADMINISTRATION AND SETTING NEGOTIATION OBJECTIVES
(A GUIDE FOR SETTING BARGAINING OBJECTIVES THROUGH JOURNAL OF ARBITRATION AND GRIEVANCE DECISIONS)

Arbitration and Grievance Settlements			Evaluation of Settlement		Bargaining Objectives for Next Negotiations	Comments and Cross References
Number of Case	Item	Clause Identification	U	S		

Department, other than on a temporary basis as provided for in Section 14.9, employees oldest in terms of Departmental seniority will be retained as needed in such Department provided they have the required skill and ability to efficiently perform the work required.

(d) An employee on lay-off from a Department lasting ten (10) work days or more may exercise his plant seniority across department lines on common labor or base rate jobs.

When the reduction in force was concluded, 130 employees had been laid off from Department A. Of the 130 employees, twenty had been able to avail themselves of Section 14.10 (d) above and had bumped into common-labor or base-rate jobs in another department.

One month after the reduction in force and resulting layoffs, business began to pick up again and the employer was faced with the problem of recall. Section 14.11 of the agreement, *Rehire After Lay-Off*, covers the recall procedure:

(a) When employees in Departments other than in the . . . Department . . . are recalled to work therein following lay-off then shall be called back to work in the reverse order to that in which they were laid-off giving due consideration to their skill and ability to satisfactorily perform the required work and efficiency of operation. Such re-employment privilege, however, shall not exceed twenty-four (24) months following their date of lay-off. The refusal or failure to respond within five (5) calendar days to such offer of re-employment shall terminate any obligation of the Employer hereunder.

It was readily apparent that the provision above adequately covered all employees who were laid off not only from the department but also from the company because they did not have enough seniority to exercise the bumping right of Section 14.10 (d). There was, however, a real question as to what sections of the agreement covered recall of the twenty employees who had bumped into jobs in another department and were still working. The question was whether Section 14.11 (a) above applied to the recall of these employees or whether they were to be considered as transfers subject to Section 14.8, *Inter-Departmental Transfers*, which states:

(a) *Departmental Transfers at Employee Request.* Employees transferred from one department to another at their own request shall be considered new employees with regard to Department seniority standing in the Department to which transferred. Employees transferred back to their former Department at their own request will begin to accrue Department seniority in the Department to which transferred as of the date of such transfer.

When the matter could not be resolved of which section, 14.11 (a) or 14.8 (a), applied to the recall of the twenty employees still working but in another department, the parties answered the question of the immediate situation by means of a "Memorandum of Understanding," which established a recall method satisfactory to both parties. This memorandum was to apply to the specific recall of the twenty employees and had no future implications with respect to establishing precedence. When the district organization of the union later filed an exception to the use of the memorandum, the problem went to arbitration. The arbitrator ruled that the memorandum was legally established and proper within the agreement as it applied to the one-time situation.

In using Form 18–1 to record for the union the situation above, the first step is to identify the decision with some kind of a numbering system. A simple way is to label all arbitration or grievance settlements consecutively in order of their chronological appearance. The case above, if it were the first, would be number 1 (see Form 18–2). It is also of value to record the date of the case or the settlement, providing a quick

FORM 18–2

CONTRACT ADMINISTRATION AND SETTING NEGOTIATION OBJECTIVES
(A GUIDE FOR SETTING BARGAINING OBJECTIVES THROUGH JOURNAL OF ARBITRATION AND GRIEVANCE DECISIONS)

Number of Case
I 8/8/74

way to relate cases chronologically. In column 1 would also be entered the date—say, 8/8/74.

To preserve a record and to identify items promptly, the next step in the use of the contract-administration journal is to list the nature of the item or issue involved. In column 2 (Form 18–3), "Recall from layoff" would be entered in this case. In others, the entry might be seniority, discharge, leave of absence, job bidding, promotion, or any number of other issues.

A further useful type of identification is to note the specific contract clause(s) or section(s) involved in the case. Using the example, the union would enter the numbers of sections 14.8 (a) and 14.11 (a) in column 3 (Form 18–4).

FORM 18–3

CONTRACT ADMINISTRATION AND SETTING NEGOTIATION OBJECTIVES
(A GUIDE FOR SETTING BARGAINING OBJECTIVES THROUGH JOURNAL OF ARBITRATION AND GRIEVANCE DECISIONS)

Number of Case	Item
1 8/8/74	Recall from Layoff

FORM 18–4

CONTRACT ADMINISTRATION AND SETTING NEGOTIATION OBJECTIVES
(A GUIDE FOR SETTING BARGAINING OBJECTIVES THROUGH JOURNAL OF ARBITRATION AND GRIEVANCE DECISIONS)

Number of Case	Item	Clause Identification
I 8/8/74	Recall from Layoff	14.11 (a) 14.8 (a)

The next entry based on the case example results from the union's assessment of the relationship of the decision to the interest of employees in the bargaining unit or to the union. If the decision were judged adverse to these interests, the column labeled "U" (unsatisfactory) would be checked; if satisfactory, the column labeled "S" (satisfactory) would be checked. In the particular example cited, the immediate results of the decision would have to be listed as satisfactory to the union; hence, the column labeled "S" (Form 18–5) would be checked. But because the particular case decision was only stopgap and the problem of recall might return to plague the union, the long-run implication of the case settlement would have to be listed as U (unfavorable). For this reason, it would be well to check U in addition to S, to indicate that the immediate meaning of the decision was satisfactory but the long-run implications were unsatisfactory.

The danger to the union in the current construction of the contract is that employees who exercised their bumping rights to move into other departments during a reduction in force might well be construed to be transfers (14.8 [a]) rather than layoffs (14.11 [a]). If this were to happen, the union members who chose the route of bumping into other departments would at that point lose seniority accumulated in their original department instead of retaining seniority for 24 months as provided in Section 14.11 (a). When a recall to their original departments was announced, the workers who bumped into other departments would have to bid in as new employees without seniority. In effect, they would have been reduced from the head to the bottom of the seniority list among those who had been laid off from the department.

FORM 18–5

CONTRACT ADMINISTRATION AND SETTING NEGOTIATION OBJECTIVES
(A GUIDE FOR SETTING BARGAINING OBJECTIVES THROUGH JOURNAL OF ARBITRATION AND GRIEVANCE DECISIONS)

Arbitration and Grievance Settlements			Evaluation of Settlement	
Number of Case	Item	Clause Identification	U	S
I 8/8/74	Recall from Layoff	14.11 (a) 14.8 (a)	U	S

Because of the possibility of this situation's arising again, the union decides that in the next negotiations, it must seek a modification in the language of 14.11 (a) to cover the situation. The modification to be sought is new language to the effect that layoff for purposes of recall under 14.11 (a) is to be construed as layoff from the dapartment—and/or the plant. It is also to include or cover those employees who bump during a reduction in force into base-rate or common-labor jobs in other departments as well as those who are on layoff from all plant work because of the reduction in force. This decision then becomes an objective for the next negotiations and is recorded in column 5 (Form 18–6).

The important point is that the objective be established in writing at the time of the arbitration decision that raised the problem of language in the contract covering recall from layoff from the department. Recording the needed information at the time of occurrence, the union is more keenly aware of the implications of the case and what is needed than at a later time when the memory may have dimmed.

FORM 18–6

CONTRACT ADMINISTRATION AND SETTING NEGOTIATION OBJECTIVES
(A GUIDE FOR SETTING BARGAINING OBJECTIVES THROUGH JOURNAL OF ARBITRATION AND GRIEVANCE DECISIONS)

Number of Case	Item	Clause Identification	U	S	Bargaining Objectives for Next Negotiations
I 8/8/74	Recall from Layoff	14.11 (a) 14.8 (a)	U	S	Modify 14.11 (a) to the effect that layoff for purposes of recall is to be construed as layoff from the Department and is to include those employees who during a reduction of force have exercised their plant seniority to bump into base rate and common labor positions in other departments.

It should also be observed that, at this point, only the general objective is recorded. No attempt is made to establish optimistic (O), realistic (R), and pessimistic (P), as is done when the time arrives for setting objectives and making strategy plans for the actual negotiations. When negotiation time does arrive, then, based upon the bargaining climate and the strategy agreed upon, it is more sensible and the party is in a much better position to take each of the objectives recorded in the contract-administration journal and set them up in the familiar O, R, and P framework.

The final column (Form 18–7), "Comments and Cross References," serves a variety of purposes. First, it would be wise to enter here any official number used for the case. For example, when the parties request a list of arbitrators from the FMCS, the agency not only responds with the requested list of names but identifies the case as, for instance, "RE 75K07915—Recall from layoff." Since this becomes a means of identification in the FMCS records and to the parties concerned, it should be listed in the last column.

Finally, as other settlements or decisions are recorded in the manner shown in this example, there is a need for cross-referencing. For example, case number 50 may be one involving recall from layoff. In order to have quick reference from one issue to similar issues that have been recorded, number 50 should have a notation in the last column cross-referencing it to number 1, which is also a recall-from-layoff issue. Any other information the party thinks is worth recording to enhance the usefulness of the journal of contract-administration settlements and decisions should be duly recorded at the time of the event.

FINAL CAUTION AND EXPLANATION

Checking unsatisfactory (U) for a particular decision or settlement does not automatically mean that an objective must be set to modify the contract language. For example, in discipline and discharge cases, checking U to indicate an unsatisfactory result may only indicate that the case was lost on a "just-cause" basis. Changing a contract clause will probably not be a remedy if the same situation occurs in the future. The remedy is to be sure that it does not. Similarly, checking satisfactory (S) does not automatically mean that there is no need for a modification in the language of the contract at the next negotiations. What it may mean is that the settlement was satisfactory to the party but, on the other hand, the party feels that even though its side won the case, it would be better in terms of future relations to prevent the recurrence by establishing an objective to change the contract language appropriately to remedy the situation in the future. Each decision or settlement must be thought through carefully to determine whether an objective should be estab-

CONTRACT ADMINISTRATION AND SETTING NEGOTIATION OBJECTIVES
(A GUIDE FOR SETTING BARGAINING OBJECTIVES THROUGH JOURNAL OF ARBITRATION AND GRIEVANCE DECISIONS)

Number of Case	Arbitration and Grievance Settlements		Evaluation of Settlement		Bargaining Objectives for Next Negotiations	Comments and Cross References
	Item	Clause Identification	U	S		
I 8/8/74	Recall from Layoff	14.11 (a) 14.8 (a)	U	S	Modify 14.11 (a) to the effect that layoff for purposes of recall is to be construed as layoff from the Department and is to include those employees who during a reduction of force have exercised their plant seniority to bump into base rate and common labor positions in other departments.	FMCS File RE 75K07915

lished requiring modification in the language of the contract, whether the objective will receive opposition by the other party at negotiations (a conflict item), or whether it is one that will be mutually supported by both parties as necessary (a mutually advantageous item). If preparation is an asset during negotiations, then keeping an accurate record with first-hand reactions becomes a major input for proper preparation.

SELECTED REFERENCES

Bambrick, James J. Jr., and Marie P. Dorbandt, "The Use of Bargaining Books in Negotiations," *Management Record,* XIX (April 1957), 118–21, 143–45.

The use of a bargaining book does not obviate the use of the objectives approach. A bargaining book may be used as a useful support to CBO.

Morse, Bruce, *How to Negotiate the Labor Agreement.* Detroit: Trends Publishing Co., 1971.

Morse describes and illustrates how to prepare a clause book for negotiations.

Collective Bargaining Process— Resolution of Conflict

So long as the parties to a bargain are free to agree or not to agree, it is inevitable that, human nature being as it is, there should now and again come a deadlock, leading to that trial of strength and endurance which lies behind all bargaining. We know of no device for avoiding this trial of strength except a deliberate decision of the community expressed in legislative enactment.

Sidney and Beatrice Webb   *1902*

PART FOUR

Resolution of Conflict—
Negotiation

CHAPTER 19

Collective bargaining, as covered in Parts I, II, and III, is viewed as a joint process by which labor and management in a free society resolve their differences with a minimum of conflict. Two aspects of collective bargaining have been considered: first, the negotiation of contract terms that will cover the relationships of labor and management for a specified period of time; second, the means used to administer the agreement on a day-by-day basis.

Approximately 25 million workers and their employers operate under the constitution of the workplace known as the collective bargaining agreement. The process works, and works well. This is attested to by the lack of viable alternatives to collective bargaining to develop in a free society and by the large portion of the total agreements that are renegotiated regularly without strife.

Jack Conway notes:

> At this moment, collective bargaining has larger claim to vitality and utility than ever before in the history of the American society. Neither side of the American bargaining table is haunted by an uneasiness over what has been called the end of ideology or the exhaustion of the uses of collective bargaining.[1]

NEED FOR IMPROVEMENT

Nevertheless, there has been ever-present on the labor–management scene a desire on the part of the advocates of free collective bargaining

---

[1] Jack Conway, *Ideological Obsolescence in Collective Bargaining* (Berkeley: Institute of Industrial Relations, University of California, 1963), p. 3. Printed for private circulation.

to discover techniques and methods collective bargaining can adopt to resolve conflict more effectively. Some of the more important reasons for the search for improvement of the collective bargaining process are these:

1. Collective bargaining in the traditional sense—negotiation, grievance procedure, and grievance arbitration—works well but not perfectly. Impasses occur. Crisis bargaining continues in some negotiations. Personal animosities develop. And the strained relations accompanying such situations could result in work stoppages and other interferences with the flow of production and services. The Bureau of Labor Statistics notes, in addition, that "while legal bans and public opinion may deter strikes, shorten them, make them suicidal ventures for any sponsoring organization, and possibly result in the discharge of all strikers, they cannot entirely prevent strikes in a free society."[2]

2. As long as there is unresolved labor–management conflict, there will be economic pressure to find improved collective bargaining techniques and methods for its resolution. The company loses production and income. The employee loses employment and wages. Government agencies are under public pressure when they fail to provide tax-financed services. Federal and state governments lose tax revenue. The government employee, denied the right to strike, seeks an equitable alternative to this denied right. This mix of motives to resolve labor–management conflict in both private and public sectors, while not enough to override the need to strike in every case, remains a powerful force to encourage the development of constructive methods and techniques to bolster the effectiveness of traditional collective bargaining.

3. Off scene, there is always the spectre that if there should be a major breakdown in the ability of traditional free collective bargaining to resolve conflict, or if collective bargaining should not prove viable in its ability to adjust to changing times and institutions, the public or the government will be forced to move in the direction of compulsion. Every step in the direction of compulsion is a step toward the demise of free collective bargaining.

4. The special challenge is to find ways and means to prevent or resolve conflict in specific problem areas of work without weakening the basic fabric of free collective bargaining. Such problem areas are those with a critical impact on the health, welfare, or safety of the public and those, such as the federal, state, and local public sectors, where most employees have no statutory right to strike. In these areas, denial of the right to strike has not eliminated strikes. Moreover, without the right to strike or a suitable alternative, negotiation often becomes an exercise in frustration. Wingsinger of the Machinists notes the frustration of representatives of federal government workers: "Since Federal workers cannot strike, the representatives

2 *Work Stoppages—Government Employees, 1942–1961*, U.S. Bureau of Labor Statistics, Department of Labor, Report No. 247, 1963, p. 1.

cannot exert the kind of leverage that makes collective bargaining work in private industry. They come to the bargaining table as supplicants, not as equals."[3] The special challenge then becomes one of finding alternatives to the strike (as distinguished from the right to strike) while at the same time preserving the incentives in traditional collective bargaining to resolve conflict.

Part IV should, therefore, be viewed as an extension of preceding discussions that have been concerned with traditional collective bargaining as viewed through the processes of contract negotiations, grievance handling, and grievance arbitration. The common themes of all the techniques of conflict resolution to be covered in this and the following chapter are (1) a basic commitment to the efficacy and desirability of free collective bargaining, and (2) a dedication by the believers in free collective bargaining to develop ways and means of increasing the effectiveness of collective bargaining without destroying the basic instrument. This writer hastens to disclaim the presumption that any single technique or combination of techniques among those to be discussed constitutes a cure-all for labor–management conflict. Each method has its merits in a given situation and at a given period of time. Choice of any of the techniques or any combination of techniques must be carefully weighed against the particular circumstances involved in the conflict situation.

It should be emphasized that the procedure used in the techniques is also only a means to an end. The solution of conflict vitally depends upon the disposition of the parties toward peaceful labor–management relations.

TYPES OF CONFLICT

It should also be noted that "conflict" in labor–management relations is a multifaceted concept. It is not easily classified. It can be overt or covert. The latter type, because it is less easily identified, may be more damaging. Moreover, the conflict may arise at the organizing stage, during the negotiating stage, or during the period when the contract is in the process of being administered. Conflict in labor–management relations may also vary according to its source: It may be motivated by economic or financial considerations (wages, overtime, vacations, holidays, pensions, insurance), by matters of principle (management rights, union and employee rights), by personal reasons (discharge, discipline, promotion, rapport between supervisors and employees), by institutional problems (survival needs of the union and the company or agency as

---

[3] William W. Wingsinger, "There Is No Alternative to the Right to Strike," *Monthly Labor Review,* September 1973, p. 58.

institutions), by political desires (internal company or union politics; federal, state, or local politics related to conflict situations), or by legal requirements (establishing precedence, determining the meaning of a contract).

Looked at in another way, the conflict may vary as to participants: an individual employee and one or more members of management, an individual or group of employees and the employer, the bargaining representative (union or association) and the employer, or any number of combinations of these individuals and groups. Finally, if overtly expressed, the conflict may be evinced by anger, animosity, coolness, or physical violence. Overtly expressed conflict may also assume the form of picketing, boycotting, taking excessive but legal sick leave, enforcing rules and regulations to the letter (ticketing by police, prescribing all possible tests in a hospital, establishing strict safety rules), or performing duties perfunctorily (bus drivers driving but collecting no fares). Other ways conflict may be demonstrated more covertly are by committing sabotage (causing a breakdown in machinery or defective products), effecting slowdowns, being deliberately inefficient, sowing seeds of dissension, or denigrating a product or firm.

PREVENTING IMPASSE IN NEGOTIATIONS

Attention is first directed to wide-ranging techniques and methods broached but never tried, those used and later abandoned, and those now operative. Introduced over several decades but at an accelerated rate during the last decade and a half, their purpose has been to improve the effectiveness of traditional collective bargaining in the resolution of contract negotiation disputes. Simkin notes that "only a cynic could deny the fact of substantial progress in collective bargaining techniques over the past 30 years."[4]

The format followed emphasizes the nature of the tool or technique rather than the particular area of its use. Because of the wide variation in techniques, finding a simple means of classification and a systematic method of presentation is extremely difficult. Some techniques are formal; some are informal. In some instances, the particular technique allows flexibility of action; in others, it is quite inflexible. Some techniques are part of a structured process; others are unstructured. Some of the techniques are the result of actions of the parties themselves; some are the results of legislation or administrative orders; others are the work of a government agency, such as the Federal Mediation and Conciliation

---

[4] William E. Simkin, "Positive Approaches to Labor Peace," *Industrial and Labor Relations Review,* Cornell University, October 1964, p. 37.

Service. Neutrals are used in some cases as resource and technical experts; in other situations, neutrals are used to resolve conflict through a binding decision. In some instances, the technique involves only the parties themselves; in others, a neutral or neutrals from the private sector are involved; in still others, the intervention of a government body occurs. Finally, the technique may be aimed at preventing conflict, or it may be aimed at resolving conflict evinced by an impasse or overt action such as a strike.

Range of Techniques

The format that seems easiest to follow is to classify the techniques and methods into two general types: (1) those aimed at *prevention* of work stoppages, impasses, and crisis kinds of bargaining, and (2) those aimed at *resolution* of an impasse or work stoppage once it has occurred. Within each of these major classifications is a number of subclassifications, each considered a basic technique that is by nature uniquely different from others used, such as mediation, fact-finding, and arbitration, to name those more commonly known. Within each of the basic subclassifications, attention will be given to the variations in its use as a preventive device or as a resolution device. Prevention is the first area to be covered.

MEDIATION. Chapter 6, "Players," briefly described the role of the mediator in the more traditional sense. It was emphasized there that the major use of the mediator in the past has been to "put out fires." It is his function to use his good office to provide a positive environment for dispute resolution. In doing so, he draws on his personal experience (mediators are drawn mainly from professionals in the field of management or labor), his knowledge of the issues and settlement patterns, and his ability to suggest innovative solutions to break a deadlock. He must have a facility for effective communication, a keen sense of timing, and, above all, the confidence of the parties. His primary purpose is to act as a catalyst. He has no authority to dictate a solution. The late Arthur Meyer describes the mediator as struggling alone:

> The sea that he sails is only roughly charted and its changing contours are not clearly discernible. Worse still, he has no science of navigation, no fund inherited from the experience of others. He is a solitary artist recognizing, at most, a few guiding stars and depending mainly on his personal power of divination.[5]

The mediator's only objective is the prevention or settlement of a dis-

[5] Arthur S. Meyer, "Function of the Mediator in Collective Bargaining," *Industrial and Labor Relations Review*, January 1960, p. 160.

pute. He is not required to moralize about the specifics of the settlement.

Influenced by the rapidly changing and more complex nature of collective bargaining and an increasing willingness of both parties to adopt alternatives to the strike within the collective bargaining framework, the mediator, over the last decade especially, has been extending himself into many new activities. These activities, while new, do not stray from the fundamental charge of the mediator, and that is to seek to resolve impasse by peaceful means. Probably the most significant move of the mediation service, in contrast to its earlier "putting out fires" assignments, is to involve itself increasingly in activities that are aimed at preventing bargaining problems that could lead to impasse. This effort, under the strong encouragement and effective leadership of W.J. Usery, until recently the director of the FMCS, has resulted in increasing emphasis upon some programs started earlier but not fully implemented and upon new programs aimed at preventing conflict.

PREVENTIVE MEDIATION.   The most familiar technique, not particularly new but receiving increased emphasis, is that known as "preventive mediation." Using this technique, federal and state mediators become involved in the labor–management relations well in advance of negotiations. It is a process in which problem solving, as a basis for developing a healthy relationship between the parties, receives major concern. Included are such functions as special consultation and advisory services that, taking the parties as the mediator finds them, attempt "to provide a basis for restoring healthy labor–management relations by bringing problems into focus and confronting the conflict contained in them so that their cures are designed and implemented."[6] Techniques used are conducting joint and separate conferences with the parties, encouraging and establishing joint labor–management meetings and committees on a continuing basis, sustaining liaison before and after the contract is signed, holding post-contract consultations to smooth out unsolved problems, and conducting training seminars to assist the parties in more realistically assessing their problems and to turn an ineffective relationship into a problem-solving relationship.

In recommending extension of the preventive-mediation program, the National Labor–Management Panel of the Service, in its second annual report, called special attention to the unique function of the FMCS:

—to observe the status and viability of the bargaining relationship

—to identify underlying sources of conflict likely to persist

---

[6] Jerome T. Barrett and James F. Power, "FMCS and the Expanding Dimensions of Mediation Services," *Viewpoints*, published by the Society of Professionals in Dispute Resolution, Summer 1975, p. 6.

—to assess the need and usefulness of continuing discussion and problem exploration

—to assist in the early and critical stages of such joint ventures

—to make available, when requested, professional and experienced consultation[7]

The panel concluded by noting that it is the relationship of the parties, in the final analysis, that determines the "success or failure of the effort to anticipate and to solve problems through continuing dialogue, study, and exploration."[8] It is to improve the relationship of the parties that the work of the mediator is dedicated.

These preventive activities were broadened in 1974 to include a model of total mediation activity aimed at making the mediator available to assist the parties through the whole range of their bargaining activities. Included also were organizational changes at the federal level to make FMCS services more responsive to needs. Three operating offices were created: the Office of Mediation Service (including an assistant director for the public sector), the Office of Arbitration Services (see Chapter 20), and the Office of Technical Services. The last-named service is given the primary charge for preventive mediation through its service in technical assistance, professional development, research planning and development, and technical information.

For small firms, government agencies, and employee organizations new to the game of collective bargaining, using the mediator in this fashion provides real rewards. They are provided expert, impartial aid over a broad range of activities by an experienced individual. This helps the parties to avoid the pitfalls of decisions and actions based on emotions, personal biases, and inadequate sources of information. The focus is on the prevention of disputes.

In its report for 1974, the FMCS correctly objected to the use of the term "preventive mediation" as a general description of its prenegotiation activities. Although it is preventive in nature, since the major objective is labor–management peace, the broader approach of the service encompassing the full range of relationships between the parties is not fully expressed by the older term "preventive mediation."

RELATIONS BY OBJECTIVES. Finally, the latest in innovative techniques initiated by the FMCS Office of Technical Services for preventing disputes is the experimental program called "Relations by Objectives" (RBO). Joining management by objectives (MBO) and collective bargaining by objectives (CBO), the RBO program is aimed at improving relations and communications between the parties by a process of (1)

[7] *Eighteenth Annual Report*, FMCS, fiscal year 1965, p. 85.
[8] *Ibid.*

identification of problems, (2) establishment of target goals or objectives necessary to correct the problems, (3) joint discussions on implementation, and (4) agreement on an action program. Precise time limits are established for the process. Joint action up and down the line is required to achieve the final goal of a problem solved. The key to the success of this process of improving relationships is that it requires interaction. It provides a systematic framework for problem solving, and it establishes a positive program for the joint solution of problems.

EARLY-BIRD NEGOTIATION. A more limited, but nevertheless important, version of the continuous-bargaining concept that Simkin called the "early-bird" approach to negotiation has been actively promoted by the FMCS and converts among the parties to negotiations. This means establishing negotiations far enough ahead of the contract deadline so as to be able to discuss items at issue in a calmer, more deliberate environment. Whereas the parties are normally enjoined by the NLRA to give sixty days' notice of intent to modify the contract (ninety days, in health-care industries), the "early-bird" converts start their deliberations sometimes a full year ahead. The consequence of such action is that the negotiations are quite often completed well before the contract deadline and do not run into the last-minute, crisis type of bargaining that ends either in impasse or in a hurried and poorly constructed contract. By substituting calm, unhurried negotiations for the emotion-creating, hurried negotiations of crisis bargaining, the early-bird approach is a positive technique in the prevention of impasses and resultant work stoppages. Moreover, the reduction of impasse situations through the early-bird concept involves more than just getting a head start; it evinces an attitude that is vital to peaceful settlement of contract problems: a desire to make the concept work.

The New York hotel-industry method of negotiating illustrates one way early-bird bargaining has been used. Although the usual contract negotiated up to 1959 was for three years, it was actually terminated a year early through the use of the early-bird concept. It had been customary for the union to request a reopening of the contract for wage and hour negotiations on a yearly basis. Healy notes, "Of particular significance, at the second reopening of the three-year agreement, the parties have negotiated a completely new agreement instead of discussing only wages and hours."[9] By the opening up of the entire contract at the end of the second year, a full year was provided for negotiations before its formal expiration date.

Matthew Kelly refers to an interesting approach to the early-bird arrangement. Under this concept, the parties agree in advance that if the

[9] James Healy, ed., *Creative Collective Bargaining* (Englewood Cliffs, N.J.: Prentice-Hall, 1965), p. 83.

contract is negotiated and ratified in advance of its formal termination date, the new contract will be "preactivated" to take effect as of the date of ratification, which would give the employees any new benefits a number of weeks in advance.[10]

Employees of a Northeastern manufacturing company established a pattern as early as 1959 of engaging in a short strike during each negotiation. As the FMCS reported, this happened with monotonous regularity. At the instigation of the federal mediator, the parties finally agreed to enter into early negotiations in order to avoid this annual pattern. Prenegotiation meetings began in March, some five months ahead of the July 31 contract deadline. Presumably because of the less hurried atmosphere, the negotiations were so successful that the contract was signed four months ahead of the deadline. In addition, the parties agreed upon a three-year contract instead of the traditional one-year contract.

The 1974 steel negotiations, although given most publicity for the binding-arbitration agreement, were also an example of an early-bird negotiation approach. With a contract deadline of August 1, 1974, the parties started negotiations in February and finished in April, over three months early.

Finally, mediators have found success with a technique of securing agreement of the parties to postpone issues that might result in an impasse during negotiations to the calmer and more deliberate atmosphere of special postnegotiations. This still involves negotiations but not under the pressure of contract deadline, and therefore it has the same attributes as the early-bird negotiation approach.

JOINT LABOR–MANAGEMENT STUDY COMMITTEES.   In an article in the *AFL-CIO Federationist* of November 1963, entitled "New Directions in Bargaining," the comment was made:

> Joint study groups and human relations committees created by unions and employers have stirred interest as a new development in collective bargaining. As an innovation to meeting changing problems, this approach reflects a vitality and flexibility in collective bargaining.[11]

The list of industries making use of this technique to prevent conflict reads like a "Who's Who" and includes newspapers, automobiles, farm equipment, airlines, meat-packing, steel, maritime, glass, rubber, electrical manufacturing, clothing, machinery, and utilities, to name only a few. As the title suggests, these are committees established jointly by

---

[10] Matthew A. Kelly, "Techniques for Minimizing Crisis," Bureau of National Affairs, 14: 454, 5–29–69.

[11] "New Directions in Bargaining," *AFL–CIO Federationist*, November 1963, p. 18.

the parties to function primarily outside the limited time capsule of the traditional negotiation period, to serve broadly as a basis for establishing a better understanding between the parties, and to carry out long-range assignments. Some are organized on a bilateral basis, the participants thinking that more can be accomplished toward finding the right answers if outside parties are not present. Some are organized on a tripartite basis, with a neutral or neutrals participating. These groups reason that the neutral can serve important functions, such as representing the public's viewpoint, maintaining objectivity in the discussion of common problems, acting as a catalyst, and using his experience and expertise to introduce and encourage creativity in the approach to problem solving. Some of the committees are broadly conceptualized in their activities, ranging in their discussions over many problems; others are constrained more narrowly to deal with a specific problem. In their activities, some of the committees function on a continuing basis, meeting regularly, year after year, while others are one-time operatives, disbanding after they have completed their assigned task. It is significant that some one-time committees, after experiencing the rewards of better understanding and better communications, are then maintained for broader continuing problems of the first type of committee.

The primary difference between these joint committees and the labor–management teams engaged in traditional bargaining is that they do not operate under the time restrictions or the crisis atmosphere of the regular negotiation teams. One additional difference in concept among the committees is their relationship to contract negotiations. In some cases, the committees are involved in a continuous negotiation process as problems arise, and agreements arrived at, once approved by the parties, become a part of the contract. Other committees are specifically excluded from any direct involvement in contract negotiations; rather, their functions are to deal with broader problems of a long-range nature and to emphasize the improvement of relations that create a better overall climate of understanding for negotiations without being involved with the specifics of negotiations.

A direct influence on the success of these committees is the kind of climate they establish for their deliberations. The following composite of ground rules reflects the sort of atmosphere that the parties agree has been so vital to the success of such committees:

1. Informality is the rule, in a relaxed setting, away from everyday pressures.
2. No formal record is kept of the discussions.
3. Opinions, views, and positions expressed by the parties can be later withdrawn or revised. Statements made may not be quoted at later negotiations.

4. Emphasis is upon brainstorming. Attitudes with respect to collective bargaining matters are not indicated by the nature of the discussions.
5. Proceedings are confidential. There is no exchange of papers and no publicity.
6. Emphasis is upon the parties' becoming fully acquainted.
7. Free and open exchange is emphasized, with a full and candid exploration of issues.
8. Issues are mutually selected.
9. Suggestions of neutrals, where used, are advisory only.
10. Conclusive agreement is not sought. This allows the parties to explore difficult and complex, even explosive, issues.
11. There can be experimentation with ideas and procedures without any kind of a permanent commitment.[12]

Although these ground rules are a composite, a perusal of them can lead to only one conclusion—that the parties hope to encourage, through a nonthreatening, free, and open atmosphere, discussion on a level impossible in the formal structure of negotiations or in the daily employer–employee relationship.

Given this open atmosphere for candid and frank discussion, what do the parties hope to attain, or what do they think they have attained? Again using the composite approach, the following indicates varying results expected from joint-committee action:

Communication problems are eased.

When a committee is allowed to engage in continuous bargaining, mistakes in the contract can be taken care of on the spot, and contract modifications in response to problems, if approved by the parties, can be allowed at any time, a flexibility not found in the regular process of contract negotiation. This is a "living-document" concept.

There is provided an excellent forum for innovation and creativity that is lacking in the more confined framework of regular negotiations.

[12] Healy, *Creative Collective Bargaining;* Simkin, "Positive Approaches to Labor Peace"; R.W. Fleming, "New Challenges for Collective Bargaining," *Wisconsin Law Review,* May 1964; Richard P. McLaughlin, "Collective Bargaining—The New Trend," *Labor Law Journal,* August 1964; Frederick R. Livingston, "Avoidance and Settlement of Disputes," BNA, No. 572 (1967) Di-D7; *FMCS Annual Report* for Fiscal Year 1965; "The Kaiser–Steelworkers Agreement," *Monthly Labor Review,* December 1959 (also February 1961); Kelly, "Techniques for Minimizing Crisis"; Executive Order 10946, Title 3, "Establishing a Program for Resolving Labor Disputes at Missile and Space Sites"; Clark Kerr and George Halverson, *Causes of Industrial Peace under Collective Bargaining: A Study of Lockheed Aircraft Corporation and the International Association of Machinists,* Reprint No. 17, University of California, Berkeley, 1950. Kerr notes, "One technique for expeditious settlement has been on-the-spot investigation of grievances by the union's business representative and a representative of the company's Industrial Relations Office . . . only the essential issues are left for higher levels." p. 17.

Frankness and realism are fostered, with candid and objective exploration of issues unclouded by the face-saving, political atmosphere of the bargaining. Sham and artifice are foreign to this environment.

This allows an objective study of matters too complex or too emotionally loaded to settle under the pressures of bargaining deadlines.

It generates mutual trust and confidence and a genuinely mature bargaining relationship.

The composite approach avoids the rigidity and crisis-loaded contract deadline and provides a flexibility inimical to frozen positions.

Because it is continuous, it provides a means of anticipating and solving problems before they generate a crisis.

Preconceived ideas can be discussed in a rational, nonthreatening atmosphere.

Longer-range consideration of problems is possible.

Flexibility of the committee process replaces the rigidity of traditional bargaining.

Not only a better forum for determining the facts, but the time to determine the facts, is possible.

Because it is continuous, this method avoids the accumulation of problems, a real bottleneck in traditional last-minute negotiations.

It creates a positive attitude toward peaceful resolution of problems, a cooperative approach to problems rather than an "arm's-length" relationship.

Through constancy of contact, regular communication, and problem-solving orientation, more understanding at the bargaining table is effected. Behavior at the bargaining table becomes more mature, responsible, and sophisticated.

The joint-committee approach personalizes relations between management and union representatives.

A forum for dialogue in advance of technological change eases its impact.

The committee can serve as a release valve for relieving pressures that may arise during formal negotiations.[13]

There is no doubt about the importance of these joint committees in giving fresh vitality to the collective bargaining process. Commitment to a continuing dialogue by labor and management over mutual problems is a commitment to the concept of collective bargaining as a continuous rather than intermittent (contract-deadline) process.

RESOLVING IMPASSE IN NEGOTIATIONS

The preceding section concerned itself with techniques devised to replace crisis bargaining and prevent negotiation impasses leading to work

[13] *Ibid.*

stoppages and other interferences with production and employment. In addition to these preventive types of techniques, several innovative techniques have appeared that have as their objective the resolution of impasse after it occurs. These will be discussed under the headings of mediation, fact-finding, arbitration, bag of tools, and the nonstoppage strike. A final subsection will be addressed to the role of the strike in resolution of impasse in order to give completeness and balance to the total discussion of conflict prevention and resolution.

Mediation

In the preceding discussion, mediation was presented as a technique for preventing conflict. The main focus of the discussion was directed to the concept of preventive mediation, but in a much broader framework than that conceived when the term was first introduced in the 1950s. The focus here is to direct attention to yet another aspect of mediation: its innovative use in resolving conflict, in contrast to its traditional use.

Mediation in the traditional sense has been regarded as a process that should be kept quite separate from such techniques as arbitration and fact-finding. With the increasing flexibility being introduced in attempts to develop more viable ways of resolving labor–management disputes, this strict division between the functions of mediation, fact-finding, and arbitration is undergoing change and is no longer as sacrosanct as in the past.

MEDIATION–ARBITRATION. One method, used successfully by Sam Kagel and given the title of "med-arb," breaks with precedent by incorporating both mediation and arbitration functions in one individual.[14] As the term indicates, the total process is a blending procedurally of both mediation and arbitration. Simply stated, med-arb involves calling in an experienced person who is given both mediation and arbitration authority. His first responsibility is to attempt to help the parties resolve their differences through mediation. But while attempting to resolve by mediation, he also has in reserve authority to arbitrate any unresolved issues. The process includes urging the parties to settle through negotiation but holding a terminal procedure in reserve if this fails.

It is important to emphasize that the arbitration part of the process is voluntary, not compulsory arbitration, since the parties must have voluntarily agreed to it beforehand. And if the parties have voluntarily agreed to the process, it also means that they prefer a peaceful solution over open conflict. This is important itself in creating the setting for successful med-arb. It logically follows that the parties must have jointly pledged no strike, no lockout for the process to work.

---

[14] Sam Kagel and John Kagel, "Using Two New Arbitration Techniques," *Monthly Labor Review*, November 1972, p. 12.

The key to the success of the med-arb approach, according to the Kagels, is that it "gives the med-arbiter 'muscle' which is not available to him if he acts solely as a mediator."[15] He performs a mediation function in attempting to assist the parties to reconcile their differences, but mediation in a special sense. He does not, as the Kagels point out, "transmit messages between labor and management. He, in effect, becomes a party to the negotiations in the sense that, while negotiating, each of the contending parties must necessarily seek to convince him that their position is reasonable and acceptable,"[16] knowing that he might play a terminal role on unresolved issues as an arbitrator. The process, as one participant stated, "keeps both parties honest."[17] The reason for this is that the mediation hearings are, in a sense, also arbitration hearings, because the med-arbiter must use the information and arguments brought out in the mediation session to make a terminal judgment if any issues remain unresolved. In this way, the med-arb process utilizes the best of both mediation and arbitration procedures while leaving freedom to the parties to determine how far they want to go.

Last, it should be apparent that it is not the type of process in which inexperienced individuals should be used, since to perform both mediation and arbitration functions within the same setting requires not only experience but specially developed skills.

MEDIATION–FACT-FINDING.   The proscription of the right to strike by a number of the states as well as the federal government has given impetus in a few instances to a combined process of mediation–fact-finding of somewhat the same nature as the med-arb technique, except for the final and binding terminal procedure of the latter. The distinction between this type of process and the more usual mediation–*then*–fact-finding is that here, both processes (mediation and fact-finding) are carried out by one mediator or mediation board in a continuous process. As in the med-arb process, the person or persons involved are at first confined to the mediation function (go-between, catalyst, confidant, knowledgeable advisor) and nothing more. If this function does not result in a resolution of the impasse, then the mediator automatically or, in some instances, with the permission of the parties moves to the role of fact-finder. As H.S. Block notes, the value of the combined mediation–fact-finding function is that the mediator "possessing an insider's knowledge obtained as an intermediary . . . is in a peculiarly advantageous position to make fact-finding recommendations which should encompass both the equities and the realistic expectancies of the parties."[18]

A few examples will illustrate the use of the process. Under the 1975

---

[15] *Ibid.*
[16] *Ibid.*
[17] *Ibid.*
[18] Howard S. Block, "Criteria in Public Sector Disputes," in *Arbitration and the Public Interest* (Washington, D.C.: Bureau of National Affairs, Inc., 1971), p. 179.

Washington Educational Employment Relations Act, the mediator also acting as a fact-finder is open as a possibility, if the parties wish to move in this direction. Section 13 of the act reads:

> The mediator shall meet with the parties or their representatives or both, forthwith, either jointly or separately, and shall take such other steps as he may deem appropriate in order to persuade the parties to resolve their differences and effect a mutually acceptable agreement. The mediator, without the consent of both parties, shall not make findings of fact or recommend terms of settlement.

In South Dakota, the commissioner of labor, under Section 3-18-8.1 of the Public Employees' Unions Act, upon the request of either party attempts first to conciliate a dispute; then, if this is unsuccessful, he is required to "impartially investigate the matters in difference between the parties" and make a report to them "of the issues involved and his recommendations for settlement of the controversy. "The commission also has the option to call in "two capable citizens not directly connected with the dispute, one to be named by each party, to assist in the investigation and advise with him as to his recommendations." North Dakota follows a tripartite mediation–fact-finding procedure with findings and recommendations. If the recommendations are turned down by either party, the party representatives may ask the board for further consideration of the issues. Finally, in Georgia, under the Fire Fighters' Mediation Act, Section 9, a tripartite mediation board is provided to hold hearings. Within ten days after these hearings:

> . . . the mediators shall make written findings and a written opinion upon the issues presented a copy of which shall be mailed or otherwise transmitted to the bargaining agent or its attorney or other designated representative and the corporate authority. A majority decision of the mediators shall be advisory in nature and shall not be binding upon either the bargaining agent or the corporate authorities.

PARTISAN MEDIATION AND MEDIATION TO FINALITY. Of these two other mediation concepts, the latter can be dispatched with little discussion at this point, since it will be taken up more appropriately under compulsory arbitration. It is mentioned here only to clear up any confusion concerning real meaning. In the 1967 rail dispute, the final action taken by Congress was the establishment of a board to decide the issues. Donald Cullen notes, "Although the Administration delicately termed this last step 'mediation to finality,' few observers could discern how it differed from compulsory arbitration."[19]

---

[19] Donald E. Cullen, *National Emergency Strikes,* ILR Paperback No. 7, October 1968, p. 75.

The term "partisan mediation" has real meaning. It refers to the strong role played by central labor councils in the San Francisco–Oakland Bar Area. A procedure has been established whereby no AFL-CIO union goes on strike without approval of the central labor council. Before this approval is forthcoming, there is triggered a waiting period for notification of other employers and unions that may be affected. The executive committee of the labor council then takes an active role in trying to work out an agreement, or it "appoints a small subcommittee to function with the parties in a mediating capacity. This is not impartial mediation—a better description would be partisan mediation."[20]

Fact-Finding

The proscription of the right to strike in the public sector has given a tremendous impetus to the use of fact-finding as one of the alternative techniques to the right to strike. Nothing has more hastened the inclusion of procedural machinery such as fact-finding and voluntary arbitration than the realization that, even though proscribed from striking by statute, public employees do strike. Executive Order 11491 does not mandate fact-finding but does provide for its use in federal-sector negotiation impasses under Section 17: "Third party fact-finding with recommendations to assist in the resolution of an impasse may be used by the parties only when authorized or directed by the [Federal Impasses] Panel." In contrast, virtually all the states covering public-employee collective bargaining either mandate fact-finding as a part of the procedure or provide it on a voluntary basis.

Fact-finding comes in many forms and operates under many operational rules. Most fact-finding panels are tripartite, although a "panel" may be just one person. The panel may be constituted by choosing one member from each side and having these two in turn select a third, who is usually chairman. Or all three members may be chosen from the public or the government agency. In most instances, the fact-finding panel is charged with findings of fact through a hearing, with the right, in some cases, to subpoena and to render an opinion or to recommend settlement of the dispute on the basis of the facts. The majority of fact-finding recommendations are advisory only and may at some point be made public by either the fact-finder or the parties. The hoped-for result of fact-finding is that, either highlighting the facts through neutral third-party action or placing the parties in the glow of public opinion by making the facts public, these recommendations will enable the parties to see the light and reach an agreement. Finally, while fact-finding has seldom been used in private industry in the normal course of events, it has played

[20] Richard A. Liebes, "Partisan Mediation by the Central Labor Council," *Monthly Labor Review*, September 1973, p. 56.

a prominent role in the emergency procedures of both the Railway Labor Act (fact-finding without recommendations) and the Taft-Hartley Act (fact-finding without recommendations).

A few rather interesting fact-finding approaches have been incorporated into state statutes or suggested by interested parties that were not covered by the composite descriptions above. For example, under the Nevada Local Government Employment–Management Relations Act, Section 288.200, fact-finding, if invoked, may result in recommendations that are advisory or binding by agreement of the parties, or:

> If the parties do not mutually agree to make the findings and recommendations of the factfinder final and binding, the governor shall have the emergency power and authority, at the request of either party and prior to the submission of the dispute to factfinding, to order . . . that the findings and recommendations on all or any specified issues of a factfinder in a particular dispute will be final and binding.

Under the Connecticut law of October 1975, Extending Bargaining Rights to State Employees, Section 8 provides for regular fact-finding with nonbinding recommendations, but then, in addition, authorizes the fact-finder to use mediation if he so chooses: "Nothing in this section shall be construed to prohibit the fact-finder from endeavoring to mediate the dispute for which he has been selected or appointed as fact-finder." Fact-finding in disputes involving public employees in Oregon also provides that the fact-finding committee "may attempt to mediate a dispute at any time prior to the submission of its findings and recommendations." (Section 50-030, Rules of Practice and Procedure.) It is also true that under New York law, fact-finders are not only authorized and encouraged to mediate, but do mediate.[21]

Two other proposals are advanced by Sam Zagoria and Donald H. Wollett. Zagoria would tie the fact-finder's recommendations to public referendum by allowing either party to place the recommendations on the next special ballot or regular election, the results to be retroactive.[22] Wollett suggests a process by which any taxpayer or affected consumer could, upon the refusal of the parties to accept the recommendations of a fact-finder, bring a court suit. The court would then, if it found public health or safety threatened and no other means of resolving the suit, rule the fact-finder's recommendations binding. Wollett reasons that the unpredictability of the court's course of action would create an atmo-

---

[21] Charles M. Rehmus, "An Overview of Labor Relations in the Public Service," *Collective Bargaining and Dispute Settlement in the Public and Private Sectors*, Industrial Relations Center, University of Hawaii, July 31, 1969, p. 50. Comment by Anderson.

[22] Sam Zagoria, "Referendum Use in Labor Impasses Proposed," *LMRS Newsletter*, September 1973, pp. 2–4.

sphere of "mutual anxiety" and cause the parties to think twice before rejecting the fact-finder's recommendations.[23] Finally, under the Taft-Hartley Act amendments covering health-care institutions, the law provides, as a part of a delay of strike procedures, for the use of a board of inquiry. After mediation and upon recommendation of the local mediator, the FMCS may appoint such a board—which in theory can be tripartite, but in practice has meant the appointment of a single person experienced in the field and drawn from such groups as former mediators and arbitrators from FMCS panels. The responsibility of the person acting as a board of inquiry is to meet with the parties at impasse, ascertain the points at issue and the positions of the parties on each issue, draw on or even have present the federal mediator, and utilize mediation techniques if that method seems promising. Issues remaining unsettled at the close of the hearing, which may be all or a reduced number of the original issues, are then to be considered by the board of inquiry, and within a two-week period, recommendations for settlement are to be forwarded to the parties. The recommendations are advisory only and may be accepted or, if not accepted, serve as a basis for further efforts of the federal mediator.

Arbitration

Developments in recent years importantly, but not exclusively, influenced by public-sector bargaining needs have given a new emphasis to the use of voluntary arbitration as a terminal procedure in contract negotiation disputes. In special circumstances, such as health and safety, there has also been renewed effort in types of legislated arbitration.

Legislated arbitration has been the butt of much criticism in the past. And the government seemed to agree that bargaining should be aided by mediation, with a little prodding on occasion through fact-finding, but stopping short of terminal arbitration procedures. Yet, the use of binding arbitration as the terminal point in impasse procedures is not without significant precedents. From the late nineteenth century, there have been a number of instances where arbitration of interest disputes has been used either on a one-time basis or as part of a permanent procedure. The reader is referred to the Amalgamated Street Railway Unions, and the anthracite coal-mining, hosiery, men's clothing, newspaper, book and job printing, electrical, and hotel industries, to cite a few. Starting with the Arbitration Act of 1888 and continuing through the Erdman Act of 1898, the Newlands Act of 1913, and the Railway Labor Act, voluntary arbitration was a fixed feature of the dispute-resolution procedures. David Cole also recalls that in the twelve years following World War II,

---

[23] Donald H. Wollett, "Mutual Anxiety: A California Proposal," *Monthly Labor Review*, September 1973, pp. 50–51.

he was involved at least fifty times in arbitration of interest disputes.

The increased attention to arbitration in resolving interest disputes has also been given impetus not only by more flexible attitudes toward varied techniques of using arbitration, but also by the increasing preference of labor leaders such as Meany, Abel, Wurf, and others for the use of alternatives to the strike. Nor has the public reaction to strikes gone unnoticed. Former Secretary of Labor Hodgson notes that "in at least one sphere the American public will no longer tolerate bargaining failure. I have in mind the big strike situation."[24] Rehmus points out that although "arguments against arbitration may sound plausible, none appears to be strongly supported by the available data."[25]

For the purpose of clarity, although the fact has been covered earlier, the reader is reminded that *arbitration* as used in this chapter is confined to interest disputes or disputes that have arisen during contract negotiations. This is to be distinguished from *grievance arbitration*, to be discussed in the next chapter, which is a contract-interpretation procedure. Moreover, care should be taken to distinguish clearly between voluntary and compulsory arbitration. The former is established by the voluntary agreement of the parties; the latter is imposed, usually by law or court order. Arbitration may also be binding or advisory. The former leaves the parties no recourse; under the latter, they may choose whether or not to accept. Finally, there are other variations to be found in the use of arbitration to resolve interest disputes. The arbitration may be conducted by a board, usually tripartite, or a single arbitrator. The tripartite board, more often than not, is made up of a member from each party and a neutral chosen by an agreed-upon procedure. In some important arbitration-board actions, the parties have considered it important to have more than one neutral on the board, or even to have the board entirely composed of neutrals.

The scope and procedures of the boards may also vary. In some instances, the board is to resolve all unresolved issues still standing at some point in the negotiations. In others, the board must choose from final offers on unresolved matters of the parties to the negotiation. In still others, the board is given some discretion to combine other techniques and skills with the arbitration process, such as mediating, remanding the issues for further negotiation, or a procedure that involves less of a judicial proceeding and more of a search for accommodation.

The essence of these variations, in contrast to arbitration of interest disputes in the traditional sense, is that arbitration has assumed a refreshing viability in meeting the collective bargaining problems of the

[24] James D. Hodgson, "Stretching Out the Duration of Labor Contracts," *Monthly Labor Review*, September 1973, p. 55.

[25] Charles M. Rehmus, "Legislated Interest Arbitration," *IRRA 27th Annual Winter Proceedings*, December 28–29, 1974, p. 309.

present day. Consideration will now be given in more detail to some of the nontraditional ways in which arbitration of interest disputes is being used.

One attitudinal shift toward interest-dispute arbitration is significant. Increasingly, practitioners are becoming convinced that arbitration in the contract negotiation areas must become more viable and flexible if it is to meet the needs. This line of thinking views arbitration of interest disputes as a process in which adjustment, accommodation, and acceptability will be more common goals, rather than a win-lose type of adjudication. In skilled hands, it will also be considered as a "continuation rather than a replacement for the negotiation process."[26] More latitude is being allowed during the arbitration procedure for simultaneous or alternative use of other techniques. Illustrative of this more flexible type of arbitration are the following: (1) public members of a tripartite arbitration board using industry and union members as a sounding board "against which the public members could rattle ideas, concepts, and specifics" in arriving at a decision acceptable to the parties;[27] (2) allowing parties to sit down with alternate members of a bipartite arbitration panel while awaiting hearing, in a continuing effort to resolve their differences; (3) representatives of the parties on a tripartite arbitration panel using the leanings of the neutral member to initiate further negotiations; (4) arbitration *cum* mediation—the arbitration board at its option resorting to mediation any time during the arbitration process; (5) arbitration *cum* negotiation—the arbitrator or arbitration board remanding some issues to further negotiation.

A significant step was taken by the steel industry in the use of regular arbitration to solve unresolved issues during contract negotiations. This was important not only because of the strategic function and size of the industry involved but also because of the pattern-setting possibilities if the step taken continues to be successful. On March 29, 1973, the major steel companies and the 600-member Basic Steel Industry Conference of the Steelworkers signed what is known as the Experimental Negotiation Agreement (ENA) and by their signatures agreed to submit all issues remaining unresolved no later than April 20, 1974, to final and binding arbitration by an impartial arbitration panel. Excluded as issues for arbitration were local working conditions, union membership and check-off provisions, cost-of-living adjustment provisions, matters concerning uniformity of wages and benefits, no-strike and no-lockout provisions, and management rights. In addition, employees were guaranteed a minimum 3 percent wage increase for each of the three years of the agreement

[26] Charles M. Rehmus, "Binding Arbitration in the Public Sector," *Monthly Labor Review*, April 1975, p. 54.
[27] William E. Simkin, "Limitation of Arm's-Length or Adversary Arbitration," *Monthly Labor Review*, September 1973, p. 56.

and a one-time $150 bonus on August 1, 1974, the day when the new three-year contract would go into effect. The results of this agreement are that the process worked; agreement was reached on April 12, 1974; no recourse was necessary to the impartial arbitration panel; and the parties agreed in advance to implement the same procedures for their 1977 contract negotiations.

FINAL-OFFER ARBITRATION. Receiving most of the attention during the past decade in the literature is a process that has been called variously *final-offer, last-offer, final-position, best-offer, either-or, one-or-the-other,* and *forced-choice arbitration of interest disputes.* This process has elicited much interest among those seeking alternatives to the strike in the public-employee areas but has also been recommended by its advocates for wider use. The essence of final-offer arbitration is simply that in making a decision on a contract negotiation dispute, the arbitrator or board must select one or the other of the final offers of the two parties. There are variations, of course, but the most common approach is that each party makes a final package offer of the unresolved issues at the point of invoking arbitration, and the arbitrator must choose one of the two packages. He has no flexibility to vary the items within the packages or to modify the terms in a way he might consider more fair and reasonable.

Fred Witney, a panel member, reported on the procedure used by the city of Indianapolis and the AFSCME, based on a bill introduced in the Indiana state senate in 1972 that (1) required the arbitration panel to "select the most reasonable, in its judgment of the final offers submitted by the parties, and such final offer shall be the binding contract between the parties," and (2) stated, "The Board is expressly precluded from selecting individual terms and conditions from each package so as to direct a composite consisting of elements selected from both proposals."[28] From this basic form, final-offer arbitration procedures vary. Under the Michigan procedure covering policemen and firemen, the final offer is on an issue-by-issue basis. The Michigan law, Section 423.238, states that "the arbitration panel shall identify the economic issues in dispute, and direct each of the parties to submit . . . its last offer of settlement on each economic issue." The law then directs the arbitration panel, "As to each economic issue, the arbitration panel shall adopt the last offer of settlement which, in the opinion of the arbitration panel, more nearly complies" with the statute. Under the Iowa procedures, the panel has two routes by which it may arrive at a decision. First, it may select from the final offers of the parties on each impasse item. Second, the panel may alternately choose the recommendation of the fact-finder

---

[28] Fred Witney, "Final-Offer Arbitration: The Indianapolis Experience," *Monthly Labor Review*, May 1973, p. 20.

on each impasse item. Eugene, Oregon, provides still another selection package: Each party is allowed to make two final offers for the arbitration board's consideration, in the form of a complete contract proposal or in the form of the items at impasse only.

Another variation concerns the point at which the final offer(s) must be rendered for the decision of the arbitration panel. In some instances, the final offers are those made at the time arbitration is invoked. In others, the parties have the option of waiting until the end of the hearing to reveal their positions. And in other instances, the parties may make a final offer at the beginning of the hearing, but subject to modification at the end of the hearing if either party wishes.

Although there is a noticeable lack of guidelines upon which the arbitration panels can base their decisions, a few statutes have pointed the way. Among the criteria mentioned that the arbitrators are expected to use in arriving at the choice of the final offers are bargaining history; financial ability; interests and welfare of the public; comparison of wages, hours, and employment (public and private); cost of living; overall compensation; stipulations of the parties; and the power of the public employer to levy taxes and appropriate funds.

COMPULSORY ARBITRATION. The final category is that of compulsory regular arbitration. This is by its very nature a legislated type of arbitration. Two examples will suffice to illustrate this approach.

In 1967, a rail stoppage occurred, involving the six shopcraft unions and the major railroads. The emergency procedures of the Railway Labor Act were invoked and an emergency board appointed. The emergency board made its findings and recommendations. The shopcrafts rejected the recommendations. In sequence then, the no-strike period was extended 20 days by congressional action; a special mediation panel failed to bring a resolution; the no-strike period was extended an additional 47 days by Congress; at its conclusion, the union struck for two days; and Congress then established a final board to determine the issues. This is what the administration called "mediation to finality," but in reality this was nothing more nor less than compulsory arbitration.[29]

In determining the impasse procedures to be activated, Alaska includes a rather novel approach to regular terminal arbitration. Public employees are classified into three groups, according to the service they perform, under Section 23.40.200 of their Arbitration Act:

(1) Those services which may not be given up for even the shortest period of time;

(2) Those services which may be interrupted for a limited period but not for an indefinite period of time; and

29 Cullen, *National Emergency Strikes*, pp. 74–75.

(3) Those services in which work stoppages may be sustained for extended periods without serious effect on the public.

In definition of these areas, the first group includes police, firemen, and employees of jails, prisons, other correctional institutions, and hospitals; the second group includes public-utility, snow-removal, sanitation, and educational-institution employees; and the third group includes all other employees. The Alaskan act provides that the first group may not strike and that binding arbitration is the terminal procedure. The second group, after mediation and a majority vote to strike, may strike on a limited basis, but if the strike endangers the health, safety, or welfare of the public, the matter may end in binding arbitration the same as with group 1. Group 3 employees may engage in a strike upon a majority vote of the employees in the collective bargaining unit. The interesting aspect of the Alaskan act, and perhaps a forerunner of things to come, is that a serious attempt has been made to differentiate on a public-impact basis between the situations when the right to strike should be allowed and when it should be prohibited. The act separates employees functionally in terms of the critical or noncritical nature of the service they perform. For too long we have retained the artificial distinction of critical versus noncritical on the basis of public- versus private-sector employees. These artificial distinctions should give way, and are slowly doing so, to more meaningful criteria in which critical and noncritical are based upon the actual service or productive effort and its impact on public safety, health, or welfare, regardless of the location of the work, whether in the public or the private sector.

Bag of Tools

When I was a graduate student in industrial and labor relations in the late forties and early fifties, the so-called *bag-of-tools* approach to impasse resolution was an interesting concept but not much more. Although still not as formalized as other impasse procedures, this approach —also variously known as the *choice-of-procedures, mutual-anxiety, arsenal-of-weapons, multiple-tool,* and *uncertainty* approach—has received revived interest more recently. This interest has resulted in legislation such as that of Massachusetts, in congressional hearings on emergency disputes in transportation, and in increasing emphasis in professional writings. Most of the interest to date in the use of a multiple-tool approach has related either to impasses of major public concern or to emergency strike legislation. However, it is also receiving more attention as a possible impasse procedure in public-sector disputes.

The logic behind the multiple-tool approach is that, if no uncertainty is raised in the minds of the parties as to the procedures they might be faced with in case of impasse, then they avoid responsible bargaining in good faith and move perfunctorily through the legislated emergency-procedure steps to what they anticipate will be a favorable government handout. If uncertainty *is* introduced as to what procedures the government might eventually take, ranging from compulsion to a continuation of a work stoppage, then there might be an incentive for the parties to use the regular bargaining process rather than risk a negative result because of the impasse procedure selected. The way the multiple-tool approach would operate would be for the government to establish an impartial, independent, widely representative, and knowledgeable board with authority to utilize any one of a number of tools in attempting to resolve the impasse. The tools suggested range from those of a more compulsory nature to those with little or no compulsion. The following list, while not exhaustive, is representative of the types of choice:

1. A system of graduated penalties
2. Extending the no-strike period through use of an injunction
3. Further mediation
4. Advisory arbitration
5. Compulsory arbitration—all issues
6. Compulsory arbitration—issues at impasse only
7. Fact-finding with recommendations—nonbinding
8. Fact-finding with recommendations—binding
9. Final-offer arbitration
10. Partial strike or lockout
11. Nonstoppage procedure
12. Seizure
13. Unlimited strike allowed
14. Limited strike allowed

It is interesting to note that both the Taft-Hartley emergency procedures and the EO 11491 impasse procedures are flexible enough to provide for the multiple or bag-of-tools approach. Section 210 of Taft-Hartley provides for a final step that the president must take if the emergency dispute is not settled at the termination of the 80-day injunction. It reads: ". . . the President shall submit to the Congress a full and comprehensive report of the proceedings, including the findings of the board of inquiry . . . , together with such recommendations as he may see fit to make for consideration and appropriate action." Appropriate action in the hands of Congress certainly allows for the multiple-tool approach, among others, should Congress adopt the concept. The Railway Labor Act does not include such a provision, although it has been the practice of the president when he has exhausted all the procedures to place the dispute in the lap of Congress if it remains unsettled. Under EO 11491, the resolution of impasse is of such major concern that, rather than its just providing for emergency procedures, a special panel, the Federal Service Impasses Panel, was established with direct responsibility for handling disputes not resolved by the normal procedures of the order. Section 17 states:

> When voluntary arrangements, including the services of the Federal Mediation and Conciliation Service or other third-party mediation, fail to resolve a negotiation impasse, either party may request the Federal Service Impasses Panel to consider the matter. The Panel, in its discretion and under the regulations it prescribes, may consider the matter and may settle the impasse by appropriate action. Arbitration or third-party fact finding with recommendations to assist in the resolution of an impasse may be used by the parties only when authorized or directed by the Panel.

Up to the end of 1976, the arbitration option has not been among the tools used by the panel in resolving impasses, although, as noted above, it certainly is an option. However, in resolving a 1974 dispute, the panel for the first time moved to binding impasse-settlement recommendations. The options the panel currently elects to choose from are:

—To direct the parties to return to the bargaining table.

—To direct the parties to avail themselves of mediation assistance.

—To direct the parties to utilize other established voluntary settlement procedures; or to appoint a fact-finder to conduct a hearing for the purpose of establishing the facts of the dispute and the positions of the parties, and to otherwise develop a complete record upon which the panel may base impasse settlement recommendations to the parties.

—If recommendations are issued, the parties have 20 days to consider them. Should the dispute remain unsettled after the expiration of the 20-day period, the panel "will take whatever action it deems necessary to bring the dispute to settlement."[30]

Admittedly, the Impasses Panel has not administered its functions through a bag-of-tools plus uncertainty approach. The reason for coverage here is that the framework effects such an approach should the Impasses Panel choose to go in that direction. Functionally, the activities and approach of the panel fit more closely to the next technique to be discussed—the *superneutral* or what might be called the *variable-technique* approach.

[30] Reports of the Federal Service Impasses Panel, July 1, 1970–December 31, 1973, p. 4, and January 1, 1974–December 31, 1974, p. 1.

VARIABLE-TECHNIQUE APPROACH.   The reason for separating this from
the bag-of-tools approach is that the bag-of-tools technique emphasizes
the uncertainty created by the authority's selecting at some point one
of a number of tools or techniques available to it that the parties, until
that point, would have had no way of predicting. Hence the possibility
that, as a result of the uncertainty, they might deem it more advisable
to negotiate to a settlement. In contrast, under the variable approach,
a neutral or an impasse board has a number of techniques at its option
and uses them in any way it deems most productive at any particular
stage of the negotiations. This means that it may use mediation, move
to fact-finding with recommendations, remand the matter to negotiations based on the recommendations, move back to the mediation,
proceed to some form of arbitration with flexibility for the parties to continue negotiations, or turn to mediation while the arbitration is in process. The point is that it is an ad hoc procedure in which success
depends upon the willingness of the parties to use various techniques
and upon the ability of the neutral to handle with expertise and a good
sense of timing and judgment the movement from one technique of
impasse resolution to another.

Support for such a process, whether it is called the variable-technique,
the superneutral, or the pragmatic and flexible administration approach,
should be forthcoming in the now-emerging climate of approval of more
flexible approaches to conflict resolution. It is in a sense the breaking of
the old conventional lines of demarcation that imposed a strict separation
between the traditional impasse techniques of negotiation, mediation,
fact-finding, and arbitration, in order to permit the viability and flexibility in techniques of impasse settlement necessary to handle effectively
today's types of impasse problems. It should also be emphasized that
responsibility for much of the shift and change in attitudes that effect a
more flexible approach to impasse resolution results from the new challenges of public-sector unionism and collective bargaining. David Cole
points out that the variable-technique procedure has been used, and he
vigorously supports a voluntary version of it:

> My strong preference is for an indefinite combination of all these pro-
> cedures, together with any others the parties may devise that they be-
> lieve may be helpful. I would favor a course in which they move by
> agreement step by step from one procedure to another until their differ-
> ences are ended. I would exclude nothing nor would I compel them to
> go forward if either chooses not to do so. This is because of the very
> nature of agreement making. . . . My suggestion is a combination of
> all the possible procedures to be used step by step, with emphasis on
> the constant mutual desire of the parties to move ahead.[31]

[31] David Cole, "The Evolving Techniques," *AFL-CIO Federationist*, May 1974
(a reprint).

In essence, the variable approach is the technique being used by the Impasses Panel in the federal-employee bargaining sector. Of 116 cases before the Impasses Panel between 1970 and 1974, 39 were withdrawn before final action of any kind by the panel; 8 were declined because of jurisdictional matters; 7 were returned for more negotiation; 12 were returned for more mediation; 1 was returned for other voluntary arrangements; 10, because there was a question as to whether the proposal being considered was contrary to law, regulation, controlling agreement, or the executive order, were referred to other procedures under EO Section 11 (c); 19 were settled prior to fact-finding; 19 were settled after the panel report and recommendations; and 1 was resolved upon the issuance of a decision and order by the panel.

Nonstoppage Strike

Another technique has been around a long time but has not found much usage. I remember well being exposed to the concept in Neil Chamberlain's *Social Responsibility and Strikes* in 1953, while attending a seminar with Prof. Jean McKelvey. At that time, Chamberlain noted that he had arrived at the nonstoppage-strike proposal independently but subsequently found three other, prior instances in which a similar proposal had been made: Marceau and Musgrave, in "Strikes in Essential Industries: A Way Out," *Harvard Business Review,* May 1949; Goble, in "The Non-Stoppage Strike," *Labor Law Journal,* February 1951; and Bakke, in a radio address over station WTIC, Hartford, June 15, 1952.[32] From time to time the nonstoppage strike, sometimes called the *statutory strike, semistrike,* or *income-work time gradual pressure strike,* has received renewed attention. The first known application of the technique was in 1964 as a result of an agreement between the Dunbar Furniture Company and the Upholsterers International Union, AFL-CIO.

In contrast to a regular stoppage strike, the nonstoppage strike requires the parties to continue production while being subject to financial forfeits for the time the dispute remains unresolved. Several different proposals have been made for invoking the nonstoppage-strike process: by statute through the use of an injunction procedure, by voluntary agreement of the parties, or by voluntary agreement of the parties and congressional approval. The goals various writers identify are to ensure continued production; to attempt to promote collective bargaining by the disputants; to establish a way for the parties to fight it out without negative impact on customers, the community, or the public generally; a way of taking the public out of the middle; and a method

[32] Neil W. Chamberlain, assisted by Jane M. Schilling, *Social Responsibility and Strikes* (New York: Harper & Row, 1953), p. 279.

by which there can be an accurate countdown of losses to the parties as a result of the continuation of the dispute.

The assumptions on which the nonstoppage approach is based are that an incentive to settle differences will be provided by requiring the parties to forfeit income to a lesser degree than in a full strike but nevertheless enough to be significant, and that, even though each party will receive some advantages by continuation of production and employment, both will also incur some losses.

The various forfeiture proposals require that both parties incur some financial loss:

1. 25% of employees' wages, 25% of salaries of specific officers of the company, and an amount paid by the company equal to its net profit to be forfeited

2. 50% of wages to be forfeited by the employees and a matching amount by the company

3. 33⅓% of employees' wages and a matching amount to be forfeited by the company

4. Forfeit of wages by employees to range from 10% to 100% (40% a good standard), to be determined by executive (government) discretion, the company to forfeit a matching amount

5. 50% of wage income of employees plus a forfeiture by the company of everything above operating expenses plus one-half of fixed costs

6. A 50% forfeiture of wages by employees plus a company forfeiture of one-half of what company's change in net earnings would have been had a regular work stoppage been instituted[33]

The various proposals also outline procedures whereby all or a portion of the forfeiture may be returned:

1. If the dispute is settled within 90 days, all the forfeited money is returned. If not, a new 90 days begins.

[33] Cyrus F. Smythe, "Public Policy and Emergency Disputes," *Labor Law Journal* (Chicago: Commerce Clearing House, 1963), p. 830; Kenneth G. Slocum, "Working Strikers," *Wall Street Journal*, May 20, 1964, pp. 1, 15; Damon W. Harrison, Jr., "The Strike and Its Alternatives: The Public Employment Experience," *Kentucky Law Journal*, Vol. 63 (1975), 464–65; David B. McCalmont, "The Semi-Strike," *Industrial and Labor Relations Review* (New York: New York School of Industrial and Labor Relations, 1962), January, pp. 191–211; George W. Goble, "The Non-Stoppage Strike," *Current Economic Comment* (Urbana: University of Illinois, Bureau of Economic and Business Research, August 1950), pp. 3–11; LeRoy Marceau and Richard A. Musgrave, "Strikes in Essential Industries: A Way Out," *Harvard Business Review*, Vol. 27, May 1940, 27; Chamberlain, *Social Responsibility and Strikes*, pp. 279–86; Stephen H. Sosnick, "Non-Stoppage Strikes: A New Approach," *Industrial and Labor Relations Review* (New York: New York School of Industrial and Labor Relations, Cornell University, 1964), pp. 73–78; "The Right to Strike and the General Welfare," Committee on the Church and Economic Life, National Council of Churches of Christ in the U.S.A. (New York: Council Press, 1967), pp. 4–39.

2. If the dispute is settled within six weeks, all monies are refunded; if settled in seven to nine weeks, 75% is returned; if settled in ten to eleven weeks, 50% is returned; if settled in the twelfth week, 25% is returned; if the dispute is continued beyond twelve weeks, parties may strike or lock out; if strike is not called by the thirteenth week, the old contract is automatically renewed.

3. Establish 20 periods of seven days each, or 140 days in all. At any point within the 140 days, if the dispute is settled, all monies not paid will be refunded.

4. No refund of monies paid. Permanent loss to both company and employees.

5. Monies refunded at end of statutory strike.[34]

The proposals also include directions as to where the forfeited monies are to be paid:

1. To the U.S. Treasury

2. Deposited in a bank

3. To a community project agreed upon by the parties; if they cannot agree, to the Ministerial Association

4. To the local school board or community (In this proposal there were no refund provisions; assumption was that employee–company loss is community's gain.)[35]

A few of the proposals also took into consideration the fact that the nonstoppage technique might not result in a resolution of the dispute. In this contingency, the suggestions were that:

1. After twelve weeks, a strike may be called, but if it is not called by the thirteenth week, the contract is automatically renewed.

2. After the 140 days elapse without a resolution of the dispute, a work stoppage may take place.

3. Seizure is suggested as a final step, but not as a part of the nonstoppage-strike procedure. It would be a separate penalty that might be imposed upon the parties.[36]

THE RIGHT TO STRIKE

Although the right to strike is hardly to be considered as a part of the innovative techniques and methods discussed in prior sections of this

[34] *Ibid.*
[35] *Ibid.*
[36] *Ibid.*

chapter, the discussion of resolution of contract negotiation (interest) conflict would not be complete without some mention of it. It is hoped that the reader understands from the preceding material that what most of the proposed techniques are aimed at is not the elimination of the right to strike, but ways and means of reducing or eliminating the desire or need to strike. Almost unanimous support is given to a preservation of the democratic right to strike. Most observers agree that without this right, there would be no collective bargaining and no democratic way of resolving conflict. Even where the technique established by statute seems more one of compulsion than of voluntarism, careful consideration is given to finding alternate procedures to preserve the equities toward which strike pressures are directed but without the actual need of a strike. The strike-prohibition concept, although mandatory in instances of critical areas such as health, welfare, and safety, must be considered mandatory only in the light of the new environment that has emerged in the last decade—not that of preceding periods. The mandatory approach is more and more looked upon not as a completely unilateral process disregarding all the elements of a good labor–management relationship but as a step that has been taken only after careful consideration and implementation of alternative procedures. Prohibiting the right to strike without meaningful alternative procedures would avail little, since experience has shown that strikes do occur despite bans.

SELECTED REFERENCES

Aaron, Benjamin, and K.W. Wedderburn, eds., *Industrial Conflict—A Comparative Legal Survey*. New York: Crane, Russak & Co., 1972.

A comparative legal survey of industrial conflict in the United States, Great Britain, Sweden, West Germany, France, and Italy.

Blackman, John L., *Presidential Seizure in Labor Disputes*. Cambridge, Mass.: Harvard University Press, 1967.

In the foreword, John T. Dunlop notes that relatively little is known about seizure as one of the arsenal of tools in resolving conflict that vitally affects the public interest, and yet there have been 71 instances of its use. Professor Blackman provides a definitive account of the experience in these 71 seizure situations.

Chamberlain, Neil W., assisted by Jane M. Schilling, *Social Responsibility and Strikes*. New York: Harper & Row, 1953.

For the reader who is interested in the social implications of the strike, this is a classic in the field. From the initial point of defining social responsibility, the author moves to a thoughtful consideration of public opinion and strikes, social control of strikes, and social and legal sanctions.

Davey, Harold W., *Contemporary Collective Bargaining*, 3rd ed. Englewood Cliffs, N.J.: Prentice-Hall, 1972.

Professor Davey, in his inimitable way, discusses industrial conflict and industrial peace.

Dunlop, John T., "The Function of the Strike," in John T. Dunlop and Neil W. Chamberlain, eds., *Frontiers of Collective Bargaining*. New York: Harper & Row, 1967.

Professor Dunlop explains the functional classification of strikes and the decline of the strike. More important, he anticipates the developments that are now taking place: "The parties to collective bargaining may be reasonably expected to experiment more and to devote their attention to the design and perfection of procedures and machinery to resolve disputes. . . ."

"Exploring Alternatives to the Strike," *Monthly Labor Review*, 96, No. 9 (September 1973), 35–66.

Included in this section are a series of articles based on papers presented at the fifth annual Collective Bargaining Forum of the Institute of Collective Bargaining and Group Relations. An excellent and informative series by some of the field's most astute professionals in both the academic and practicing areas. Addressed in the papers are such topics as the role of the strike, alternatives in the public sector, alternatives in the private sector, and alternative techniques. The articles range through all the traditional forms of alternatives such as mediation, fact-finding, and arbitration, but even more important, they delve into new uses and combinations such as med-arb, binding arbitration in interest disputes, partisan mediation, mutual anxiety, and binding fact-finding.

Fleming, R.W., "New Challenges for Collective Bargaining," *Wisconsin Law Review*, May 1964.

Concise discussion of new techniques being used to resolve problems of technological change and to render resolution of conflict a more rational, continuing process.

Flynn, Ralph J., *Public Work, Public Workers*. Washington, D.C.: The New Republic Book Co., 1975.

Through interviews and case histories, Flynn probes the feelings of government workers that are moving them to a new militancy, especially at the state and local levels. The author states that the first step toward a solution to the disorder of strikes is a new national law for public workers, on the order of the Wagner Act.

Gomberg, William, "Special Study Committees," in John T. Dunlop and Neil W. Chamberlain, eds., *Frontiers of Collective Bargaining*. New York: Harper & Row, 1967.

Interesting and informative discussion of special study committees (joint study committees) with emphasis upon the historical perspective. The author refers to such committee efforts as the National Civic Federation, the Protocol of Peace, the Cleveland Ladies' Garment Industrial Experiment, the Chicago Amalgamated Experiment, and the Pequot Mills Experiment.

Healy, James J., ed., *Creative Collective Bargaining*. Englewood Cliffs, N.J.: Prentice-Hall, 1965.

The most definitive work to date on innovative and creative approaches to the improvement of the collective bargaining process. Included are discussions of such plans as the American Motors Progress-Sharing Plan, General Motors, United Air Lines, New York Hotel Industry, Electrical Contracting Industry, Hart Schaffner & Marx, International Harvester, Swift and Company, Allegheny Ludlum, Armour Automation Committee, West Coast Longshore, Basic Steel Human Relations Committee, and the Glass-Container Industry.

Hutt, W.H., *The Strike-Threat System—The Economic Consequences of Collective Bargaining*. New Rochelle, N.Y.: Arlington House, 1973.

A penetrating and provocative analysis of the strike, in which Professor Hutt concludes that fear of strikes inflicts far greater damage on the economic system than actual strikes do. The author reiterates an earlier view that the "mere right to disrupt the continuity of the productive process is having deplorable effects, regarding both the size of real income and equity in the distribution of income."

Indik, Bernard P., and Georgina M. Smith, *Resolution of Social Conflict through Collective Bargaining: An Alternative to Violence?* Reprint No. 22, Institute of Management and Labor Relations, Rutgers University, 1969.

The authors examine the similarities and differences between the labor movement and the racial movement and the possibility of transferring the working elements of collective bargaining to the racial scene as a possible way of reducing conflict. They conclude "it does seem reasonable to expect that some modified bargaining scheme, adapted to the civil rights revolution, can provide a device, or an armament of devices superior to calling national guardsmen or police riot-control groups."

Knowles, K.G.J.C., *Strikes—A Study in Industrial Conflict*. Oxford: Basil Blackwell, 1952.

This book stands as a classic on the strike and covers the British experience from 1911 to 1947.

Lester, Richard A., "An Alternative Strike Procedure," in Neil W. Chamberlain, ed., *Sourcebook on Labor*, p. 756. New York: McGraw-Hill, 1958.

A sort of presidential bag-of-tools approach to emergency strikes with ad hoc hearings, voluntary arbitration, fact-finding, injunction, and seizure with financial penalties as options.

Maggiolo, Walter A., *Techniques of Mediation in Labor Disputes*. Dobbs Ferry, N.Y.: Oceana Publications, 1971.

Complete description of the philosophy of mediation, the mediator, the mediation function, and when to use the mediator.

Northrup, Herbert R., *Compulsory Arbitration and Government Intervention in Labor Disputes—An Analysis of Experience.* Washington, D.C.: Labor Policy Association, Inc., 1966.

Professor Northrup provides an informed basis by which those interested in compulsory arbitration may measure its usefulness.

Simkin, William E., *Mediation and the Dynamics of Collective Bargaining.* Washington, D.C.: Bureau of National Affairs, Inc., 1971.

The former director of the FMCS brings to the reader his unusual perception of the mediation process and its function in crisis bargaining, emergency disputes, preventive mediation, fact-finding and mediation, and the use of mediation in public-employee disputes.

Stephens, Elvis C., "Resolution of Impasses in Public Employee Bargaining," *Monthly Labor Review,* 99, No. 1 (January 1976), 57–58.

Professor Stephens reports on the developments in impasse resolution and the types of issues in dispute.

Stern, James L. et al., *Final-Offer Arbitration.* Lexington, Mass.: D.C. Heath, 1975.

The authors describe and analyze what has happened in Pennsylvania, Michigan, and Wisconsin in dispute-resolution procedures for public safety employees. Called upon for information are the labor and management negotiators and neutrals involved in dispute resolutions in these states. From this study the authors project future trends and speculate about possible consequences of transferring various procedural arrangements to other bargaining situations. The study provides an excellent view of the final-offer arbitration technique.

Stern, James L., and Barbara D. Dennis, eds., Industrial Relations Research Association Series, *Proceedings of the Twenty-Seventh Annual Winter Meeting,* December 28–29, 1974, pp. 307–8.

Papers delivered by Charles M. Rehmus and R. Theodore Clark, Jr., concerning legislated interest arbitration in the public sector.

Stevens, Carl M., "Mediation and the Role of the Neutral," in John T. Dunlop and Neil W. Chamberlain, *Frontiers of Collective Bargaining.* New York: Harper & Row, 1967.

Professor Stevens spells out the functions and tactics of mediation.

Tanimoto, Helene S., *Guide to Statutory Provisions in Public Sector Collective Bargaining—Impasse Resolution Procedures,* Occasional Publication No. 95, Industrial Relations Center, University of Hawaii, 1973.

Excellent coverage of the statutes, ordinances, and personnel rules and regulations covering all the states and the District of Columbia as they apply to impasse procedures. Three major techniques are considered: mediation, fact-finding, and arbitration. Included in the appendices is a chart of employees covered under state statutes and orders.

————, and Joyce M. Najita, *Guide to Statutory Provisions in Public Sector Collective Bargaining—Strike Rights and Prohibitions,* Industrial Relations Center, University of Hawaii, 1974.

A state-by-state examination of the right to strike under state statutes.

Yaffe, Byron, and Howard Goldblatt, *Factfinding in Public Employment in New York—More Promise Than Illusion*, ILR Paperback No. 10, New York State School of Industrial and Labor Relations, Cornell University, June 1971.

Yaffe and Goldblatt are part of a five-state study to evaluate the usefulness of fact-finding as a strike deterrent in public employment. In concluding their study, the authors note that William E. Simkin's comments about successful fact-finding are borne out by their survey: "Where fact-finding has been successful, I would suggest—but cannot prove—that the factfinder has mediated deliberately, instructively or surreptitiously." Their conclusion is that the New York situation affirms that where fact-finding is so viewed, it is a relatively successful mechanism in resolving bargaining impasses.

Yoder, Dale, and Herbert Heneman, Jr., eds., "Employee and Labor Relations," *ASPA Handbook of Personnel and Industrial Relations*. Washington, D.C.: Bureau of National Affairs, Inc., 1976.

This section of the PAIR handbook includes an article by Harold Davey on "Third-Party Mediation, Arbitration." Based on the author's more than thirty years' experience in the field and extensive research, the article is well worth the reader's attention.

Resolution of
Conflict–Contract
Administration

CHAPTER 20

The principal concern of this chapter is not with conflict that results in strikes or work stoppages. Where a contract includes grievance procedures with arbitration as the terminal step, as most of them do, the parties have already agreed that the terminal step is to be a substitute for, not an alternative to, the right to strike or lock out. However, less obvious forms of retaliation may and still do occur because of hostility arising from grievances. These manifestations of conflict (slowdown, low productivity, sabotage) are definitely a part of the meaning of conflict.

Since almost 100 percent of firms and agencies subscribe to the grievance process as the most efficient means of resolving contract-interpretation problems, primary attention has been directed, not at replacing or finding alternatives for the grievance process, but at developing more effective procedures. This involves consideration of matters such as timeliness, cost, and quality.

Following the format of Part III, the material here is divided into two parts: grievance procedure and grievance arbitration. Care will be taken not to repeat material covered in Chapters 15, 16, and 17 on these subjects in their more traditional forms. Emphasis will be on techniques and methods that have been introduced to develop more effective grievance administration.

GRIEVANCE HANDLING

A primary problem in grievance administration has been the length of time consumed between the filing of a grievance and its resolution by the parties. When this is coupled with a grievance system that encourages employees to file a grievance whenever they have a minor gripe or complaint, the result is even more delay and a subsequent stacking up of unresolved grievances many of which should never have been filed in the first place. As a consequence, some firms have found themselves with literally thousands of grievances clogging the grievance machinery. In such instances, grieving for the sake of grieving has become more the pattern than has promoting peaceful and cooperative relations between the parties.

Arbitrators are often dismayed at being blamed for inordinate delays in the resolution of grievances when, all too often, the grievances have followed a slow, tortuous route that may have delayed submission to arbitration for a full year or longer. This is especially annoying and unfair to the grievant where issues such as discipline and discharge are concerned. Additionally, grievants are often discouraged by the dispatch with which a grievance is taken from the personal, first-level, employee–supervisor focus to the higher and more impersonal institutional grievance steps. Too often, continued communication with the grievant or foreman concerned becomes more remote and impersonal and less enlightening at the higher steps. These kinds of problems have led to some rather interesting methods aimed at rendering grievance handling more effective, more responsive to needs, and less time-consuming and costly. It must be admitted that, because grievance administration is almost totally supported by the parties and rather comfortably structured against overt conflict by its terminal step of arbitration, not as much attention has been given to its improvement as to that of the negotiation process.

LOWEST-LEVEL APPROACH. The lowest-level approach is not a formal technique but rather a combination of actions taken to maximize settlement of grievances orally at the shop level. The program requires the following:

1. Top leadership of both the union and management must agree that the best settlement is a settlement at the shop level, and preferably before the grievance is reduced to writing.
2. Those normally involved at higher levels of the grievance procedure must actively support the lowest-level settlement policy through their willingness to move down to the problem in order to assist in the shop-level settlement, instead of allowing the problem to move up to them.
3. All involved must commit themselves to a program of immediate response, frank discussion, factual but equitable judgment, and expedited settlement.
4. An active training program must be established to provide information continuously to lower supervisors and union stewards as to contract content and meaning.

The whole idea of the lowest-level approach is that of a "grass-roots" resolution process in contrast to an "institutional" resolution process. The UAW–Harvester experience has been that it can work and that it can also improve relations between the parties at the same time.

GRIEVANCE MEDIATION. Use of mediation at some point in the grievance procedure, prior to grievance arbitration, has in some instances been a successful technique and has been incorporated into a few labor agreements. Its use has appeared in several forms. In cases where a backlog of unsettled grievances has occurred, a form known as "intensive mediation" has been successful. An oft-repeated example is the time David Cole, with the assurance of full authority, plunged into an International Harvester–UAW backlog of thousands of grievances pending arbitration and dramatically reduced it through the technique of intensive mediation. In the Coos Bay region of Oregon, a federal mediator was called in to help reduce a backlog of some 150 grievances through intensive mediation. Avoiding a decision-making role, the mediator, through intensive mediation over a period of two weeks, "got the parties back on the track" and at the same time resolved more than 120 of the grievances.

Mediation is also used in a more conventional sense when it is formally recognized in the agreement as a step in the grievance procedure prior to arbitration. It is a distinct step in the sense that the mediator does not also act as arbitrator, as in med-arb; his job is to facilitate the settlement of the grievance by making suggestions or by advising the parties. He does not make a decision as the arbitrator does. His is the usual function of a mediator—to persuade, to facilitate, to act as a catalyst, not to force. Typical of this contractual procedure are the following excerpts from public- and private-sector contracts:[1]

> If the grievance is not settled, it may be submitted first at the union's option to mediation by a State mediator from the State Board of Mediation and Arbitration.

> Either party to this agreement may, by giving written notice to the other party prior to arbitration as herein provided, request the Federal Mediation and Conciliation Service to send a Commissioner of Conciliation . . . to assist in a settlement of the grievance.

> Either the City or the union may petition the State Board of Mediation and Arbitration to appoint a mediator.

> The mediator shall have 10 days . . . to help the parties reach agreement. If . . . he is unable to resolve the dispute, he shall give a verbal

---

[1] See *Grievance and Arbitration Procedures in State and Local Agreements,* Bulletin 1833, U.S. Department of Labor, 1975; and BNA, *Collective Bargaining Negotiations and Contracts,* No. 626 (1969).

and written report to the Board stating the steps that he has taken in attempting to reach an agreement and his recommendation for resolution. Information copies of his recommendation shall be sent to the Association and the aggrieved person. The mediator shall then be dismissed.

If the grievance is not resolved through mediation within five (5) days after the conference as provided . . . above the grievances may then be submitted to arbitration.

Should this outlined [grievance] procedure fail to obtain a satisfactory settlement, there will be declared a sixty (60) day Mediation Period during which time the Union agrees not to strike or stop work, and the Company agrees that there will be no lockout of any of its employees. This Mediation Period will be used by a Mediation Committee representative of both the Union and the Company to thoroughly investigate the complaint, and render a recommendation acceptable to both the Union and the Company. . . . At any time during the Mediation Period, either party may request the aid and assistance of the Federal Mediation and Conciliation Service in resolving the dispute.

GRIEVANCE HANDLING *cum* FACT-FINDING. Sam Kagel underscores an inherent weakness all too evident in grievance handling, which frequently leads to appeal to arbitration when such a step is not really necessary. This is the failure, in preparing for an arbitration hearing, to obtain the facts necessary to settle the grievance until forced to. Kagel supports a fact-finding step that is triggered at the point where the grievance is reduced to writing. The advantage of such an interim step in the grievance procedure is that it disciplines the parties to obtain their facts earlier in the procedure and thus may obviate the continuing to arbitration of many unnecessary grievances. Such a step is already evident in some agreements in public- and private-sector contracts. The following are illustrative:[2]

(a) One factfinder shall be designated by the employer and one factfinder shall be designated by the union.
(b) The object of the factfinders is to thoroughly investigate the grievance so that their report could be the basic source of stipulated facts concerning the grievance.
(c) The factfinders shall put into writing all the facts upon which they agree and these will be considered stipulations. . . .

Upon request of the grievant and the union, the unresolved grievance will be referred to advisory fact-finding. A single fact-finder will be used. If the Board and union are unable to agree upon a fact-finder

[2] See *Grievance and Arbitration Procedures*, Department of Labor Bulletin 1833; and Sam Kagel and John Kagel, "Using Two New Arbitration Techniques," *Monthly Labor Review*, November 1972.

within 7 days, a panel of 5 or 7 names will be obtained from the American Arbitration Association, and starting with the grievant the parties shall alternately strike names until a single name is left.

The committee, after deliberate and thorough review of all available testimony and information, shall make its findings and recommendations to the parties in writing.

The findings and recommendations of the advisory committee may be made public by either party. The findings and recommendations of the advisory committee are not binding upon either party but shall serve as a basis for further good faith efforts on the part of both parties to negotiate and settle any remaining issue.

The advisory panel shall review the grievance and within 20 days from date of appointment of third member, recommend a solution to the Mayor and City Council. The Mayor and City Council shall render the final decision.

GRIEVANCE HANDLING AND JOINT STUDY COMMITTEES. As a final note under grievance handling, it should be indicated that the joint labor–management committees discussed in Chapter 19 also serve an important function in developing an atmosphere for both negotiations and grievance handling in which facts and objectivity become highlighted and problems are anticipated. The emphasis is not on a litigious stance by the parties, but upon personal relations, understanding, and a commitment to peace. The FMCS annual reports emphasize the continuing value of joint study committees as a tool in preventing collective bargaining conflicts of all types.

GRIEVANCE ARBITRATION

Criticisms raised with respect to grievance arbitration are not usually directed at the basic value of the technique. Indeed, grievance arbitration, as noted in Chapter 17, is almost universally included as the terminal point in the grievance procedure and is the basic reason for there being few work stoppages over issues submitted to the grievance procedure. Peter Seitz notes that "Grievance Arbitration (despite the banshee-like howlings of a few dyspeptics . . .) is a marvelously acceptable and generally satisfactory institution."[3]

Most of the criticisms have been directed at the mechanics of grievance arbitration. As with other legal processes, there are many contrasting opinions as to what grievance arbitration does not do and what it

---

[3] Peter Seitz, "How to Succeed in Killing Arbitration without Really Trying," *Seminar on Collective Bargaining, 1967—Emerging Characteristics* (Jamestown, N.Y.: Jamestown Community College Press, 1968), p. 95.

ought to do. Some people feel that the process is too expensive; others
point out that it is much less expensive than following the alternate
route, that of resorting to the courts. Some accuse arbitrators of unnecessary delay; others pin the delay mainly on the parties themselves. Some
think that delay can be reduced by drastically reducing or eliminating
opinions; others argue that it is the obligation of the arbitrator to articulate his logic and reasoning to effect an acceptable award and to clarify
contract intent for similar instances that might arise. Some persons
think that transcript of proceedings and the posthearing brief should be
eliminated; others respond that in some complicated cases, the transcript
is a positive need, and that the transcript is a device to keep witnesses
honest and the arbitrator's award relevant to the issue presented. Criticism is also raised that there are too few arbitrators; a response is that
there are not too few arbitrators but too few *qualified* and *experienced*
arbitrators *acceptable* to the parties. Then there are those who criticize
arbitrators for not being legalistic enough—for introducing problem solving to arbitration; others respond that the arbitration process is a problem-solving and a legalistic process, and that with good judgment, both
can be used without weakening the process.

While not an exhaustive list, these attitudes indicate something of the
give-and-take of published and verbal comments on grievance arbitration. The substance of the complaints, proposals, and discussions concerning grievance arbitration generally centers upon two major needs:
(1) to increase the number of qualified, experienced, and acceptable
arbitrators; and (2) to reduce the time and cost of arbitration. It is to
meet these two general needs that most of the innovative activity of
the Federal Mediation and Conciliation Service, the National Academy
of Arbitrators, the American Arbitration Association, the Society of
Professionals in Dispute Resolution, and the parties themselves is directed.

More Qualified, Experienced, and Acceptable Arbitrators

To place the matter in proper perspective, it should be pointed out that
there is some controversy over whether there *is* a shortage of arbitrators,
even of qualified arbitrators. This question arises because of the reluctance of the parties to use younger, newer, or less experienced arbitrators even when they are qualified—indeed, many of these arbitrators have
been accepted for the panels of the AAA and FMCS. Since final selection of the arbitrator who will hear the case is still a matter of mutual
agreement between the parties, inclusion on a list submitted to them
by the services (FMCS and AAA) does not mean selection by the parties.
Because of questions such as this, the efforts to increase the number
of arbitrators acceptable to the parties involve both an encouragement

to the parties to use less experienced but qualified arbitrators already in the field, and also an attempt to increase the numbers of trained and qualified arbitrators in the field as a whole. It is a program, then, of increasing acceptability, increasing quality, and increasing numbers.

Two projects illustrate the attempts of various interested groups to increase the number of trained arbitrators. In a project funded by the Labor–Management Services Commission, the Department of Labor initiated training programs at UCLA and Berkeley to increase the numbers of experienced third-party neutrals. Each program, consisting of 15 candidates, was a combination of classroom training and on-the-job or counterpart training. Experienced arbitrators directed the programs, and more were recruited to assist in the apprenticeship aspects of the program. Cooperation of referral agencies in fact-finding and arbitration was obtained in order to ensure immediate exposure and experience for the candidates upon graduation. It was intended that the experience be first in community-type disputes and that, once experienced, the candidates should then be able to move over into labor relations, especially in the public sector. The concept of using working arbitrators was to provide a framework for actual exposure to arbitration processes while in training.[4]

Another program, one of several sponsored by the NAA, AAA, and FMCS, was established in cooperation with Cornell University. Under this program, nine daylong sessions, one a month, were scheduled. Twenty practitioners from labor and management and seven attorneys were selected, based on criteria that included preferences (although not exclusively) for younger persons, five years' experience with labor or management or both in labor relations work, location in western New York, and no discrimination as to race, creed, color, or national origin. Exceptions could be made for highly qualified persons. In addition to the nine academic sessions, each trainee was assigned to accompany an experienced arbitrator to hearings (with approval of the parties) and to prepare an award for the evaluation of the experienced arbitrator after a formal award had been made in the case. The key concepts in the program were active and total involvement of the parties, establishment of a need for arbitrators in the region, use of candidates with experience in the field, and provision of a program that not only stressed procedural and substantive aspects of arbitration, but exposed the candidate to the actual process of arbitration.[5]

These examples indicate the kind of positive programs that are emerging under the auspices of interested professional groups, universities, and

---

[4] W.J. Usery, Jr., "Some Attempts to Reduce Arbitration Costs and Delays," *Monthly Labor Review*, November 1972, p. 5.

[5] James F. Power, "Improving Arbitration: Roles of Parties and Agencies," *Monthly Labor Review*, November 1972, pp. 19–20.

labor and management. The distinctive feature about these is that there is a deliberate effort to give potential arbitrators experience by an on-the-job type of training with experienced professionals. It was also intended that exposure of the trainees to the parties would subsequently increase their opportunities to be selected for actual cases.

Another approach to increasing the use of less-experienced but qualified arbitrators has been promulgated by the FMCS under its new ARBIT system (Arbitration Information Tracking System). Although ARBIT was designed primarily to provide a more immediate response to those using the FMCS arbitration services, it also includes features that it is hoped will stimulate the use of newer arbitrators. ARBIT contains complete biographical information on each arbitrator, which is automatically updated with each case the arbitrator decides. Further, as requests are made to FMCS for arbitration panels from which the parties may choose the arbitrator they will use, an "active memory" in the ARBIT system ensures that there will be an equitable distribution in referrals among all names on FMCS lists. This means that newer arbitrators will have as much opportunity as older ones to have their names submitted by the FMCS to the parties on the panel referrals. (Usually, seven names are submitted.) Including the name of a newer arbitrator on these panels does not guarantee that he will be selected, of course, but it does increase the odds in his favor by presenting his name more frequently to the parties. Each time a newer arbitrator is selected and decides a case, his biographical data reflect this new information, thus increasing even more his opportunity to be again selected.

The mediators in the field, because of their constant contact with the parties, may also be a positive force in encouraging the use of newer arbitrators, by suggesting names when it is appropriate. Experienced arbitrators too have a responsibility; they could take newcomers under their wings in a kind of on-the-job training relationship. This means allowing newer arbitrators to sit in on hearings, where the parties do not object, and letting them try their hands at writing sample decisions for the arbitrators' perusals. This would be similar to the Cornell and Berkeley programs but on a voluntary and individual basis. The NAA, AAA, and FMCS consider the responsibility of regular arbitrators to train newer ones important enough to include it as an obligation in their new *Code of Professional Responsibility for Arbitrators*, Section 1 (C) (1) of which states, "An experienced arbitrator should cooperate in the training of new arbitrators." Through their *Code*, the three groups also seek to ensure high-quality performance among arbitrators by establishing standards that spell out not only ethical principles but what is considered good practice in the arbitration profession. The FMCS, while encouraging the use of newer arbitrators, has also instituted a quality-control program through the use of stricter criteria for new arbitrators seeking to be added to the FMCS roster. This means that while encouraging the use of newer arbitrators by listing them on its roster, the FMCS is also attempting to ensure that they will be qualified. The final check upon quality performance by arbitrators is through the parties themselves. This is simply a matter of exercising their right of choice to exclude arbitrators who, in the opinion of the parties, do not do a good job in terms of quality and/or the time consumed to render decisions.

Reducing Time and Cost of Grievance Arbitration

A number of programs have been instituted to reduce the time and cost involved in grievance arbitration. Through ARBIT, the FMCS has been able to provide panel names to the parties much faster. The AAA has also established an expedited procedure for the arbitration process itself. And the parties have begun to incorporate expedited arbitration procedures in their agreements.

The FMCS ARBIT system has already had phenomenal success in reducing the time it takes to respond to a party requesting an arbitration panel. For years, the average interval between a request and the forwarding of a panel of arbitrators was twenty days. In the first two years of ARBIT, the time was reduced to fifteen days, and by the end of fiscal year 1974, it was ten days. The new standard of expediting panel names to parties is one working day.

Along with this, the FMCS through ARBIT is pledged to:

Establish better controls of arbitration activities

Create a capability of maintaining the new response-time standards even with increased work load

Respond more precisely to requests

Ascertain national arbitration requirements

Determine substantive trends

These standards are all conducive to a speedier and better referral service by FMCS and, through this, a reduction in both time and cost involved in grievance arbitration.

The American Arbitration Association has also been significantly involved in establishing expedited arbitration procedures. In response to concern over rising costs and excessive delays, a subcommittee of the AAA in 1971 recommended the establishment of an expedited grievance-arbitration procedure "under which cases could be scheduled promptly and awards rendered no later than five days after the hearings."[6] In

---

[6] Expedited Labor Arbitration Rules of the American Arbitration Association.

return for eliminating certain features traditionally associated with grievance arbitration, the parties were assured that they could obtain quicker discussions at some cost savings. The Expedited Labor Arbitration Rules of the AAA include appointment of the arbitrator by the AAA rather than selection by the parties; selection of the place and time of hearing by the AAA; oral notice of a hearing not less than 24 hours in advance; elimination of transcripts or briefs; expeditious handling of hearings in whatever manner will permit full presentation by the parties; and no filing of documents after the hearing. The award, in writing, is to be made promptly—unless agreed upon otherwise by the parties, within five business days after the closing of the hearing. If the arbitrator determines that an opinion should accompany the award, it should be in summary form. Other features added by the AAA in New York are that Fridays are set aside on a regular basis for hearings, and that the parties must be available when called.

The concept of expedited grievance arbitration received a major boost by the steel-industry settlement in August 1971. For the first time, a two-year experimental expedited arbitration procedure (renewed in 1974) was founded, to be implemented on a regional intercompany basis. The procedure provides two routes for appeal of grievances to arbitration. All grievances may be appealed either to expedited arbitration or to regular arbitration. Regular arbitration would proceed in the traditional way under the agreement. To handle expedited cases, an arbitration panel was established in each of twelve major steel areas. Arbitrators selected for these panels were drawn from relatively young lawyers in practice or on university staffs. An administrative officer was established for each locality to receive referrals to arbitration from the parties and to assign a member of the panel on an alphabetical rotation basis. A 1975 "Memorandum of Understanding" establishing the procedure used by the Steelworkers Union and a major corporation best illustrates this:

REFERRAL TO EXPEDITED ARBITRATION:

All grievances appealed to the last step of the grievance procedure shall be reviewed by the Union Relations Administrator and the Representative of the International Union. After such review either may communicate with the other and jointly determine whether such grievance does not warrant disposition in that step but is rather appropriate for expedited arbitration and, therefore, agree to refer such grievance back to the local parties at the preceding step for review and disposition.

. . . any grievance referred back to the preceding step the local parties . . . shall . . . meet and again attempt to settle the grievance . . . if they are unable . . . the grievance may then be appealed by the chairman of the Grievance Committee to the Expedited Arbitration Procedure.

GRIEVANCE ISSUES WHICH MAY BE APPEALED:

Any grievance appealed to this Expedited Arbitration procedure must be confined to:

a. Issues which do not involve novel problems.
b. Issues which do not have extensive contractual significance.
c. Issues which are not unusually complex.

PROCEDURE FOR APPEAL TO EXPEDITED ARBITRATION:

As soon as it is determined that a grievance is to be arbitrated under this expedited procedure, the local party representatives will agree to a date and place of such hearing. They will call the Administrative Secretary for a panel Arbitrator.

. . . An arbitrator shall not be requested to hear more than four cases in one day and shall not be requested for more than two consecutive days of hearings.

DESIGNATION OF EXPEDITED ARBITRATOR:

The Administrative Secretary will maintain an alphabetical listing of the panel members. . . .

Arbitrators will be called for requested hearings on the basis of "first-up-first-out" in alphabetical order.

1. When an arbitrator is called and is not available . . . the Administrative Secretary will continue down the roster. . . .
2. When an arbitrator is called but is not in . . . he will be given not more than two hours from that point to call in before the next name on the roster is called.

THE HEARING:

The hearing shall be conducted in accordance with the following:

a. The hearing shall be informal.
b. No briefs shall be filed or transcripts made.
c. There shall be no formal rules of evidence.
d. Each party's case shall be represented by a previously designated local representative.
e. The Arbitrator shall have the obligation of assuring that all necessary facts and considerations are brought before him by the representatives of the parties. In all respects, he shall assure that the hearing is a fair one.
f. If the Arbitrator or the parties acting jointly conclude at the hearing that the issues involved are of such complexity or significance as to require further consideration by the parties, the case shall be referred to the last step of the grievance procedure. . . .

The only arbitration decisions which may be cited as part of either parties' expedited arbitration presentation are regular nonexpedited arbitration decisions involving the [company].

FEE SCHEDULE FOR HEARINGS:

1. $100 per half day of hearing if one or two cases are heard.
2. $150 per day of hearing if one or two cases are heard.
3. $200 per one-half day or day of hearing if three or four cases are heard.
4. If it is necessary for the Arbitrator to travel on a day or days other than hearing day, and if the total time required for such travel represents a significant part of the day, he shall receive an additional fee of $100.

DECISION:

. . . The Arbitrator shall issue a decision no later than 48 hours after conclusion of the hearing. His decision shall be based on the records developed by the parties before and at the hearing and shall include a brief written explanation of the basis for his decision. These decisions shall not be cited as a precedent in any discussion of grievances at any step of the grievance or regular arbitration procedure or expedited arbitration procedure.

The coal industry uses an expedited procedure called, in their agreement, "Immediate Arbitration." Under this procedure, the first three steps of the grievance procedure may be bypassed, an arbitration hearing held within five days, and a bench decision rendered on the spot, to be followed by a written decision within ten days.

Another technique labor–management groups use more frequently is to establish panels of rotating permanent arbitrators for regular cases. Although the specifics vary, the basic idea is for the parties, with the aid of such organizations as the FMCS and the AAA, to select a group of arbitrators who then, for the length of the agreement, on a rotational or random selection basis, handle all grievance arbitration. The use of a permanent arbitrator is not new. What seems to be new about the process described above is that the parties are attempting to secure the best of a combination of a permanent arbitrator and an ad hoc arbitrator system. Advantages anticipated from the permanent-arbitrators panel system are (1) experienced, well-qualified arbitrators on tap at all times, (2) a reduction of both time and costs by establishing a quick selection process and by using arbitrators who have a familiarity with the particular industry and contract, and (3) maintaining of some flexibility and fresh faces by rotating the cases among several arbitrators.

The National Bituminous Coal Wage Agreement of 1974 gave a big boost to the permanent-arbitrators panel technique. Under this agreement, panels of experienced arbitrators were chosen for each of the districts in which there are UMW agreements. A typical panel is composed of four arbitrators. A coordinating office for all the districts is established in Washington, D.C. When a grievance is appealed to arbitration, the referral is first made to the coordinator's office. The coordinator immediately selects the next arbitrator rotationally from among the four on the district panel. To save time, the arbitrator is notified by telephone, and he is told at the same time whether the process is an immediate (expedited) or a regular arbitration. If it is expedited, a hearing is held within five days and a bench decision is rendered, with a written decision to follow within ten days. If it is a regular arbitration, the hearing is held without delay (within fifteen days), to be followed later by a written decision. However, even in the regular procedure, the emphasis is upon speeding up decisions. Appeal may be made from the panel arbitrator's decision to a National Arbitration Review Board on one or more of the following conditions:

(i) That the decision of the panel arbitrator is in conflict with one or more decisions on the same issue of contract interpretation by other panel arbitrators.

(ii) That the decision involves a question of contract interpretation which has not previously been decided by the Board, and which in the opinion of the Board, involves the interpretation of a substantial contractual issue.

(iii) That decision is arbitrary and capricious, or fraudulent, and therefore, must be set aside.

Among other types of panels are one establishing three arbitrators as a permanently rotating panel for a tier of states, and a permanent panel of seven arbitrators from which the selection in any particular case is on a random basis. In all instances, the panels are for the term of the agreement, and panel members may be dropped at any time at the request of the parties. There has been a remarkable increase in the use of such panels in recent years, motivated by a desire to regularize, improve the quality of, and cut costs of arbitration procedures.

Finally, it should be noted that cost cutting and time saving in grievance arbitration may be assisted and encouraged by the AAA and FMCS, but their impact is limited. Control of costs and time is most effective when instituted by the parties themselves. Suffice it to say that costly and time-consuming procedures do not have to be endured by the parties. The parties *do* choose the arbitrators; they *do* spell out the grievance procedures in their agreements; and they may further control cost and time by joint agreement as to guidelines for hearings, transcription, documentation, and period of time for the decision.

The AAA has introduced some sound advice in its *9 Ways to Cut Arbitration Costs:*

1. *Arbitration should be prompt.* An important "hidden" cost in labor arbitration is the time lost to executives, union representatives, and

workers. The cost of legal fees can also be significant. All of these items can be reduced by expediting the procedure. Furthermore, the "back pay meter" may be ticking while you are waiting for an eventual decision. Even where financial risk is not involved, a quick decision is usually better because keeping a grievant on the hook is bad for employee relations.

2. *Don't order a transcript unless you really need it.* Court reporting is expensive. Transcripts delay the award. The arbitrator can't start writing his opinion until he gets the record. Furthermore, arbitrators feel obliged to read every word. That means study time at the per diem rate. In some cases, transcripts are worth what they cost. But most of the time they serve only to double the total expenses of arbitration.

3. *Question the arbitrator's fee if you think it is too high.* The arbitrator is serving the parties. He should be paid a fair fee. Under AAA procedures, you are told his per diem rate in advance of his appointment. By reducing travel time, the number of hearings and study time, you have some control over the amount of arbitrator's fee. When necessary, ask the AAA to speak up about an unreasonably high fee.

4. *Clarify the issues before the first hearing.* Why spend hours of hearing-room time establishing facts that aren't really in dispute? When parties come in prepared with the names and seniority dates of grievants, amounts of money involved and other details of record, it not only cuts hearing-room time but shortens the arbitrator's study time as well. In labor arbitration, the matter has already gone through the grievance procedure. A badly organized presentation serves no good purpose.

5. *Sometimes, parties don't really need long opinions.* Parties can ask the AAA to request the arbitrator to simplify or eliminate his opinion. In a few cases, it may be appropriate for the arbitrator to handwrite his award and a brief opinion at the close of the hearing, delivering it to the parties at once. If you don't need an opinion as a guideline for the future, consider the possibility of eliminating it. The arbitrator's bill will be substantially smaller. The dispute may be resolved sooner.

6. *Avoid unnecessary citations.* When parties indulge in needless citations they only compel the arbitrator to "go to the books" himself. That takes study time. Citation of awards by other arbitrators may be necessary in some situations. But be accurate. Don't rely on digests or headnotes alone. Above all, be selective.

7. *The labor arbitrator is an experienced professional.* Exercise restraint in submitting arguments about procedural matters. Generally, a simple but accurate presentation of your facts and arguments will put the sophisticated arbitrator in a position to make a decision.

8. *Don't break your date with the arbitrator.* When a hearing date is set, keep it. Don't ask for postponements unless absolutely necessary. The arbitrator is a profesional man whose time means money. He

may be turning down another case on the day when your hearing is scheduled. Some arbitrators make a charge for postponements on short notice. This custom will grow unless parties exercise restraint.

9. *Find out about an arbitrator before you select him.* A man who never arbitrated a job evaluation dispute, for instance, may have to be educated at your expense. Look up the arbitrator in the Summary of Labor Arbitration Awards and other reporting services. This will give you a better idea of his qualifications. If it's an AAA case and you need more information, don't hesitate to ask.[7]

CONCLUSION

In the excellent study edited by James J. Healy, *Creative Collective Bargaining*, the authors concluded in 1965:

> There is a small group of people in the labor–management field, how-ever, who have pioneered in breaking away from the traditional ways of bargaining and in accommodating the bargaining process to their particular needs. Their progress thus far gives cause for considerable hope and optimism that the parties can settle the great majority of their problems themselves, and that they can do so by means of the institution of free collective bargaining.[8]

Now, over a decade later, I can see no reason to question such optimism. Collective bargaining is proving to be a viable and adaptive process in all its facets. All parties—labor, management, government, and public—evince an increasing willingness to eliminate the necessity of compulsory devices or punitive means of settling differences by turning instead to imaginative and innovative collective bargaining techniques.

SELECTED REFERENCES

McPherson, William H., "Grievance Mediation Under Collective Bargaining," *Industrial and Labor Relations Review*, 9, No. 2 (January 1956).

Professor McPherson, on the basis of successful use of mediation prior to the grievance-arbitration step, advocates that more employers and unions should experiment with the technique.

Simkin, William, *Mediation and the Dynamics of Collective Bargaining*. Washington, D.C.: Bureau of National Affairs, Inc., 1971.

Chapter XII addresses itself to the role of mediation in grievance situations.

---

[7] Reproduced by permission of the American Arbitration Association.
[8] James J. Healy, ed., *Creative Collective Bargaining* (Englewood Cliffs, N.J.: Prentice-Hall, 1965), p. 283.

Stern, James L., and Barbara D. Dennis, eds., Industrial Relations Research Association Series, *Proceedings of the Twenty-Seventh Annual Winter Meeting,* December 28–29, 1974, pp. 307–40.

An informative discussion of the expedited grievance arbitration concept delivered by Michael F. Hoellering. Also included in the papers are two on the postal experience with expedited arbitration.

Conclusion

The following observations represent the author's view as to the under-lying themes of this book:

First, collective bargaining in all its aspects—negotiation, contract administration, and special strengthening techniques—has achieved a degree of acceptance and widespread respectability unmatched at any other time in its evolution.

Second, collective bargaining is both a product and a function of a free society. The rejection of alternate or substitute ways, based on compulsion, of resolving labor–management problems is a refreshing expression of faith in the free-society approach to the resolution of such problems.

Third, the negativism of the late 1950s and early 1960s toward collective bargaining, when even its continuation was questioned, has been replaced by a positiveness that finds expression in directing resources and efforts toward its improvement rather than in destroying the institution of collective bargaining.

Fourth, the most effective approach to training people for involvement in the various activities concerned with collective bargaining is through the learning experience. The various processes involved in collective bargaining—negotiation, grievance, grievance arbitration—are so inextricably woven into human relationships that one must experience the process in order to gain expertise.

Fifth, effectiveness in collective bargaining activities results from more-than-adequate preparation and experience. But preparation and experience alone are not sufficient. It is the function of the collective-bargaining-by-objectives methodology to add a third ingredient—a systematic and orderly approach to negotiations. Because it is a methodology, it is equally effective in any negotiation situation, not just that of collective bargaining. Not only does CBO introduce system into collective bargaining negotiations, but by the discipline it introduces, the level of preparation it requires, and the tangible goals that it produces, CBO provides a positive approach to collective bargaining negotiations.

Collective Bargaining by Objectives— Simulation Exercises and Negotiation Games

Beck's Brewery—A Manufacturing Game
Associated General Contractors—A Construction-Industry Game
River City Veterans Administration Hospital—A Federal-Sector Game
Sycamore City—A Municipal-Sector Game

APPENDICES

Collective Bargaining Simulation

INTRODUCTION

Development of expertise in collective bargaining negotiation is more than a process of reading about and listening to others tell about the practice of negotiation. These are important tools in learning and developing expertise but leave some important gaps in the learning process. Collective bargaining is, as much as anything else, a process that requires a sense of feel for what is going on. The sense of feel is acquired through involvement in the process of collective bargaining, not in just reading about it. The closest substitute for actual experience in negotiating labor agreements is the use of simulation, a method of learning I have used effectively for a number of years. Tying simulation bargaining to the methodology of collective bargaining by objectives has greatly improved and enhanced the learning-experience results. The participants soon find that, by this approach, learning does not have to be painful; it may even be fun, and it can be highly motivational if placed in the proper framework. Participants quickly learn that negotiation requires the application of a number of interdisciplinary skills: accounting, economics, statistics, verbal and written communication, human behavior, labor law, labor relations, politics, and administration, to name a few. I claim no monopoly on the best ways to use simulation in training potential negotiators but offer this particular approach as one obtaining beneficial results. The format to be followed is to (1) introduce the reader to the bargaining games included, which are the basis for renegotiation simulation situations; and (2) outline nine steps that carry participants as realistically as possible through all the stages of bargaining, from preparing for negotiations to the negotiations themselves, and then on to the testing of the negotiated agreement through its administration period.

THE GAMES

Four types of games are included, to be used according to the needs of those who participate in the simulation. These were selected to illustrate three basically different bargaining situations. The games use (1) a private-industry manufacturing firm, (2) a private-industry construction firm, (3) a public-sector federal agency, and (4) a public-sector state or municipal agency.

Information included in each game is sufficient for the purpose of placing participants in a simulation situation where the objective is to renegotiate an initial agreement between the employer and the union or association. Included is general information about the industry or agency, information about the union or association and the employer, information about the labor relations between the parties during the time the labor agreement has been in effect, and financial information. A copy of the initial agreement that is to be renegotiated is also included. The participants should be held to the information provided in the game and not be permitted to manufacture additional information unless it logically derives from the game information or from researched and documented sources.

INSTRUCTIONS FOR USE OF THE SIMULATION EXERCISE

Step 1. Background

Participants should as quickly as possible become acquainted with the nature of the collective bargaining negotiation process and the tools needed for engaging in negotiations. At a minimum, this should include (1) the meaning and significance of collective bargaining in the American framework (see Chapters 1–4, text); (2) the parties who are involved or may be involved in collective bargaining, including the main participants, management and labor, and others such as mediators, arbitrators, and administering boards in both public and private sectors (see Chapter 6, text); (3) the legal framework within which collective bargaining takes place (see Chapter 5, and additional and more specific information in chapters dealing with the negotiation process); and (4) the art of negotiation and introduction to the process of negotiation (see Chapter 7).

At this point, participants should also clearly understand the entire course that the simulation exercise will follow, from preliminaries to final agreement.

Step 2. Organizing Bargaining Teams

This step may actually take place sometime during the initial orientation process of Step 1. Regardless of the size of the total group, the bargaining teams, for maximum participation and results, should be kept to about four participants each. After teams are organized, an even number of union teams and management teams should be designated and pairings made. From this point on, participants should identify only with the team they have been assigned to, and teams should relate only to the opposite teams with which they have been paired for the negotiations—that is, Management No. 1 team to Union No. 1 team, and so on. For maximum benefit, locations that are entirely separate from each other should be found for the various bargaining groups. The bargaining groups should be cautioned that each member must refrain from discussing with other groups what his group is doing until the whole exercise is completed.

Step 3. Materials for Game and Introduction to a Systematic Way of Approaching and Carrying on Negotiations

Participants should be given the game being used for the simulation and referred to all other materials that will be available or sources to which they may turn in the process of the negotiations (see Chapter 10 and the appropriate appendix).

At this point, the participants should be asked to read Chapters 7–14 on the methodology of collective bargaining by objectives. The instructor should take time to be sure that they clearly understand the objectives procedure. The systematic way that this procedure leads them into the negotiations and supports them during the negotiations minimizes the mistakes they might make and will effect a much more positive approach.

Step 4. Preparation for Presentation of Positions

Using the objectives approach, the bargaining teams should quickly develop their material—items, priorities, and objectives—from which can be derived the initial position that will be presented to the other side. It is noted that this requires two steps in the process of establishing a complete list of items to be negotiated and the objectives for those items: (1) the initial position taken by the initiator party—usually, but not required to be, the union; and (2) the response of the other party. At this point it is well for the instructor to meet separately with the union teams as a group and the management teams as a group to explain different formats that may be used in presenting a position to the other party. Here, and at all points where convenient, the instructor emphasizes that the degree of benefit derived from the exercise is directly tied to the way in which the individual involves himself or herself in the role he or she has been assigned or has assumed.

The teams then establish a timetable for the presentation of positions and the beginning of actual negotiations. The importance of adequate preparation is emphasized at this point, since it is not customary for the parties to admit new items to the bargaining table once the negotiations actually begin.

Step 5.   Negotiations

Bargaining groups should be completely separated from each other if maximum results are to be obtained. To put them into various corners of a large room only inhibits the learning experience.

Although the simulation process may be condensed and framed for short exposure situations of only one or two sessions, this may prevent maximum benefit in getting participants to feel the many aspects of negotiation. All too often, the simulation becomes a once-over-lightly job when only one or two sessions are devoted to a simulation exercise. A much more productive approach is to allow as many as ten to twelve two-hour sessions, with all the outside sessions the groups find necessary. This involves enough depth of involvement so that participants not only see, but develop a sense of feel for, what the negotiation process really is: the frustrations of personality problems, the difficulties in verbally communicating with the other party, the slow, tedious, and time-consuming process of language construction, the emotionalism, and the strategies and techniques of negotiation, for example. For the full appreciation of these factors, a depth of exposure is required that brief simulation fails to achieve.

Once the negotiations begin, the most productive results can be obtained if the instructor at this point sheds his role and instead assumes any real role that the participants may require during the course of the negotiations: company official, union official, the NLRB, or the appropriate board, mediator, arbitrator, or legal counsel for either side.

During the negotiations, each participant should be asked to keep an individual log of the experience that not only relates what has happened but, more important, reveals an understanding of the forces in the negotiation process—personalities, economics, politics—that influence final results.

Participants should also be informed of the exact date when the contract will terminate, for two reasons: (1) This sets the time frame for the negotiations, and (2) it parallels the real situation by providing the participants with a date at which the 60-day period also terminates and at which time they may exercise all options allowed by the law, such as striking or extending negotiations if the contract has not been completed. I have also found that, in order to prevent artificiality from entering the negotiations in the latter part of the time period, it is best to inform the participants that, while a negotiated agreement should be their prime objective, the instructor will also accept a real impasse that meets with his approval.

Step 6.   Mediation Service

A highlight of my own use of simulation has been to take the bargaining groups to the offices of the Federal Mediation Service for a simulation session in mediation. If one of the groups is at impasse—and quite often this is the case—this group becomes a live party to the mediation process, with the mediator functioning as he would with a real union–management situation. Other participants become observers. If a mediator is not available, the instructor should take the group through a mediation session. Participants should be asked to read Chapters 19–20.

Step 7.   Testing the Agreement

At the conclusion of the negotiations, the bargaining groups should be asked to turn in a copy of the agreement (or a portion, if they were at impasse) and to read Chapters 15–18 of the text. The instructor should then carefully examine the agreements for problem areas in construction or omission, and formulate grievances to bring out these problems. Other grievances should also be formulated that show the workings of the agreement during the contract period. Through discussion relative to these grievance situations, the participants are easily brought to a realization of the importance of the construction and language of the agreement.

Step 8.   Grievance Arbitration

An extension of Step 7's application of the contract is to involve the participants in an arbitration exercise in which they may play the roles of the parties and also that of the arbitrator. If time does not allow a full simulation of the arbitration process, the instructor should be careful to explain the process to the group.

Step 9.   Windup

A general discussion of the negotiation session, observations as to what most influenced results, the use of experience gained in the use of various strategies and techniques as a base for the next negotiations, and an evaluation of the total learning experience gained through the simulation exercise should be the order of the day.

Beck's Brewery—
A Manufacturing Game

A

THE BREWING INDUSTRY TODAY

Today, the brewing process is quite automated and standard through-out the world. Cereal, malt, barley, hops, and water are mixed and filtered into wort. The wort is boiled to liquefy the sugars into easily fermentable forms, then yeast is added to start the fermentation. Once fermentation is well on its way, the yeast is removed and the wort is transferred to an aging tank, where it lagers for several weeks. The brew is again filtered and packaged. Bottled and canned beer goes through a pasteurization process before being sent to market.

Breweries have for many years been a major source of tax revenue and, through the United States Brewers' Association, have been very cooperative in policing themselves and showing great social responsibility in their antilitter and recycling programs.

The market is dominated by five national and several seminational breweries, with only minor local competition from the regional and local breweries. All breweries are closely regulated by federal and state agencies, so there is little difference in quality or price and only slight differences in product. The advantages of bulk purchasing and extensive distribution continue to give the larger breweries a pricing advantage, which has caused many of the regional breweries to go out of business. Ten years ago, there were 197 breweries in the United States, whereas in 1975, there were only 111. Competition is particularly intense in Wisconsin, where the number of breweries has declined from 35 in 1965 to only 9 today. Competition among breweries is primarily based on the

Note: At the end of this appendix are statistics of financial information on the industry and Beck's Brewery.

image their particular beer or company portrays. The image of a beer and its company is portrayed primarily through packaging, advertising, and slogans. Also, breweries have their own distinct labels to differentiate their product from that of their competitors.

Breweries are currently experimenting with new beer packaging. For example, a radically different packaging, in terms of outer container and bottle appearance, has been introduced by one brewing company in the industry. This new packaging is a plasti-shield quart bottle and a new type of 7-ounce bottle called the "pony pack." The plasti-shield bottle has a foamed polystyrene jacket that requires up to a third less glass than conventional nonreturnables and can be recycled. The 7-ounce, no-deposit-bottle "pony pack" comes in special, open eight-pack cardboard carriers.

Brewing companies tend to advertise their product heavily through the mass media, especially television. Slogans play a big part in trying to get people to remember brand names. Slogans like "When you're out of Schlitz, you're out of beer!" or, "Budweiser, the King of Beers," function to attract and keep customer awareness.

Quality is also a competitive factor. Some brewing companies emphasize the alcoholic strength of their beers, others their lightness. Quality is also determined by the emphasis companies place on the brewing process they use. Although quality seems to be emphasized less than image, quite often quality and image are inseparable. For example, a company that stresses the use of natural spring water in its brewing process wants its beer to carry the image of quality.

Pricing is still a factor in brewing-company competition. Competition has intensified between regional and national brewers, and antitrust legislation is being sought by regional brewers against alleged unfair pricing practices. The price squeeze on popular-priced brands of regional breweries has reduced their competitive advantage over national breweries because of rising costs and price ceilings. National brewers of premium beer, with greater operational and purchasing efficiencies, can brew and sell cheaper than regional brewers.

In the first part of 1975, there was at least one brewery in each of 31 states. However, breweries are essentially concentrated in four states: California with 8, Texas with 7, Pennsylvania with 18, and Wisconsin with 9.

Brewery workers are in the semiskilled employment category, with work ranging from general help and cleanup men to leadmen who determine minor variations and readiness of beer for bottling.

Unions have been very strong in the brewery industry, and pay rates on the average are high. The United States Brewers' Association reports the following:

we are very optimistic [handwritten margin note]

TABLE 1. Average Hourly Earnings: 1965–1974

Year	Malt Beverages	All Food	All Manufacturing
1974	$ 6.48	4.15	4.40
1973	5.98	3.83	4.07
1972	5.50	3.60	3.81
1971	5.11	3.38	3.56
1970	4.71	3.16	3.36
1969	4.43	2.96	3.19
1968	4.16	2.80	3.01
1967	3.93	2.64	2.83
1966	3.78	2.52	2.72
1965	3.64	2.43	2.61

Source: *Brewers Almanac, 1975*, United States Brewers' Association, Inc., Washington, D.C. Definition: Average Hourly Earnings = Gross production or non-supervisory payrolls divided by total man-hours worked. (See p. 3 in Handbook of Labor Statistics, Bureau of Labor Statistics, 1967.)

The Milwaukee area has a very large semiskilled work force of 653,000 workers, with a low unemployment rate (4.1 percent). There are nearly 17,000 food workers in the area, earning an average of $5.88 an hour, compared to the weighted average of all workers of $5.28 an hour. Although Milwaukee is known as the "Beer Capital of the Nation" (three of the five largest breweries are located there), breweries account for only about 2 percent of the work force. Inflation in the Milwaukee area has been no worse than in other areas and seems to follow the national trends fairly closely.

BECK'S BREWERY

Beck's Brewing Company is a medium-sized brewery in the Midwest region. The product is sold by lots to regional distributors, who in turn sell to grocery stores, liquor stores, restaurants, and sporting arenas. (See end of this appendix for details of production.)

Beck's beer is sold primarily in the Midwest, including the states of Wisconsin, Michigan, Illinois, Ohio, and Indiana. Its primary target is Wisconsin, since it prides itself as a "home-grown" brew.

Beck's has its home office in Milwaukee, Wisconsin, and all Beck's beer is produced in the Milwaukee plant. The state of Wisconsin charges a $2-a-barrel (31 gallons) tax on all beer produced.

The company was founded in 1945 by Michael Robertson. Robertson's success has been a result of two things: aggressive advertising, and the image of being a medium-sized company brewing exclusively for the Midwest. It was a family-owned concern until going public in 1965.

Beck's spends approximately 9 percent of sales on advertising. It advertises in magazines and newspapers, and on radio and television. Most recently, Beck's used spot announcements on television, advertising in Milwaukee Brewers baseball games. Since the theme of Beck's beer is "back to nature," the TV ads are photographed in the wheatfields of the Iowa corn belt, or in the pinewoods and lake regions of Wisconsin, stressing also the Midwest orientation. The ads or commercials are frequently interspersed with bits of information on Beck's brewing procedure, emphasizing the quality Beck's brings to its customers.

Employee Relations

Employee relations at Beck's had been fairly good for the first 20–25 years. Toward the end of 1969, however, friction developed between employees and management over wage increases, fringe benefits, and union security. The friction was intensified by the growing impersonal relationship that had developed over the years, as Beck's grew in size from a 100-employee local brewery to the present 600-employee regional concern. Beck's had been able to keep wages and benefits from rising too rapidly because of the personal relationship Robertson had with each of the employees, who knew him as "Mike." The employees had security in knowing Mike personally and feeling like part of the family. They enjoyed company outings, bowling in the company league, and being able to go to Mike, knowing he would understand their needs.

By the end of the sixties, with the increase in the size and complexity of the business, Mike had become more and more distant. The personal identification of the employees with the firm had diminished accordingly. This broadening social gap between management and labor caused employee pride in the company to diminish until almost everyone viewed his job as "just another job." There followed a steady increase in the number of complaints about the lower-than-average wage and benefit package and the lack of job security.

This seemed to be an ideal organization for the International Union of United Brewer, Flour, Cereal, Soft Drink, and Distillery Workers of America (AFL-CIO). The international had long regarded Beck's as the lone holdout in the Milwaukee area. Working slowly with the production workers of Beck's, the international union, through Local #3, reached a point in 1973 where it felt it could successfully achieve bargaining status. Consequently, an NLRB-sponsored election was requested upon a 30 percent showing of employees interested, and it was held on March 10, 1973.

The union had underestimated the employees' loyalty to Beck's and lost the election by a narrow margin, getting only 44 percent of those voting. However, the union was not to be denied. Using some of the older, more disgruntled employees as contacts, the union began a quiet campaign during the rest of 1973 and early 1974. Another election was called for in April 1974, and this time, the union won by a large majority. Local #3 was designated as the bargaining agent for Beck's production employees. The membership of the union immediately jumped from 32 to 77 percent of the 500 production employees. Contract negotiation immediately began and produced a contract for the period from May 20, 1974, through May 19, 1975 (see page 308).

Experience under First-Year Agreement

The contract turned out to be less than satisfactory to both sides in some areas. The management of Beck's Brewery and the union agree that the grievance procedure is somewhat cumbersome and needs to be renegotiated. Both also agree on the need for an effective pension plan.

Rank-and-file members of the union still complain about their wages; although greatly improved, they are still below the brewery average. They also complain that the entire benefit package is not in keeping with the industry norms, especially in the insurance and holiday areas. The union is expected to ask for more holidays, a greater amount of life insurance, and dental insurance.

Grumbling has also been heard about the distribution of overtime and slack-time hours and the lack of a wage-maintenance program. Most of this complaining can be traced to the slack production months of January and February, when thirty men were laid off for three days a week for six straight weeks. The men feel that a shorter workweek for all would be preferable to the present situation. Overtime distribution could also be improved by allowing some choice in the working of overtime hours.

The layoffs in January and February also pointed out that the term *job security* was interpreted differently by each side. The company used the term to mean "importance to the company of the job performed by an individual," whereas the union felt it meant "seniority in the department." The term was taken to arbitration, where the company definition was accepted.

The company also has its complaints about the contract. The cost of arbitration was not specified, and the company paid all costs for the first three cases taken to arbitration. The union felt this was an indication that Beck's would continue to pay all costs, but the company feels that the union has been using this flaw in the contract to take more cases to arbitration.

Management has also been dissatisfied with the job the union stewards are performing. The stewards have assumed that they can conduct most of their business on company time. The company has allowed this practice to continue, but has expressed a desire to have limits to these activities and to how long a steward may take to perform them.

Management further feels that a "management-rights" clause is necessary, as well as a revision of the "transfer and promotion" clause. Some changes instigated by management were delayed for several weeks while the union tried to challenge them through the grievance procedure.

The transfer and promotion clause prevented the company from hiring some extremely well-qualified personnel from a closing brewery, because some of the present employees were "well qualified" and had to be given preferential treatment.

AGREEMENT

This AGREEMENT made this FIRST day of May, 1974, between the undersigned firm of Milwaukee, Wisconsin (hereinafter referred to as the EMPLOYER), party of the first part, and the Brewery Workers' Local Union No. 3, Milwaukee, Wisconsin, and the International Union of United Brewery, Flour, Cereal, Soft Drink and Distillery Workers of America (hereinafter referred to as the UNION), parties of the second part, as representative of the employees covered by this Agreement.

THEREFORE, in consideration of the mutual covenants hereinafter set out, the parties hereto covenant and agree as follows:

ARTICLE 1

Union Recognition

(a) The EMPLOYER recognizes the UNION as the sole collective bargaining agent for its employees in the Brewery Department, Bottling Department and Delivery Department, as hereinafter more specifically stated.

(b) The EMPLOYER will not interfere with the right of employees to become members of the UNION. The UNION will not intimidate or discriminate against employees who choose not to join the UNION.

(c) The term "EMPLOYEE" or "EMPLOYEES," as used in this agreement, shall be construed to include only the classifications of employees specifically listed in this agreement and employed in the Employer's plant.

ARTICLE 2

Hiring of New Employees

(a) Preference in hiring of new employees shall be given in accordance with the following, provided the applicants are well qualified and physically able to perform the work:

(1) Employees requesting transfer from one department to another

(2) Employees who were employed by the Employer during the preceding year

(3) Others experienced in the brewing industry

(4) Other applicants

(b) Any employee who leaves one department to start work in another department shall lose all seniority in the department he left after thirty (30) days.

(c) Temporary summer help may be used without meeting the requirements of paragraph (a) above, provided there are no employees laid off who are willing and able to work and the duration of their employment does not exceed fifty (50) consecutive working days. All temporary help will be paid probationary wages. Employees converting from temporary summer to full-time employment will be considered in category (3) or (4) of paragraph (a) above and will not be hired before applicants in categories (1) or (2) of paragraph (a).

(d) When employees are temporarily required in one department, laid-off employees from other departments will be given first consideration for temporary employment. Acceptance or refusal of temporary work in another department shall in no way affect the job security of that employee in his own department. Temporary employment of laid-off employees shall be at the rate prevailing in the working department. Other temporary employees shall be paid probationary wages.

ARTICLE 3

Layoffs and Rehiring

Should it become necessary to lay off employees, they shall be laid off impartially according to job security. Upon rehiring, the last employee laid off shall be the first rehired, and the first laid off shall be the last rehired.

ARTICLE 4

Discharge

Employees may not be discharged, except for good cause, in the discretion of the Employer, and the Union shall have the right to investigate. Causes for discharge shall include, but not be limited to, the following: dishonesty, misuse of brewing monies and willful destruction of brewery property. No wages for time not worked shall be paid to discharged employees if the Union does not make its investigation within three (3) working days. If no investigation is made, the discharge shall be considered as accepted by the Union.

ARTICLE 5

Discrimination and Union Activity

The parties hereto agree not to use any subterfuge, coercion or intimidation, directly or indirectly, to evade or frustrate compliance with the spirit and terms of this agreement, nor cause the discharge or suspension of any member of the Union because of Union activities.

Any employee on leave of absence for Union activities or as a full-time officer shall not lose his seniority and shall on return to work be given his former position, if capable.

ARTICLE 6

Injuries and Illness

An employee who, through sickness or accident, cannot perform his work must report to the Employer and the Union, and shall after recovery be re-employed in his former position, provided such sickness or accident has not incapacitated the employee.

ARTICLE 7

Reporting Accidents and Injuries

All employees must in case of accident or injury to them report same to the office of the Employer and to the first-aid man, and procure names and addresses of all witnesses to the accident, no matter how trifling the accident may be. No employee shall refuse to go for medical service when directed by Company or first-aid man. Injured men shall be removed from the job until injuries are determined and first aid or doctor's care is supplied. Any mechanical defects shall be reported immediately.

ARTICLE 8

Safety

(a) A joint Union–Management Safety Committee will be established.

(b) The Employer reserves the right to make such rules and regulations as may be necessary to secure safety and maintain proper order. Recommendations from the Safety Committee must be considered and acted upon as soon as possible.

(c) Safety appliances for any work of a hazardous or injurious nature as may be deemed necessary shall be furnished and each employee must use same.

(d) Gas masks shall be furnished to employees while working in tanks or vats. While varnishing, kotizing and mamutizing, an employee shall be stationed outside the tank or vat where employees are working, as a safety measure.

ARTICLE 9

Hours of Labor

(a) Eight (8) hours shall consist of a day's work. The work week shall consist of five (5) days starting on Monday and which shall be consecutive except where interrupted by a holiday. Day work shall not begin before 7:30 A.M. nor later than 9:00 A.M. The starting time shall be prescribed by the Employer and the hours worked shall be consecutive, except for one-half (½) hour break for lunch which will be between 12:00 noon and 1:00 P.M. as assigned by the Employer. 11:30 AM

(b) All work performed at the request of management in excess of eight (8) hours in any day shall be paid for at the rate of time-and-one-half the regular rate. Saturday shall be considered the sixth day of the normal work week, and all work performed on Saturday shall be paid for at the rate of time-and-one-half.

ARTICLE 10

Holidays

The following holidays are recognized under this agreement:

1. New Year's Day
2. Good Friday
3. Memorial Day
4. Fourth of July
5. Labor Day
6. Thanksgiving Day
7. Christmas Day

Any employee must have worked ninety (90) days for the Employer prior to a holiday to be eligible for holiday pay. Any qualified experienced man working one (1) day in the week in which a holiday falls is to receive holiday pay.

These holidays shall not be considered as part of the regular work week if no work is done.

If work is performed on any of these holidays, it shall be paid for at the rate of time-and-one-half, and these days shall then be considered as part of the regular work week.

Employees shall perform holiday work in rotation.

When an employee is called for jury duty, the Employer shall pay the employee an amount equal to the regular jury duty pay paid by the county up to fifteen (15) days.

ARTICLE 11

Vacation

All employees in the continuous service of the Employer for —

1 year shall receive one week's vacation with pay
5 years shall receive two weeks' vacation with pay
15 years shall receive three weeks' vacation with pay

1 after 1
2 after 2
3 after 8

Vacation pay for all classifications shall be the average weekly wage for a period of 12 months in the calendar year immediately preceding the effective date of this contract, but shall, in no case, be less than the employee base pay for a 40-hour week.

Employees shall receive a maximum of three (3) lost-time days' pay in the event of the death of the following: Natural Mother, Father, Wife, Child, Mother-in-Law or Father-in-Law.

ARTICLE 12

Insurance

An insurance plan, such as that presently carried to include the Standard Semi-Private plan, an improved $300.00 Surgical Plan and a $100.00 deductible Major Medical Plan, along with the Life Insurance Plan as outlined in the present Insurance Plan booklet, shall be the only insurance plan in effect and paid for by the Beck's Brewing Company.

ARTICLE 13

Union-Made Malt and Other Materials

Union-made malt and all other union-made materials shall be given preference—price, quality and availability being equal and contract commitments permitting.

ARTICLE 14

Hauling Materials

It shall be the duty of the employees covered by this agreement to haul all bulk material required in the brewery, including hops, grains, etc., also all packages and containers such as kegs, cases, bottles, and cans, etc., said materials to be hauled from railroad cars, freight stations, boat terminals, warehouses, etc., and delivered to platform as directed.

ARTICLE 15

Wages

(a) Payment of wages due employees shall be made by the Company every other Friday for work performed during the previous two (2) calendar weeks, except when regular pay day falls on a day not worked, pay checks will be distributed on the previous day.

(b) Beginning May 20, 1974, wages shall be paid at the following rates: [Note that all employees in the Plant are referred to as brewery workers.]

Employees	Wage Rates	
Brewing	Hourly	
Leadman	$8.65	9.24
Assistant leadman	7.41	7.88
Regular worker	6.18	6.58
First-year worker	5.16	5.50
Extra help	4.53	4.82
Malting		
Leadman	$8.32	9.21
Assistant leadman	6.75	7.19
Regular worker	6.01	6.40
First-year worker	5.11	5.44
Extra help	4.28	4.56
Bottling		
Leadman	$8.28	8.82
Assistant leadman	6.72	7.16
Regular worker	5.93	6.32
First-year worker	4.94	5.26
Extra help	4.12	4.39
Power plant		
Senior first man	$8.81	9.38
First man	7.82	8.33
Operators	6.26	6.67
Maintenance men	6.26	6.67
Helpers	4.94	5.26

ARTICLE 16

Military Service

In the event that any employee covered by this agreement is called to active military service in the armed forces of the United States, such employee shall be considered on leave of absence and shall be entitled to all rights of re-employment as provided by the Selective Service and Training Act of 1948.

ARTICLE 17

Limitation of Union Responsibility for Unauthorized Strike

Except as otherwise provided in this agreement, during the term of this agreement, the Union guarantees the Employer that there will be no authorized strike, work stoppage, or other concerted interference with normal operations by its employees. The Employer guarantees that it will not lock out its employees. For the purpose of this Section an authorized strike, stoppage, or other concerted interference with normal operations is one that has been specifically authorized or ratified by the General Executive Board of the International Union.

Should an unauthorized strike, stoppage, or other concerted interference with normal operations take place, the International Union shall in no event be liable, financially or otherwise, provided that the International Union within twenty-four (24) hours after actual receipt of notice in writing or by telegram from the Employer that a strike or work stoppage has commenced will notify the Employer in writing or by telegram that such strike, work stoppage or other concerted interference with normal operations is unauthorized and that a copy of such notice has been sent to the Local officers with instructions to bring it to the attention of the employees involved. The Local Union whose members are involved in such unauthorized action shall not be held to its legal liability therefore, if any, provided it meets the following conditions. But in any event the Local Union agrees to:

(a) Promptly post notices in conspicuous places at the affected plant and at the Local Union office stating that such action is unauthorized.

(b) Promptly order its members to resume normal operations. The employees who instigate or participate in unauthorized strikes or stoppages in violation of this agreement shall be subject to discharge or discipline, in which event their sole recourse to the grievance and arbitration procedures shall be limited to the question of whether they did in fact instigate or participate in such strike or stoppage.

ARTICLE 18

Separability

Should any part hereof or any provision herein contained be rendered or declared illegal, invalid, or an unfair labor practice by reason of any existing or subsequently enacted legislation or by any decree of a court of competent jurisdiction or by the decision of any authorized Government Agency, including the National Labor Relations Board, the remaining portions hereof shall not be affected thereby; provided, however, in such contingency the parties shall meet and negotiate with respect to substitute provisions for those parts or provisions rendered or declared illegal, invalid, or an unfair labor practice.

ARTICLE 19

Arbitration of Grievances

(a) Grievances by individual employees relating to the interpretation or application of this agreement shall be first taken up by the employee affected and his foreman or by the shop steward and foreman. If they fail to arrive at a mutually satisfactory adjustment within five (5) days, unless extended by mutual agreement, the matter shall be referred to the Secretary of the Local Union, who shall attempt to adjust it by negotiations with the Employer's representatives. If a mutually satisfactory adjustment is not arrived at by them within an additional five (5) days, unless extended by mutual agreement, the matter shall be submitted to a Board of Arbitration upon written request of either party.

(b) The Board of Arbitration herein referred to shall be chosen and shall operate as follows: Two (2) arbitrators shall be appointed by the Union and two (2) by the Employer within five (5) days, unless extended by mutual agreement, after the receipt of the request for arbitration. In the event that a majority is unable to agree upon the disposition of the case, a fifth arbitrator who shall be Chairman of the Board shall be designated by the aforesaid four (4) arbitrators.

Should the four (4) arbitrators be unable to agree upon the fifth arbitrator within five (5) days, unless extended by mutual consent, he shall be designated, upon written request of either party, by the American Arbitration Association. The Board of Arbitration as so constituted shall determine the matter at issue by decision in writing signed by at least three (3) of its members, which decision shall be final and binding upon the parties.

(c) There shall be no strike or lockout while arbitration is pending; provided, however, that in the event one party should fail or refuse to appoint arbitrators or should take any action to prevent arbitration or should fail or refuse to comply with a decision of the Board of Arbitration within three (3) days after its receipt, the party in default shall automatically lose its case, and, in addition to whatever other remedies may be available to the party not in default, the first clause of this paragraph shall not be binding upon such party.

(d) Discharges may be made the subject of grievances and of arbitration.

ARTICLE 20

Termination

This agreement shall become effective May 20, 1974, and shall continue in effect until May 20, 1975, and shall thereafter renew itself automatically for periods of one year unless either party serves written notice upon the other not less than sixty (60) days before the end of the initial period or any subsequent period of its desire to terminate or modify this agreement.

TABLE 2. Income Statement (10-Yr. Trend)
(Expressed in 1,000s)

	1974	1973	1972	1971	1970	1969	1968	1967	1966	1965
Sales	56,607	54,116	53,589	52,870	45,206	44,810	42,387	41,889	42,115	36,602
C.G.S.	45,325	39,550	37,347	33,277	34,002	34,401	29,379	29,211	29,352	24,058
Labor	7,847	6,793	6,254	5,740	5,235	4,868	3,540	3,196	2,621	2,436
R.M. + O/H	37,478	32,757	31,093	27,537	28,767	29,533	25,839	26,015	26,731	21,622
Gross profit	11,282	14,566	16,242	19,593	11,204	10,409	13,008	12,678	12,763	12,544
Selling & admin, exp.	4,822	3,499	3,471	3,423	331	313	260	207	7,908	7,219
Dep'n. exp.	1,998	1,711	1,446	1,296	1,143	1,032	701	599	573	478
Other operating exp.	2,960	3,522	2,384	2,487	3,928	3,530	3,954	4,417	1,612	1,556
Income before taxes	1,502	5,834	8,941	12,387	5,802	5,534	8,093	7,455	2,670	3,291
Income taxes	644	2,468	4,077	5,859	2,895	2,789	3,885	3,444	1,255	1,579
Net income	858	3,366	4,864	6,528	2,907	2,745	4,208	4,010	1,415	1,711

Notes: 1. "Other operating expenses" includes interest expense.
2. "Labor" includes payroll for both regular time and overtime.

TABLE 3. Beck's Balance Sheet (10-Yr. Trend)
(Expressed in 1,000s)

	1974	1973	1972	1971	1970	1969	1968	1967	1966	1965
Cash & M.S.	3,432	6,177	9,026	8,923	5,765	5,456	7,859	5,045	6,452	8,477
A/R	2,945	4,914	3,207	2,089	1,824	2,766	1,383	971	1,177	971
Inven.	6,732	5,520	5,049	4,173	4,308	2,827	2,356	2,490	2,154	1,548
Other C.A.	1,513	922	438	469	529	741	105	423	105	423
Total C.A.	14,620	17,533	17,720	15,654	12,426	11,790	11,703	8,929	9,888	11,419
Plant & equip.	35,627	30,639	26,363	23,870	18,169	19,951	18,882	18,526	16,744	16,388
Accum. dep'n	<12,894>	<11,475>	<10,315>	<9,283>	<6,962>	<7,736>	<6,833>	<6,706>	<6,319>	<6,190>
Net plant & equip.	22,733	19,164	16,048	14,587	11,207	12,215	12,049	11,820	10,425	10,198
Other assets	1,271	1,131	1,347	1,207	2,821	1,652	000	50	165	330
TOTAL ASSETS	38,624	37,828	35,115	31,448	26,454	25,657	23,752	20,799	20,478	21,947
Current liab.	8,193	6,718	6,062	5,653	4,791	4,424	3,604	3,173	3,359	4,342
Long term debt	4,135	3,597	2,646	2,067	1,778	1,571	1,374	000	000	000
Deferred inc. tax	378	302	230	105	000	000	000	000	000	000
Other liab.	234	2,193	1,824	481	000	337	582	293	166	182
Total liab.	12,940	12,810	10,762	8,306	6,569	6,332	5,560	3,406	3,525	4,524
Common stock and A.P.I.C.	10,544	10,333	10,122	10,122	8,622	8,516	7,989	7,567	7,462	7,146
R/E	15,140	14,685	14,231	13,020	11,263	10,809	10,203	9,826	9,491	10,277
TOTAL LIAB. & S.E. & R.E.	38,624	37,828	35,115	31,448	26,454	25,657	23,752	20,799	20,478	21,947
Average shares outstanding	2,943	2,751	2,720	2,708	2,311	2,298	2,223	2,210	2,154	2,137

Note: The appropriate accounting methods which minimize taxes were used in all cases (i.e., depreciation methods, inventory valuation methods, etc.).

318

TABLE 4. Statement of Retained Earnings (10-Yr. Trend)
(Expressed in 1,000s)

	1974	1973	1972	1971	1970	1969	1968	1967	1966	1965
Beg. retained earn.	14,685	14,231	13,020	11,263	10,809	10,203	9,826	9,491	10,277	11,258
+ Net income	858	3,366	4,864	6,528	2,907	2,745	4,208	4,010	1,415	1,711
− Dividends	403	2,912	3,653	4,771	2,453	2,139	3,831	3,675	2,201	2,692
Ending retained earn.	15,140	14,685	14,231	13,020	11,263	10,809	10,203	9,826	9,491	10,277

TABLE 5

	Wages per Hour (Avg.)	No. Employed in Category
Leadman	$8.42	26
Assistant leadman	6.97	30
Regular	6.04	288
First-year worker	5.06	40
Extra help	4.30	30
Senior first man	8.81	15
First man	7.82	15
Operators	6.26	21
Maintenance men	6.26	20
Helpers	4.94	15
		500

wt ave = $6.16

TABLE 6.   Employees by Yrs. of Service Seniority and Average Ages

Years of Seniority	No. of Workers	Average Ages
20 or more	26	51 yrs.
15–20	130	38
10–15	160	33
5–10	40	27
4– 5	30	25
3– 4	20	22
2– 3	20	22
1– 2	28	21
0– 1	46	20
	500	

Note: 6% of all production employees are women.

TABLE 7. Labor Turnover — Malt-Liquor Industry Averages

Year	Accessions /100 Employees	New Hires /100 Employees	Separations /100 Employees	Quits /100 Employees	Layoffs /100 Employees
1974	4.4	1.6	4.5	.6	3.2
1973	3.6	1.6	3.9	.6	2.6
1972	3.7	1.5	4.1	.5	3.1
1971	3.4	1.1	3.9	.4	3.0
1970	3.9	1.5	4.1	.5	3.0
1969	4.0	1.9	4.1	.8	2.9
1968	3.7	1.7	3.9	.8	2.6
1967	4.4	1.9	4.4	.9	3.1
1966	4.7	2.1	4.7	.8	3.3
1965	4.1	1.5	4.3	.6	3.2

DEFINITIONS

Spendable Average Weekly Earnings

Spendable average weekly earnings in current dollars are obtained by deducting estimated federal Social Security and income taxes from gross weekly earnings. The amount of income tax liability depends on the number of dependents supported by the worker and his marital status, as well as on the level of his gross income. To reflect these variables, spendable earnings are computed for a worker who has no dependents and a married worker who has three dependents. The computations are based on gross average weekly earnings for all production or nonsupervisory workers in the industry division, excluding other income and income earned by other family members.

The series reflects the spendable earnings of only those workers, with either no or three dependents, whose gross weekly pay approximates the average earnings indicated for all production and nonsupervisory workers. It does not reflect, for example, the average earnings of all workers with three dependents; such workers in fact have higher average gross earnings than workers with no dependents.

Since part-time as well as full-time workers are included, and since the proportion of part-time workers has been rising in some industries, the series understates the increase in earnings for full-time workers. As noted, "fringe benefits" are not included in the earnings. For a more complete discussion of the uses and limitations of these series, see the article by Paul M. Schwab, "Two Measures of Purchasing Power Contrasted," in the *Monthly Labor Review* for April 1971. Reprints of this article are available from the Bureau of Labor Statistics.

"Real" earnings are computed by dividing the current Consumer Price Index into the earnings averages for the current month. This is done for gross average weekly earnings and for spendable average weekly earnings. The level of earnings is thus adjusted for changes in purchasing power since the base period (1967).

Average Hourly Earnings Excluding Overtime

Average hourly earnings excluding overtime premium pay are computed by dividing the total production-worker payroll for the industry group by the sum of total production-worker man-hours and one-half of total overtime man-hours. Before January 1956, these data were based on the application of adjustment factors to gross average hourly earnings (as described in the *Monthly Labor Review*, May 1950, pp. 537–40). Both methods eliminate only the earnings due to overtime, paid for at 1½ times the straight-time rates. No adjustment is made for other premium-payment provisions, such as holiday work, late-shift work, and overtime rates other than time and one-half.

Indexes of Aggregate Weekly Payrolls and Man-Hours

The indexes of aggregate weekly payrolls and man-hours are prepared by dividing the current month's aggregate by the monthly average for 1967. The man-hour aggregates are the product of average weekly hours and production-worker employment, and the payroll aggregates are the product of man-hour aggregates and average hourly earnings. At all higher levels of aggregation, man-hour and payroll aggregates are the sum of the component aggregates.

Labor Turnover

Labor turnover is the gross movement of wage and salary workers into and out of employed status with respect to individual establishments. This movement, which relates to a calendar month, is divided into two broad types: *Accessions* (new hires and rehires) and *separations* (terminations of employment initiated by either employer or employee). Each type of action is cumulated for a calendar month and expressed as a rate per 100 employees. The data relate to all employees, whether full- or part-time, permanent or temporary, including executive, office, sales, and other salaried personnel, and production workers. Transfers to another establishment of the company are included, beginning with January 1959.

Accessions are the total number of permanent and temporary additions to the employment roll, including both new and rehired employees.

New hires are temporary or permanent additions to the employment roll of persons who have never before been employed in the establishment (except employees transferring from another establishment of the same company) or of former employees not recalled by the employers.

Other accessions, which are not published separately but are included in total accessions, are all additions to the employment roll that are not classified as new hires, including transfers from another establishment of the same company and former employees recalled from layoff.

Separations are terminations of employment during the calendar month and are classified according to cause: quits, layoffs, and other separations, as defined below.

Quits are terminations of employment initiated by employees, failure to report after being hired, and unauthorized absences, if on the last day of the month the person has been absent more than 7 consecutive calendar days.

Layoffs are suspensions without pay, lasting or expected to last more than 7 consecutive calendar days, initiated by the employer without prejudice to the worker.

Other separations, which are not published separately but are included in total separations, are terminations of employment because of discharge, permanent disability, death, retirement, transfers to another establishment of the company, and entrance into the armed forces for a period expected to last more than 30 consecutive calendar days.

Month-to-month changes in total employment in manufacturing industries reflected by labor turnover rates are not comparable with the changes shown in the bureau's employment series for the following reasons: (1) Accessions and separations are computed for the entire calendar month, whereas the employment reports refer to the pay period that includes the 12th of the month; and (2) employees on strike are not counted as turnover actions, although such employees are excluded from the employment estimates if the work stoppage extends through the report period.

Job Vacancies

Job vacancies are the stock of unfilled job openings as of the close of the last business day of the reference month. Openings for all kinds of positions, classifications, and employment, full-time, part-time, permanent, temporary, and seasonal, are included. Excluded are jobs to be filled by recall from layoff, transfer, promotion, demotion, or return from paid or unpaid leave; jobs unoccupied because of labor–management disputes; job openings for which "new" workers were already hired and scheduled to start work later; and openings with future starting dates, which are requested as a separate item.

Job vacancies are defined as vacant jobs that are immediately available for filling, and for which the firm is actively trying to find or recruit workers from outside the firm.

"Actively trying to find or recruit" means that the establishment is engaged in current efforts to fill the job vacancies by means of orders listed with public or private employment agencies and school placement offices; notification to labor unions and professional organizations; "help wanted" advertising (newspaper, posted notice, etc.) recruitment programs; and interview and selection of applicants.

Long-term job vacancies are those current vacancies that have continued unfilled for 30 days or more.

The reporting establishment is also asked to indicate the number of openings with future starting dates for which the firm is actively trying to recruit workers from outside the firm.

Job openings with future starting dates may exist for such reasons as: job unavailable until expected separation of present incumbent occurs; work will not start until some future date; new branch to be opened in the future; or anticipated increase in business.

The *job vacancy rate* is computed by dividing the number of current job vacancies by the sum of employment plus vacancies, and multiplying that quotient by 100.

ESTIMATING METHODS

The principal features of the procedure used to estimate employment for the industry statistics are (1) the use of the "link relative" technique, which is a form of ratio estimation, (2) the use of size and regional stratification, and (3) periodic adjustment of employment levels to new bench marks.

The "Link Relative" Technique

From a sample composed of establishments reporting for both the previous and current months, the ratio of current-month employment to that of the previous month is computed. This is called a "link relative." The estimates of employment (all employees, including production and nonproduction workers together) for the current month are obtained by multiplying the estimates for the previous month by these "link relatives." Further details (including (2) and (3) above) are given in the *Handbook of Methods*, BLS Bulletin 1711 (1971), Chapters 2 and 3. Reprints are available upon request.

Associated General Contractors— Construction-Industry Bargaining Game

B

SPECIAL INSTRUCTIONS—CONSTRUCTION GAME

Because arrangements vary considerably from one region to another in the construction industry, it was not thought wise to tie the game to a particular situation. Furthermore, since the negotiation is between a single union (the Carpenters) and an association of employers (the Associated General Contractors), it is impossible to provide financial statements as in the other games. On the other hand, this is exactly the reason for including a negotiation game based on a construction-industry contract—the fact that it is a unique negotiation situation.

Construction is an industry in which flexibility must be the key word. In most instances, the process requires assembling of workers and materials at separate and diverse locations. Labor is specialized by trades, and part of the problem the contractor faces is assembling the required skills as needed for short periods of time. The worker identifies with his trade and union rather than with a particular employer. The union becomes his entry into work, and as a result, the union plays a particularly important role in his life. The unity this brings among the members allows the union to exert a tremendous influence on the industry. Through the contract, the union attempts to act as a stabilizing agent for its members in a fluctuating and mobile job situation, in matters such as wages, policing the work, supplying labor, and disciplining the work force.

In the contract that follows, there are two variables that the instructor or leader in the negotiation exercises should feel free to modify: the period of time of the contract, and the wage rate. The year that the contract is in effect is left open to fit the particular renegotiation exercise established by the group leader. An $8-an-hour wage rate is inserted, but the instructor may modify this to meet the local situation.

AGREEMENT

THIS AGREEMENT, MADE AND ENTERED INTO THIS 14th DAY OF JULY, 197– BY AND BETWEEN ASSOCIATED GENERAL CONTRACTORS, HEREINAFTER ALSO REFERRED TO AS THE EMPLOYER, AND THE UNITED BROTHERHOOD OF CARPENTERS AND JOINERS OF AMERICA, AFL-CIO, ON BEHALF OF ITS LOCAL UNION HAVING JURISDICTION OVER THE WORK IN THE TERRITORY COVERED BY THIS AGREEMENT, HEREINAFTER REFERRED TO AS THE UNION.

I. JURISDICTION

A. Territory Covered:

The area covered by this agreement shall be . . . .

B. Work Covered

All carpentry work on building construction including but not limited to construction, erection, alteration, repair, modification, demolition, addition or improvement of or to a building structure within the recognized jurisdiction of the United Brotherhood of Carpenters and Joiners of America. Included is work in connection with new methods of construction or use of materials established or developed during the term of this Agreement. Also included shall be the use and application of tools, devices, procedures, mechanical, power driven or otherwise customarily and regularly used by carpenters whether continuously or intermittently and which are regarded tools of the carpentry trade.

C. Owners

On any construction project, only one (1) owner working with the tools shall be recognized as the contractor. All others working with the tools shall be members of the Union, subject to all of the provisions of this Agreement, including, but not limited to, the payment of contributions to all Trust Funds.

II. EMPLOYER MEMBERSHIP

This Agreement is made for and on behalf of, and shall be binding upon all persons, firms or corporations that at the time of the execution of this

Agreement are, or during the term hereof become, members of the Employer, which members are individual employers of carpenters in the above mentioned areas.

III. INDEPENDENT AGREEMENT

This Agreement is separate and distinct from, and independent of, all other Agreements entered into between the Union and other employer organizations.

IV. UNION SECURITY AND HIRING

A. Union Security

Every person performing work covered by this Agreement who is a member of the Union and in the employment of an individual employer on work covered by this Agreement on the effective date of this Subsection 4A shall, as a condition of employment or continued employment, remain a member in good standing of the Union. Every other person covered by this Agreement and employed to perform work covered by this Agreement shall be required, as a condition of employment, to apply for and become a member of (within ninety days) and to maintain membership in good standing in the Union.

B. Hiring

1. The Union shall establish and maintain open and non-discriminatory employment lists for the use of carpenters desiring employment on work covered by this Agreement and such carpenters shall be entitled to use such lists without charge.
2. The individual employer shall first call upon the Union for such men as he may from time to time need, and the Union shall furnish the individual employer the required number of qualified and competent carpenters of the classifications needed by the individual employer.
3. When ordering carpenters, the individual employer will give notice to the Union, if possible not later than 2:30 P.M. of the day prior (Monday through Friday) or, in any event, not less than seventeen and one-half (17½) hours, if possible, before the required reporting time and in the event that twenty-four (24) hours after such notice (Saturdays, Sundays and recognized holidays excluded), the Local Union or District Council shall not furnish such a carpenter, the individual employer may procure carpenters from any source or sources. If carpenters are so employed, the individual employer shall promptly report to the Union each such carpenter by name.

4. Subject to the foregoing, the individual employer shall have complete freedom of selectivity in hiring and the individual employer retains the right to reject any job applicant referred by the Union for any reason. The individual employer may discharge any employee for any cause which he or it may deem sufficient, provided there shall be no discrimination on the part of the individual employer against any employee for activities in behalf of, or presentation of, the Union not interfering with the proper performance of his duties.

V. WORK DAY AND WORK WEEK

A. Eight (8) hours between 8:00 A.M. and 5:00 P.M., except as provided under shift work, excluding meal period, shall constitute a regular day's work at straight time rates, unless otherwise agreed upon by the parties hereto.

   The regular work week shall consist of forty (40) hours, Monday through Friday at straight time.

B. When part of an eight (8) hour day is worked, pro-rata rates for such shorter periods will be paid. A carpenter shall be entitled to pick-up time of five (5) minutes at the end of each work day.

VI. OVERTIME

Overtime shall be paid as follows:

On all building construction: for any extra time worked after the regular eight (8) hours have been worked between the hours of 8:00 A.M. and 5:00 P.M., time and one-half shall be paid. All work on Saturdays, Sundays and recognized holidays shall be paid time and one-half. When men are required to report for work before 8:00 A.M., they shall be paid time and one-half prior to 8:00 A.M., except on shift work or when, by mutual consent of the employer and the Union, they render it desirable to start the work day earlier, due to existing traffic, weather or similar conditions.

VII. SHIFT WORK

Where two (2) or more shifts are worked in any twenty-four (24) hours, each shift shall work eight (8) hours and receive eight (8) hours' pay. No multiple shift shall be established or started for less than five (5) consecutive regular work days.

VIII. HOLIDAYS

The following are recognized holidays: New Year's Day, Washington's Birthday, Decoration Day (Memorial Day), Independence Day, Labor Day, Thanksgiving Day, and Christmas Day.

IX. REPORTING TIME, DISCHARGE AND INJURY

A. Men ordered to report for work for whom no employment is provided, shall be entitled to two (2) consecutive hours' pay, except in cases where bad weather or other conditions beyond the individual employer's control prevents employment.

B. Except as hereinafter provided, carpenters who start work, but are discharged between the hours of 8:00 A.M. and 12:00 noon, shall receive four (4) hours' pay; carpenters starting work at 8:00 A.M., but who are discharged between the hours of 12:00 noon and 5:00 P.M., shall receive eight (8) hours' pay. Carpenters discharged on the first day of employment for inefficiency, insubordination or intoxication shall receive pay only for hours worked. Carpenters who voluntarily quit shall receive pay only for hours worked.

C. Discharged employees. Employees receiving notices of discharge shall be allowed a reasonable time (not less than fifteen [15] minutes) before the end of the regular work day to assemble their tools in addition to the normal pick-up time prevailing on that job.

D. Employees who are, as a result of an industrial injury, unable to complete a full day's work, shall nevertheless be paid for the full day on which such injury occurred; provided, however, that said injury requires the attention of a licensed physician and said physician has certified to the employee's inability to complete work on that day because of such injury.

E. An employee who works the full regular work week, Monday through Friday, shall receive on said Friday of that work week pay for not less than the number of hours worked on the Monday of that same work week.

X. CRAFT DEFINITIONS

A. Journeyman Carpenter

The term "Journeyman Carpenter," as used herein, means an employee qualified by experience and ability to perform work with carpenters' tools, carpenters' level and such other tools or survey instruments as are normally used by carpenters in the performance of carpenters' work.

The term "Apprentice Carpenter," as used herein, means an employee as defined from time to time as an apprentice in the Apprenticeship Standards for the Carpentry Trade, who shall be permitted to perform any work done by a Journeyman Carpenter. The term of apprenticeship shall not exceed a period of four (4) years.

An individual employer who is entitled to employ apprentices may employ not more than one (1) apprentice for the first two (2) journeymen regularly employed by him, and not more than one (1) additional apprentice for each three (3) additional journeymen employed by him. The first apprentice may not be employed by the individual employer. Any individual employer employing five (5) journeymen, shall, while employing five (5) journeymen, also employ at least one (1) apprentice. For each additional ten (10) journeymen then in his employ, he shall employ at least one (1) additional apprentice.

XI. CONTRACTING AND SUBCONTRACTING

No work covered by this Agreement shall be performed at piece rates and no work shall be let by piece, contract or lump sum for labor services only. The only method of payment shall be on an hourly basis according to the provisions of this Agreement.

XII. TOOLS

A. Carpenters and apprentices shall furnish their own tools, but shall not furnish, rent or lease saw horses, ladders, mitre boxes, electric drills, automotive equipment to be used for the purpose of hauling or delivering individual employers' materials or equipment, or any kind of power operated machines or saws. Each employee shall arrive on the job with tools in proper condition. To implement this Section, the individual carpenter shall provide a tool box with a lock. If necessary, the employee shall be allowed a reasonable amount of time during the work week to sharpen tools on the individual employer's time.

B. Reasonable Secure Places for Tools. The individual employer shall provide on each job site a reasonably secure place where his employees may keep their tools.

XIII. GRIEVANCE PROCEDURE

A. In the event that a dispute arises on the job, it shall be first reported to the business agent of the Union who shall then attempt to adjust said grievance or dispute with the individual employer or his representative.

B. The Union business agent shall specify the date(s) of alleged violation(s) of the sections(s) of the Master Agreement which gives cause for the dispute.

C. If said grievance or dispute is not satisfactorily adjusted by the authorized Union representative and the individual employer or his representative within three (3) days after the date when it was reported, it shall be referred to a Board of Adjustment in writing within five (5) days, unless the time is mutually extended by both parties.

D. In the event a dispute arises, a Board of Adjustment shall be created for the settlement of such disputes. It shall be composed of two (2) representatives selected by the Union and two (2) representatives selected by the Employer. Said Board shall organize at once and shall elect a Chairman and a Secretary and shall adopt rules of procedures which shall bind the contracting parties. Said Board shall have the power to adjust any differences that may arise regarding the meaning or enforcement of this contract. Within twenty-four (24) hours of the time any dispute is referred to it, the members thereof within three (3) days shall choose a fifth member who shall have no business or financial connection with either party. If the parties are unable to agree on a fifth member, he shall be chosen by lot from a list of five (5) names provided by the Federal Mediation and Conciliation Service. The decision of said Board shall be determined by a majority of its members and shall be rendered within five (5) days after such submission. The Union and the employer shall prepare a written submission agreement which shall be presented to the Board. The submission agreement shall specify the issue in dispute and the section or sections of the Agreement that are involved. In the event that the parties cannot agree on a joint submission agreement, then each party shall make its submission separately and supply the other party with a copy of such separate submission. The decision of said Board shall be determined by a majority of its members and shall be rendered within five (5) days after such submission. Said decision shall be within the scope of this Agreement, and shall not change, delete or add to any such terms and shall be final and binding on all parties hereto. The expense of employing said fifth person shall be borne equally by both parties.

E. Pending the decision upon any dispute or grievance, work shall be continued in accordance with the provisions of this Agreement.

XIV. WAGE RATES

A. The following shall be the classification and minimum hourly wage rates during the term of this Agreement from the effective dates noted below:

July 16, 197–

Journeyman Carpenters—$8.00

B. Foremen's Wage Rates. If the individual employer determines to use any foremen, they shall be paid seventy-five cents (75¢) an hour above the current journeyman's wage rate. The individual employer shall continue to have the right to determine, in his sole and unlimited discretion, the need for and number of foremen.

C. Apprentices' Wage Rates. The wage rates for apprentices shall be the following percentages of the journeyman rate:

0 to 6 months	60%
6 to 12 months	65%
12 to 18 months	70%
18 to 24 months	75%
24 to 30 months	80%
30 to 36 months	85%
36 to 42 months	90%
42 to 48 months	95%

XV. HEALTH AND WELFARE

Each individual employer covered by this Agreement will contribute to the Carpenter's Health and Welfare Trust Fund the sum of fifty cents (50¢) per hour worked by each employee covered by this Agreement for the purpose of providing Health and Welfare benefits for such employees.

XVI. PENSION PLAN

For the purpose of providing pension benefits to employees covered by this Agreement, the individual employer will contribute fifty cents (50¢) for each hour worked by carpenters in his employ under this Agreement to the Carpenter's Pension Trust Fund.

XVII. VACATION AND HOLIDAY PLAN

Each individual employer covered by this Agreement shall contribute fifty cents (50¢) per hour for each hour paid for or worked by each carpenter in his employ under this Agreement to the Carpenter's Vacation and Holiday Plan.

This contribution shall be allocated as follows: Thirty-five cents (35¢) to holidays and fifteen cents (15¢) to paid vacation.

XVIII. LIABILITY OF THE PARTIES

It is mutually understood and agreed that neither the employer, any individual employer, the Union or any local union shall be liable for damages caused by the acts or conduct of any individual or group of individuals who are acting or conducting themselves in violation of the terms of this Agreement without the authority of the respective party, provided that such action or conduct has not been specifically authorized, participated in or ratified by the employer, the individual employer, the Union or the local union as the case may be.

In the event of any unauthorized violation of the terms of this Agreement, responsible and authorized representatives of the Union, local Union, the employer or the individual employers, as the case may be, shall promptly take such affirmative action as is within their power to correct and terminate such violation for the purpose of bringing such unauthorized persons into compliance with the terms of this Agreement. Such individuals acting or conducting themselves in violation of the terms of this Agreement shall be subject to discipline.

XIX. EMPLOYEES NOT TO BE DISCHARGED FOR RECOGNIZING AUTHORIZED PICKET LINES

No employee covered hereby may be discharged by an individual employer for refusing to cross a lawful picket line established by an International Union affiliated with the Building and Construction Trades Department of the American Federation of Labor, or a local union thereof, which picket line has been authorized or sanctioned by the Local Building and Construction Trades Council having jurisdiction over the area in which the job is located and after the individual employer involved has been notified and has had an opportunity to be heard. Said notice shall be in writing and mailed to the individual employer at his address. This Section shall not apply to jurisdictional disputes.

XX. TERM OF AGREEMENT

This Agreement shall remain in full force and effect from the 15th day of June, 197–, and shall continue thereafter unless either party within sixty (60) days prior to the 15th day of June, 197–, or sixty (60) days prior to the 15th day of June of any subsequent year serves written notice on the other of its desire to change, modify, amend or supplement this Agreement.

While this Agreement continues in effect, neither party will make demands upon the other party for any changes in conditions or benefits except at the time and in the manner provided above.

For the UNION:

For the EMPLOYER:

River City Veterans
Administration Hospital–
A Federal-Sector Game

C

Labor relations programs in all but a very few federal agencies are controlled and governed by the provisions contained in Executive Order 11491.

Executive Order 11491 was issued by President Nixon in the fall of 1969. It was based on recommendations given to the president by a select committee of cabinet officers, following an extensive review of labor–management relations as practiced under President Kennedy's pioneering Executive Order 10988.

Executive Order 11491 was amended in August 1971 and again in February 1975. The order permits labor organizations that have been designated by secret vote of the majority of the employees in an appropriate unit to be the exclusive representative of those employees for collective bargaining purposes. The right of exclusive representation entitles unions to negotiate collective bargaining agreements with agency managements, although no agreement may contravene applicable laws and regulations or published agency policies and regulations for which compelling need exists, or apply where controlling collective bargaining agreements have been negotiated at higher levels. The order also prohibits certain unfair labor practices on the part of both agencies and unions.

The Federal Labor Relations Council administers the order and decides major policy questions. A Federal Service Impasse Panel has authority to resolve negotiation deadlocks, and the assistant secretary of labor for labor–management relations has authority to determine appropriate units for bargaining, to supervise elections, and to decide cases alleging unfair labor practices or violations of the standards of conduct for labor organizations.

This order provides the legal framework for all the negotiations that take place between the union and the employer and ought to be reviewed carefully by the participants before entering into any negotiations.

THE EMPLOYER

The Veterans Administration Hospital is located in a large metropolitan Midwestern city, River City. It employs 1,350 nonprofessional hourly and salaried employees. The hospital actually has two facilities, a new one located on the outskirts of the city and an old one located in the midtown district.

THE UNION

The American Federation of Government Employees (AFL-CIO) is the largest federal-employee union in the country. It is currently recognized as the exclusive representative in 1,627 federal bargaining units, representing over 650,000 employees. Of the 1,627 units, 1,111 have successfully negotiated at least one agreement, and these agreements cover 550,000 employees.

The AFGE has organized two locals at the River City VA Hospital. Local 1000 represents about 800 employees at the new suburban facility, and Local 2000 represents 550 employees at the midtown center. Both locals are recognized as exclusive representatives for their respective unit locations, having been properly certified after winning bitterly contested unit elections 2½ years ago.

THE AGREEMENT

The first agreement was negotiated with the assistance of two highly experienced negotiators advising the union. The representatives for management were much less experienced and felt as though they were outmanned in the first contract negotiations. In fact, the consensus of most management personnel is that the management team has given the union almost everything it wanted.

This time around, the negotiation procedures, Article XI, should provide a better balance for both sides of the bargaining table.

Highlights of the first agreement are as follows:

The prerequisites of exclusive recognition are detailed in several clauses. Monthly union–management meetings are required (Article IV, Section 4), and the union may be granted permission to hold membership meetings on VA premises during nonduty time (Article VIII, Section 2). The union also enjoys the right to announce its meetings in the hospital's daily bulletin (Article IX, Section 3). There is dues checkoff at a cost of 2 cents per transaction (Article V, Section 3). New hires will receive a copy of the brochure describing the union's health-benefits plan and be informed that one must be an AFGE member to enroll (Article X, Section 1); presumably, distribution of the brochure can help union organizing at the facility.

Ground rules for any future negotiations are set forth in Article XI. Teams are to be limited to six persons each, including one alternate and one advisor each (Section 1). Sessions are to be closed (Section 4). Caucuses are to be permitted as required, the caucusing party withdrawing to a room specified for that purpose (Section 5); caucuses and rest periods are not to exceed 15 minutes' duration each (Section 5).

Section 6 of Article XI describes a noteworthy "self-help" impasse-resolution technique. Whenever an impasse—defined as the inability of the team "to arrive at a mutually agreeable decision, through the bargaining process"—is reached, a homegrown fact-finding committee is to be appointed. The union and management teams each nominate one member, and these two pick the third. No fact-finder may be a member of a negotiating team. "The issues in dispute will determine the amount of time to be granted the Committee in securing the facts," Section XI-B (2) says. The committee report, without recommendations, is to be submitted to the bargainers, who will then make another attempt to resolve the dispute. If they fail, they will call upon the Federal Mediation and Conciliation Service, and following that, the Federal Service Impasses Panel (Sections XI-C and XI-D).

A four-step grievance procedure ending in arbitration is provided for general schedule and wage grade employees, and a two-step procedure for nonappropriated-fund (NAF) employees of the Veterans Canteen Service (Article XIV, Section 2).

Article XV, Section 2, on "washup time," says in full:

"Personal cleanup time, usually not to exceed ten (10) minutes in each instance, may be granted by the supervisor when a need for cleanup during scheduled work time is apparent. Apparent need is defined as gross soiling of employee's person or clothing which is visually noticeable and known to exist because of the nature of the work accomplished, such as work in contact with grease, excreta, bacterially contaminated materials, acids, dusts or other clinging materials. Longer time may be authorized in specific instances to meet identified need."

Article XXI, "Vacations," requires employees entitled to lengthy vacation time to schedule much of it in advance, with the balance in reserve for emergency or incidental use (Sections 1 through 3). Individual sick-leave usage may not be publicized, but employees with much accumulated leave may have their names posted on boards as members of the "500 Hour Club" (Article XXII, Section 3). Section 4 of this article pledges both supervisors and union officials to encourage sick-leave saving.

An Equal Employment Opportunity Committee is established (Article XXIV, Section 4). Moreover, the union president "may review the computer prepared minority statistical reports in the Office of the Personnel Officer" (Article XXIV, Section 7).

The complete text of the agreement follows.

AGREEMENT BETWEEN

VETERANS ADMINISTRATION HOSPITAL
River City, U.S.A.

And

AMERICAN FEDERATION OF GOVERNMENT EMPLOYEES
Locals 1000 and 2000
Nonprofessional Unit

ARTICLE I

Parties to the Agreement

Section 1. This agreement is entered into between the Consolidated Veterans Administration Hospital, River City, U.S.A., hereinafter referred to as the "Employer," and the American Federation of Government Employees, Locals 1000 and 2000, hereinafter referred to as the "Union."

ARTICLE II

Authority

Section 1. This agreement is entered into under the authority of Executive Order 11491, as amended by E.O. 11616 (hereinafter referred to as "Order"), and pursuant to letters of exclusive recognition accorded AFGE Locals 1000 and 2000 (AFL-CIO).

ARTICLE III

Bargaining Units

Section 1. Unit Identification and Coverage. The Employer recognizes the American Federation of Government Employees Locals 1000 and 2000

(AFL-CIO) for exclusive recognition purposes. The unit is comprised of all regular work force employees of the VA Hospital, River City, U.S.A. *except* Manager Officials, Supervisors, professional employees and employees engaged in personnel work in other than a purely clerical capacity. This agreement shall apply to all the employees included in the Units of Recognition, including Canteen Service employees, police officers and guards. This agreement applies to all part-time employees working a regular schedule, but excludes temporary employees. The Union has an obligation to represent the interests of all employees in the exclusive Units of Recognition without regard to membership.

ARTICLE IV

Purpose

Section 1. The purposes of this agreement are to foster employee–management cooperation, to promote and improve the efficient administration of the hospital, and to encourage employee participation in the formulation of station personnel policies and procedures affecting employees in the Unit of Recognition.

Section 2. The public interest requires high standards of employee performance and the continual development and implementation of modern and progressive work practices to facilitate improved employee performance and efficiency.

Section 3. The parties to this agreement recognize that these goals can be accomplished through mutual understanding. It is therefore agreed that the parties will meet and confer, at reasonable times, with the objective of reaching agreement.

Section 4. It is further agreed that Management's representative and the officers of the Union will meet on a regular recurring monthly basis for consultation purposes and to promote mutual cooperation.

ARTICLE V

Rights and Obligations

Section 1. In the administration of all matters covered by the agreement, officials and employees are governed by existing or future laws and the regulations of appropriate authorities, including policies set forth in the *Federal Personnel Manual;* by published VA policies and regulations in existence at the time the agreement was approved; and by subsequently published VA policies and regulations required by law or by the regulations of appropriate authorities, or authorized by the terms of a controlling agreement at a higher agency level.

Section 2. Nothing in this agreement shall restrict the VA in exercising the right, in accordance with applicable laws and regulations, to: direct employees of the VA; hire, promote, transfer, assign, and retain employees in positions within the VA, and to suspend, demote, discharge, or take other disciplinary action against employees; relieve employees from duties because of lack of work or for other legitimate reasons; maintain the efficiency of the Government operations entrusted to the VA; determine the methods, means, and personnel by which such operations are to be conducted; and take whatever action may be necessary to carry out the mission of the VA in situations of emergency.

Section 3. Nothing in this agreement shall require an employee to become or to remain a member of a labor organization, or to pay money to the organization except pursuant to a voluntary, written authorization by a member for the payment of dues through payroll deductions.

ARTICLE VI

Orientation of New Employees

Section 1. A copy of this agreement together with a current list of Union officers and Stewards furnished by the Union appropriate to the work unit will be included in the orientation folder given to new employees by the Personnel Service at the time of hire.

ARTICLE VII

Manpower Planning

Section 1. Personnel will send print-outs of employees eligible for retirement to the Service Chief for their use in the advance selection and training of skilled and shortage category employees through the merit process. When it is determined that it would be in the best interest of the hospital to fill a position through training, Management will establish and advertise a trainee position with the ultimate goal of promotion. This will be done in accordance with existing policies on training, development and promotion.

Section 2. Employees at all levels are encouraged to participate in activities and training both in and outside of the VA which will further their development and/or opportunity for promotion. A record of such training should be forwarded by the employee to Personnel Service for inclusion in the Personnel Folder.

Section 3. RIF. The employer agrees to make every effort to reassign, including retraining for vacant positions if available, to minimize RIF actions resulting from the introduction of new equipment and changes in staffing requirements.

ARTICLE VIII

Internal Union Business

Section 1. Solicitation of membership or dues and other internal union business shall be conducted during the nonduty hours of the employees concerned. Employees outside their regular working hours may solicit membership, or collect membership dues on VA premises provided such activities do not interfere with VA operations and are not conducted during official working hours of the employees contacted. Nonemployee representatives of AFGE, with the prior approval of the Director, may hold organization meetings to solicit membership on VA premises subject to the aforementioned restrictions. Official working hours for these purposes include rest periods, but do not include luncheon periods.

Section 2. Subject to safety and security regulations and where facilities for holding meetings are available on VA premises, the Union may be granted permission by the Hospital Director to use such facilities for business and membership meetings outside the regularly scheduled working hours of the employees involved, provided such action will not interfere with proper functioning of VA activities. Such meetings may be attended and conducted by nonemployees. Request for use of VA facilities will be submitted in writing giving the date and time.

ARTICLE IX

Literature

Section 1. Bulletin Board. Space will be reserved on each designated official bulletin board at the hospital for the Union to post notices and literature for the attention of all employees consistent with procedures in VA Manual MP-5.

Section 2. Distribution of Literature. Distribution of literature by employee Union members will be permitted, provided, (1) employees distribute the literature outside their regular working hours, (2) the placing of the literature on the desks or at the workplaces of employees is done outside the employees' working hours. Similar distribution privileges to nonemployee representatives of labor organizations are subject to these same restrictions. All nonemployee AFGE representatives are required to secure prior Hospital Director approval before entering VA premises for the purpose of conducting any type of labor organization business. The Union President will submit such request in writing to the Hospital Director.

Section 3. Daily Bulletin. Short articles may be furnished the Editor, Daily Hospital Bulletin for publication to include announcements of meetings of the Union. Such notices will indicate clearly that the announcement is made at the request of the local concerned.

ARTICLE X

Health Insurance—AFGE Plan

Section 1. A copy of the brochure of the "AFGE Health Benefits Plan" will be included in the Green Employment Folder given to each employee of the unit along with all other applicable plans. The new employee will be informed that he must be or become a member of AFGE to enroll in the AFGE plan. The Union will furnish a supply of brochures to the Hospital Division's Personnel Offices.

Section 2. Supervisors. When a member of the unit has AFGE Health Insurance and is promoted to a supervisory position he no longer is a member of the unit and dues deduction will cease. However, the supervisor can continue to have AFGE Health Insurance so long as he pays membership dues direct to the Union. If the supervisor elects to terminate membership in the Union he has 31 days after such termination for enrollment in another Health Insurance Plan by contacting Personnel Service.

Section 3. Nonsupervisory. Employees of the unit of recognition who terminate Union membership and have an AFGE Health Insurance Plan may change enrollment plans within 31 days after termination of AFGE enrollment by contacting the Personnel Service.

ARTICLE XI

Negotiation Procedures

Section 1. Each party will designate not more than four persons to serve as members of its negotiating team, plus one alternate member and one advisor. A spokesman for each party will be appointed within this group. During negotiations, he will be the only person authorized to speak for his team. The names of the team members will be exchanged by correspondence between the Hospital Director and Presidents of AFGE Locals 1000 and 2000 no later than 15 calendar days after notification of intentions to amend this agreement.

Section 2. Negotiation time authorized will not exceed 40 hours of official time for each Union negotiation representative to negotiate during regular working hours. This includes all activities in connection with the negotiation of an agreement, from any preliminary meetings on ground rules through all aspects of negotiation including mediation, and impasse resolution. All negotiation and preparatory caucuses shall be conducted during normal working hours. The Employer will not pay any overtime, premium pay, or travel expenditures for negotiating time.

Section 3. The Employer or the Union may invite, when both parties agree, an employee to a negotiation meeting concerning interpretation or clarification of laws, policies, regulations or directives pertinent to the particular subject matter under discussion. Persons serving in the capacity will be recognized only to the extent as herein agreed.

Section 4. No one other than those designated above will be permitted to attend negotiation meetings except by mutual consent of both parties to cover specific circumstances.

Section 5. Caucuses may be held as required, and may be called by either spokesman at his discretion. The team requesting a caucus will withdraw to a specified caucus room furnished by the Employer. The caucusing party shall make every effort to avoid unwarranted delays in negotiations. Caucus periods will not exceed fifteen (15) minutes in duration. Rest periods during negotiation sessions shall be called by mutual consent and shall not normally exceed fifteen (15) minutes in length.

Section 6. Negotiation Impasse Procedures.

A. For the purpose of this agreement, the definition of an "impasse" is as follows: "the inability of the Negotiating Teams representing the Employer and the Union to arrive at a mutually agreeable decision, through the bargaining process."

B. *Fact-Finding Committee*—When it has been determined that an impasse has been reached, the item first shall be referred to a joint Fact-Finding Committee.

   (1) The Committee shall consist of three VA employees; the Hospital Director and the Unions shall each appoint one member and these two shall select the third member. No member of the Negotiating Team shall serve on the Fact-Finding Committee.

   (2) The issues in dispute will determine the amount of time to be granted the Committee in securing the facts. The parties will, upon submitting a disagreement to the Fact-Finding Committee, set a specific date for the Committee to report. Official duty time shall be allowed the Committee for discharging its function.

   (3) The Committee shall, by inquiry, research, and conference, ascertain the exact facts at the base of the dispute and submit their findings, without recommendations, to the negotiating parties for consideration.

   (4) The parties will consider the facts submitted to the Committee and will make at least one more effort to reach agreement within 30 days of receipt of the report.

C. *Federal Mediator*—In the event an agreement is not reached after reviewing the findings of the Fact-Finding Committee, upon agreement in writing of both Union and Management, a joint request will be made for the services of a Federal Mediator by both. A request will be addressed to the Regional Director, Federal Mediation and Conciliation Service.

The use of FMCS Mediators is subject to the rules of the FMCS as outlined in title 29, CRF, Chapter XII.

D. *Federal Service Impasses Panel*—In the event the parties are still unable to reach agreement, negotiations on the disputed issue will be terminated or referred by either party to the Federal Service Impasses Panel.

ARTICLE XII

Meetings

Section 1. Union President. The Union President may leave his work area during regular duty hours for reasonable periods of time to attend Committee meetings and consultation with Management. A mutual agreement as to time will be worked out with the Supervisor before leaving the work area.

Section 2. Steward. The Union Steward of the appropriate local will be notified by the Service Chief of the date, time and place, either orally or in writing, when a group type meeting is to be called, which affects employees in the unit of recognition, for the purpose of discussing proposed changes in working conditions, personnel policies and procedure.

ARTICLE XIII

Stewards

Section. 1. Management recognizes the Union Steward System for the express purpose of promoting an effective relationship between supervisors and employees by helping to settle problems at the lowest possible level of organization. It is further agreed that supervisors and designated Stewards will work together in a spirit of friendliness, cooperation and a positive desire to solve problems of mutual concern. The Union and the Steward as representative of the Union recognize that the Supervisor is responsible to higher Management for the quality, quantity and timeliness of patient care and work performed in the unit. Before attempting to act on any employee complaint, the Steward shall first determine that the employee has made a reasonable effort to resolve the matter informally with his supervisor.

Section 2. Absence from Work. Stewards will be permitted to leave their jobs to transact authorized functions as described above after first receiving permission from their immediate supervisor. In making the request, the Steward will inform the supervisor only where he will be and for approximately how long. Assigned workload at the time of the request will be the controlling factor in granting the request. The Union recognizes its responsibility to insure that its representatives do not abuse this authority by unduly absenting themselves from their assigned work areas, and that they will make every effort to perform representational functions in a proper and expeditious manner. Upon entering a work area other than his own, the Steward will advise the appropriate Supervisor of his presence and the name of the employee he desires to visit.

ARTICLE XIV

Grievance Procedure

Section 1. This procedure will be the sole procedure for processing grievances over the interpretation or application of this negotiated agreement. It may not be used for any other matters, including matters for which statutory appeal procedures exist. In those instances where the parties have decided, for purposes of information, understanding, or otherwise, to incorporate by paraphrase, reference or repetition, provisions of law or higher level policies or regulations, such provisions will not be within the scope of this grievance procedure.

Section 2. The only representative an employee may have while processing a grievance under this procedure is the exclusively recognized Union or a representative approved by the Union. An employee may pursue a grievance under this procedure without representation, but the exclusive Union should be given an opportunity to be present at each step.

A. *For General Schedule and Wage Grade Employees.*

> *Step 1*—In the event an employee has a grievance, he shall have the right to present the grievance to his immediate supervisor orally or in writing within fifteen (15) calendar days of the date the employee has knowledge of the action or first learned by the employee. The grievance will be discussed informally with the Supervisor. The Supervisor will make every effort to resolve the grievance immediately but must provide an answer within ten (10) calendar days. This answer will be oral unless the employee has presented the grievance in writing.

> *Step 2*—If the grievance is not satisfactorily resolved, it may be presented to the Service Chief in writing within ten (10) calendar days of the supervisor's decision. The grievance must state the section or sections of the agreement the party feels have been violated, the nature of the violation and the corrective action desired. The Service Chief shall answer, in writing, within ten (10) calendar days.

> *Step 3*—If the grievance is not satisfactorily resolved at Step 2, it may be presented to the Hospital Director in writing within seven (7) calendar days of the decision of the Service Chief. The Hospital Director will issue a decision within ten (10) calendar days.

Step 4—In the event the Director's decision does not satisfactorily resolve the grievance, the Union or Management may, within fifteen (15) workdays, indicate they are taking the issue to arbitration. Within this fifteen (15) workday time period, the parties will request the Federal Mediation and Conciliation Service to submit a list of five (5) arbitrators. Each party will alternately strike one name from the list of arbitrators until one name remains and he will be the arbitrator. Who will strike the first name will be determined by lot. Arbitration may extend only to interpretation or application of the agreement, and the costs of arbitration will be shared equally by the two parties. Either party may file exceptions to an arbitrator's award with the Federal Labor Relations Council under regulations prescribed by the Council. The Arbitrator will be notified by Management to conduct his hearing during the normal duty hours of each employee contacted, to avoid change in the employee's work schedule and involvement in overtime. If a hearing is held it will be during the administrative business hours of the hospital. Employees called to the hearing will be excused without charge to annual leave. The Arbitrator will be requested to render his decision as quickly as possible, but in any event not later than 30 calendar days after conclusion of the hearing unless both parties agree to extend the 30 day limitation.

B. *For Veterans Canteen Service.*

Step 1—In the event an employee has a grievance, he shall have the right to present his grievance to the Canteen Officer orally or in writing within fifteen (15) calendar days of the date of the act or occurrence. The grievance will be discussed informally with the employee. The Canteen Officer will make every effort to resolve the grievance immediately but must provide an answer within ten (10) calendar days. The answer will be in writing.

Step 2—If the grievance is not satisfactorily resolved in Step 1, the grievance may be presented to the Canteen Field Director in writing through the Canteen Officer. The VCS Field Director will review the case and issue a decision in writing within fifteen (15) workdays.

C. *Compliance with Time Limitations.* Failure of the Supervisor or the Service Chief to answer grievances within the time limits will permit the grievance to be referred to the next succeeding step of the procedure. Failure of the employee or the Union to take action within the prescribed time for each step gives the Employer the right to cancel the grievance. Extensions of time limitations may be granted by mutual consent for good cause provided the request is made within the initial time limitations.

D. *Availability of Records Related to a Grievance.* In the execution of the grievance procedures, the Employer will, upon request, produce pertinent records as permissible without violating laws and regulations, for the purpose of substantiating the contentions or claims of the parties.

E. An employee, and employee representative if desired, is entitled to a reasonable amount of official time to prepare and present his case if he is otherwise in an active duty status. This excludes overtime and travel expenses.

F. The use of this grievance procedure is the right of an employee in the unit. This right may not be interfered with, nor may an employee be treated in any way prejudicially for using it; on the other hand, employees are expected to use it reasonably and in good faith.

ARTICLE XV

Dressup and Washup Time

Section 1. A station policy will be issued specifying which categories of employees are authorized to wear uniforms to and from work. Employees permitted to wear uniforms to and from work are not authorized time for changing clothes within their scheduled tour of duty. Employees not authorized to wear uniforms from the hospital will be given ten (10) minutes dressup time.

Section 2. Washup. Personal cleanup time, usually not to exceed ten (10) minutes in each instance, may be granted by the supervisor when a need for cleanup during scheduled work time is apparent. Apparent need is defined as gross soiling of employee's person or clothing which is visually noticeable and known to exist because of the nature of the work accomplished, such as work in contact with grease, excreta, bacterially contaminated materials, acids, dusts or other clinging materials. Longer time may be authorized in specific instances to meet identified need.

ARTICLE XVI

Hours of Work

Section 1. The administrative workweek shall be seven (7) consecutive days, Sunday through Saturday. The basic workweek may not extend over more than six (6) days in the administrative workweek. Break in work hours for a full time employee shall not be more than one hour in any one basic workday. Generally the employee will be scheduled to work no more than two tours of duty in the workweek. The occurrence of holidays shall not affect the designation of the basic workweek. Establishment of different tours of duty will be kept to the minimum possible and will be made only when needed by mission requirements, and approval of the Hospital Director.

Section 2. Posting Work Schedules. Employees involved in rotational shifts/tours of duty will have their schedule posted in their work area two weeks in advance. Tours will not be changed arbitrarily and only in case of emergency. The employee will be notified as soon as the change is made in his tour by the Supervisor.

ARTICLE XVII

Holidays

Section 1. When a holiday falls on a day that is within an employee's administrative workweek and his day of duty is included in the holiday work schedule, the employee will be scheduled to work and receive holiday compensation, unless he can be excused for the holiday.

Section 2. The scheduling of holiday work, when required, will be done on an equal basis consistent with good operations. Volunteers will be used as a first source to staff operations concerned. In the event there is not sufficient number of volunteers for a particular shift on a given holiday, any selections necessary will be made from those employees who are regularly assigned to that shift. Such selections will assure equal treatment insofar as reasonably possible taking into consideration all nine holidays within the leave year.

ARTICLE XVIII

Overtime

Section 1. Overtime work is emergency work officially ordered and approved by authorized officials in excess of the eight-hour day or forty-hour workweek, whichever is the greater for full-time GS and WG employees. Overtime will be used only when necessary work cannot be performed through planned coverage by on-duty personnel during their regular forty-hour basic workweek. GS employees will be offered a choice of either compensatory time off or overtime pay except for an employee whose basic pay exceeds the maximum of GS-10. Wage Grade employees must be paid for overtime work, as compensatory time off cannot be given. Overtime assignments will be equitably distributed consistent with qualifications of the employee's job assignment.

Section 2. Opportunity for overtime and call-back for assignments will be distributed and rotated equitably among qualified employees by specialty or service by Hospital Division in accordance with their particular skills. Overtime will not be assigned to employees as a reward or penalty. In the assignment of overtime, the Employer agrees to provide the employee with advance notice when possible. Any employee designated to work overtime on days outside his basic workweek will be notified by the Supervisor as soon as the overtime emergency is known so the employee can make arrangements for personal needs. When work is scheduled on a holiday, as much advance notice as possible will be given to the employees affected.

Section 3. Records. Suitable records of overtime worked or declined by the employee will be maintained by the Supervisor to assure that each employee receives substantially the same consideration. An overtime record shall be maintained by the supervisor and can be reviewed or discussed by the Steward.

Section. 4. Employees who work overtime shall be allowed a 10 minute break during each consecutive four-hour period worked.

Section 5. Call-Back (Full Time). Call-back is irregular or occasional overtime work performed by a GS/WG employee on a day when work was not scheduled for him or for which he is required to return to his place of employment. Pay will be at least two hours in duration, either in money or compensatory time off, at the request of the employee, for GS employees and pay for WG employees. Overtime immediately before or after regular duty hours, even with meal break, is not call-back for pay purposes.

ARTICLE XIX

Details

Section 1. A detail exists when an employee continues in his current status title, grade and pay and is temporarily assigned to:

A. An established position, or an identical one with a higher or lower basic pay rate, or one requiring different qualifications from those now required in his official position.

B. An unestablished position, that is, one whose duties and responsibilities have not been graded under a classification system and the necessary approvals for its establishment have not been obtained. This type could be in a different occupational line of work, or one that requires different qualifications from those now required in his official position assignment.

Section 2. Selection of an employee for detail will be fair and equitable in relation to all employees available for detail. Such matters as assignments that enhance qualifications, offer promotion possibilities, or entail other benefits will be fully considered.

Section 3. Requests for detail, or extension over 30 calendar days, to unestablished positions will contain a brief description of the specific duties and tasks to be assigned and the reasons for the detail.

ARTICLE XX

Leave

Section 1. Annual Leave. It is mutually agreed that annual leave accrual is a right of the employee. However, the determination as to the time and amount of annual leave granted at any specific time is the responsibility of the employees' immediate supervisor. Every reasonable attempt consistent with the workload will be made to satisfy the desires of the employees with respect to approval of short periods of annual leave for birthdays, religious holidays, funerals, etc. Decision to approve or disapprove annual leave must be based upon workload and emergency conditions in relation to the number of employees and types of skills available to perform work. If for any reason an employee's request for annual leave cannot be granted, the supervisor will notify the employee of the reason.

Section 2. *Advance of Sick Leave.*
    A. An employee serving a probational period will not be advanced more sick leave than would accrue during the probational period.
    B. An employee who has completed his probational period with a career conditional/career appointment may be advanced NTE 30 days (240 hours).
    C. Such approvals will be subject to receipt of the following by the Chief of Service:

Step 1—Statement from the physician indicating the serious disability of ailment and the beginning and expected ending dates of sick leave absence.

Step 2—Statement from the physician of reasonable expectation the employee will be able to return to his regular position.

Step 3—The above be attached to SF-71, "Application for Leave," signed by the employee and submitted to his Service Chief.

Step 4—The Service Chief will give notification to the employee of the action taken on his request.

ARTICLE XXI

Vacations

Section 1. Supervisors will plan and schedule the more substantial periods of annual leave on a yearly basis. Employees are encouraged to take at least two consecutive weeks of vacation each year for the purpose of rest and relaxation.

Section 2. Employees who have accumulated the maximum, who earn five weeks of leave a year, will have at least four weeks scheduled—two weeks used by the Saturday following the second Sunday in June and two weeks the last half of the leave year. The remaining five days will be used for emergency, occasional or incidental use. (This scheduling will not apply when the employee wishes to and can legally carry leave over to the next leave year.)

Section 3. The employee who must use four weeks' leave will have three weeks scheduled, and at least one week will be used by the Saturday following the second Sunday in June, leaving one week for occasional use.

Section 4. Employees will be requested by their supervisor on November 1 to submit SF 71 or similar data to the supervisor by December 1, so that vacation scheduling can be completed and posted by the last week of the year for the ensuing leave year. Employees who do not submit a request for vacation will be scheduled by the supervisor so the employee will not forfeit leave.

Section 5. In scheduling, first consideration will be given to employees who earn 5, 4 and 2 weeks' annual leave a year. In the event of ties the VA Service Computation data is applicable. Repetitive requests for summer month and holiday leave will be rotated in order of VA Service Computation data and mutual agreements among the employees concerned and the supervisor. Supervisors may restrict granting of long-term vacations during the Thanksgiving, Christmas and New Year's Holidays so that more employees may be granted one to three days of annual leave.

Section 6. Planned and approved vacation schedules will not be changed except in case of emergency and only upon the supervisor or employee being informed and approved by the highest supervisory level below the Service Chief. When the emergency occurs the employee or supervisor will be notified immediately. Supervisors may approve exchange of vacations between employees when both employees agree and the work level is interchangeable.

Section 7. Tours of duty of an employee will not be changed prior to beginning or returning from a period of leave to the disadvantage of other employees.

ARTICLE XXII

Sick Leave and Disabilities

Section 1. Requesting Leave. When, due to unforeseen circumstances, employees are unable to request leave in advance, it is their responsibility to notify, or to have a responsible person notify the place designated to receive calls in their service, of the reason and expected duration for their absence. The request for leave should be made as early as practicable, before or at the beginning of their tour of duty, but in any event within the first 2 hours of absence. An employee who expects to be absent more than one day will inform his supervisor of the approximate date that he thinks he will be able to return to duty. Requests will be considered and a decision will be made as to how this absence will be charged.

Section 2. If a supervisor believes an employee is abusing sick leave, the employee will be notified in writing in advance of the requirement that each request for sick leave must be supported by a certification from the attending physician of incapacity to work. Otherwise, a physician's certificate will be required only in excess of three work days. Notices to employees requiring a physician's certification for every sick leave request will have a follow-up every thirteenth pay period to determine whether additional action is to be taken or the requirement withdrawn.

Section 3. Counseling. A preliminary step to invoking the requirement for a physician's certificate for all sick leave absence will be a counseling session between the employee and supervisor. This will include furnishing the employee the dates sick leave was taken and the cause to suspect abuse of sick leave privileges; i.e., sick leave before or after days off or on a holiday scheduled to work; repetitious one day sick leave requested on, before, or after paydays; or before or after approved annual leave. Tardiness and approved annual leave will not be listed in the charges as justification for suspected abuse of sick leave. The supervisor will not publicly post individual sick leave used but may post sick leave savers; i.e., "500 Hour Club."

Section 4. Employees will be encouraged by supervisors and Union Officers of the advantages in saving sick leave for bona fide causes and of the advantages in accumulating sick leave to increase their service computation credit for annuity purposes on retirement or death.

Section 5. Limited Duty Assignments. Supervisors will make every effort to assign employees who are injured on the job to other duties until able to return to their regular positions.

Section 6. Disabilities. Supervisors, Personnel Officials and Union Officers will work cooperatively in efforts to effect the reassignment to other occupations in lieu of disability retirement, when an employee becomes disabled in his regular position and is recommended by the VA Personnel Physician for a specific occupation. Personnel Officials will give a physically impaired employee top priority in referral for reassignment to a vacant position to the same grade or lower grade position.

Section 7. Supervisors will use good judgment in the referral of employees to the Health Unit who become ill on the job and are returning from sick leave. The Health Unit Physician or Officer of the Day will use VA Form 5-3831b to inform the supervisor of the employee's condition. If he is sent home, the physician will be requested by the supervisor to indicate approximate length of time and other matters which the supervisor should have for planning and approving leave.

ARTICLE XXIII

Safety and Health

Section 1. Maintenance of Safe Working Conditions. The Employer and the Union shall maintain a continuing cooperative effort to provide and maintain safe working conditions and shall encourage employees to work in a safe manner. When a safety question is raised which the supervisor or Service Chief cannot resolve, the final decision on the matter will be the responsibility of the Hospital Director after consultation with the Union and appropriate Management officials. The Union will designate an employee to serve as a member of the Hospital Safety Committee.

Section 2. Special Clothing and Equipment. It is agreed that any protective clothing and/or equipment which the employer requires will be furnished to the employee by employer.

Section 3. Lifting and Pushing Assignments. Supervisors will assure that employees have had training in lifting and pushing prior to assignments to such duties requiring heavy tasks. The supervisor will make equitable distribution of assignments to such tasks with sufficient manpower on heavy assignments to avoid injury.

Section 4. Weather Dismissal.

A. *Hazardous Conditions*—The Employer recognizes the hazards inherent with severe weather conditions and is concerned with the safety and welfare of employees during these conditions. Therefore, the Employer will, on each occasion of severe weather conditions, consider the pertinent factors related to the current conditions and determine whether the VA Hospital or any segment of the hospital shall be closed or administrative leave granted. The decision of the Employer will be based on the following factors:

Step 1—Weather conditions in the immediate vicinity of the Hospital.

Step 2—Weather and road conditions along main traffic arteries to and from the Hospital.

Step 3—Forecast of weather conditions.

Step 4—Related intentions of other Federal agencies in the immediate vicinity of the Hospital.

The employee will be notified as soon as the excused decision is reached by Management. Employees shall make every effort to come to work even though conditions might not be ideal. On each occasion, supervisors will be furnished information of granting appropriate leave to employees who are delayed due to traffic or weather during hazardous weather situations. In order to assure coverage of hospital activities and to safeguard the VA's interests when hazardous weather conditions develop, the Employer reserves the right to designate individual employees who must remain on duty in the event of a group dismissal and who are to report for duty in the event of an office closing. Individuals so designated will be given advance notice and clearly advised of their responsibility.

B. The Employer recognizes that on extremely unusual and rare occasions certain work areas of the hospital may develop heat conditions which could adversely affect the physical well being of employees performing work in the affected area(s) which would warrant the employees being excused from work. The final decision on dismissal will be made by the Hospital Director.

ARTICLE XXIV

Equal Employment Opportunity

Section 1. The Employer and the Union agree to cooperate in providing equal opportunity for all qualified persons without regard to age, handicap, race, color, religion, sex or national origin and to promote the full realization of equal employment opportunity through a continuing affirmative program.

Section 2. The Employer will conduct a continuing effort to avoid prejudice or discrimination based upon age, handicap, race, color, religion, sex or national origin, from the Employer's personnel policies and practices and working conditions, including disciplinary action for employees and supervisors where discrimination is proven.

Section 3. The Employer will utilize to the fullest extent the present skills of employees including the redesigning of jobs where feasible to employ at lower grades, provide the maximum opportunity for employees to enhance their skills through on-the-job and classroom work so that they may perform at their highest potential and be qualified to advance in accordance with their abilities.

Section 4. The Employer will establish an Equal Employment Opportunity Committee to foster within the hospital and community level a cooperative action to improve equal employment opportunities and community conditions. The Committee shall meet at the call of the Chairman and will advise the Hospital Director in establishing affirmative programs to promote equal employment opportunity, including the implementation of the Upward Mobility Program.

Section 5. The Chairman of the EEO Committee will prepare a quarterly progress report on the Equal Employment Opportunity Plan of Action and publish it in the daily bulletin.

Section 6. Management will request nominations for EEO Counselors from the Union for consideration in making selections. Candidates selected shall meet the criteria established by the U.S. Civil Service Commission and will be trained in accordance with the provisions of applicable regulations. Counselors will serve under the direction of the Equal Employment Opportunity Officer (Hospital Director).

Section 7. The Union President may review the computer prepared minority statistical reports in the Office of the Personnel Officer.

ARTICLE XXV

Duration, Amendment and Termination

Section 1. This agreement shall remain in full force and effect for two (2) years from date of approval by the Chief Medical Director and is automatically extended for two (2) year periods unless either party gives written notice to the other not less than sixty (60) days, but not more than ninety (90) days prior to the expiration date that the party desires to terminate or modify this agreement. In this event, the parties shall begin negotiations within thirty (30) days. Each such renewal will create a new duration period with a new effective date. If negotiations are not concluded by the expiration date, the provisions of this agreement shall continue in effect until the existing agreement is renegotiated.

Section 2. This agreement will be terminated in the event exclusive recognition is discontinued. Termination of this agreement will not of itself terminate the grant of exclusive recognition to the unit.

Section 3. This agreement, except for its duration period, as specified in Section 1 of this Article, is subject to opening only as follows:

A. After the effective date of this agreement, amendment to this agreement may be required because of changes in applicable laws or executive orders which significantly affect any of the terms of this agreement. In this event, the parties will meet within thirty (30) calendar days after receipt of a written request from either party for the purpose of negotiating new language that will meet the requirement of such laws or executive orders. Such amendment will be duly executed and will become effective on the date approved by the Chief Medical Director.

B. It may be opened for amendment by mutual consent of the parties at any time after it has been in force and effect for at least one year. Any requests for amendment shall be in writing and must be accompanied by a summary of the amendment proposed. Representatives of Hospital Management and the Union shall meet within thirty (30) calendar days after receipt of such request to reopen the agreement for amendment and negotiations shall be limited to those proposals concerned in the summary. Agreement shall be evidenced by written amendment duly executed by both parties, and will become effective on the date approved by the Chief Medical Director.

ARTICLE XXVI

Federal Mediation and Conciliation Service

Section 1. The Federal Mediation and Conciliation Service will be given notice of the desire by Management or the Labor Organization to amend, modify or terminate the agreement in accordance with the rules of the Service.

In witness hereof this Agreement has been signed by the Parties hereto this 1st day of July 1974.

For the UNION:

For the EMPLOYER:

Sycamore City— A Municipal-Sector Game

D

Private-sector employees have had protected rights to collective bargaining under the National Labor Relations Act since 1935. This has not been the case for state and local government employees. Many states provide no statutory framework for collective bargaining, although in most it is occurring on a de facto basis. The majority of the states, however, have enacted some legislation to regulate collective bargaining in some form for one or more categories of employees. Sycamore City is governed by a state public-employee collective bargaining statute.

The essential features of the statute applying to collective bargaining are as follows:

1. Public employees have the right to form, join, and participate in the activities of labor organizations of their own choosing for the purpose of representation and collective bargaining with their employer on matters concerning employment relations.

2. A labor organization certified by the Public Employee Relations Board or recognized by the public employer is the exclusive representative of the employees of a public employer for the purposes of collective bargaining with respect to employment relations.

3. It is an unfair labor practice for an employer to refuse to bargain collectively in good faith with the exclusive representative. The same responsibility is placed upon the employee bargaining representative.

4. It is also an unfair labor practice for the employee representative or the employer to refuse to reduce to writing an agreement reached as a result of collective bargaining, and to sign the resulting contract.

5. A public employer may enter into a written agreement with the employee representative, setting forth a grievance procedure with a terminal step of

binding arbitration. The parties may also negotiate, if they choose, a binding-arbitration clause for negotiation impasses.

6. If after a reasonable period of time of negotiation the parties have failed to reach an agreement on a contract, either or both parties are to notify the Public Employee Relations Board of the status of their negotiations. If the board feels that the parties have failed to achieve agreement through negotiation, it may, either upon its own motion or a motion from either party, assign a mediator from the State Conciliation Service. If the dispute is not settled after 15 days of mediation, one or both of the parties, or the board on its own motion, may initiate fact-finding. A tripartite board will be selected from seven names secured from the State Employee Relations Board. Each party may eliminate two names from the list, leaving three for the tripartite board. The fact-finding board will hold a hearing and, within 30 days from the conclusion of the hearing, make written findings of fact and recommendations for resolution of the dispute. If the fact-finding board's recommendations are not accepted, the recommendations will be made public. The parties may agree at any point in the preceding process to submit their disputed issues to final and binding arbitration.

7. Participation in a strike is unlawful for any public employee who is not part of an appropriate bargaining unit for which an exclusive representative has been certified by the board. Public employees who are not prohibited from striking by the preceding restriction may engage in a strike only after the following conditions have been met:

   a. The procedures of number 6 above have been fulfilled.

   b. Thirty days have elapsed since the fact-finding board's recommendations were made public.

   c. The exclusive employee representative has given ten days' notice by certified mail.

8. Where the strike constitutes a clear and present danger or threat to the health, safety, or welfare of the public, the public employer concerned may sue for relief, including injunctive relief. If the court agrees with the employer's contention, then its relief is to include an order establishing final and binding arbitration.

Sycamore City, with a population of 200,000, is located close to a major population center in the western United States. The employer universe competing with Sycamore City for workers is distributed in approximately the following fashion:

Manufacturing	26%
Logging	7%
Transportation, communications, gas transmission	10%
Trade	11%
Finance	8%
Service	6%
Government (federal, state, city, and county)	32%

The distribution of full-time employees by department in Sycamore City is as follows:

Public affairs and finance	142
Public safety (not including police and fire)	181
Police	367
Firemen	327
Streets and public improvements	416
Parks and public property	126
Auditor	16
General government	4
Legal and judicial	22
Water department	254
Airport	53
Personnel	6

The mean age of the employees is 39.6 years, and the mean length of service is 9 years.

Elected officials' and appointed officers' salaries for 1975–76 were as follows:

Mayor	$19,440.00
Commissioner	17,760.00
Commissioner	17,760.00
Commissioner	17,760.00
Commissioner	17,760.00
Auditor	16,656.00
Personnel director	15,624.00
City engineer	19,968.00
City attorney	19,968.00
Superintendent of water works	19,008.00
Traffic engineer	16,416.00
Planning director	19,968.00
City treasurer	15,624.00
City recorder	15,624.00
Purchasing agent	12,864.00
Chief deputy auditor	14,880.00
Deputy auditor	12,864.00
Accounting coord. for spec. FDS	13,512.00
License assessor	12,864.00

These officials are not counted in the prior listing of distribution of employment. Their salaries are determined by other means than collective bargaining.

FINANCIAL HISTORY

A continued rise in expenditures, matched by a healthy but unexpected growth in selected revenues, characterized the operation of the city's general fund, resulting in a small excess (almost $250,000) of revenues over expenditures for the preceding fiscal year ended June 30, 1975.

The water and airport funds each enjoyed a financially successful year, but net income in the golf-course fund experienced a sharp decline for the first time in a full decade of expanding operations.

The advent of federal revenue sharing rescued the city's general fund from a genuine crisis in its budget for the last fiscal year. Without federal revenues amounting to $6,200,000, the city fathers would have been compelled to raise several new taxes and make a sizable hike in the general property tax, since a state statute proscribes deficit spending.

However, the city fathers are very concerned that the present general fund relies upon state and federal revenue to make up 33 percent of the total fund.

The following depicts the changes in the budget over the last five years:

1972	$16,976,331
1973	18,283,386
1974	21,463,769
1975	25,693,785
1976	28,383,864

Although there have been changes in property values and other taxable entities, the mill-levy level has not been changed in about ten years. The city can, by law, increase the mill levy by 11.5; the only limitation is that the commissioners must hold a public hearing before the increase.

After many difficult budget sessions, which included substantial requested budget reductions for each department, the city commission adopted a budget for the fiscal year ending June 30, 1976, that included a 10 percent cost-of-living increase for all full-time employees, with the understanding that the total number of employees would be trimmed by 100, through attrition or layoffs or both, before the beginning of the next fiscal year. At this point, most of the decrease has been accomplished. The 10 percent cost-of-living increase was over and above the built-in (approximately 3 percent) merit increase.

Sycamore City
Budgets for Fiscal Year
Ending June 30, 1976
Estimate of Property Tax Revenues

1974 assessed valuation		$352,133,614	
Based on 97% collection	Mills	100%	97%
General fund	18.5	6,514,472	$6,319,038
Based on 95% collection	Mills	100%	97%
Debt service fund	5.5	1,936,735	1,878,633
Governmental immunity		100%	97%
Trust fund	.5	176,067	170,785

Budget for Fiscal Year Ending June 30, 1976
Estimated Revenues

Account	Amount
Property taxes, current year	$6,319,038
Property taxes, prior year	140,000
Sales taxes	4,400,000
Franchise taxes	2,200,000
Business licenses	650,000
Non-business licenses and permits	400,000
Parking meter revenue	200,000
Fines and forfeitures	1,600,000
Interest on investments	500,000
Rents and concessions	26,000
State liquor fund allotment	332,086
Class "C" road fund revenue	576,263
Federal and state road grants	800,000
Federal grants—police program	460,298
Comprehensive employment and training act	880,000
Federal shared revenue	6,185,000
Street replacements and cuts	60,000
Sewer service charges	1,400,000
Charges for current service	400,000
Contribution from water utility fund	500,000
Contribution from airport fund	350,000
Sundry revenue	6,179
Total revenues	$28,384,864

Budget Appropriations

Department or Account	Amount
Public affairs and finance	$ 1,795,192
Public safety	1,366,914
Police department	5,392,738
Fire department	3,817,655
Streets and public improvements	6,141,555
Parks and public improvements	1,921,827
City auditor	150,670
Total departments	$20,586,551
Reserve for city's share of federal and other programs	100,000
Federal and state road programs	800,000
City's share of special improvement districts	400,000
General government	6,198,313
Departmental capital	300,000
	7,798,313
Total appropriations	$28,384,864

A rough breakdown of this budget is:

Salaries	56%
Operations	40%
Capital	4%

Sycamore City Corporation
Budgets for Fiscal Year
Ending June 30, 1977
Estimate of Property Tax Revenues

1975 assessed valuation		$372,006,006	
Based on 97% collection	Mills	100%	97%
General fund	18.5	6,882,111	$6,675,648
Based on 97% collection	Mills	100%	97%
Debt service fund	4.5	1,674,027	1,623,809
Governmental immunity		100%	97%
Trust fund	.5	186,003	180,422

General Fund No. 1
Budget for Fiscal Year Ending June 30, 1977
Estimated Revenues

Account	Amount
Property taxes, current year	$ 6,675,648
Property taxes, prior year	100,000
Sales taxes	6,600,000
Franchise taxes	2,600,000
Business licenses	630,000
Non-business licenses and permits	495,000
Parking meter revenue	180,000
Fines and forfeitures	1,600,000
Interest on investments	800,000
Rents and concessions	30,000
State liquor fund allotment	332,086
Class "C" road fund revenue	473,277
Federal and state road grants	1,100,000
Federal grants—police program	75,000
Comprehensive employment and training act	1,150,000
Federal shared revenue	5,578,677
Street replacement and cuts	120,000
Sewer service charges	1,500,000
Charges for current service	505,000
Contribution from water utility fund	664,210
Contribution from airport fund	300,000
Sundry revenue	6,000
Sub-total	$31,514,898
Loan from revenue sharing fund	1,000,000
Total revenues	$32,514,898

Budget Appropriations

Department or Account	Amount
Public affairs and finance	$ 1,864,223
Public safety	1,472,380
Police department	5,645,414
Fire department	4,032,903
Streets and public improvements	6,258,492
Parks and public improvements	2,015,935
City auditor	149,685
Total departments	$21,439,032
Comprehensive employment and training act	936,729
Reserve for city's share of federal and other programs	100,000
Federal and state road programs	1,573,277
City's share of special improvement districts	400,000
General government	7,765,860
Departmental capital	300,000
	11,075,866
Total appropriations	$32,514,898

This projection does not include any salary increases above the merit or step increment of 3–4 percent for the eligible employees.

The city personnel director has provided the commissioners three different salary-increase options of 7.7, 10, or 15 percent, with corresponding reductions in personnel, in an attempt to reduce the projected deficit while at the same time allowing the commissioners to place a reasonable salary-increase figure on the bargaining table.

These options are as follows:

General Fund
Optimal Plans for Salary Increases and Solutions for Reducing Revenue Deficiency for Year 1976–77

Revenues		
Revenues per statement	$31,514,898	
Add:		
Loan from 1976–77 revenue sharing funds	1,000,000	
Elimination of proposed 2 1/2-mill property tax reductions	902,115	
Adjusted estimated revenues		$33,417,013

	Salary Increases		
	7.7%	**10%**	**15%**
Appropriations per statement	$32,514,898	$32,514,898	$32,514,898
Salary increases	1,402,468	1,820,840	2,731,260
	$33,917,366	$34,355,738	$35,246,158

Adjusted estimated revenues

(from above)	33,417,013	33,417,013	33,417,013
	($ 500,353)	($ 918,725)	($ 1,829,145)
Less reduction in personnel			
Increase of 7.7%, reduce 56	504,000		
Increase of 10 %, reduce 97		921,500	
Increase of 15 %, reduce 183			1,830,000
	$ 3,647	$ 2,775	$ 855

WAGE AND BENEFIT HISTORY

Prior to the enactment of a state collective bargaining statute, Sycamore City used for a compensation policy the practice of paying "prevailing rates insofar as possible" of similar jobs found in local private industry.

The determination of "prevailing rates" was made by a Citizen Advisory Board appointed each year by the city commission. This group was formed in 1972 to provide an outside viewpoint to the commission in its collective bargaining activities. The board is composed of 6–8 members drawn from city taxpayers who are representative of both labor and management elements of the private-sector labor market.

A wage and salary study of the area is first conducted by the board. This information is compared to Department of Labor statistics concerning wages, fluctuations in the Consumer Price Index, and average wage settlements, to aid in the setting of bench-mark positions. Before the board presents its findings to the commission, the employees' union is invited to present its position to the board. This process is not, however, intended to be a "practice round" of collective bargaining—it is simply an information-gathering process for inclusion in the board's final report.

Three years ago (1973), the Citizen Advisory Board recommended a 7.75 percent cost-of-living adjustment to the salary schedule with no increase in fringe benefits. A settlement very close to this was implemented by the city commission as of July 1, 1973. Year before last, the advisory board recommended lower increases for the AFSCME members and higher increases for supervisory, fire, and police employees, in order to bring parity to the system.

Although the AFSCME union is by far the largest, the police and fire fighters' unions are quite strong, and are typically more militant in their endeavors to reach parity with national averages.

In 1975, the Citizen Advisory Board recommended a 9 percent increase across the board, responsive to the increasing cost of living. For this year (1976), the board recommended 8 percent across the board for all bargaining groups. This includes benefits and takes into account the 3–4 percent merit (step) increase already built into the budget.

A few years of historical wage information is provided in Addendum A.

Last year, a contract was negotiated for the first time, covering all city employees except policemen and fire fighters, with the American Federation of State, County and Municipal Employees. The complete text of the contract, which has covered the employees during the year and is now up for renegotiation, follows.

AGREEMENT

This Agreement made and entered into the first day of July 1975 by and between Sycamore City, which is hereinafter called the employer, and the Sycamore City Employees' Union, which is hereinafter called the union, WITNESSETH:

In consideration of the mutual covenants herein set forth, the employer and the union agree and shall be bound as follows:

ARTICLE I. RECOGNITION

The employer recognizes the union as the bargaining agent for all employees of Sycamore City with the exception of the following: Police, Firemen and all other elected and appointed officers of the City.

ARTICLE II. DUES DEDUCTION

The employer agrees to accept and honor voluntary written assignment of union dues from wages or salaries due and owing employees covered by this Agreement, provided that such assignments can be grouped and the total made payable to one assignee.

ARTICLE III. NONDISCRIMINATION

The employer recognizes that the desire of the employees to join the union and to be represented by the union will repose greater confidence in the execution of fair personnel relations. Therefore, the employer agrees to take no action which may tend to discourage the desire of the employees to join the union or frustrate the union in its activity. No employee shall be discharged or discriminated against by the employer for upholding union principles or working under the instructions of the union, so long as such activity does not interfere with the efficient operations of the City. The employer shall grant reasonable leaves of absence without pay to employees whenever required in the performance of duties as "duly authorized representatives of the union." "Duly authorized representative" means members of regularly constituted committees and/or officers of the union. Two employees are to be compensated at regular rate of pay for attending City-union negotiations during normal working hours when set by mutual agreement of employer and the union.

ARTICLE IV. SENIORITY

The employer shall follow the practice of giving preferable consideration to employees having seniority service rights in each department, in making promotions or effecting demotions that are not for cause, where there is no material difference in ability. If a department is terminated, the employees of the terminated department shall have seniority that will prevail in other departments. In cases of layoffs or recall, seniority will prevail.

ARTICLE V. FILLING OF VACANCIES

Current City employees will have the opportunity to apply for vacant positions if they so desire. Positions so filled that constitute a promotion or acquirement of new skills will be filled on a probationary basis. Probationary time for current employees with at least one year of service will not exceed ninety (90) days. Probationary status for new employees will not exceed one year. Employees to retain the position must show capability to satisfactorily perform all duties required. Employee to be paid at higher rate if approved after probationary period in higher skill.

ARTICLE VI. MANAGEMENT RIGHTS

The employer reserves the right to employ and to dismiss and to direct the working force, subject to the terms of this Agreement.

ARTICLE VII. WORK DAY—WORK WEEK

A regular work day shall consist of eight (8) hours continuous except for a normal lunch period not to exceed one (1) hour. A regular work week shall consist of forty (40) hours, five (5) regular work days, Monday through Saturday, inclusive. A designated work week shall consist of forty (40) hours composed of any five consecutive work days. The schedule for a designated work week shall be established by the employer, in advance. If other than a Monday through Friday work week is designated, schedules will be rotated among affected employees within a department.

ARTICLE VIII. OVERTIME

All time worked in excess of eight (8) hours in any one work day, or all time worked in excess of forty (40) hours in any one work week, or on days other than the designated work week, shall be paid at the rate of one and one-half times the regular rate. All Sunday work will be paid at the rate of one and one-half times the regular rate. Time and one-half shall be paid for work performed prior to or after a designated shift.

ARTICLE IX. CALL TIME

When an hourly employee is called back to work at a time other than his regular shift, he shall be paid a minimum of two (2) hours for each call back.

ARTICLE X. HOLIDAYS

The following Holidays shall be granted without loss of pay:

1. New Year's Day—1st of January
2. Lincoln's Birthday—12th of February
3. Washington's Birthday—3rd Monday in February
4. Memorial Day—last Monday in May
5. Independence Day—4th of July
6. Labor Day—1st Monday in September
7. Columbus Day—2nd Monday in October
8. Veteran's Day—4th Monday in October

9. Thanksgiving Day—4th Thursday in November
10. Christmas Day—25th of December
11. Any other day declared a legal Holiday by the President of the United States, or the Governor of the State.

It is understood that when any of these Holidays fall on a Sunday, the following Monday shall be considered as the Holiday. Any employee who is scheduled for a day off on a day which is observed as a legal Holiday, shall be entitled to receive a day off either on the day preceding or the day following the Holiday, whichever allows a day off in addition to the employee's regularly scheduled days off. Employees will be eligible for holiday pay after they have completed six (6) months of service. All holiday work shall be paid for at time and one-half the employee's regular rate of pay in addition to Holiday pay.

ARTICLE XI. VACATIONS

1. *Annual Vacation Leave.* Each full-time employee of the City is entitled to and shall earn annual vacation leave credits from the first full pay period of employment. For calculating vacation leave credits, two thousand eighty (2,080) hours (52 weeks × 40 hours) shall equal one (1) year. Proportionate vacation leave credits shall be earned and credited at the end of each pay period. However, employees are not entitled to any vacation leave until they have been continuously employed by the City for a period of twelve (12) calendar months. Persons regularly employed nine (9) or more months each year, but whose continuous employment is interrupted by the seasonal nature of the position, shall earn vacation credits. In order to qualify, such employees must immediately report back for work when operations resume in order to avoid a break in service. However, such persons must be employed twelve (12) qualifying months before they can use the vacation credits. Vacation leave credits shall be earned in accordance with the following schedule:

   a. From one (1) full pay period through ten (10) years of employment at the rate of fifteen (15) working days for each year of service.
   b. After ten (10) years through fifteen (15) years of employment at the rate of eighteen (18) working days for each year of service.
   c. After fifteen (15) years through twenty (20) years of employment at the rate of twenty-one (21) working days for each year of service.
   d. After twenty (20) years of employment at the rate of twenty-four (24) working days for each year of service.

   Permanent part-time City employees are entitled to prorated annual vacation benefits if they have regularly scheduled work assignments and normally work at least twenty (20) hours each week of the pay period and have worked the qualifying period.

2. *Separation from Service or Transfer to other Departments; Cash for Unused Vacation Leave.* An employee who terminates his employment with the City for reason not reflecting discredit on himself, shall be entitled upon the date of such termination to cash compensation for unused vacation leave, assuming that the employee has worked the qualifying period set forth in 1 above. However, if a City employee transfers between agencies of the City, there shall be no cash compensation paid for unused vacation leave. In such a transfer the receiving City department assumes the liability for the accrued vacation credits transferred with the employee.

3. *Absence because of Illness Not Chargeable against Vacation.* Absence from employment by reason of illness shall not be chargeable against unused vacation leave credits unless approved by the employee.

ARTICLE XII. SICK LEAVE

1. *Sick Leave—Effective Date, Qualifications Generally, Cumulation of Credits.* Each full-time employee is entitled to and shall earn sick leave credits from the first full pay period of employment. For calculating sick leave credits, two thousand eighty (2,080) hours (52 weeks × 40 hours) shall equal one (1) year. Proportionate sick leave credits shall be earned and credited at the end of each pay period. Sick leave credits shall be earned at the rate of twelve (12) working days for each year of service without restriction as to the number of working days he may accumulate.

A City employee may not accrue sick leave credits during a continuous leave of absence without pay which exceeds fifteen (15) calendar days. City employees are not entitled to be paid for sick leave until they have been continuously employed for ninety (90) days. Upon completion of the qualifying period, the employee is entitled to sick leave credits he has earned.

Permanent part-time City employees are entitled to prorated leave benefits if they have a regularly scheduled work assignment, and normally work at least twenty (20) hours each week of the pay period, and have worked the qualifying period.

Full-time temporary and seasonal City employees are entitled to sick leave benefits provided they work the qualifying period.

2. *Sick Leave—Discharged, Suspended, etc., Employees.* An employee who terminates his employment with the City is entitled to a lump-sum payment equal to one-fourth (¼) of the pay attributed to his accumulated sick leave. The pay attributed to his accumulated sick leave shall be computed on the basis of the employee's salary or wage at the time the sick leave credits were earned. Accrual of sick leave credits for calculating the lump-sum payment provided for in this section begins July 1, 1971. However, no employee forfeits any sick leave rights or benefits he has accrued prior to July 1, 1971. However, where a City employee transfers between departments within the City he shall not be entitled to a lump-sum payment. In such a

transfer the receiving City department shall assume the liability for the accrued sick leave credits earned after July 1, 1971, and transferred with the City employee.

3. *Sick Leave—Re-employment.* An employee of the City who receives a lump-sum payment pursuant to this act and who 'is again employed by the City shall not be credited with any sick leave for which he has previously been compensated.

4. *Abuse of Sick Leave.* Abuse of sick leave is cause for dismissal and forfeiture of the lump-sum payments provided for in this act.

5. *Application of Sick Leave.*

   a. Employees who become ill will be paid for all days lost, to the extent of their accrued sick leave, provided they may be required to furnish a medical certificate.

   b. Employees may take sick leave, aside from personal illness, for the following reasons:

      (1) A serious affliction on one of the employee's immediate family, requiring employee's presence, not to exceed three (3) days in any one (1) month.

      (2) Death in employee's immediate family, not to exceed five (5) days in any one month.

      (3) Attendance at funeral of a fellow City employee or attendance at funeral of a close personal friend; however, the use of sick leave for funerals as recited in this paragraph shall not exceed four (4) hours per funeral or eight (8) hours per month.

      (4) Contact with, or exposure to a contagious disease which might spread to other City workers, only if the family has been placed under quarantine by the proper authorities.

      (5) Sick leave taken will be deducted from the sick leave accumulated prior to July 1, 1971 until such accumulation is exhausted.

      (6) The immediate family is judged to consist of a wife or husband, child, father, mother, brother, sister, grandparent, or guardian, or relative of employee's wife or husband in like degree.

ARTICLE XIII. OTHER LEAVE OF ABSENCE

Employees who have been in the service of the employer for at least twelve (12) months may be entitled to take leave of absence without pay for good and sufficient reason. Leaves of absence will be granted up to six (6) months. Request for leave of absence must be submitted in writing and approved by the labor committee of the City Commission.

ARTICLE XIV. JURY DUTY

1. *Jury Duty.* Each City employee who is under proper summons as a juror shall collect all fees and allowances payable as a result of the service and forward the fees to the appropriate accounting office. Juror fees shall be applied against the amount due the employee from his employer. However, if an employee elects to charge his juror time off against his annual leave he shall not be required to remit his juror fee to his employer. In no instance is an employee required to remit to his employer any expense or mileage allowance paid him by the court.

2. *Service as a Witness.* An employee subpoenaed to serve as a witness shall collect all fees and allowances payable as a result of the service and forward the fees to the appropriate accounting office. Witness fees shall be applied against the amount due the employee from his employer. However, if an employee elects to charge his witness time off against his annual leave he shall not be required to remit his witness fees to his employer. In no instance is an employee required to remit to his employer any expense or mileage allowances paid him by the court.

3. Employers may request the court to excuse their employees from jury duty if they are needed for the proper operation of a unity of City government.

ARTICLE XV. GRIEVANCE AND ARBITRATION PROCEDURE

A Grievance Committee of three (3) members shall be selected from the membership by the union. These three members shall select their Chairman.

STEP 1. When an employee has a grievance against the employer, he will submit such grievance in writing to the Committee within three (3) working days of its occurrence.

STEP 2. The Committee shall hold a hearing within five (5) working days and make a determination as to whether such grievance is justified. If the Committee determines such a grievance is not justified, the matter shall be closed, provided however that the employee retains the right to appeal to the union membership in case he disagrees with the Committee.

STEP 3. If the Committee determines that such grievance is justified, it will notify the appropriate supervisor forthwith and will try to settle the grievance satisfactorily at that level of authority. In no case, however, shall a decision require more than five (5) working days.

STEP 4. Should the union Committee decide that the decision of the immediate supervisor is unsatisfactory, the Committee may then appeal directly to the Mayor, who shall conduct a hearing within ten (10) working days of such appeal, and notify the Grievance Committee in writing within five (5) working days of the results of such hearing.

STEP 5. Should a majority of the union membership present and voting at the next regular meeting decide that the decision of the Mayor is unsatisfactory, then the grievance will be submitted for final and binding arbitration to an arbitration committee composed of one member selected by the union, one member selected by the employer, and one member selected by the other two. This process of selection of the arbitration board shall be completed insofar as possible within five (5) working days, and its process of deliberations and decision within thirty (30) working days.

ARTICLE XVI. HEALTH AND WELFARE

The employer shall contribute an amount equal to the full health insurance premium for a single employee. This amount shall be $17.72 per month.

ARTICLE XVII. RETIREMENT

The employer shall contribute 10% of every eligible employee's salary to the public employees' retirement system for the benefits provided by law. Half of this amount shall vest immediately to the employee.

ARTICLE XVIII. STRIKES AND LOCKOUTS

During the term of this Agreement the employees shall not strike against the employer and the employer shall not shut out the employees for any cause.

ARTICLE XIX. TERMINATION

This Agreement shall supersede all rules and agreements in conflict with this Agreement, and shall remain in full force and effect from the 1st day of July 1975 until the 30th day of June 1976, and shall renew itself for one-year periods thereafter unless either party notifies the other at least sixty (60) days prior to the expiration date.

ARTICLE XX. WAGE SCHEDULES

Wage scales of employees covered under this Agreement are to be found under Addendum "A," which is attached hereto and thereby made a part of this Agreement.

ARTICLE XXI. SAVINGS CLAUSE

If any section, subdivision, paragraph, sentence, clause, phrase or other part of this Agreement is determined or declared to be contrary to or in violation of any State or Federal Law, the remainder of this Agreement shall not hereby be affected or invalidated.

IN WITNESS WHEREOF the parties hereto, acting by and through their respective and duly authorized officers or representatives, have hereunto set their hand and seal the day and year first written above.

For the Union:

For the Employer:

ADDENDUM A. City of Sycamore Employee Group Wage and Benefit Adjustments Since July 1, 1970 Cost-of-Living Increase

	"A" Group AFSCME Unit	"B" Group Supervisory & Management, General	Police Unit	Police Supervisory	Fire Unit	Fire Supervisory
July 1, 1970	5.0%	5.0%	5.0%	5.0%	5.0%	5.0%
July 1, 1971	5.0%	5.0%	5.0%	5.0%	5.0%	5.0%
July 1, 1972	5.5%	5.5%	6.95%	8.0%	6.45%	8.5%
July 1, 1973	8.0%	7.5%	9.85%	9.1%	13.0%	13.0%
July 1, 1974	5.0%	8.5%	8.7%	9.7%	10.7%	11.0%
July 1, 1975	10.0%	10.0%	10.0%	10.0%	10.0%	10.0%

ADDENDUM B.
Class Titles and Ranges of "A" Schedule

Range No.	Class Title
3A	Clerk I
3A	Library Page
4A	Bookmender
5A	Clerk II
5A	Library Assistant I
5A	Recreation Leader II
6A	Clerk-Messenger
6A	Duplicating Equipment Operator Trainee
6A	Bindery Assistant
6A	Police Service Aide 1
7A	Utilities Service Representative I
8A	Clerk III
8A	Secretary I
8A	Centrex Operator
8A	Bookkeeping Machine Operator
8A	Accounting Clerk I
8A	Parking Control Attendant
8A	Advocate I
8A	Library Assistant I
9A	Offset Printer
9A	Engineering Aide
9A	Custodial Worker I
9A	Laborer
10A	Senior Parking Control Attendant
10A	Police Service Aide II
11A	Secretary II
11A	Accounting Clerk II
11A	Stores Clerk
11A	Intern
11A	Water Meter Repairman I
11A	Water Meter Reader
11A	Custodial Worker II
11A	Bookmobile Operator
11A	Equipment Operator I
11A	Maintenance I
11A	Automotive Serviceman
12A	Transit Operator
13A	Accounting Clerk III
13A	Utilities Service Representative II
13A	Water Meter Repairman II
13A	Equipment Operator II
13A	Maintenance II

14A	Advocate Planner
14A	Engineering Technician I
14A	Library Assistant III
14A	Tree Trimmer
14A	Utilities Service Representative III
14A	Utilities Serviceman
14A	Water Source Attendant
14A	Sewage Treatment Plant Operator I
14A	Maintenance Welder
14A	Parking Meter Technician
15A	Storekeeper
15A	Graphics Technician I
15A	Sewage Treatment Plant Mechanic
15A	Equipment Operator III
15A	Maintenance Carpenter
15A	Maintenance Electrician
15A	Automotive Mechanic
16A	Public Information Specialist
16A	Advocate II
16A	Engineering Technician II
16A	Housing Assistance Counselor I
16A	Community Services Counselor I
16A	Financial Counselor I
16A	Business Assistance Counselor I
16A	Park Ranger I
16A	Sewage Maintenance Technician
16A	STP Operator II
16A	Field Representative
16A	Maintenance Technician
16A	Communications Technician I
16A	Transit Foreman I
17A	Accountant
17A	Buyer
17A	Housing Safety Inspector I
17A	Rehabilitation Counselor I
17A	Graphics Technician II
17A	Water Source Supervisor
17A	Sanitary Analyst
17A	Airport Safety and Operations Manager
18A	Housing Assistance Counselor I
18A	Community Services Counselor II
18A	Park Ranger II
18A	Landscape Designer
18A	Communications Technician II
18A	Signal Technician
19A	Engineering Technician III
19A	Building Inspector
19A	Sign Inspector
19A	Housing Safety Inspector II
19A	Business Assistance Counselor II

19A	Rehabilitation Counselor II
19A	Assistant Planner
19A	Librarian I
19A	Utilities Inspector
19A	Senior Communications Technician
19A	Senior Signal Technician
20A	Engineering Technician Specialist
20A	Civil Engineer I
20A	Assistant Traffic Engineer
20A	Senior Building Inspector
20A	Plans Examiner I
20A	Senior Housing Safety Inspector
20A	Hearings Examiner
20A	Community Services Counselor III
20A	Financial Counselor II
20A	Project Coordinator I
22A	Real Estate Specialist
22A	Associate Planner
23A	Civil Engineer II
23A	Plans Examiner II

Schedule of Salary Ranges
"A" Schedule

Range No.	1	2	3	4	5	6
3A	400	412	425	439	455	472
4A	412	425	439	455	472	489
5A	425	439	455	472	489	507
6A	439	455	472	489	507	525
7A	455	472	489	507	525	544
8A	472	489	507	525	544	564
9A	489	507	525	544	564	585
10A	507	525	544	564	585	608
11A	525	544	564	585	608	632
12A	544	564	585	608	632	657
13A	564	585	608	632	657	684
14A	585	608	632	657	684	713
15A	608	632	657	684	713	744
16A	632	657	684	713	744	776
17A	657	684	713	744	776	810
18A	684	713	744	776	810	846
19A	713	744	776	810	846	884
20A	744	776	810	846	884	924
21A	776	810	846	884	924	966
22A	810	846	884	924	966	1009
23A	846	884	924	966	1009	1054
24A	884	924	966	1009	1054	1101
25A	924	966	1009	1054	1101	1150
26A	966	1009	1054	1101	1150	1201
27A	1009	1054	1101	1150	1201	1255
28A	1054	1101	1150	1201	1255	1311
29A	1101	1150	1201	1255	1311	1370
30A	1150	1201	1255	1311	1370	1432

Class Titles and Ranges of "B" Schedule

Range No.	Class Title
5B	Clerk II—Confidential
8B	Clerk III—Confidential
8B	Secretary I—Confidential
11B	Secretary II—Confidential
12B	Secretary III—Confidential
12B	Police Service Aide III
13B	Deputy City Recorder
13B	Recreation Leader III
14B	Office Supervisor
14B	Word Processing Center Supervisor
16B	Payroll Supervisor
16B	Central Services Supervisor
16B	Personnel Technician
16B	Administrative Assistant I
16B	Parks Foreman I
16B	Water Meter and Equipment Foreman
16B	Custodial Foreman
16B	Maintenance Foreman I
16B	Garage Foreman
17B	Treasury and Investment Accountant
17B	City Recorder
18B	Recreation Coordinator
18B	Parks Foreman II
18B	Building Maintenance Foreman
18B	Maintenance Foreman II
18B	Transit Foreman II
19B	Accounting Supervisor
19B	License and Parking Control Supervisor
19B	Administrative Assistant II
19B	Graphics Technician III
19B	Chief Service Representative
19B	Equipment Supervisor
20B	Affirmative Action Officer
20B	Housing Assistance Counselor III
20B	Housing Maintenance Supervisor
20B	Street Supervisor
21B	Training Coordinator
21B	Administrative Assistant III
21B	Chief Engineering Technician
21B	Chief Surveyor
21B	Chief Housing Safety Inspector
21B	Program Manager EHAP
21B	Rehabilitation Counselor III

21B	Librarian II
21B	Recreation Supervisor
21B	Parks Supervisor
21B	Plant Maintenance Engineer
22B	Financial Counselor III
22B	Business Assistance Counselor III
22B	Librarian III
22B	Sewage Collection Superintendent
22B	Building Maintenance Supervisor
23B	Purchasing and Services Supervisor
23B	Personnel Analyst
23B	Referral Center Supervisor
23B	Management Analyst
23B	Civil Engineer II—Supervisory
23B	Chief Building Inspector
23B	Property Manager
23B	Project Coordinator II
23B	Water Superintendent
23B	Assistant STP Superintendent
23B	Communications and Signal Supervisor
23B	Equipment Superintendent
24B	Assistant City Attorney I
24B	Safety Officer
24B	Housing Assistance Manager
24B	Community Services Supervisor
24B	Rehabilitation Supervisor
24B	Senior Planner
25B	Civil Engineer III
25B	Traffic Engineer
25B	Real Estate Services Supervisor
25B	Development Engineer
25B	Architect
25B	Neighborhood Development Supervisor
25B	Recreation Superintendent
25B	Parks Superintendent
25B	Parks Planner
25B	STP Superintendent
25B	Street Superintendent
26B	Planning and Development Supervisor
27B	Chief Accountant
27B	Inspections Division Administrator
27B	Sanitary Engineer
27B	Airport and Transit Superintendent
28B	City Engineer
28B	Planning Administrator
29B	Housing Administrator
29B	Assistant City Attorney, 11
29B	Renewal Administrator

Schedule of Salary Ranges
"B" Schedule

Range No.	1	2	3	4	5	6
3B	500	522	541	556	580	605
4B	522	541	556	580	605	627
5B	541	556	580	605	627	651
6B	556	580	605	627	651	682
7B	580	605	627	651	682	710
8B	605	627	651	682	710	738
9B	627	651	682	710	738	768
10B	651	682	710	738	768	799
11B	682	710	739	769	804	840
12B	710	739	769	804	840	880
13B	739	769	804	840	880	921
14B	769	804	840	880	921	963
15B	804	840	880	921	963	1008
16B	840	880	921	963	1008	1061
17B	880	921	963	1008	1061	1113
18B	921	963	1008	1061	1113	1165
19B	963	1008	1061	1113	1165	1223
20B	1008	1061	1113	1165	1223	1289
21B	1061	1113	1165	1223	1289	1355
22B	1113	1165	1223	1289	1355	1419
23B	1165	1223	1289	1355	1419	1492
24B	1223	1289	1355	1419	1492	1564
25B	1289	1355	1419	1492	1564	1637
26B	1355	1419	1492	1564	1637	1714
27B	1419	1492	1564	1637	1714	1798
28B	1492	1564	1637	1714	1798	1891
29B	1564	1637	1714	1798	1891	1985
30B	1637	1714	1798	1891	1985	2084

Schedule of Salaries

Class Code	Class Title	Range No.	1	2	3	4	5	6
450	Fire Fighter	1C	841	885	929	979	1,031	1,083
452	Fire Equipment Operator	2C	885	929	979	1,031	1,083	1,138
454	Fire Captain I	4C					1,229	1,290
455	Fire Captain II	5C					1,290	1,350
462	Fire Prevention Officer	3C	929	979	1,031	1,083	1,138	1,195
472	Dispatcher	2C	885	929	979	1,031	1,083	1,138

Employees will be eligible for progression from Step 1 through Step 6 in increments of 6 months, 12 months, 24 months, 36 months, and 48 months.

Sycamore City Revised Pay Schedule A

Class Code	Class Title	Range No.	1	2	3	4	5	6
410	Animal Control Officer I	1E	737	774	813	854	896	941
411	Animal Control Officer II	2E	752	789	829	871	914	960
412	Animal Control Officer III	3E	766	805	846	888	932	979
413	Animal Control Officer IV	4E	781	820	862	905	950	997
415	Sr. Animal Cont. Officer I	5E	774	813	854	896	941	988
416	Sr. Animal Cont. Officer II	6E	789	829	871	914	960	1008
417	Sr. Animal Cont. Officer III	7E	805	846	888	932	979	1028
418	Sr. Animal Cont. Officer IV	8E	820	862	905	950	997	1047
420	Jailer I	9E	737	774	813	854	896	941
421	Jailer II	10E	752	789	829	871	914	960
422	Jailer III	11E	766	805	846	888	932	979
423	Jailer IV	12E	781	820	862	905	950	997
425	Police Officer I	13E	857	900	945	992	1042	1094
426	Police Officer II	14E	874	918	964	1012	1063	1116
427	Police Officer III	15E	891	936	983	1032	1084	1138
428	Police Officer IV	16E	908	954	1002	1052	1105	1160
430	Corporal I	17E	900	945	992	1042	1094	1149
431	Corporal II	18E	918	964	1012	1063	1116	1172
432	Corporal III	19E	936	983	1032	1084	1138	1195
433	Corporal IV	20E	954	1002	1052	1105	1160	1218

Index